Now Playing at the

Valencia

PULITZER PRIZE–WINNING

ESSAYS ON MOVIES

Stephen Hunter

Simon & Schuster Paperbacks
New York   London   Toronto   Sydney

For my superb editors at The Washington Post,
David Von Drehle, John Pancake, Peter Kaufman, and Leslie Yazel,
with a special nod to Robin Groom,
with thanks

SIMON & SCHUSTER PAPERBACKS
Rockefeller Center
1230 Avenue of the Americas
New York, NY 10020

First Simon & Schuster paperback edition 2005

SIMON & SCHUSTER PAPERBACKS and colophon are registered trademarks
of Simon & Schuster, Inc.

For information regarding special discounts for bulk purchases,
please contact Simon & Schuster Special Sales:
1-800-456-6798 or business@simonandschuster.com.

Designed by Elliott Beard

Manufactured in the United States of America

10   9   8   7   6   5   4   3   2   1

Library of Congress Cataloging-in-Publication Data
Hunter, Stephen.
    Now playing at the Valencia : Pulitzer Prize–winning essays on movies /
Stephen Hunter.
        p.   cm.
    Includes index.
    A collection of essays previously published in Washington Post, 1997–2003.
    1. Motion pictures—Reviews. 2. Motion pictures. I. Title.
PN1995.H855 2005
    791.43'75—dc22   2005050008

ISBN-13: 978-0-7432-6125-8
ISBN-10:   0-7432-6125-9

CONTENTS

INTRODUCTION

*I*n the fifties, Evanston, Illinois, was a paradise distinguished by a million leafy elms, a beautiful lake, a world-class university, a block-by-block array of stately homes. But who the hell even noticed? I certainly didn't.

Far more interesting were its three movie theaters.

It was in one of those theaters that I misspent my youth. From the first second I'd seen a movie, I knew I had discovered a home far more nourishing than the one into which I had been born. I had an immediate imaginative connection with the images on the screen. What happened up there was as real to me—more real, in fact—as anything in the otherwise unglamorous career in mediocrity better known as my childhood. I should have been in school, I should have been doing my homework, I should have been mastering sports, small talk with girls, simple arithmetic, all skills that to this day elude me. But I was at the Valencia, fifteenth row, right-hand aisle seat.

The Valencia was the tawdry B-house of Evanston, located in the southern end of the small downtown, where the class and elegance of the Sherman Avenue corridor had begun, ever so gently, to decay. Architecturally, it expressed its affinity for the Spanish motif of its namesake by a style called "El Cheapo." The screen was set in a ludicrous papier-mâché castle wall, complete to parapets and ramparts, all painted a dreadful mauve. The floor was eternally sticky, the bathrooms eternally smelly. Jujubes sealed in mucus dotted its ceiling. In the lobby, the Affy Tapples snared flies in their caramel tar, the Coke cup came out of the machine crooked and wasted a nickel's worth of sugary bubbles, and the popcorn had been popped before the Second World War.

Naturally, the place showed films appropriate to its location in the movie food chain: all the crumb-bum double features, a new one every week, the raw, the violent, the cheap, the sensational, the pitiful, the inept. Guns fired, blood splattered, mules talked, monsters mashed, pies flew, throats spurted, cities flattened, and planes crashed. Everyone said it was ridiculous. And, as is so often the case, everyone was wrong.

To me, the stories were thrilling, the stars—the Ken Tobeys, the Frank Lovejoys, the Rory Calhouns, the Stephen McNallys, the Dan Duryeas— gigantic, the themes of heroism and male supremacy utterly convincing. I also liked the guns. Those movies were filled with guns, used in every creative way. Swords were neat too, as were airplanes, but not as neat as the guns, which dangled in low-slung gunfighters' holsters or were carried with a tough sergeant's insouciant I-don't-know-what as part of the cool messy GI look.

You couldn't see guns elsewhere, at least not in such weekly profusion. You couldn't see them at the posh Varsity slightly uptown, abutting that temple of Sherman Avenue upscale consumerism, Marshall Field's. The Varsity was a cathedral of swank with twinkly lights in its dome suggesting stars in the firmament. It exhibited the A pictures of the decade, the MGM musicals, the inspirational biblical dramas, the blubbery Douglas Sirk melodramas, the big-budget Broadway and literary adaptations, like *Marjorie Morningstar*, which I didn't and still haven't and happily never will see. They actually cleaned the urinals at the Varsity. But there were very few guns—much less gunfights, fistfights, sword fights, dogfights, and monster attacks—at the Varsity.

Nor were there many guns at the Coronet further downtown, boldly located in a yet more decayed area which was dangerously closer to the actual Berlin Wall between black and white Evanstons. This was the art house where Bergman first played, and Kurosawa, where small, dark wonderful pictures changed world cinema but no cities were ever squished flat under a prehistoric paw. Immediately upon entering it— my insane father took me a couple of times, to films he couldn't get my mother to go to; I remember *Samurai* and *The Magician*—you understood you were in a different culture with different expectations. You had left the mainstream, a daring thing to do in the fifties, and were grasping at something strange. I picked up on this even if I couldn't articulate it, and I suppose I responded. But still: It was provocative, it was mind-spinning, it was different. But it wasn't me.

Left to my own devices, I far more happily spent my time in the Valencia. And that perhaps explains why I became the second film critic in America to win the Pulitzer Prize in 2003. I was—here's the Cap-I irony—educating myself exactly to the job I would someday be lucky enough to hold. I learned more in the Valencia than I did anywhere on earth, in any school, in the army, in a marriage, and in the features departments where I would spend my life. And that's also why I still prefer to sit in the fifteenth row, right-hand aisle seat.

This volume collects what I believe to be my best work from *The Washington Post*, but as I assembled it, I was astounded by how much more it seemed to do with what was playing at the Valencia in the fifties than with the present; it ends up examining in a loosey-goosey way the process by which the genre pictures of the forties and fifties became the mainstream movies of the late twentieth and early twenty-first centuries. It shows why the Valencia *was* America in the fifties and how America of the oughts came out of the Valencia.

I've organized by genre, which of course is never quite neat enough (nothing is) and leads to a certain untidiness at the margins. Each genre corresponds to a lost pleasure of the Valencia—those vulgar categories that still proclaimed that movies were meant to be fun, not art, without really realizing that the fun *was* the art. I must say rereading my own work wasn't much fun, and I kept coming across little tricks that seemed funny two minutes before a deadline but now seem pretty dreadful. And at a certain point it became clear to me that maybe I don't have the true movie-mind that believes there is no other life than the life on the screen. If you want that, plenty of critics can provide it, geniuses all. I don't thrive on arcane cinema data and can't remember entire crews down to third assistant grip. I'm not even sure what a grip is. Even as a critic, I've never really left the Valencia: I want the Valencia's pleasures, which are escape, excitement, provocation, most of all an emotional journey. Otherwise, I lose interest and don't care what lens was used.

So I'm really only selling one product: my attempt to convey the awe and joy at what's on screen, and the bitterness when it's absent. It's not much, I admit. You won't learn a lot, except by accidental inference: a sense of why we go to the movies, what we want from them, what we in fact get from them, and why they are so damned important to us. And the answer, I suspect, has much to do with your childhood and how you first saw them. Lord help you if *The Beast from 20,000 Fathoms* was your first experience.

—S.H.

One

WESTERNS

Stand on a hilltop in this widest of open spaces and look a hundred miles in every direction, and there's not a human construct in existence except the vehicle that brought you there.

But John Wayne is here. You can feel him in the wind, you can see him through the mirages, in the clumps of cottonwoods, you can sense him where the streams cut the rolling land. He's here in the landscape.

The skies are magnificent: No artist born since 1900 could capture the subtlety of tone fused with the vastness of scope. The green of prairie, unnatural this late in the summer, runs toward forever. Antelope actually play. Buffalo actually roam.

It's a land for big men, almost a cathedral. In *The Searchers*, Wayne's greatest film, the Comanche chief Scar called him "Big Shoulders," and only an emptiness like this, vaulted by a sky like that, seems capable of accommodating those shoulders, that distinctive, graceful way of carrying so much muscle and authority, the look of ferocity that came so quickly to his face and warned all and sundry to steer clear or face lethal consequences. Ask Liberty Valance: He found out the hard way.

Indoors, John Wayne is even more prominent. Here in Ingomar, Montana, population 125 people, 17,650 cattle, 20 bison, 2 llamas, and 247,532 prairie dogs, the town center is an agreeable old bar called the Jersey Lily, where the beer is cold, the steaks tough, and the beans plentiful. On the dust-blown streets it always looks as if a gunfight is about to erupt, but inside it's warm and friendly. Discouraging words are not heard; folks smile a lot more than they frown and will generally drink to or with anyone.

But here's the cool part: If you close your eyes after a beer or two, or a bean or 700, you can see him standing there at the end of the long stretch of bar. He's wearing that pinkish bib shirt, that leather vest, that dirty pale-tan hat. He's got beef everywhere on his body, but not fat. The gun, worn high on his hip in working cowman's practicality, not low after the gunslinger style, is the Colt Single Action Army .38-40, with the yellowing ivory grips. The eyes are wary, rich in wisdom, impatient with pilgrims, tenderfeet, and blanketheads, possibly incapable of expressing love because they are so fixed on duty. He is what for decades was a vision of the ideal man.

Now it gets even cooler: Put down that beer, relax those eyes, and you can see that it's not a writer's florid fantasy. The Duke is there, as I've described him; well, a full-size movie cutout, from the days when the studios advanced their products by sending such cardboard images of the star to stand sentinel in the nation's movie houses. Somehow the Lily got one—it's from early-seventies Wayne; I would guess *Chisum* or *Big Jake* or possibly *The Train Robbers*.

But that's not all. Look in the other direction, and he's there, too. His portrait hangs at the bar's other end, though it's not the classic Duke from the pictures, but the mature, prosperous rancher Duke, with a lot of miles on him, but a sense of abiding peace in his eyes as well. You're in a bar but you're also in a sacred glade, a place of worship, pilgrim.

And the Duke is back there in your swank, stuffier East, too. I saw him on the tube there. A beer commercial, just as clever as previous versions, in which by some digital magic he is computer-inserted into a modern scenario, demonstrating that 20-odd years after his death, he's still a star. His antagonist is some kind of yuppie entrepreneur who wants to close a neighborhood bar. The Duke—the images appear to be purloined from the great John Ford classic of Irish schmaltz, *The Quiet Man*—appears and gives him a good going-over. The beer's on him, literally, as someone douses the yup with a pitcher of brew, wilting his $4,000 Armani suit, and it's so wonderful!

Wayne's a staple on AMC and TCM, those two wondrous small-screen custodians of the movie past, where you'll encounter him at various ages, in various positions of command or valor, fighting on till the end. In fact, American Movie Classics featured a thirty-six-movie Duke package during its Film Preservation Festival last month.

He's even there in his absence. I had a professional obligation ten days ago to sit through a film called *American Outlaws*, which was a horror so intense it would have frightened Joseph Conrad, connoisseur of horror. Among the things it lacked, besides plot and character and intelligence and emotion, was a star. It was full of Peter Pans who walked ever so light in their boots, almost as if flying. The hero looked to be about seven. Soaking wet, with pockets full of nickels, he might have weighed 100 pounds. He had the gravitas of a minnow.

The old Hollywood knew and the new Hollywood doesn't: You don't get gravitas by pointing a camera at a pleasant young face and turning it on. You get gravitas by some special alchemy between face and film as transmuted through lens and tweaked by light, until what registers is larger and more powerful than what is. Wayne had this, though not at the start and possibly not at the end. Still, along with Bogart and Monroe and Grant and maybe one or two others, his physical radiance—that is, the accumulation of face and body and movement, small things like the carriage of the hands and the tilt of the jaw—he imprinted himself upon the consciousness of a generation.

So many of us rode the big wave in baby flesh that rolled across the country between 1946 and 1960, and those were the Duke's best years, when he ruled at the box office and in the imagination. He was the man we wished our fathers were, and of course they were too busy to notice, too busy catching up for the four years the Nazis and the Greater East Asian Co-Prosperity Sphere stole from them. So he raised us more than they did.

As I say, he did not come to this point easily. His career, in fact, may be divided into six parts. In the beginning, he was merely beautiful; then he became heroic if still simple; then, a full adult in command of his considerable powers, he was complex; then, like an angry, disappointed father, he turned bitter and contentious; he was finally avuncular, a self-parody, a king during an idyll, I suppose. And we are in the sixth stage right now.

Wayne, born Marion Michael Morrison in Winterset, Iowa, in 1907, came west as a child and grew up in California. The story of his rise is well enough known: As a college student, he was a movie roustabout when not playing football for USC. That devil-genius in the guise of Irish blarney and guile known as John Ford took a liking to him. As Ford would later say, "I never knew the big son of a bitch could act."

Well, at first he couldn't. His early roles in cheesy westerns—*Randy Rides Alone* would be my favorite, not that I've seen it—are negligible. He got a break in 1930, when Raoul Walsh, under Ford's urging, starred him in *The Big Trail*. It was a catastrophe, and if you've been able to sit through four or five minutes of it, you know why: He has almost no resources, as an actor. He just sits there; his untrained voice, particularly, is a disgrace, a light, wispy thing that cracks often and is almost uninflected. You think: Really, this guy should go back to pushing the props around the set.

That humiliation gone by, he then endured nine more years of near-starvation in the poverty-row westerns. But as he aged, he got less pretty and far more interesting. His face acquired weight, density, and a webbing of creases; it came to appear geologic, as fissures of wisdom ruptured its serenity. His eyes grew savvy; when the camera came on, you didn't sense panic, and before he spoke, he didn't take a deep breath; he'd learned to avoid two early flaws.

The new Wayne was defined as a star in a single movie, Ford's *Stagecoach* in 1939. Talk about a moment. Nobody ever got one like the Duke in this picture. The camera finds him, in buckskins, wary and tired, on the run. His horse has been shot and he stands by the side of a Monument Valley road, carrying a saddle and a rifle, as the titular vehicle approaches. The camera zooms in—the only zoom in the picture—and Wayne, as the Ringo Kid, does this cool move with his sawed-off, large-levered Winchester (a '92, also .38-40 for all of you who demand to be in the know); he spins it, cocking it as it flashes under his armpit. Only a 6-foot-4 guy could do that; Chuck Connors had the same move on fifties TV in *The Rifleman*, and he was another honest 6-foot-4.

It was a moment of such grace and power and masculine majesty, rivaled by only a few others. It contained in an instant all that would become classic Duke: the Westerner, lean, laconic, isolated, grandly picturesque but totally repressed, graceful, and direct. He'd never be a sex guy: His movie love affairs were more like buddy deals, where love was expressed in affectionate needling, but never the abject statement of pure emotion. He was most usually a duty guy, doing what had to be done. If it involved killing, as it so often did, the killing was done out of necessity, not out of pleasure. He acquired wisdom that built toward a command presence like no other. And this was at a time when the gift of command was so important.

The war arrived—Wayne was thirty-four, with four kids at home, so he fought it on the home front—when his maturity and natural authority made him the perfect officer or sergeant. He commanded marines and Seabees, fighter pilots, paratroopers, submarines, naval vessels, almost every single fighting contrivance in almost every theater of war, though he did miss the Aleutians. I suppose he missed North Africa, too.

Our fathers cheered him then; we cheered him later. In the fifties, that is, when these movies were rerun endlessly on TV, which also carried ads for his new movies, so that it was a Duke-rich environment wherever you turned. I discovered him during commercials for *Hondo,* one of his lesser pictures, but even shrunk small by a black-and-white TV, his charisma was vivid enough to leap from the small screen and ensnare a kid's inner brain. Joan Didion said it best: John Wayne "would control the shape of our dreams."

When Wayne worked with excellent directors, the result, embarrassing for everyone, was that rare thing called art. He said (I love this quote): "I never had a goddam artistic problem in my life, never, and I've worked with the best of them. John Ford isn't exactly a bum, is he? Yet he never gave me any crap about art."

That may have been true. But the best directors—Ford in at least six great movies: *Stagecoach, The Long Voyage Home* (1940), *They Were Expendable* (1945), *She Wore a Yellow Ribbon* (1949), *The Quiet Man* (1952), and, of course, *The Searchers* (1956), but also Howard Hawks in *Red River* (1948), and William Wellman in *The High and the Mighty* (1954)—located a darkness within him. They saw through the delusions of the über-male's perpetual righteousness, and found a tragic dimension in his stubborn strength, his insane heroism, his need to dominate and rule.

That's why, of all the performances, I like best his Ethan Edwards in *The Searchers,* for here is a man so crippled by hate, so riddled by anger and the need for blood vengeance, that he loses his way. His will is titanic; his rage is more titanic; it dries up his love, and though he performs an *Odyssey*-scale task of heroism in finding the kidnapped daughter of his dead brother and though in the end he steps back from the cruelest savagery, it is too late. He is exiled, and that sad last scene lingers forever: The door closes and he's condemned, like the Comanche brave whose eyes he shot out earlier, to wander between the winds.

We knew, somehow, that Wayne had a darkness in him. But we trusted he would use it only against enemies. He would protect us. That is why we loved him so. Then we thought he used it against us. That is why we hated him so.

The war in Vietnam, of course, sundered families everywhere. It sundered, too, the metaphorical family of John Wayne the father and his children, the baby-boom generation. He insisted that the war that would kill us was a war like the one he had known, where the enemy was absolute, where the nation itself and its way of life were at stake, where the necessary killing and inevitable dying were sanctified by its higher justification.

We believed it was a new thing, a war of national liberation, and that it didn't endanger our culture. We also believed—I think it's safe to say this now—that we didn't want our asses wasted in some jungle hellhole.

Who was right? That fight still goes on, and if I have an answer I will keep it to myself. Symbolically, however, it was waged most bitterly over Wayne's film—he starred and directed—*The Green Berets*, which was loathed by millions of kids and loved by millions of other Americans. (Did you know it was the fourth-top-grossing movie of 1968? It was really quite a hit.)

Well, it is pretty awful. The first half is a not-quite-convincing account of the defense of a Special Forces camp (the pine trees of Fort Bragg, where it was shot, somewhat dilute the illusion that we're in Vietnam) and the wooing of a liberal journalist to the hawk side; the second is an even lamer secret mission behind enemy lines to snatch a general, complete with a dragon-lady secret agent and some of the most condescending sequences of Asian culture ever shot. In its way, it answers the question: Why are we in Vietnam? But the answer is not the one Wayne thought he was giving; it was: because we thought that Vietnam was North Carolina and our Asian allies were children or seductresses, and that the sun sets in the east.

Wayne was truly damaged by the outrage his film stirred, and the bitterness his presence engendered. From then on, he just played John Wayne over and over again, in a series of unpersuasive but occasionally amusing films (*True Grit*, for Henry Hathaway, was his Oscar winner, but lord, I wish Pappy Ford had directed it!), growing older and fatter and somehow more ridiculous. His two most absurd films occur in this period (I am discounting 1956's insane *The Conqueror*, where he played Genghis Khan): his two *Dirty Harry/Bullitt* rip-offs, *McQ* and *Brannigan*. John Wayne should never wear a suit coat, because his shoulders are so big it looks like a monkey jacket; he should wear his gun outside, where it can be part of his posture, not in a concealment holster; he should ride a horse, not a Mustang; he should never be forced to act against weightless performers like Eddie Albert or Richard Attenborough.

And that hairpiece. It looked like he'd mugged Howard Cosell in an alley and stolen his cigar, his wallet, and his rug!

He had one great performance left, and how sad that it's not in a great movie: a kind of summing up, directed by old pro Don Siegel, called *The Shootist*. He was dying then, after his fifth operation, from lung cancer. But he never showed it, in a dignified adult performance of an old gunfighter with a crab in his guts, determined to go out the way he came in, with guns in hand. Not a great movie, but there's so much mythic lionhood up there you think: "Boy, that big son of a bitch can act."

What is going on now, I believe, is something quite magnificent: It's not a rediscovery of John Wayne or a rebirth or a renaissance. It's something like a reconciliation.

I see in the Duke's reemergence something I never thought I would see: some healing of the scars of Vietnam. Maybe enough time has passed. We forgive him. He forgives us. It's okay now. We can be blanketheads and pilgrims again, though we're in our fifties, and he can be the wise, tough old scout who knows what has to be done. In our old age, his old age is comforting. Daddy's home. It's fabulous.

(AUGUST 26, 2001)

*A*fter all these years, my darling *High Noon* has not forsaken me on this, our viewing day.

Fred Zinnemann's revered 1952 Western, which is opening today in a dandy new 35mm print at the AFI's cathedral to the religion of the Old Movie out in Silver Spring, remains, now as then, a terrific piece of filmmaking. It's taut, believable as it unspools. It's charismatic, with a slow buildup of tension in near-real time that finally explodes into a blast of violence. Then it's over; then it goes away.

Regarded as fifties melodrama, it's nearly perfect: I love the strokes of the deceptively simple plot, the way each incident magnifies the dramatic situation without waste or frill. I love Gary Cooper's tight, controlled performance, which achieves mythic poetry without a single moment of hamminess or self-indulgence. I love the formality of Zinnemann's camerawork until he reaches a key moment and then abandons formality for pure German expressionism—I'm thinking of a weirdly angled shot of the clock's pendulum, photographed so that it looks like a descending blade from a Poe story, lowering itself to slice our noble hero in two.

The premise is simplicity itself: Will Kane, the retiring marshal of a town called Hadleyville, somewhere in the West, is about to marry a pretty Quaker gal (the luminous Grace Kelly) when he learns that three men are in town, awaiting the arrival of the fourth on the noon train (an hour and a half away). The four men will kill him to settle an issue of vengeance. His first reaction is to flee. Then he returns, believing in the power of community to stand together. But the community, faced by naked force from the outside, disintegrates, and the sheriff is left alone to face the four as high noon draws ever closer. Tick-tock, tick-tock.

Of course the movies has entered our lore for extra-cinematic reasons. It's seen as metaphor as well as melodrama. For many—particularly the writer, Carl Foreman, who was blacklisted shortly after completing the script—it was an allegory of McCarthyism, with a committee of gunmen, like a committee of congressmen, coming to town to destroy someone innocent, and nobody in the community with the guts to stand up to them.

But both producer Stanley Kramer and Zinnemann have denied that such a meaning was intended, and the anger between Kramer and Foreman was so intense that the two never spoke after the project. As recently as last year, a second generation of combatants—Foreman's disciple Lionel Chetwynd and Kramer's widow, Karen—were still fighting bitterly over the issue, which was raised in a PBS documentary Chetwynd had made on the two men, called explosively *Darkness at High Noon*.

But, as others have pointed out, *High Noon* is so simple and nuance-free, with its brute division of good and evil, that it can support any number of meanings.

It pretty much means what you want it to mean, open-endedly. Given its placement in time in 1952, it's just as easy to argue a conservative, rather than a liberal, metaphorical meaning. In this case, the evil gunman Frank Miller and his gang of three are Commies and the town is Korea. Guess what, nobody wants to fight to stop the Commies. Come on, it's only Korea, for God's sake. So the hero, Gary Cooper and obviously standing in for the U.S. of A., has to go it alone, as the country did (largely, but not entirely) in Vietnam. In this respect, *High Noon*'s true fifties brother would be Howard Hawks's *The Thing*, a cautionary fable (closing line: "Watch the skies!") that offered the wisdom that it was so much more sensible to blow strangers and strange ideologies away than to attempt to understand them.

Yet watching the film in the AFI Silver, another possible meaning forced itself on me. So, for the hell of it, here it is: If you look at *High Noon* without assumptions, it seems to me that the dichotomy it describes falls along rural vs. urban lines, rather than political lines. It's about the wicked city taking over the pristine rural town, and implicitly returning vices—prostitution, gambling, drinking, the Tenderloin—to a middle-class dream. And in that light, certain things that have made no sense suddenly fit together neatly.

I've always been disappointed in Ian MacDonald, who played the evil Frank Miller. When we finally see him, after an hour and a half of buildup, he's a major disappointment. Far from an icon of towering Western evil—think, for example, of Jack Palance's gunslinger in *Shane*—he's a squirrelly little man in pressed pants and shirt, with a bow tie. He looks about as cowboy as Sonny Corleone.

And that's it, exactly. He's not a cowboy, he's a gangster. Look at that face, with its acne, its dark, feral eyes, its quickness. He looks as though he should be a hit man, a loan shark enforcer, not a Western outlaw. In fact, MacDonald came to the film after a long career as a character actor. He was far from a Western icon, with roles in such films as *Joe Palooka in the Big Fight*, *Malaya*, and *Where the Sidewalk Ends* to his credit; after *High Noon*, of course, he became a Western staple, but not before.

As the film has it, he's clearly been sponsored by some sort of big political machine with an interest in taking over and restoring Hadleyville to its former corrupt glory as a profitable sin town. Originally sentenced to hang, Frank was spared the gallows when that sentence was commuted to life, and now he's been pardoned "by the politicians up north"—clear indications of a kind of political clout or favor of the sort endemic to big cities.

His mission is to kill Will Kane and reopen the town for exploitation. That's why the townsmen are so frightened. They realize that Frank stands for the process of urban corruption, not just a force of random violence in the world.

Perhaps the most vivid visualization of this meaning is Frank's arrival. He arrives by train (itself suggesting modernity), but as the train pulls across the prairie into the station, it issues a horrendous belch of smoke, dark and roiling, that defiles the beauty of the land. That's the smoke of city and industry, the smoke of modernity, coming to Hadleyville.

In this sense, *High Noon*'s closest sibling would be *It's a Wonderful Life*, where another man, George Bailey (the great Jimmy Stewart), stood alone against an avaricious force that came to destroy the beauty of the small town. Frank Miller may have been bringing to Hadleyville what Jimmy Stewart prevented in *It's a Wonderful Life*: Potterville, the squalid den of avarice Bedford Falls would have become under the rule of the film's greedy nemesis. I suppose another irony is this: Look out the window, or on TV, and where are you in America in 2003? Well, you're in Potterville, despite the efforts of Cooper and Stewart.

Well, whatever it means or doesn't mean, it sure is nice to see this old classic on a screen the right size, in perfect focus, and with its heroes and villains bigger than life, as they were.   (MAY 30, 2003)

*L*isten here, pilgrims. Kevin Costner's *Open Range* talks too much talk, but it walks enough walk. And it's got great hats. So it's a pleasure to report, minor caveats aside, that it's a fine, old-fashioned two and a half hours at the Bijou.

The movie basically represents a balancing act of some considerable courage and grace. It's poised between corny and mythic and between vanity project and work of art. How close it comes to parody, and how much it yearns to memorialize the great Costner mug—but for the most part, the artist in this guy overpowers the egoist, at least until the final scenes.

The myth that underlies *Open Range* is the primal American definition of freedom as space. We're a people who like to move about. When we see an empty horizon, we yearn to know what's beyond it. That freedom is what's resonantly at stake in this account of a brutal range war between cattle-industry factions in a vast green cathedral of 1882.

Somewhere beyond the mighty Mississip, a big rancher (Michael Gambon, sporting muttonchops and brogue) claims all that verdant protein under all that blue sky is his, even if he doesn't own or hasn't fenced it. A gypsy crew of "free-grazers" meanders onto his self-claimed sea of grass with their pitiful herd and their four men, meaning but to let the cows feed, then move them on. They are attacked for their transgression; one man dies, another is seriously wounded. The two unhurt survivors—Costner's laconic, embittered ex-gunhand Charley Waite and Robert Duvall's more avuncular cracker-barrel speechifier Boss Spearman—are told to git.

But there ain't no git in these boys, so they strap on the long guns, chat up a pretty gal, buy a chocolate bar, smoke a real nice cee-gar so as to sample a little of life's pleasures at what they suspect is its end, and head down to the O.K. Corral. Okay, okay, it's not the O.K. Corral, but for all the fat blobs of lead that are slung in its confines, pardner, you wouldn't want to live on the difference.

Has Costner the director seen other westerns? And how. Clearly he's studied the majestic pictorialism and languid story rhythms of George Stevens's *Shane.* He's loved the bickerin' and feudin' that marked the internal dynamics of *The Wild Bunch.* He's watched the young Clint Eastwood saunter down the ramshackle street of a Roman cow town, and draw first and shoot faster than greased mercury. He's seen the dark interiors of John Ford's *My Darling Clementine*, and noted how in the movie the old black powder cartridges left seething fumes in the air. He remembers how much the Duke's *Hondo* loved his dog. He may even have seen his own *Dances With Wolves*, with its appreciation of thorny warrior psychology.

But even as you feel the self-conscious manipulation of these influences, you are taken aback by how brilliantly the movie tweaks them to its own uses. In fact, that's the strategy behind the whole picture: to recreate the traditional but find an unconventional expression for it. It's a revisionist western whose main revision is to de-revise the western back to its original form.

That aesthetic finds its fullest deployment in the issue of design: *Open Range* is a superb piece of movie construction that achieves a near-perfect balance between the remembered and the seen-anew. It re-creates the traditional structures—the main street, the townies' restaurant, the stable, the marshal's office—yet it finds ways, continuously, to make them fresh. I note with particular satisfaction that site of endless oater confrontations as well as ritual consumption of rotgut from unlabeled bottles of amber liquid, the Saloon.

If you're of a certain age, you've been in at least 10,000 saloons, usually called the Long Branch and usually with the Marshal, the tall feller with the star played by James Arness. But Marshal Dillon is nowhere to be found, and this saloon is different: It's dark and paneled, with wickered windows. It has mirrors, like the Long Branch, but the glass is definitely nineteenth-century for the wavery reflection it casts. Stop and reflect a bit: Someone has thought about the quality of glass in 1882. (Smeary glass is a visual motif of the movie.)

In other ways, the movie is full of bold, original, seemingly authentic details: I loved the river of mud that runs down the main street, and the collapsed, out-of-kilter building frame that tilts toward surrealism in the middle of a gunfight, and the way the blacksmith (Michael Jeter) rides a rope in and out of the frame. I love the joke the two heroes play on the unstated homoerotic meanings of the partner-western, when Duvall's yakky Boss says to Costner, "Hell, we're just like a old married couple."

Yet the movie isn't quite realistic. While it sports enough true grit and gloppy mud for a dozen anti-sentimental westerns, it's also reaching forever to the universal. There's more mythic posing against that beautifully evoked, endless green landscape than the four presidents on the mountain in the Black Hills. And all that hazy glass: Perhaps that's a way of documenting the process by which myth blurs reality toward an ideal. The music is grand, stirring and shows the influence of too much Elmer Bernstein. And maybe even too much Leonard Bernstein. The writing— or is that overwriting?—occasionally feels built for sound bite: "There's some things," says Costner's Charley, just before the elegant launch of a gleamy tobacco gob into the mud, "gnaw on a man worse than dying." Or, he says, "Boss, I'm all right with killing. I've always been all right with killing." His romantic interest, played by a handsome if underused Annette Bening, says, "I have had my disappointments."

The story progresses, but it never hurries. Each scene plays out in real time (admittedly, a lot of it), as the actors speak in one continuous shot, until they're finished, without a lot of jazzy editing. Costner insists, perhaps overdogmatically, on spelling out motives and emotions. He's not one for new-movie shorthand techniques. He may be the best director of 1957.

Possibly the screenplay, by Craig Storper, is too clunky. Or possibly the original novel, by Lauran Paine (author of 899 other books!), was too clunky. In either case, Costner, an earnest plodder much of the time, frequently can find no way to cinematically express ideas, so his characters just baldly state them in revelatory oratory. Charley, for example, confesses that he's an ex-guerrilla (presumably of the Confederate psycho Quantrill's sponsorship), too used to killing. How much better if Boss had simply noticed his spectacular dexterity in handling the Colt, asked how Charley came by it, and was rewarded with a guerrilla's thousand-yard glare more telling and more chilling than all the speeches in the world.

The tendency to explain rather than dramatize reaches its apex in the too many minutes left in the movie after the big gun-down, when Charley pitches woo toward the movie's least satisfactory character, Sue (Bening). I suppose Costner is making a good-faith effort to portray the realities of Victorian courtship, but on and on it goes, in dialogue too wooden to be believed. Anyone can write this stuff, which almost sounds something like, "Why, ma'am, I jist wanted to tell ya, my heart's thrummin' like a butterfly at the prospect that you might look with favor upon my petition to come spoonin' sometime when all this cruel fracas has at last come to a just finish." Meanwhile, the poor gal only wants a date. She seems to age a decade or so while he spits out his speeches.

I hate to point that out, given the general fabulousness of the film, but until the end, Costner has been content to let Duvall's spunky Boss be the show. Boss has the good lines and is the driving force, while Charley broods in the distance, a sullen, beautiful Achilles with issues. At the end, however, Costner reclaims the center of the movie with that solid fifteen of unnecessary face time. It feels ever so slightly indecent.

But the movie is psychologically insightful enough to make Charley's issues interesting, in the modern way. Unlike the thousand heroes of Republic Pictures and other Poverty Row factories, he's reflective enough to feel unworthy. He's a man who has killed, a lot; he feels himself to be an infection upon society and has sought to purify himself in the isolation of the cattle drive and to spare civilization his predations. It isn't stated, but one assumes he's the whoring kind of man, not the marrying kind. But in the spasm of violence that concludes the action arc of the movie, he sees a different possibility. Instead of being one of John Ford's facilitators, destined tragically to restore order and then be exiled to wander bitterly between the winds (Wayne in *The Searchers*), it's his humble need to return. Too bad the movie can't find a more eloquent way to express that.

But as an action director, Costner is at his best. What a fine shootout to bring it to an almost-end. Maybe you have to have a taste for this stuff to see the distinctions, but in my narrow mind, he finds many ways to reinvent a stock occurrence. It's actually three gunfights in one, or one gunfight in three acts. The first is pure O.K. Corral action, men at close range, shooting straight-up, a lot, in a few seconds, until only a few are standing. Then it's a running gun battle, through streets and buildings (someone has seen *High Noon*). And finally it's almost an expression of community will, as the bloodied Charley faces antagonists at the font of corrupt civic power, the marshal's office (in Eastwood's *Joe Kidd* it was a judge's office), and the townsfolk have joined in an act of revolutionary restoration.

Flawed and talky, sinuous and violent, funny and warm, the movie does it's main thing, its raison d'être, brilliantly: It tells you how the West was won. (AUGUST 15, 2003)

The Hi-Lo Country is the movie that the late, great Sam Peckinpah yearned to make all those years ago. Under other guidance, it has finally reached the screen and unsurprisingly it turns out to be about a one-man wild bunch.

That Big Boy Matson, he's a heroic sumbitch, wild, crazy, free, smart, tough, violent, and of course funny in that needley sergeant's way, infinitely amused at the scrabblings of the less testosterone-endowed. As played (or should I say occupied) by Woody Harrelson, he's all of a piece, all man, and all trouble. He's too big to play by rules or adjust to the changes coming across the West. That makes him interesting, dangerous, and doomed.

His primary misfortune is that it's not old Mexico, 1914, just before a big war; it's New Mexico, 1946, just after a big war. The times they are a-changing; fellow can't just up and do what he wants. Cowboying across an open range is a dying profession. Makes more sense to ship the critters by truck to the railhead. That is, if some corporate Jimmy-gimme hasn't bought up all the cattle.

Big Boy's story is conventional, as derived from a novel by an authentic cowboy named Max Evans. One can certainly see the elements that attracted Peckinpah, a specialist in the double-edged weapon of machismo, so attractive, so tragic, and the elegiac sense of a frontier slowly closing down. And Peckinpah's most successful screenwriter, Walon Green (he wrote *The Wild Bunch*, among other films), is behind the keyboard on this project. Green writes exceptionally good pick-a-fight dialogue; he loves those little cosmic riffs of antagonism where two cowpokes pick at each other's scabs in incrementally escalating scorn until violence is inevitable. (*The Wild Bunch* was full of such nasty pleasures, too.)

But what's the Britisher Stephen Frears doing behind the camera; does the director of *Dangerous Liaisons* seem an ideal choice for a western? Well, remember that *Liaisons*, as well as another film in the Frears oeuvre, *The Hit*, were about male predation at its ugliest. Frears may not know the geography, but he certainly knows the territory.

The story is narrated from the point of view of Pete Calder (Billy Crudup, who looks astonishingly like Tommy Lee Jones before his face crinkled up like the floor of the Mojave Desert). Pete loves Big Boy and almost becomes his little brother, but there are complications: The first is that Big Boy already has a little brother, called Little Boy (Cole Hauser); the second is that as much as he loves him, Pete hates him, too, for Big Boy is currently having a big whoopee with the beautiful Mona (Patricia Arquette), whom Pete secretly lusts after. Now, just to keep it interesting, Mona is the wife of Les (John Diehl), the foreman of big greedy ranch owner Jim Ed Love (Sam Elliott).

Does the foregoing suggest there's enough material in *The Hi-Lo Country* for any three or four movies? And I didn't even mention the blizzard, Jim Ed's ambitions to buy up all the cattle and range, the poker scene, a long rodeo sequence, and a final blast of squalid domestic violence.

Way too much movie. Not enough time. It's a kind of triangle-o-rama, in which Jim Ed and Big Boy both love the land; Big Boy and Pete both love Mona; Big Boy and Les both love Mona; Pete and Little Boy both love Big Boy; Big Boy and Pete both love a horse called Old Sorrel; Hoover Young and Jim Ed both love the cattle business; Mona and Josepha both love Pete (a little, at least). And I don't even have room to tell you who Hoover Young (James Gammon) is.

By the end, the film has lost all the semblance of coherent narrative and become a collection of almost random episodes. Each is amusing or powerful, but they don't connect into something meaningful. The theme about Big Cattle taking over, in the form of Sam Elliott? Forgotten, utterly. Elliott, after dominating every scene he's in with that squint-eyed look of ironic superiority, vanishes. The love affair between Pete and Josepha (Penélope Cruz, a big Spanish movie star in her first American film)? Lost. Blown away.

But for a long time, the movie's some kind of fun. It has a wonderful sense of not one but two distinct styles in American history: the West and the forties. It offers some crackerjack fight scenes, and a gut-busting rodeo thing when two crazed stuntmen actually get in the ring with one very large, angry bull that doesn't know it's in the movies.

And, bless his soul, Frears has studied the iconography of the American western with enough attention to offer some old, lost movie thrills: the sweep of prairie giving away to blue mountains in the distance, the course of a lone rider across the plains, a sense of the incredible dynamism and danger in cattle ranching, particularly as it applies to large bovine morons who also don't know they're in the movies and don't like the rope just tossed around their necks. On that score alone, I took some pleasure from the film. Too bad, in the end, it was all hat and no cattle.

(JANUARY 15, 1999)

Those who have seen it know that the old Sergio Leone western *The Good, the Bad and the Ugly* should more accurately be called *The Not Very Good, the Pretty Darn Bad and the Sort of Ugly.*

The movie, which arrived on these shores in 1966, was the third of the Leone westerns that established Clint Eastwood as a world star, after *A Fistful of Dollars* and *For a Few Dollars More.* Then, it was about seventeen hours and twenty-nine minutes long. Now a completely restored version of the film has arrived and it is at its full length, nineteen hours and forty-seven minutes.

I exaggerate, but not by much. Actually, about fifteen minutes of film has been added, and the print looks terrific. And the movie, which will be shown September 4, is otherwise the movie exactly as it always was: not a narrative so much as a folk opera on western themes as interpreted by an Italian director somewhere amid what appears to be a giant construction project outside Rome. It ambles, it riffs, it indulges: It lacks the toughness and precision of the first two films (with their plots stolen from the Japanese), and guess what—it's not even really about Clint Eastwood's character!

It's magnificent, but is it a western? Or, to put it another way, is it a great western or is it a great Italian western? I would hold to the latter interpretation out of pure nativist pride. No damn furriner has made as good a tale of cowboy life and culture, of courage and conflict and cattle, of race and hate and bitter spite, of horses and Indians and lawmen and Colts, as John Ford's *The Searchers* or Howard Hawks's *Red River* or any of the dozens of smaller, but hardly remembered films, like the Anthony Mann–Jimmy Stewart jobs or the Randolph Scott–Budd Boetticher series or the great run of Sam Peckinpah films.

But . . . this is a great movie, whatever strange estuary of the western river it occupies. To see it in the old (but restored) AFI Silver, that cathedral of art moderne, that vault of streamline, to see it big on the big, big screen, to hear that total screwball electrified music—waa-WAA-waa—belching out and filling the lit space above your eyes: Baby, it doesn't get much better than that.

Leone's genius was both big and small, an astonishing mix of gifts. He was really good on faces and, in fact, this film begins with a close-up out of Brueghel: one of the countless Italian extras Leone chose for warts, bumps, crevasses, swellings, scars, and wattles. In fact, the close-up is so gigantic that you are astonished to learn that this guy is there merely to die, rather ignominiously, too, at the hands of the Sort of Ugly, Eli Wallach's Mexican bandit Tuco.

In short order—no, actually, in long order—Leone introduces us to the other components of his film: The Not-So-Good, i.e., Eastwood, as a nameless adventurer who will grow into *A Fistful of Dollars*'s Man With No Name (this is a prequel to that film), and then the Pretty Darn Bad, played, in his greatest role, by American expat Lee Van Cleef, who had one of the most feral of faces in all of human genedom. Van Cleef, a minor character actor in Hollywood westerns (he's the second guy to die in *High Noon*), got to Italy early and, God bless him for his enterprise, hacked out a pretty good and completely unanticipated career in the spaghetti oaters, where he became a big star. Once it has established these three faces, the movie then tracks them across the Southwest in search of a lost payroll shipment. However, the Civil War keeps getting in the way.

And you say: Uh, Steve, the Civil War, she was not fought in the Southwest. Don't tell me; tell Signor Leone. If he knew, he didn't care. So amid desert cactus and Mexican villages (which were really outside of Rome), the Civil War is refought, and Leone is far more interested in that than in his story, which is pretty incomprehensible also.*

That lets him express his genius for the big, as in probably the best Civil War battle sequence ever filmed, with its moving subtext of bitter commitment to duty—very powerful stuff in 1966, during the height of Vietnam. A mad colonel, men dying on the scale of that scene in *Gone With the Wind* where the camera pulls back to show Scarlett standing amid thousands of wounded, towns bombarded, trains pulling across the bleak landscape and, of course, through it all, the Good, the Bad and the Ugly hunting each other and the gold. Waa-WAA-waa.

(AUGUST 22, 2003)

*F*or Roy Rogers, the compass always read true west, the clock always said high noon and every town was Dodge City. And the good guys—notably himself—always won.

The West was a dream of decency and justice, manifest destiny was the better path, men were noble, women were schoolmarms or best pals like Dale Evans, children were li'l pioneers. As glorious as the past had been, the future looked even better. Happy trails to you and you and you. That's what Roy stood for, that's what Roy meant.

---

*Wrong, wrong, wrong. As many readers wrote to correct, indeed a Civil War campaign *was* fought in the Southwest. Señor Leone knew better than Señor Hunter.

And if now we no longer believe it, maybe that's our problem, not Roy's, and that gives us no license to laugh at the great cowboy star, who died yesterday at the age of 86 at his home in Apple Valley, California, after a long illness.

Still, it can be a little hard to stifle a snicker today, particularly if you've seen the dusty, bitter, haunted things that westerns became. After all, after the trashy killers of *The Wild Bunch* or even sweaty, shaky Gary Cooper in *High Noon*, Roy always looked a little foolish, like some Eastern dude's view of the campy Westerner. Sophistication wasn't in him: He was foursquare, forthright, but without tragic foreboding.

Yet to laugh at him, and to feel smugly superior to the uncomplicated virtues he represented, is to somehow miss the point. He was exactly what he seemed: courtly, gentlemanly, a man of the Old West—even if he'd been born under the graceless name Leonard Slye in Cincinnati in 1911—who did all the cowboy things with sure, convincing ease.

His wardrobe was almost as lovingly assembled as the armor of a knight about to joust for his lady. He wore two engraved, highly polished six-guns in a double-holster rig, the leather engraved in the high Mexican style and adorned with silver conchos. He never wore jeans, but tight whipcord pants, with squared pockets sporting bright piping to make them stand out. His boots were tall and shiny, also elaborately engraved, usually brightly colored. He often wore a peculiar shirt, dazzling to Easterners, with buttons and pockets at strange angles, contrasting patterns of checks, a flutter of fringe spangling the chest.

Such shirts! Sometimes they had drawstring necks and sometimes that double placket of buttons running in a V up the torso. Fascinating shirts, like feats of engineering, shirts that took a blueprint to put on each morning. And of course he always wore a neckerchief tight about his throat and a white hat unstained with sweat. He rode a magnificent palomino, a horse so golden it could have come from an argonaut's dream, and he commanded it—Trigger, "the smartest horse in the movies"—atop a saddle as magnificent as a king's, festooned with silver as well. And when he rode, he was sentimental poetry in motion, with that easy Western authority, posture rigid yet flexible, standing in the stirrups, the wind battering him but never blowing that white hat away. Like all the great cowboys, he was great on horseback, good with animals and guns and the elderly, infinitely courtly to women, and steady of gun hand or fist with bad guys, all of whom, by some weird code of etiquette, forgot to shave that morning.

Of course he was the ceremonial cowboy; each of his implements or accouterments had its roots in authentic cowpoke or cattle-drive culture, but each had been removed from it, shined, polished, turned to artifact, almost as if to be inserted into a museum. His was the blemishless West, a museum West, a boy's West.

So it was not merely consistent but also mandatory that although he was man of justice, he was never a killer, a gunman, a shootist, a so-ciopath. He was never a man with no name and no past or future: He had a name and a past and a future—it was America. He hailed from the age where they didn't know the prefix to "hero" was necessarily "anti-." When he drew and fired it was never to kill, but only to knock the firearms out of his opponent's hands.

And this played well. It's easy to forget that for nearly a decade before the box miniaturized him and made him a mere touchstone in the pop-cult meltdown of baby-boomer prepubescent memory, he was a genuine movie star. After migrating to California in 1929 and spending time as a fruit picker and truck driver, he tried to convey his sweet but hardly overpowering singing voice into a radio career.

"Leonard Slye" sounding like a child molester in a novel by Dickens, he changed his name to Dick Weston, to little avail, but when he changed it again, to Roy Rogers, and founded the western singing group the Sons of the Pioneers, he began to get radio jobs.

As a singer, he's credited as one of the founders of the western sound, and has been voted into the Country-Western Hall of Fame twice, first as part of the Sons of the Pioneers (in 1980) and then as a solo artist in 1988. His standards included "Tumbling Tumbleweeds," "Cool Water," "I'm an Old Cowhand (from the Rio Grande)," and, of course, "Happy Trails," which he recorded with his second wife, Dale Evans, who wrote it and who survives him.

He broke into films in 1935 with four Sons of the Pioneers movies, when the concept of the Singing Cowboy wasn't cornball but deadly earnest. His competitors included Gene Autry and even John Wayne, who was reduced to playing "Sandy the Singing Cowboy" in late '30s B-westerns.

Rogers, with his low-key skills and pleasant singing voice, prospered, getting his first starring role in *Under Western Stars* in 1938. Soon he began his association with the avuncular, bewhiskered, and comical George "Gabby" Hayes. In his few mainstream films, like *Dark Command*, he hardly registers, but in the lively, informal world of the B-westerns, he found his milieu and the perfect outlet for his talents. In 1942 he starred in and earned the nickname "King of the Cowboys," beginning a run that lasted throughout the forties and into the early fifties, when he was voted the No. 1 western star for nine consecutive years.

Always a shrewd businessman, he understood early on that TV would kill the B-westerns, so he got into it as soon as possible, beginning a TV series that would last from 1952 until 1957.

As an actor, his prime virtue was his low-key likability. There was something open and uncomplicated in his face, and he seemed unplagued by deeper states of anxiety. Nothing ever fazed him, nothing ever perturbed him. He was without doubt or hesitation. His sureness of character, his lack of rancor and pain, his lack of complex sexual or masculine edge made him the ideal small-screen star. He took to television without a crumb of trouble and quickly rose to prominence just when the new medium was taking over the American family. He assembled a superb cast of second-line comic players, as well as the wonderful animal sidekicks, like Bullet, a German shepherd, and Trigger, that golden horse. And there was always Pat Brady, struggling with his fickle jeep Nellybelle, good for a laugh.

With other theatricalized cowboys like Autry and Hopalong Cassidy and the Lone Ranger, he starred in hundreds of televised morality plays, usually sponsored by a cereal company or a chocolatey milk enhancer, and in less than an hour led justice to triumph. As such, he became part of the collective unconscious of the baby-boomer generation, a lodestone memory so intense that men in their fifties who make hundreds of thousands of dollars a year will this day feel just a little chill of mortality as they look down from the city from behind the tinted glass of their fifty-fifth-story corner offices. If death can come to the King of the Cowboys, they'll think, it can come for me, too.   (JULY 7, 1998)

Two

CRIME AND SUSPENSE

For connoisseurs of the paradox, here's a good one: The best film noir of the past decade doesn't even know it's a film noir.

That can only be Curtis Hanson's superb *L.A. Confidential*, which just opened to an almost universal chorus of praise and looks to be one of the big fall films. No wonder: The movie is a font of the old Bijou pleasures of that most bracing of all American genres. In the density of its plot, it recalls such noir classics as *The Big Sleep* and *Chinatown*. In the intensity of its violence it recalls *The Big Heat* and *The Killers*. In the bleakness of its perspective—the titillation of nihilism, don't you know?—it recalls *Out of the Past* and the oh-so-juicily depressing *Body Heat*. Even its really cool title allies it with previous noirs, like *Kansas City Confidential*, *New York Confidential*, and *Miami Expose*. It's everything a film noir ought to be, except that in one very firm sense, it's not a film noir at all.

But perhaps we are ahead of ourselves. Some weeks ago, I confidently threw the term into a piece and was confounded with enough calls from baffled readers the next day to realize that what is a staple of the professional movie-viewing business and this particular critic's key trope may not be widely understood by those among you who live in the real world, you poor things. So let us begin with this: What is film noir?

And here's the answer from someone who once taught a course in it at a prominent educational institution so elite that it would never have admitted him as an undergraduate: I don't know.

Note that I don't say: I have no idea. In fact, I have too many ideas. This would all make much more sense if I knew less about it. But it's all so confusing.

The crux of the issue seems to come down to a debate over style versus meaning. Is noir both, or is it only one or the other? The style is familiar: the shadowy night look, almost abstract urban landscapes, a surreal sense to the play of light and dark, highlights of neon and reflections off puddles or dampness; fog; tilted angles; the visual correlative of a diseased or excited mind. The themes are also familiar: urban decay, moral compromise, powerful, evil women (the "femme fatale"), corruption and conspiracy everywhere. Like pornography, you know it if you see it.

As a concept, we can certainly root film noir in time. The term—from the French, meaning "black film"—refers to a genre of movies that dominated the American film industry in the late forties and early fifties, which many ascribe to the exhaustion and depression that necessarily followed a massive social effort to win a global war. The films had one other attribute in common—almost always they boasted a title that had a hard urban lyricism, a tough guy's poesy: *The Big Clock, Criss Cross, He Walked by Night, The Asphalt Jungle, D.O.A., Cry Danger.*

What is so fascinating about film noir is that it just will not go away. Even after other genres like westerns, biopics, costumers, monster movies, and space operas come, blossom and wither, film noir in some form or other retains its intrinsic power to shock and unsettle, and young filmmakers persist in making their reputations through it. Lawrence Kasdan got his start with *Body Heat*, which some believe remains his best film; more recently John Dahl has worked out a very decent niche with *Kill Me Again, Red Rock West,* and the unforgettable *The Last Seduction.* Quentin Tarantino must have certainly seen every film noir ever made, as *Reservoir Dogs* and *Pulp Fiction* make clear; Joel and Ethan Coen broke into the big time with *Blood Simple* and then reached greatness in *Fargo,* both films as noir as it comes; and even Oliver Stone has noir impulses, indulged in *Natural Born Killers* and in the upcoming *U Turn.*

Of course in their original form, the movies did not just pop into existence from nowhere. Indeed, their emergence after the war may be viewed as a congruence of disparate cultural themes that met, commingled, struck sparks in the night, and somehow amalgamated into something that felt entirely new. But that simply points out the truism that everything used to be something else, and that something else also used to be something else.

Part of the "something else" was German expressionism, that gaudy expression of Weimar decadence that flowered in the rubble of the defeated German empire. The Key Theatre in Georgetown is still showing *M*, Fritz Lang's sublime 1931 film set in the Berlin underground, about the search for a child murderer, and to see it is to be present at the creation of what would become noir. Lang had the look and the feel down pat: a dark world of twisty alleys and wet pavement, the milieu of professional crime and the games between hunter and hunted. He would eventually emigrate to the United States, where he made *You Only Live Once*, *The Big Heat*, *While the City Sleeps*, and *Clash by Night*, among others, and Lang's career, in this sense, is not only brilliant in its own right but also highly symbolic. It stand for the careers of dozens of other film artists (like directors Raoul Walsh, Michael Curtiz, André de Toth, Anthony Mann, Billy Wilder, and Otto Preminger, and cinematographers Joseph Biroc, Karl Freund, Russell Metty, Ernest Laszlo, and Karl Struss) who were dislocated by Nazism, fled to the New World, and, under the sunny California skies, let their pessimism and world-weariness leak into the American body filmic. They shot L.A. through a lens of Weimar and made it look like a city invented by Kafka. Fair enough. But noir's European antecedents must be considered to go back even further than that.

Surely a key concept in noir is the importance of the subconscious and of unknowable motivations like guilt, compensation, envy, even out-and-out psychopathology (like Lang's driven, terrifying, yet pathetic child murderer). The imagery from which noir is largely built is a visual metaphor for the unconscious. The very concept of the flashback, such a key noir narrative ploy, is Freudian, for it is founded on the idea of the subconscious as a kind of eternal tape recorder, always absorbing information and able to re-create entire scenes from out of the past when necessary to advance the plot. All this, of course, dates back to Herr Doktors Freud and Jung, and their discoveries that the rational world that we so trusted and its neat order that we so believed in really rested on a teetering internal edifice that could collapse at any second. Yes: the edifice complex!

Noir movies, therefore, tend to emphasize highly anxious states of being; noir heroes are always haunted, or terrified, or desperate, or suicidal. They live in baths of clammy sweat and their eyes always bulge; they swallow, smoke, drink, have white dry gunk on their lips, and probably could use a shower, but at your house, not mine. They're like Edvard Munch's screamer on the bridge in the orange fog, their heads distended as a howl of despair tears out of their lungs like a burning rat fleeing a fire. It's so damned European it makes you hunger for Gauloises, espresso, a beret, and nice Luger to pet under your trench coat.

All that is certainly true. But then again, to complicate matters even more, it is equally if contradictorily true that much of the energy that came into noir had American literary antecedents as well. (I told you this stuff was hard.) Noir, in a sense, was the arrival into film of an American literary movement called hard-boiled, itself descended from Raymond Chandler and James M. Cain and Dashiell Hammett out of Ernest Hemingway and Mark Twain and Herman Melville before them. For what the hard-boilers represented was a reclamation of the vernacular American language, poetic not in its complexity of structure or the ornamentation of its rhetoric, the loftiness of its thought, the delicacy of its imagery, but in its blunt precision. "He looked like a tarantula on a piece of angel food," Chandler wrote in an early novel, a simile so powerfully American it almost brings tears to the eyes.

With the clarity in language came a clarity of vision toward the city and the body politic: The hard-boiled writers refused to sentimentalize and they saw through things. They knew how stuff really worked. They didn't see downtown as a magic place but as a cesspool with a skyline, and they knew that all politicos were just bagmen in suits, with "4 Rent" tattooed on their foreheads. They saved their sense of romance for heroes who kept their higher morality hidden desperately and survived among the sharks only by pretending to be sharks. The last thing a Philip Marlowe or a Sam Spade would want known about himself was how honest he really was and what a code of honor he secretly adhered to. These guys survived in the jungle by taking on the leopard's spots.

And because so much of noir was visual in its meaning, some painters must be hauled in here, too. Certainly the visual poet laureate of noir is Edward Hopper, who painted the haunting emptiness in the city, something that the best noirs always get. His *Nighthawks* could be a poster from any of dozens of forties movies, with its all-night sentinels pouring down cups of joe in a bath of hot light against a night so empty it appears as if the Reds had gone ahead and dropped the neutron bomb. Reginald Marsh is another artist of the lost city who captured the sense of death in the streets, and he haunted New York for urban vistas.

Two of the earliest and best noirs were drawn directly from Hammett and Chandler, and both starred the greatest hard-boiled dick of them all, Humphrey Bogart. The first was 1941's *The Maltese Falcon*, where Bogart's Spade tracks down the killer of a partner he didn't even much like (he was sleeping with the jerk's wife), not out of honor or vengeance but because it's what you did when your partner got killed. Spade is a smart piece of work, all right, tough and resilient, and he looked good smoking a Camel in a trench coat under a slouchy fedora, three now-lost American arts. But, man, as good as *The Maltese Falcon* was, it couldn't hold a match, much less light a Camel, to *The Big Sleep*.

Directed by Howard Hawks, co-written by William Faulkner (probably drunk at the time) from the novel by Chandler, it's the movie to which *L.A. Confidential* owes the most. Bogart's Philip Marlowe, private shamus and ex-DA's man, sees through everything. Hired by the dying old millionaire General Sternwood to find Sean Reagan, a missing chauffeur, he cuts through a plot surprisingly like *Confidential*'s, involving gangsters, a high-end porn ring, beautiful decadent women, corrupt cops, all of it so headily mixed it would take a graduate student to figure out. Yet it works, much in the same way that *Confidential* works, primarily in the sureness of its storytelling and the swagger of its star and the pizzazz of its style. It is said—possibly apocryphally—that there's still one murder in the plot that Faulkner couldn't figure out and that Chandler, who later became a very fine scriptwriter himself, was of no help. But that's no matter: *The Big Sleep* caught the allure of Los Angeles and made you see how its pleasure eroded character and sense and how it took a very special kind of honor to survive them. That's *Confidential*'s point, too.

You can see how complicated all this gets. Is any crime film a film noir? No. Not if it's merry, witty, in color, its view of the universe optimistic, its vision epic as opposed to claustrophobic. Are the first two *Godfathers* film noir? No. For two reasons: The first is that they are too great, too expansive, too humanistic, too Shakespearean, too resonant, and their pleasures too powerful for film noir. That's the difference between a great genre film and a great film. It's also the difference between Chandler's *Farewell, My Lovely* and Dostoyevsky's *Crime and Punishment*, a great genre novel and a great novel. The second reason is that I say so, and what I say goes, because I'm a film critic, and we rule.

That, in fact, is another cause of the persistence of noir: its intellectual fascinations to a certain justly despised class of American scum—film critics. We crits won't let it die because the movies are so rich in meaning and texture and so useful as a way of explaining other movies that they continue to be evoked and studied by pointy-heads who write on film professionally, and much that has been written is brilliant. Before he was a director and screenwriter, Paul Schrader wrote something like the ultimate noir essay, called merely "Notes on Noir," in which he traced the genre's rise and fall through three distinct stages, and judging Robert Aldrich's *Kiss Me Deadly* (1955) as the final noir masterpiece. But Schrader was writing as if the genre were gone—in the early seventies, even before he himself wrote *Taxi Driver*, and he didn't foresee noir's next development, which might be called ironic noir.

That is the film noir we have been seeing lately—films by directors like Dahl and Tarantino and Schrader and Kasdan that are different from the films that came before them chiefly because they are aware of them. By now, noir has been codified into a certain look, a certain set of thematic concerns, a certain philosophical stance, a certain set of permitted permutations, and those are played with endlessly, almost achieving a state of parody. They are, in other words, post-film-school noirs, noirs made by men who love movies more than they love stories and themes more than they love characters. They get everything about noir except what's so cool about it, and the results are almost always sterile and inert. The movies aren't bad, but in some way they're not serous; they're playful, witty, full of sight gags and visual jokes (the Coens in particular and also Tarantino), but they lack weight. You feel about them the same way you feel after watching an impersonator do a famous movie star; you yearn for the real thing.

And that is exactly, to make a game attempt to bring this around to where it started, what is so fine and so fresh about *L.A. Confidential*—the wondrous Hanson, either through stupidity or blind luck or lack of a proper education, hasn't thought terribly hard about the conventions of noir and has made a movie as if he's completely unaware of them. Maybe he is. But he hasn't overdirected: The movie doesn't have that studied, grad school look to it, where it's consciously aping other films, even quoting from them, and there's no moment when you can sit up and say, "Oh, that's just like the moment in *The Asphalt Jungle* where Sam Jaffe ogles the little girl."

Particularly, he's avoided the self-conscious visual trappings of the style, like the alleys, the neon, the puddles, the wet streets, what Pauline Kael called "the candy of filmmaking." We don't have a feeling of a style imposed from without, but rather one emerging, spontaneously, from within, as was so true of the original noirs. So what we get is an oddly paradoxical creation: a movie that bears an intense resemblance to noir in its substance, in its attitudes, in its ideas, and that jacks energy out of those connections; but at the very same time it has consciously disconnected itself from the visual conventions of noir.

Hanson is straight-ahead and showy; he wants every vintage car he's rounded up to get on screen, every wide, loud tie and pleatless fifties trouser, every woman's Joan Crawford red nails, all the guns right (it was an all-Colt world back then: Detective Specials and .45s); his universe is sun-filled, and even the night shots are abnormally bright and lustrous.

The despair at the core of *L.A. Confidential* comes from within. Like the great film noirs, it's not a product of art direction or fog machines, but an examination of souls rubbed raw by evil and pain. It wears its nihilism proudly, because it takes itself so seriously. It doesn't look like a film noir, but in the most important way, it feels like one.

(SEPTEMBER 21, 1997)

L.A. *Confidential* has the lowdown, the true gen, the inside skinny all right, but not merely behind the news; it knows what goes on deep in the heart and the reptile part of the brain as well. It's a look at L.A. in the fifties, before Disneyland but after the Fall of Man, and it sees a city so seething with corruption and squalor one wonders why the God who fried Sodom hasn't issued a cosmic eviction notice for this blighted burg as well.

"Down these mean streets," another surveyor of this moral miasma once wrote, "a man must go who is not himself mean, who is neither tarnished nor afraid." Well, that was L.A. in the forties, the author was Raymond Chandler, and one man was enough, especially if his name was Philip Marlowe. In James Ellroy's L.A. of the fifties, as Curtis Hanson's brilliant adaptation of Ellroy's best novel has it, it takes three men to work the mean streets, all cops, and ironically one is mean, one is tarnished and one is afraid.

Bud White (the Aussie Russell Crowe) is the mean one, tough and fearless, formed by pain. His sense of life is pain: He can dish it out and if need be take it. He likes to break things and men, and when New York thugs come west to sniff around the paradise left unguarded by Mickey Cohen's incarceration, they get a meat sandwich courtesy of Bud's fists and are sent home with smashed mouths and broken jaws. But maybe under his beef, his scarred knuckles, and the well-worn Colt Detective Special he carries, he has a brain, a heart, and a primitive sense of justice.

Ed Exley (another Aussie, Guy Pearce), by contrast, is afraid, at least in the beginning, when his lack of force, his nervousness, prevent him from stopping a police riot. Lacking strength, he is a creature of intellect: Bespectacled and quick of wit, he looks more like a grad student than a cop, and his greatest strengths are investigation and interrogation. He sniffs weakness and inconsistency. He tracks men best not on the streets but through files and documents. He's a reader, a thinker, and aggressively ambitious. He also has well-oiled political instincts and knows which butts to kiss, which backs to stab.

And finally there's Jack Vincennes (Kevin Spacey), as tarnished as an old urn. He stands for corrupt charm. He has the social ease indicative of a narcissistic personality disorder, the ability to mingle, cajole, and schmooze. He's oleaginous and smooth, a dapper boulevardier of a cop who supports himself in style—he has great clothes—by doing favors for a sleazy tabloid reporter, wrecking this or that career for the sake of a buck. But possibly he, too, has the potential for redemption.

In fact, redemption is the central theme of *L.A. Confidential,* for each of the main characters will perform a beastly act and each will face his own evil and recoil from it and try to atone, thereby becoming heroic. In a city named for its angels, they and they alone seem to believe in Heaven and hope for a ticket to it.

One thing they know from the get go: They are not there yet and that's because of where they are. What the film gets best of all is the sense of L.A. as a paradise lost, a land of milk, honey, and sex turned rancid in the sun, as the harshly held Puritan disciplines of the East yield to the temptations of the city's nighttime fragrances.

What galvanizes the three not-yet-heroes is the infamous Nite Owl massacre. Six people in an all-night eatery, three killers, three shotguns: The result is Edward Hopper's *Nighthawks* with blood spatters by Jackson Pollock on an amphetamine high. When quick detective work suggests three black men might be the culprits, L.A.'s finest act with the brutal decisiveness that would make them so famous many years later when the quarry was Rodney King. It falls to Bud and Ed to arrest them and to Ed to break them in interrogation rooms; when they escape—hmmm, wasn't that a bit easy?—it's Ed who tracks them down and deals with them.

That's exactly what the city loves the cops for. They are heroes. The important captain Dudley Smith (James Cromwell) approves, and with his approval the brass happily get into the reception line. But even ambitious Ed, whose career has been made by the episode, begins to suspect that maybe what happened was a little too pat. Bud, who hates Ed for his rectitude, begins to look into the same case, even while he's falling in love with a prostitute (Kim Basinger) who looks a little too much like Veronica Lake. At the same time, the charming Jack has begun to tumble to an odd little racket going on behind the curtains of the stylish mansions of the Hills: Someone's running a vice network so pricey that it can afford to use hookers who've been surgically altered to look like movie stars. Gradually, as each cop begins to pick at his own private loose ends, a deeper, darker picture emerges.

The plot's not a conspiracy theory but a conspiracy actuality. Everything is a front concealing a cynical ruse where smart, vicious sociopaths are running a mean-spirited, lethal scam, taking over L.A. from the inside. In truth, there's probably too much plot, and even then it's been simplified from Ellroy's original, a text so thick with confusion that you needed to carry a compass to find the next page. But the screenplay, which Hanson wrote with Brian Helgeland, cross-pollinates clues, and we watch as the wrong cop learns the right thing, and we know, before the three cops do, that if they actually could put their spite aside, they could figure it out.

The movie may actually make sense if you take careful notes and hire three graduate students to diagram it in cyberspace, but more to the point, it feels coherent and pleasing as it builds to a big moment when the master player is revealed and ultimately a form of justice achieved. And getting there is the fun.

Hanson delivers something even rarer in film culture, not a new film noir but an old-fashioned total movie, somehow of a single piece. Nearly everything works, with the possible exception of Danny DeVito, vainly clinging to his star persona and unwilling to be truly loathsome as a publisher of a sleazy proto-tabloid. But the actors are fine, particularly Crowe's doughty, stolid, brave Bud Smith, the cinematography (by Dante Spinotti) appropriately lurid with the colors of the night, and the action sequences well-designed and compelling. I particularly like the climactic gunfight, in which heroes cower in a San Berdoo motel while bad guys shred the walls with machine-gun fire, suggesting the complete fragility of the universe and the strength it takes to stand against such reality.

L.A.*Confidential* isn't a great film, but it plays one in the movies.

(SEPTEMBER 19, 1997)

*T*here are seven kinds of cool, and *Jackie Brown* celebrates all of them. It is, at its most basic level, a symphony in the key of cool, with various hipster stylings interweaving on a tiny field of conflict, syncopated to seventies rock (very cool) and occasional gunplay (even cooler), from Quentin Tarantino out of Elmore Leonard. It's the coolest damn thing you ever saw.

Cool No. 1: Urban Street Cool.

Samuel L. Jackson plays Ordell Robbie, who's so cool he's scary. He looks more like a sax man than a gunman and arms merchant, with a braided goatee, large wardrobe of hats, shades, and magenta clothes, and Miles Davis's processed leonine mane of reddish hair. Mood indigo, Ordell? No, Ordell's mood is survival. He's got the throaty rap of a player and one of those cunning street-honed brains that see three moves ahead. No psycho, he kills as a business matter, usually those he knows will betray him, even before they know it. But his real medium of expression is language, specifically the N-word, which he uses as five of the eight parts of speech, always with a poetic flourish that stings like the tip of a whip. The movie's No. 1 moving target, he's being hunted by ATF for weapons violations—the killings feel incidental—and it's the agent's ambition that gets us to—

Cool No. 2: Beautiful-Women-Who-Are-Also-Wise Cool.

We men are such fools. We respond to women with our loins and hearts and they respond to us with their shrewd brains. So it is with Jackie Brown (Pam Grier), a flight attendant fallen on hard times who is making a little pickup change by smuggling money to Ordell's Mexican accounts. Everybody who looks at Jackie, magnificent in carriage, sculptural in body, sultry in movement, thinks she can't be smart. Bad career move. She's the smartest of them all, and is able to secretly commandeer the caper that all the guys think they're controlling, tilt it to her own benefit and, to the complete surprise of her supervisor, the ATF's Ray Nicolette, who represents—

Cool No. 3: Ruthless Cop Cool.

With his feral eyes and deadpan face camouflaging the burning fury within, Nicolette (Michael Keaton) wants to bring Ordell down and thinks he can use Jackie to do so. It's classic cop stuff: Cut into the outfit, turn an underling, play the underling against the big man by setting up a caper that's compromised from the start—in this case, smuggling Ordell's half-mil back into the country so he can invest it in some machine guns. Use people, advance toward a greater good while secretly enjoying the sheer pleasure of the hunt and the kill. But like so many, Ray thinks he's a puppet master when he is actually the marionette. What's so cool about Keaton's Ray, though, is his patience; he's a background guy for the longest time, muted and muttering and seemingly a nobody. But gradually, as the film whistles along, he looms larger and larger until finally in the end, his gun locked in a pro's two-handed grip, he's the Man, not even aware of how he's been cast in the part. In fact, the only one who'll know besides Jackie is someone who is the essence of—

Cool No. 4: Old Coot Cool.

This is Robert Forster, who had another of the ruined careers Tarantino loves to repair, as a smart bail bondsman named Max Cherry with a crush on Jackie, but smart enough to see how smart she is. His coolest thing, besides quiet loyalty and willing acceptance of a lieutenancy in her two-person unit, is that he knows himself, exactly. It doesn't bother him that he's fifty-six and has a hair transplant and that it's not going to get a whole lot better. The movie's center of moral decency, he's the one guy you hope survives, with the possible exception of Exhibit A of—

Cool No. 5: Wasted-Junkie-White-Trash Cool.

Robert De Niro. How cool is he? He's way cool. You wonder, what's he doing here? An ex-cellmate of Ordell's, his Louis Gara is the new man in the outfit, but the comic trope of his appearance is that he just sits there. His is the cool of utter indifference. As Ordell, with his preacher's fire and brimstone and his pimp's delight in manipulation, explains things to Louis, you can tell none of it is registering. He's done so much junk that his eyes are dead as old pennies and his brain is obviously as holey as a wheel of Swiss. He just gets high off a bong he shares with Bridget Fonda (see Cool No. 6), and she also talks fast and he appears not to get it. When at last he swings into action, he fails with such a resounding thud that it's the comic punch line of the film and the ultimate expression of the feckless Tarantino universe, a place of grand plans, shot nerves, capers that don't scan, and existential squalor everywhere in the dingy buildings, comic riffs, and beat-up cars. And predators, as in—

Cool No. 6: Surfer Bimbo Cool.

She's beautiful, young, smart, and mean. Fonda's Melanie is so beautiful and damned, she hates everything and everyone. Lounging about in a bikini and toe rings and subsisting on a diet of marijuana, Evian, and old movies on daytime TV, she's like a harpy put on Earth to fire bolts of grief at all the hopeless wankers who fancy her. She's probably every girl who would never go out with the director when he was a vid-store geek. Tarantino expertly charts the angst she releases into this hermetically sealed world with her utter superiority and the playful though ultimately wasteful way it redounds upon her, causing everything to fall down go boom, as expertly coordinated by the foremost practitioner of—

Cool No. 7: Vid-Geek-Turned-Director Cool.

He's annoying. He talks too much, too fast. His jaw sticks out too far. There's no way he should be dating Mira Sorvino. He's been hiding from his talent for years, acting in and producing crap. But he's revitalized the business and he's profoundly talented, and this film, one of the year's absolute best, despite a dull stretch or two, restores him to his proper place in the universe, which is behind the typewriter and then the camera. Quentin Tarantino: He's baaaa-aaack!　　　　　(DECEMBER 25, 1997)

*I*t is said that the average police gunfight takes place in the dark at a range of seven feet, in which four or fewer shots are fired. The whole thing lasts less than two seconds.

The rules for surviving such an encounter would therefore seem to be:

1) Shoot first.
2) Shoot first.

And of course,

3) Shoot first.

That is not how they do it in the movies, where the gunfight has been a staple of human interaction for ninety-five years, since *The Great Train Robbery*. As the movies have it, these to-dos almost always take place in daylight or at least in a clean, well-lighted place—a nightclub full of big-breasted dancers or a steel foundry where sparks pour from the rusty struts overhead or on Main Street at high noon. It's always one against many, which means that the many are seriously outgunned and have no chance. The whole thing has the air of Mardi Gras, Fellini, and NFL instant replays. It almost never looks scary. It never looks like it would leave you shaken for life. It doesn't look like you'd have trouble sleeping for years afterward.

It just looks like fun.

What compels these observations is the arrival of *The Replacement Killers*, directed by Antoine Fuqua in the style of John Woo. Its gunfights are so far beyond realism that to use them in the same sentence with the word "realism" is somehow an affront to logic. Instead, they're so expansive and madly choreographed that they resemble Busby Berkeley numbers with guns.

For the current variation of Wooified Hollywood gun fighting, the survival rules are also three:

1) Shoot two guns with two hands while diving through the air in slow motion.

2) Use the very best in industrial-strength mousse.

And of course,

3) Choose really cool sunglasses.

But gunfights are like anything else in film culture—subject to the laws of fashion and consequently expressive of considerable evolution over the years. They didn't just start where they are now. Nothing could be that spontaneously stupid. No, they've had to work hard to get stupid.

Ironically, the first filmed gunfight remains one of the most realistic. That's a scene in *The Great Train Robbery* that is notable for its artlessness. For, of course, gun battles must be artless. But in Edward M. Porter's version, two groups of men—a posse and a gang of robbers—just blaze away through the trees at each other in a wild panic. The guns—little smokeless powder in 1903!—belch thunderous clouds of dense, white fog, obscuring the battlefield, turning everything to chaos. Every once in a while, someone spins to the ground, arms flung out, mouth wide open. Then, just as abruptly, it's over. The sequence is hard to watch. Nobody has thought about directing it. It's in one continuous shot, and it just happens, untidy and almost ridiculous. There's no beauty to it, and as the art form developed, beauty became the governing aesthetic in gunfire exchanges.

For the longest time, gun violence was the province of the western. It unspooled by certain rules, all of them having more to do with dramatic camera placement than with reality. But for nearly fifty years, it was the same: the slow stride of two gladiators down a deserted main street, the intense gaze as each shootist met the other's eyes, then, at an agreed-upon signal, the blur as each man reached for iron. Inevitably, one was a bit faster, and the other fell to the ground.

Within this small compass, amazing variations were worked. In *Vera Cruz*, for example, Burt Lancaster smiled, spun his guns, returned them to his holster, then dropped dead. In *A Fistful of Dollars*, Clint Eastwood shot first. In *The Tin Star*, Anthony Perkins drew and fired both guns, toppling Neville Brand. In *High Noon*, Gary Cooper killed the gang that was hunting him in reverse order of hierarchy: little guys first, big guys last. In *Silverado*, Kevin Costner stood at a corner and took out an opponent down each intersecting street. On and on it went, all of it bogus.

There's very little evidence that such friendly encounters ever happened in the Old West, where the real-world rule prevailed, and he who shot first usually won. That's clear merely from the holsters. The Buscadero-style holster, holding the gun low, with all of grip, hammer, and trigger guard exposed, and tied down to facilitate the fast draw, wasn't invented until the 1920s—for the movies. Old-time gunmen, according to historical photos, carried their revolvers in high holsters mounted at waist level, in the Mexican style, where the point was to protect and carry the gun, not access it quickly. The gun was sunk deep, almost completely encased in leather. If trouble was brewing, the owner took it out. Billy the Kid and John Wesley Hardin, for example, were both slain by men who had already removed and cocked their pistols. That's not to say frontier gunmen couldn't shoot fast and well, but that gunfights then were like gunfights now: nasty, brutish, and short.

It's clear, however, that the fast-draw ritual was expressive of chivalric values that underlay the western for much of its time as America's reigning genre. It spoke of the magnificence of virtue, the malevolence of evil. In the crunch, morality would express itself in the swiftness of hand to gun, and evil would doubt itself, slow down, fumble or miss. The better man would be the faster man, so fast he could react and still beat his opponent. There was a connection between reflexes and morality, as if a just God were the true director. Even John Wayne, down to his last four rounds, lets the bad guys shoot first in *Stagecoach*. Coop, facing four men in a naked street under a remorseless sun, lets them make the first move.

Even in other genres, it was clear nobody really cared about reality. Think about some of the famous shootings in movie history. Remember Rick Blaine drilling Major Strasser at the end of *Casablanca*? He holds the gun low, down by his hip. The range is about fifteen feet. He doesn't aim, he just shoots. I tried the same shot with the same gun (a Colt hammerless .380) on a man-size silhouette once. It's hard. (I missed the first six times and finally, by trial and error, got it right on the seventh. Would the major have allowed Rick six tries?) He hit because he was a Good Guy, not because it occurred to him to aim the pistol.

What about the shot Chico takes on Tony at the end of *West Side Story*? It's about fifty feet, in the dark, with an unfamiliar handgun on a moving target. Bang, he nails Tony cold, just as he's about to hug Maria. Only in the movies.

Chaos in gunfights arrived at just about the time chaos arrived in society—in the sixties. Suddenly, gunfights became swirling whirligigs, most notably in *The Wild Bunch,* the magnum opus of gunfight movies. Expressing the ambivalent morality of the Bunch, director Sam Peckinpah plunged the dying shootists into a world of complete craziness. The clarity of action broke down as absolutely as the clarity of morality, as the fights became mad skeins of fast and slow motion knit together in a thousand microcuts, and the bloody strike of bullet on flesh was fetishized. But how realistic was this?

Well, probably not very. Again, the exchanges were governed more by an aesthetic sensibility than by a realistic one, despite the increased quotient of gore. The increasing percussiveness of the editing and the new rhythm of fast motion–slow motion excited your respiratory system and had the effect of exhilaration. The fights were no longer simple, but there was no sense of danger to them, even though we saw people die, perforated a dozen times. Peckinpah gave a dozen interviews pointing out that the film—quite controversial in 1969—was "anti-violence." All spin: In fact, one sees those fights and is drawn to them so totally that it's the pleasure centers of the brain that are being stimulated, not the flight-or-fight centers. They mesmerize you, take you in, like a thunderous symphony. They're gun music, and that's why *The Wild Bunch* was one of the most influential movies ever made, its theories of aesthetic violence dominating American movies for decades afterward.

It's that pleasure center stimulation that Woo and his Hong Kong acolytes have played with in their depictions of gun violence. At their purest, the Hong Kong gunfight films are a combination of the Western obsession with gun violence and the Eastern tradition of martial arts. They are informed not merely by incredible gore but also by an acrobatic freedom from gravity, physics, and reality. Woo does them spectacularly, and his influence had spread even before he moved to the United States. Even a film from so stoic a craftsman as Walter Hill showed the imprint of the Woo style in the absurd *Last Man Standing,* which featured Bruce Willis as the diving two-handed shooter. That seems to be where we are now, so far from reality that the meaning of violence has all but vanished.

For the truth is that despite the incredible number of gunfights that have been filmed, almost nobody in movies ever thought about a violent exchange rigorously. That is why the exchanges are so inflated and preposterous.

Here are some of the things about guns that Hollywood doesn't care about, and never gets right. First off, they are very loud. If you shoot them without ear protection, you deafen yourself. If you are surprised by their sound at close range, you flinch wretchedly. Your ears ring for hours or, as in my case, forever. Guns are also large, heavy, and dirty. Carrying one, despite the immense evolution in holster technology, is no fun; it's always slipping this way and that, and it gives you a backache. A shoulder holster, so beloved in the movies, is really more like a brassiere with a brick in it. Most detectives take theirs off in the office. Guns wear out your clothes, either by abrasion or oil stain. They smell of oil. They go off accidentally far too often. (I've only seen one accidental shooting in movies, in *Pulp Fiction*, where John Travolta accidentally shoots the guy in the backseat.)

And what about the event itself? Probably the most filmed act of all time, the gunfight has almost never been portrayed accurately. Hollywood has still taught us that it's slick and beautiful. It's not. It's short and ugly. Filmmakers know nothing about it. We never get the dump of a ton of adrenaline into the blood that necessarily accompanies the presentation of weapons. We never get the auditory exclusion, as the hearing shuts down. We never get the tunnel-vision effect, as time slows down and the world closes down almost all visual information except the gun in the hands of the man shooting at you. We never get the kicking-in of the fight-or-flight mechanism where, beyond your will, you turn instantly into tiger or pussycat. We never get the coarse thickness of the hands as small motor movements become impossible. We never get the brain fog as the skull overloads with blood and the IQ drops a hundred points in the firing of a single synapse.

And the aftermath: We never get the blood, the pain, the screams of the hit. We never get the immense squalor that attends an act of violence and the ripples of revulsion that spread out from it, unsettling all who see it or are affected by it. We never get the post-combat stress syndrome, which is composed of nightmares, remorse, crying jags, flashbacks, irrational fears, sleeplessness, intense fatigue, inability to communicate, disinterest in sex or food. We never get the months, even years, it takes to come back from such an event, if you ever do.

Only one movie, to my way of thinking, has ever captured a taste of that experience. At the end of *Bullitt* (1968), Steve McQueen, as a San

Francisco police detective named Frank Bullitt, has to shoot an armed man in the lobby of an airport. It's probably the best movie shooting, at least in terms of realism and impact on society. McQueen is very close, he aims carefully after finding the good shooting position, and he fires fast, three times. The shots are incredibly loud, and people dive and shriek; they are shaken to their essence. The gunman is hit and falls forward with all the dignity of a sack of flour going off a shelf. He hits the ground and in seconds is an island in an ocean of blood as people scream in disgust. Bullitt keeps him covered, his own face a mask of frozen tension. Finally, he walks over, kicks the gun away and, irrationally but believably, sheds his sports coat to cover the dead man's face and blood from the crowd. He looks shocked, spent, used, finished, washed out. We sense his life has changed forever. There's no triumph, only survival.

Let's see that in a movie, one more time, instead of dances with guns.

(FEBRUARY 8, 1998)

*I*magine that someone is watching you. He's intimately familiar with your family, with the particular dynamics of love and hate and fear that occur only behind your closed doors; you have no secrets from him. He's insinuating himself more deeply into your life, and he's come to have profound feelings about you.

Now here's the scary part: It's Robin Williams.

AIEEEEEEE!!!

That's *One Hour Photo,* which develops into something extremely queasy. This is good, not bad. Queasy is harder than scary, subtler than creepy, and more powerful than smarmy. It's the one that lingers for days, eroding your confidence in your ability to cope, wrecking your sleep, making you snap at loved ones. I love it when that happens.

For Williams it's a tour de geek: He plays one of those apparently anonymous men bathed in the perpetual glow of a retail store's fluorescents, so helpful in their little uniforms behind their little counters, an essay in banality written in unprepossessing flesh.

Seymour "Sy" Parrish: To know him is to ignore him. Does he exist? Is there a man behind the blue apron and the "Sy" nametag? Sy runs the one-hour photo department at Valuebuy—or perhaps it's Sav-A-Lot or Markets-R-Us or Goods-A-Plenty.

In fact, he is the department. He's clean, obedient, organized, on time, and friendly. He smiles. He cares. He knows his customers by name. He cares about his customers. He loves his customers. Isn't it wonderful?

No, not actually. Behind it all, Sy is the poster boy for inappropriate emotional attachment. Under that retail blandness and apparent love lurks the heart and soul of a twisted puppy. Sy—for reasons that become heartbreakingly vivid at movie's end—has given himself over to the worship of an ideal family: a handsome, smiling husband, successful and capable; his beautiful and kind wife, who always remembers Sy's name; and their spunky li'l kid. He knows these people through two media: their snapshots and his fantasies.

Too bad that the Yorkin family is real, and that their pathetic reality—alcoholism, promiscuous consumerism, infidelity, career difficulties, child neglect bordering on abuse—can never live up to the fabled model that floats so majestically in Sy's mind. So of course, they must be punished.

What a spooky conceit. It gets at the evil power of the ideal, and the fact that no one, not even the fabulous Yorkins, can live up to it. And it gets at the insidious ways in which fantasy as a substitute for life works: Sy invests totally in his notions of the Yorkins as perfect, based on his habit of duplicating every shot they've had him develop, and now those dupes paper a whole wall of his lonely-guy apartment. So when photographic evidence emerges that Will Yorkin (Michael Vartan) is cheating on the fabulous Nina Yorkin (Connie Nielsen) and ignoring poor li'l Jake Yorkin (Dylan Smith), Sy goes ballistic. His carefully modulated life begins to teeter out of control.

The movie is cast as a madman's confession. Sy, so meek and polite, sits in the police interrogation room while a detective quietly played by Eriq La Salle asks probing questions, and we sink back through Sy's memory, illuminated by the foreknowledge that something terrible has happened.

Williams has a special gift for this sort of character. He conveys ever so subtly what we have suspected of this gentleman since the days of Mork: Under the id-driven scream of consciousness of that crazy stand-up and talk-show persona, there's a delicate, shy, meek little man. Oh, he's still crazy as a loon, or course, but it's a different kind of crazy. It's the smirky crazy of the man who pays too much attention and who shows too much empathy. Oooh, that's the scary one.

But the brilliance of the film isn't just in Williams's ultra-disturbing performance. It's that the movie has been extremely thoroughly thought out by writer-director Mark Romanek. This young man appears to be the rare music-video director who has a solid sense of character to go along with his glib visual brilliance. He may have read a book or two. He develops a coherent theory of Sy's pathology: Sy isn't strange just because the movie's better that way. His strangeness has been manufactured by various stresses; he's been machined toward the deviant.

It is, therefore, no accident that he's the one-hour-photo man: He is a man who lives through photography because reality is so disappointing. Even his hobby is snapshots, and his fantasy history, when he shares it, is built around snapshots. At one point he shows Nina a photo of a kindly, matronly figure in a sepia-tinted old print. "My mom," he says to her, eyes all melty with remembered love—and it's clear that he believes it, even though we've seen him buy it for a buck five minutes earlier.

Somewhere in his life, somehow, for some cruel reason, he has inappropriately concluded that the ultimate act is the act of photography. When he acts out, as when he merely sits and dreams, it will be in terms of photography. So the true mystery of *One Hour Photo* is who has made him such a creature, and why? And that is also the movie's most astonishing achievement: It begins by scaring you to death by evoking a monster, and by the end it has seduced you into caring for him.

(AUGUST 30, 2002)

*B*rian De Palma's new film, *Femme Fatale*, is a passionate film buff's valentine to the two directors he loves most: Alfred Hitchcock and Brian De Palma.

The film that this worship has inspired is pretty amusing when the director apes Hitchcock, and pretty awful when he apes himself.

On the principle that nothing succeeds like excess, the movie opens with its best sequence, a completely over-the-top heist narrative in which a team of professional thieves tries to strip a comely actress of the millions of dollars of jewels she is wearing (which is practically all she's wearing).

However, the setting isn't her apartment or a hotel room or some other easy-take venue; rather, it's the Grand Palais at the Cannes Film Festival, where the young woman is appearing on the arm of real-life director Régis Wargnier as he attends the festival screening of his film *East-West*, which is, incidentally, far better than *Femme Fatale* can ever hope to be.

But the gimmick is impressive: De Palma, whose reputation in Europe is obviously a lot higher than it is here, talked the French into letting him film with the actual 2001 festival as a backdrop, and those are actual French film personalities in the background, that's the actual Grand Palais, the famous red-carpeted steps, real people smoking indoors and other astonishments and so forth and so on.

Maybe you have to have logged some time at the festival, a famous orgy of movielust, to be amused by the clever, rather mean-spirited goings-on that De Palma charts for his (and our) prurient delectation. Or maybe you just have to love beautiful women. Whatever, the prime mover in this drama is the American beauty Laure Ash (Rebecca Romijn-Stamos), who penetrates the Cannes celebration disguised as a photographer. The next move is typical of De Palma's eighth-grade sexual imagination: Evidently a lesbian, Laure whispers a come-on to the actress (Rie Rasmussen), who agrees to join her in the ladies' loo for a quickie. While there, the clever Laure strips her of the diamond-encrusted golden breastplates and passes them to a henchman in the next stall, who soundlessly replaces them with duplicates. The idea is that the actress will return to her seat unaware that she now wears fool's gold and glass, but at least she's well satisfied.

But of course it goes wrong and the end result is that the henchman—a nasty chap well played by Eriq Ebouaney—is nabbed, while Laure escapes unscathed with the loot. Number of words of dialogue in this first forty minutes of film: 0. Number of words of dialogue in the next hour and ten minutes: 4,567,231, give or take a few thousand.

It's also a remarkable sequence in that it's a director imitating himself imitating another director. More than 20 years ago in *Dressed to Kill*, De Palma worked up a nearly as impressive dialogue-free half-hour (with Angie Dickinson), which was a homage to an even more brilliant dialogue-free half-hour Hitchcock created in the classic *Vertigo*, when Jimmy Stewart tracked Kim Novak. That gives you some idea of *Femme Fatale*'s knotted heritage, and it gets worse, with homages to Hitchcock's

Rear Window battling homages to his own *Obsession*. You need to be a film school graduate to figure out who De Palma is imitating in any given scene.

But he's not without some moves. For one, he understands what a limited actress his star is, and he contrives to keep her mouth shut for the longest time. For an interval after that, he lets her speak only in a clumsy Mitteleuropean accent, like Boris's Natasha. He does not permit her to actually "act" until about the halfway point, which pretty much destroys the illusion that this is an actual professional production.

The beautiful Romijn-Stamos also lacks one other key attribute besides talent: stature. Not in height (hers seems to be immense, soaring off legs 11 feet long), but stature as power, on the set. Thus it is true that De Palma exploits her, and she's asked to do a lot of things a more experienced actress might refuse. I'd love to see him say to Meryl Streep, "Meryl, here's the scene where you undulate topless in a black thong in a café full of French motorcycle thugs." La Streep would whack him so hard he'd wake up in Anne Arundel County, asking if anybody got the number of that bus.

Romijn-Stamos soldiers on, always more model (comfortable with display) than actress (uncomfortable with emotions). The plot doesn't progress arithmetically, but rather it squares and cubes, becoming so dense with developments it loses all contact with the known world. It seems to have something to do with a fortuitous opportunity to take over someone else's personality and life, while only an aggressive paparazzo (Antonio Banderas) is paying attention and trying to figure out who's really who. It's so dense, that it's another signpost of many saying: This is a goofy movie, not reality.

You can't say *Femme Fatale* isn't interesting, however. It's so full of astonishments, cornball revelations, succulent camerawork, vivid angles into the action, and all the other candy of movies, that you forget how stupid it is. But the next morning: What a headache.

(NOVEMBER 6, 2002)

*C*atch *Catch Me If You Can* today, if you can.

Steven Spielberg's wonderful new movie is something rare: It's a warm thriller. Even rigorously hewing to the old cat-and-mouse game between a super-criminal and a dogged detective, it's got all of the Spielberg trademark twinkles to it. It celebrates family—or, perhaps to be more exact, mourns its loss; it's vivid without being pushy; it's middle-class, middlebrow, and middle-of-the-road without ever being simpering or simple-minded; it's brilliantly acted. But best of all, it's brilliantly made.

This guy really knows how to make a movie; he's studied the old-movie formulations and effortlessly duplicates them here. One, the best, is the way old directors used to build smaller story arcs into the fabric of the larger one, weaving in small payoffs all the way through, a forgotten art in today's moviemaking. But Spielberg threads small narrative satisfactions all through *Catch Me If You Can*. To cite just one, he gives us a fabulous little essay on schoolboy revenge: The hero, a devious impostor named Frank Abagnale Jr., shows up at a new school and a bully butts him in the hall. It's a typical high school scene relived a thousand times a day when a thousand new kids show up in a thousand high schools. But Frank turns the trick; he goes into the classroom, pretends with his eerie gravity and stunning sense of self-assurance to be the teacher, even bluffs a substitute teacher out. Then he turns the tables on the bully. The whole sequence can't run thirty seconds, yet it's a mini-movie in itself, a little nut bomb of sheer pleasure.

One wonders what it is in Spielberg that so loves Frank Abagnale, who swindled about $4 million in the sixties, while masquerading as an airline pilot, a doctor, and a lawyer—all before he was nineteen. Possibly it's that like so many mega-successful people, the director also feels like an impostor, and that his great career is some sort of mistake, and that somebody is going to knock on the mansion door one morning and say, "Oh, sorry, Spielberg, you were supposed to be an English teacher in suburban Phoenix, and we of the Corrections Bureau are here to escort you into the life you know you were destined for." Yet while Spielberg may romanticize this thief of identities, and never makes him seem mean-spirited or particularly evil, he doesn't quite endorse him either. It's a tale of crime and punishment, though a charming one.

The psychology of young Frank (Leonardo DiCaprio) is pretty transparent, though it's not offered as an excuse, merely an explanation. Frank is first glimpsed at a civic association meeting, where his father is being given an award. Frank is happy, secure, a belonger. In fact, notice the look on DiCaprio's face during this sequence: The musculature is unformed, slack, the smile goofy. He looks so teenage it's remarkable; and later, as a man, his face will tighten up and acquire the focus that adulthood somehow magically confers. He has a handsome, successful father (Christopher Walken), a beautiful French mother (Nathalie Baye), and the respect of all New Rochelle, New York. He is seventeen and about to learn the world can turn upside down.

It seems his father has tried to trick the IRS and as a consequence loses it all. Thus Frank and family move into a small, grubby apartment; thus he goes to that crude new school; thus, finally, divorce arrives, and Frank has to choose which parent.

He can't. He takes off instead. He then sets out on a mission to re-unify his family, to reacquire upper-middle-class stability, to achieve respect. He even has a magic carpet. It's called a checkbook. There's no money in his account, but with a checkbook and a sense of gall, nothing can stop a boy genius.

Frank is essentially a world-class bad-paper artist. He's not really into flying, into healing, into the law; those are just dodges that get him into institutions whose financial security is poorly constructed (because, of course, it's never been tested by someone of Frank's ingenuity). I love the way Spielberg shows Frank's learning curve, absorbing the rules of the paper-money system and learning how to turn them to his advantage; all of this, of course, is driven forward by his utter sincerity in various guises, and his weird gift to make himself seem older or younger than he is.

Enter the fuzz. Enter Tom Hanks, who generously, and superbly, takes the supporting role of FBI agent Carl Hanratty, head of the Bureau's cracked (not crack; it's staffed with goof-ups) financial fraud unit. Hanratty is an earnest Boston grind, without wit or genius, but obsessed with getting his man. The best part is that a lesser director might have easily subverted social morality by turning the fed into a creepy psycho and the kid into an anti-establishment martyr. It's even the sixties!

But Spielberg is entirely too smart for such cream-puff stuff. He does something so subtle I fear it won't be recognizable: He makes a chase movie in which you root equally for chaser and chasee. Both are imperfect human beings in search of a perfection they can't have. Both are lonely.

Both are actually quite decent. Their attraction-repulsion isn't pathological, as are most chases, which come to resemble death hunts. This is an arrest-hunt. And Spielberg finds a symbol to express the FBI's essential harmlessness: It's the snub-nose Colt Detective Special all the feds keep pulling, and Spielberg keeps noticing in close-up silhouettes: a tiny little gun that seems to reflect the innocence of a world where nobody really shot anybody very often. It's a gun a man would carry who really did not want to hurt anybody.

The moves and countermoves are terrific, but the best scene in the film chronicles Frank and Carl's first meeting, which Frank in nanospeed improvises a new identity in an attempt to avoid capture. It displays Frank's talent in a way that contrapuntally fills the movie with melancholy: You think, this is so wasted. Someone with this much on the ball should end up a security consultant or a law enforcement consultant, and yet that's Frank dodging through identities and that's Carl on his tail.

Hanks is so brilliant you almost don't notice it's Tom Hanks under those el cheapo glasses and that porkpie. But the revelation is DiCaprio, who shows the range and ease and cleverness that Martin Scorsese so underutilized in *Gangs of New York*. In this movie, little Leo is a gang of one, and he's a formidable presence in one of the most enjoyable films of the year.   (DECEMBER 25, 2002)

*C*arl Franklin once made a taut little film noir named *One False Move*. At the end, everybody was dead or dying, the universe was revealed to be a stainless steel rat trap with a 4,000-pound spring, and you felt so bad you felt really good.

Here, in a similar mode, is *Out of Time*, a film noir from the same smart guy. But the bad news is that the news at the end is good: The universe is harmonious, virtue and beauty are rewarded, and life just gets better and better. What fun is that?

That's the difference between real noir and something pleasantly phony like the ersatz, bit-studio demi-quasi-noir of *Out of Time*, with its fabulous production values and its professional comedy writing. It's a great zircon, as big as the Ritz. Smile and enjoy.

Until that sugar coating at the end, *Out of Time* is clever, believable, and gripping, and seems to be headed to a wondrous, bad place as it carefully modulates classic forties themes: innocent guy set up brilliantly by a femme fatale, the universe closing in as options run out, the despair of the hero, the cleverness of those he's hunting and those who are hunting him, and, finally, a milieu of atmospheric small-town sleaze.

But its best moments aren't from the noir canon, in dark alleys or neon-painted nightclubs or on wet brick streets lit by flickering street lamps. They are, instead, illuminated by the fierce glow of overhead fluorescents: in an office just like the one you are going to and I am sitting in. There, Police Chief Matt Whitlock (Denzel Washington) maneuvers amid high-tech commonplaces like cell phones and fax machines and e-mail terminals to prevent his employees from making the obvious connection to him on a case of double murder. He has got to be fast on the SEND button.

Whitlock—Washington makes a wonderful chump who turns out to be smarter than the folks who set him up think—is carrying on with a beautiful, unhappily married local woman (played hot-hotter-hottest by sultry Sanaa Lathan). She tells him she has an advanced cancer (they go to the hospital to verify); and she needs a certain large sum of money to pay for a radical treatment her insurance company won't cover. Since she may die despite the expensive therapy, she names him the beneficiary in her life insurance policy to pay back the money, which he has appropriated—he's desperately in love, see—from the evidence vault down at the cop shop, where it was being held as evidence in a drug bust.

Then her house blows up, she and her husband (Dean Cain, once a clean-limbed Superman of TV fame, now playing a bad guy) are both killed by what turns out to be a clumsy arson, Whitlock's name is attached to the insurance policy, and a tub of money will soon be found missing. Although we know he's innocent and presume that someone blew up the home with the folks in it and stole the money and has now decamped to Belize or some such, we also know that all the signs will point to Whitlock. So he must watch as people he trained and supervised turn those honed talents loose on him. Best bet: Get outta town, Jack. But of course, he can't and doesn't. Wouldn't be much of a movie if he did, would there?

It sounds a little like *Presumed Innocent* combined with *Body Heat*, and you can bet the screenwriter, David Collard, has seen them both. He has also seen Humphrey Bogart in *Dead Reckoning* and Fred MacMurray in *Double Indemnity*. And about 600 other films noir. So that makes it familiar. Does that make it bad? No, because within the rigid strictures of tradition, Collard finds slightly new and amusing twists. For example, the head investigator in the case turns out to be Whitlock's estranged wife, played by Eva Mendes in a role that shows her off much better than *2 Fast 2 Furious* did. That gives the chase a piquant sexual tension as well.

The director, Franklin, evokes place effortlessly; Banyan Key, the small Miami suburb where the film is set, feels so real you'll be sure you stayed there once. And he stages action well: A fight between Washington and a thug in a hotel room that ends up with the two hanging six floors up from a steel balcony that is about to give way and deposit them into space is riveting and fast.

There are things not to like. A comic sidekick, broadly played by John Billingsley, is a little too Hollywood cute; there's a lazy sequence in which a character is about to get shot when, bang, out of the dark comes the shot that saves him in the nick of time; and some feds are portrayed with the subtlety of wanted posters.

But all in all, *Out of Time* is on time in its trip to the dark city of treachery and bad girls.　　　　　　　　　　(OCTOBER 3, 2003)

*W*ill all the good little boys and girls raise their hands, please? Thank you. Susie—by the way, Susie, that was a wonderful decoupage you made illustrating the Ten Commandments—Susie, why don't you get a piece of cake in the kitchen? And David—congratulations on making Eagle Scout—David, you run along with Susie.

Bye, kids.

Ah. Now for the rest of you lizardheads; geeks; mutants; twisted, pimpled dwarves; dead-eyed, beleathered, spiked freaks, boy, have I got a movie for you.

The movie would be *Kill Bill: Vol. 1*, and man, is it cool.

If any civilized humans are left in the room, let me point out I didn't say "good," much less "superb" or "great." Let someone else decide that or laugh at the inquiry two decades down the road. For now, *Kill Bill*, Quentin Tarantino's first film in six years, is pure evil bliss. It's not pulp fiction; it's pulped fiction, a crazed phantasmagoria of high craft, low taste, and middlebrow swordplay. And by middlebrow I refer to the whiz of a multifolded samurai blade as it cleaves the skull and leaves the brow on the floor. That kind of middlebrow.

Uma, meet 150 Japanese guys with swords. Guys, meet Uma. Now, Uma, kill them. Uma, very good. Why, you got all 150 of them!

That's one of the thrills of *Kill Bill*, watching the willowy, fetching Uma Thurman turn into a sword-slinging Tilt-a-Whirl that spatters, scythes, slashes, lops, and dices everything in its path. I'm surprised they didn't lose a few cameramen on the shoot. The thing is about as refined as watching someone feed hot dogs into a Cuisinart set on 10, except that it's delivered with such high panache and brio, it's mesmerizing.

Kill Bill is the story of the bride's revenge, though "story" is not quite the word. It's an ideogram of vengeance, a rebus of revenge. It's not narrative; it's graffiti. The bad guys kill the bride's family. They think they kill the bride. They kill her unborn child. They kill her husband-to-be. All this happens on her wedding day, in the chapel, where she's wearing her bridal gown.

Four years later, she awakens from a coma. First, she must dispatch, in most grisly fashion, a necrophiliac happily engaging her thought-to-be-still form. Having taken care of that little detail (why, the look on the fellow's face is positively amazing!), she escapes from the hospital. Then she tracks down the evildoers and kills them. In fact, the movie runs out of time before she runs out of people to kill, so you will have to wait for what they are calling *Vol. 2*, in February, to see her whack the last.

At one point—the movie is hazy on time, as it flits forward and backward in chronology in accordance with postmodernist mandates on the arbitrariness of narrative—every major figure was a member of something called the Deadly Viper Assassination Squad, under the command of one Bill (whose face we never see, though credits reveal him to be David Carradine). Is this outfit public sector or private? Listed on the New York Stock Exchange? Term of enlistment? All of that information is unavailable. What is available is that, for reasons unspecified, it has been determined that Uma must be purged from the outfit—production notes suggest that her pregnancy prompted her to try to quit, which is frowned upon—and so the here-comes-the-bullet-into-the-bride's-head atrocity is engineered. Its hideous reality keeps flashing back into her mind as she tracks down former colleagues for her little chats.

And how could there be any further explanation for the carnage on-screen? It would just sound silly. What would possibly be the justification in the real world for an elite assassination team, staffed by gorgeous women, that appears to work solely with samurai swords (though Bill does carry a Colt Peacemaker) and is bound up, somehow, in the rules and rituals of Bushido? Tarantino has stripped the story to its rawest, most functional element: Only motive and opportunity are chronicled, and nothing is related to any kind of wider context. It is pure outlaw art, caring not a whit what anybody thinks of it. And playing by no known rules.

At one point, *Kill Bill* suddenly becomes a cartoon—literally. When it comes time for the bride to close in on the assassin O-Ren Ishii ("Uma, O-Ren." "O-Ren, Uma"), the film diverts to vivid Japanese animation for a good 20 minutes as O-Ren's bloody history is portrayed. It's not a pretty story, involving her own set of slaughtered parents, her own revenge, her swift ascent through the Tokyo underworld. Ultimately, the animated O-Ren de-morphs into Lucy Liu in time for an epic climactic battle in the snow with Uma.

The collection of fetishes on display is pretty amazing, surely the most intense this side of Krafft-Ebing's *Psychopathia Sexualis.* Tarantino has a major thing for feet, especially Thurman's, which nearly get more screen time than her face does. He loves tart mood changes, as when a child walks in on a knife fight, and the opponents (Thurman and Vivica A. Fox) immediately hide their blades and make nice for the child, like suburban bridge club members. When she goes upstairs, it's back to slash and thrust, building to something I know I've never seen before: the gun in the cereal box (POW! Cap'n Crunch everywhere!).

And let's not mince the truth here: Tarantino is also ghoulishly attracted to the realities of bladed battle, which include limb removal, massive arterial spray, piercings at all unusual angles, and, ultimately, lakes of blood. All this stuff is weirdly sexualized; we are in a very different part of the forest. Can you imagine what it would do to Susie and David to see such spectacle?

So all Susies and all Davids, of whatever age: Do not enter. Do not pass the theater where it's playing. Don't even live in the same county where it's playing

As for the rest of you fiends, pay no attention to that guy on the aisle, fifteen rows up. That's me, and I do not want to be disturbed.

(OCTOBER 10, 2003)

*F*ace/Off, the new John Woo film, is superb late-pagan entertainment. I can see it on a double bill with *The Burning of 100 Christians* or *Watch the Alligators Eat the Slaves* at some suburban Roman multiplex, circa A.D. 212.

Almost indefensibly violent, the film is one of those whirligigs of wit, barbaric energy, blood spatters, and firepower that will be adored by the morally retarded among us—like me—and loathed by the morally superior. But who has ever cared about them?

Woo, the insanely gifted and possibly insane Hong Kong transplant, still hasn't mastered the American cultural idiom. He doesn't know it's cool to be cool. But that's not bad, it's good: He's not afraid to give vent to his Chinese heart, and amid the slaughter, the cruelty, the jovial deconstruction of civilization, stick in some homey schmaltz about the sanctity of family.

So the core of the film isn't the nerve gas bomb that looks like a hi-fi from a *Playboy* cartoon busily ticking down in the Los Angeles convention center, where if detonated it would depopulate a square mile of that town. No, it's the family of Sean Archer, FBI stud, crummy husband, mourning father, a man so blighted with grief and rage that he has blow-torched the love from his own soul, condemning his family to live in the winter of his discontent. So this is really a family values pic. To revitalize the family, about 2,000 people have to die. So? What's your problem with that? Are you against family values?

Archer—a grave, tense John Travolta—is obsessed with capturing a professional terrorist and world-class psycho named Castor Troy (Nicolas Cage at highest pitch)—because Troy shot through Archer and into Archer's son some years ago. The boy did not recover.

After that event is re-created, the film proper opens with Castor's capture at an airfield, a sequence so full of kinetic spasms and handgun acrobatics and explosions that you might think you'd walked in on the end of any other film. No. Woo knows no bounds; he's just warming up with this variation of gunfight as pie fight with tumblers.

Castor is recovered comatose after a close encounter with a jet engine. But the bomb is still ticking. Someone has to penetrate a prison where Castor's sniveling but beloved brother Pollux (read your mythology) has been shipped, and get into that young man's confidence. Since Archer knows so much, he's the likely candidate. But unfortunately he can't. Why? Because he's Archer. This is where the movie gets really kooky.

Fortunately, it takes itself so lightly you are under no obligation to believe. The characters don't even believe. It seems new medical technology has made it possible to surgically exchange faces, so that Archer can go forth under Troy's, learn where the bomb is and see to its defusing.

A face, of course, isn't just skin; it's also muscles, skull, teeth, all of which are left alone. Moreover, face isn't but a fraction of identity—what about body language, hand size, finger shape, more intimate measurements, odor, musculature? What about waist? Cage must be a good 36; Travolta's easily busting that big 40. So the whole thing is daffy from the get-go. Still, I love the ricketiness of the conceit. It's so jokey and spoofy, you just get with it on a lark.

Of course the obvious happens, cranking the movie still further into the realm of kooky: Troy recovers, claims the nearest handy face—Archer's—murderously escapes and set out to wreak havoc on the world in the guise of a righteous FBI agent and take over Archer's family life and connubial duties.

As an example of the art of casting, the movie is brilliantly engineered. It allows two major stars to each play the showy villain for a time, and also for each to do an imitation of the other. Travolta must ultimately play Cage playing Travolta, while his brother in fame must play Travolta playing Cage. It's absurd, of course, but such is the filmmaker's magic that it makes rational objection beside the point.

It's kind of amusing to watch the dueling charismatics: Both see Castor as a dancer whose body language suggests complete liberation from any save the most nihilistic adolescent impulses. But Cage works mainly through his eyes: His occasionally bulge with the rapture of madness like blackened deviled eggs. His face lengthens and tilts. He looks like a basset hound on amphetamines.

Travolta, probably a better dancer, is less physical but more into twitchy line readings. He twinkles with evil, his full Force-5 Travoltaness set to the high beam. You feel the radiance of his narcissism. And when the two confront each other, they have wondrous chemistry together. They're having so much fun you feel their glee all the way to the fiftieth row.

Yet the movie isn't quite schematic as a synopsis suggests. Each character, in subtle, surprising ways, learns a little from the impersonation. Castor-as-Sean gets off on the sexual aspects of the masquerade with perpetual good wife Joan Allen, but he seems to develop odd quirks of feeling for the FBI agent's family and seems to confront his murder of their son so many years ago. He's a strangely good father to his new teenage daughter, eschewing the temptation toward which the movie seems to be heading. Meanwhile, himself escaped (bloodily) from the prison, Sean-as-Castor hides in underworld culture, learns poignant lessons about the love of some of them—notably Gina Gershon—and the loyalties of the goon set.

But Woo is never far from the next gag. His conceit of the gunfight as gymnastics with blood, and of the universe as a soap bubble of fragility about to explode, dominates his consciousness. The film's Armageddon begins with a spinning, diving shootout in a church—a Woo tradition, complete to the doves floating through the carnage in slow motion—then transmogrifies into a speedboat race across Los Angeles Harbor and finally ends in a bit of nastiness on the beach with a vagrant harpoon gun.

(JUNE 27, 1997)

*A*mong the SIG-Sauers and AK-47s and Colts and Berettas and Smith & Wessons that decorate *Lethal Weapon 4*, the most lethal weapon of all turns out to be the script.

This curious document must have been written on one side of a postcard using a very fat red crayon. That's the amount of story the movie contains, and I know it was a fat crayon because there are four people listed in the writing and story credits and it must have taken all of them to maneuver it through those complicated zig-zaggy letters like w and x.

The rest is gratuitous violence and stunts, some quite spectacular, all resolutely meaningless. There's also a little comic banter and a lot of redundancy. Did we really need both Chris Rock and Joe Pesci? I mean, isn't one funnyman enough, especially with the bickering Bickersons of law enforcement, Mel Gibson and Danny Glover, hogging the camera in endless yammering love spats? And how many car chases can one movie hold?

All the regulars are here. The movie really should have been called

Lethal Weapon: The Reunion. Besides Pesci, Rene Russo reprises from 3. Gibson's Beretta and Glover's Smith are of course on hand, or should I say, in hand.

Does anybody remember the first film? That was an actual movie, until it went nuts at the end, and the lethal weapon of the title was Gibson's melancholy mind. He was a devastated, self-loathing Vietnam vet hellbent on spectacular self-extinction; memories of America's least favorite war filled the film, giving it an almost tragic dignity. Its arc was redemptive. It watched as the crippled loner white man was healed by the healthy black family man. It was as full of love as it was of guns, and it was very full of guns.

Four profitable editions down the line, that's all gone, to be replaced by nothing. The movie has no subtext at all, unless it's something like "orange propane explosions are really cool!" Maybe they are, but . . . every three minutes and twenty-one seconds?

When the movie finally started, about an hour or so in, it seems to be about a scam by which the Chinese triads are buying the freedom of imprisoned elders from corrupt Chinese generals with counterfeit yen. Why, you ask, as nobody connected with the production ever did, would such a thing take place on American soil, not Chinese? Possibly the movie explains it, possibly it doesn't; who could tell? The real reason, however, is that if it took place in China there'd be no excuse for Gibson and Glover to launch a car from the Ventura Freeway, plunge it through a drafting office full of blueprints, people, and desks, re-launch it on the other side, and have it land on the Santa Monica Freeway. Is this worth seeing? If you like breakage, the answer is a big yes.

Glover's Murtaugh and Gibson's Riggs literally get in the way of the Chinese caper when their fishing boat is sunk by a tramp freighter smuggling in illegals in a gambit so tertiary to the central plot that it's hardly there at all. Riggs sinks the freighter with his pistol while Murtaugh shanghais the members of one alien family and grants them his own private asylum, because he's moved by the "slavery" aspects of their plights (the illegals are indentured to Chinese gangsters for $35,000 worth of hard labor). Eventually the immigrant family is reacquired by the triad boys to use as leverage to get an engraver to complete the counterfeit job.

Everything else is riffs and racism. The director, Richard Donner, was so proud of his anti-apartheid stand that he did a whole movie about it (*Lethal Weapon 2*), and he festoons this picture with anti-NRA and anti-assault rifle messages (even though he's probably sold more Berettas to the American public then Beretta's actual ad agency). But he seems to regard Asians as amusing li'l Oriental fellers, with buck teeth and funny accents. He even uses the old "flied lice" gag! Some liberal!

The movie's one grace note is sounded by its villain, played by the Hong Kong action star Jet Li. This guy has martial arts moves that are so dynamic one can hardly believe them, some twisty scissors kick action that makes him seem like he's from another dimension, or at least another form of gravity. When he lets loose, the movie becomes, however so briefly, fascinating, even awesome. It's the power, instantly recognizable, of the authentic over the artificial.

As for Gibson and Glover, both remain likable, but nothing they do could be confused with acting. Alice and Ralph Kramden sniped at each other more funnily forty years ago than these two old wheezers.

Lethal Weapon 4 is also endless. You know the thing where you think it's over and you start to get up, and suddenly a whole new scene begins and your heart sinks? It does this twice. Twice! This is some kind of weirdness. A movie that almost forgets to start almost forgets to end.

(JULY 10, 1998)

The Third Man (1949) is so elegant, tiny, and perfect that it feels more like a watch than a movie: It should have been directed by Patek Philippe.

But it was directed by the Britisher Carol Reed, who got himself into the masterpiece category this one time out in a career that was otherwise respectable, if never quite brilliant (his second-best film was probably *Odd Man Out* in 1947, his worst, *Oliver!* in 1968). But he had great collaborators: a script by Graham Greene, and a cast that included Orson Welles at his most Wellesian, Joseph Cotten at his most Cotteny, Trevor Howard at his most Howardian (you could land a plane on that stiff upper lip), Alida Valli at her most coldly beautiful (forward the slight brigade, into the Valli of indifference!), and, best of all, Vienna at its most Viennese.

Vienna, Vienna, that strudelin' town! What a haunted burg it is in the aftermath of the last war and on the cusp of a cold one: dank, shadowy, medieval, shot through with ruins, patrolled by MPs in jeeps, full of shadows, alleys, tunnels, and sewers, the film noir city viewed through the fractured prism of European existentialism and Graham Greene's weary, bitter aversion to the possibility of love.

But despite its justified fame and worldwide success, *The Third Man* has not been seen by most Americans in its true form. That's because co-producer David O. Selznick decided it was a tad slow for audiences this side of the drink, so he commissioned a Yank version.

The result was hardly butchery, more like a deft tummy tuck, and it might have even improved the film by speeding it up just enough for us children of the Republic of Attention Deficit Disorder who even then were chronically unadaptable to the more languid pace of the European product. On the other hand, here's a chance to judge for yourself, as a newly restored version of the European version—it's eleven minutes longer—opens today at the American Film Institute for a week.

Naïve American cowboy writer Holly Martins (Cotten) arrives in Vienna to find out that his best pal, Harry Lime (Orson Welles), has just died in a mysterious accident. Discovering anomalies in the various accounts of Harry's death, and running into barely concealed boredom from British military cop Calloway (Howard), Holly vows loudly to investigate.

But his naïve hubris merely stirs the maggots that festered in Harry's wake. Hoping to vindicate Harry by finding his murderer, he finds instead that Harry is a murderer. At the same time, he falls in love with Harry's girlfriend, Anna (Valli), and even as he discovers there's something about Harry (namely, that he isn't dead), he learns there's something about love: namely that the right woman sometimes falls in it with the wrong man.

What connoisseurs will notice right away in this restored version is the scene-setting prologue being read, not as it was in the American version by Cotten in his tweedy, dithering prep-school voice but in the jaded, sophisticated voice of an Englishman, rather amused at the tale he's about to tell. As well he should be, since the voice is Reed's own. Very interesting. Still, it's better with Cotten, because he is, after all, the point-of-view character, the first-person "I" of the movie. If Reed reads it, who's talking? It lacks an organic connection to the story.

Other changes are small. Scenes are held slightly longer; tidbits of dialogue are added; Holly's tragic wait for Anna under the weeping elms in the cemetery is longer, so that it's not a dirge but an ordeal. And the famous chase through the sewers at the end is slightly lengthened. This last touch is the one heartily approved of here: This whirligig of dazzle, comparable to and even the equal of Welles's famous funhouse gunfight at the end of *The Lady From Shanghai*, is possibly the best chase ever put on film, as the forces of law and order hunt the heretofore imperturbable Harry Lime like a rat through the sewers.

And Welles! Has an actor ever made himself more vivid in less time? The first ten reels are pure setup, so he'd better deliver, and he does. He is on screen for probably less than five minutes, yet he dominates the action totally. His face somehow both taut and plump at once, his eyes merry with ironic detachment and amusement at the mess into which the world has plunged itself. He's quite a piece of work, gentleman scoundrel as mass murderer of children. He makes sociopathy seem like a witty minor vice, akin to putting two olives in a martini instead of one. And he seems to relish his chosen profession even if it causes him a little heartburn. "Please remember to bring the tablets, old man," he tells Holly, as if the world's problems could be relieved by a R-O-L-A-I-D-S.

The famous scene on the Ferris wheel, as Harry points out to Holly all the little people moving around far below and then postulates the calculus of relativism: "If I said to you, you can have twenty thousand pounds for every dot that stops, would you really, old man, tell me to keep my money, without hesitation, or would you calculate how many dots you could afford to spare?" It remains one of the most coldly chilling, yet charismatic, few seconds in movie history.

It's a movie of great scenes—the dying wiggle of Harry's fingers up through the sealed grating as the cops close in, the fat little boy with the ball who denounces Holly as a killer, Anna's utter indifference to Holly's twisted declaration of love, Calloway's bitter contempt for an amateur. But it's not just scenes. It has a unity of vision and a coherence of theme and a perfection of tone that are rarely achieved in movies, or any stories for that matter. To see it is to learn anew just how great a movie can be and what bliss ninety minutes alone in the dark can provide.

(JULY 9, 1999)

*J*he *Limey* is a kind of Stamp collection: It shows us the 1967 edition of the British actor whose first name is Terence cheek by jowl with the 1999 edition.

The movie is built around scraps from an earlier film, Ken Loach's *Poor Cow*, which yields a now-and-then of incredible contrast. We see the haggard, tough Stamp of today juxtaposed with the more slender, more callow Stamp of way back then, a man so beautiful that he soared to stardom without much in the way of talent or effort. Youth, age, all wound up together. How did this smooth beauty of a boy become this blazing icon of anger, with his tense face and lizardy eyes? The two play off each other in fascinating ways.

If only the movie had been so fascinating. But the problem is that this extremely clever device has been oh-so-feebly forced into the service of mediocre melodrama under the surprisingly lax guidance of the normally trustworthy director Steven Soderbergh.

Stamp plays Wilson, a British thief who gets out of the pen after a long term and is distressed to learn that his estranged daughter has died under mysterious circumstances in far-off Beverly Hills, California, USA. With his London underworld skills and a Cockney accent as thick as blood pudding, he arrives in Los Angeles to find out why and, if appropriate, who.

Yet almost immediately the movie succumbs to what a senior critic once called "routine movie hooey." Wilson picks up allies with absurd ease—Elaine (Lesley Ann Warren), who was a friend of his daughter's, then a driver (Luis Guzmán) with underworld connections who also knew her. Both bond with him instantly and become allies in his quest, offering a place to stay and strategic hints on how to deal with the obstacles that lie ahead.

In a few easy minutes, he has established a connection to Terry Valentine, a sleazy record producer, played by Peter Fonda, who is under the impression that he's the picture's hero. Beaten, shot at, dumped, hunted, and spoken to sharply, Wilson just keeps on coming. Clearly, here's where Soderbergh had the most fun: watching the sheltered, self-indulgent, sublimely smug Hollywood big shot being slowly deconstructed by the shrewd and plucky British crook.

And Fonda's Valentine is exactly the kind of man you love to hate: a smirky ex-hippie who rode the counterculture wave to immense wealth and power and is now a kind of professional sybarite who always has a disposable young woman around as a playtoy. Evidently, Wilson's daughter was one such playtoy who learned too much and had to be disposed of.

This is a classic pulp fiction formula—the return of the avenger. Sometimes it's the father or the brother or the son; sometimes it's even the victim himself, who has miraculously survived. In all cases, it's a requirement that the avenger's talents far outstrip those of the local mobsters, whom he mows down like overripe shafts of wheat.

This device has enlivened such classics as Mike Hodges's *Get Carter*, John Boorman's equally classic *Point Blank*, Clint Eastwood's *High Plains Drifter*, and Edwin Sherin's *Valdez Is Coming*, which starred Burt Lancaster, and even the recent Mel Gibson vehicle *Payback* (a knockoff of *Point Blank*).

Yet given such a sturdy, familiar underpinning, Soderbergh doesn't get much out of it. Not one scene plays with the sharpness of *Out of Sight*, and the movie conspicuously lacks a single cleverness except the frequent reminiscences in Wilson's head that enable us to glimpse back at a young man so perfect that he could—and did—play Melville's Billy Budd. And it gives us a chance to feel his regret and ambivalence about a life that went a certain way when now, as an older man, he realizes it could have just as easily gone another, better, way.

But Soderbergh fumbles all the genre's obligations. He seems to have very little gift for action set pieces, and the ones he concocts feel so generic that they leach energy from the movie. Hasn't this guy ever heard of style? The movie is a festival of gunfights that aren't cool, car chases that don't convince, plot twists that don't astonish, revelations that aren't that revelatory.

The climax is a particular botch, with all the sides of the too-complicated-by-far plot—besides Stamp and Fonda, there's a DEA interest and a young-professional interest—showing up at a darkened California beach house and blowing the heck out of everything that moves.

The idea of this movie is fabulous, and there's something mythic in the contrast between those two great old faces—Stamp's and Fonda's—

that seems to sum up and amplify the meanings in the two cultures: One is handsome, ironic, refined, yet weak and terrified; the other tough, remorseless, driven by love and memory and far more cunning than can be believed. These great old guys deserved so much better.

(OCTOBER 8, 1999)

*B*oys Don't Cry cuts deep, to where the bullet breaks the bone.

The movie follows the melancholy vector of Teena Brandon, 1971–1993. Teena, a live-wire Nebraskan with proclivities she herself did not fully understand, swaddled her breasts in Ace bandages, pulled on a pair of jeans and boots, threw on a cowboy hat, left Lincoln and hitched to the hinterlands, reinventing herself as a wiry, rawboned, tough-talkin', beer-swillin' young fella named Brandon Teena.

There, in the heart of the heart of the country, the newly christened "Brandon" met new friends, messed around in pickup trucks, fell in love, had sex (sort of), and, for her efforts, was raped and subsequently murdered.

The movie is, to be sure, the longest, hardest sit of the season—you are stuck there, a single tube of puckered muscle, waiting for the extremely ugly violence to occur—but it is driven by performances of such luminous humanity that they break your heart.

Place it in that small genre of true-crime stories set on the pitiless plains of the great, raw middle of the country, where the wind is always sharp and the roads are all bad and the miles between comforts are many indeed. It belongs with *In Cold Blood* and *The Executioner's Song,* tales of human malfeasance under a sky so big that it makes what happens under them seem insignificant, if it wasn't so damned painful.

The singular brilliance of Kimberly Peirce's film is that it makes you believe on its own terms. It doesn't turn Teena or Brandon—wonderfully portrayed by Hilary Swank—into a cardboard saint or an icon of victimization, but instead sees her as a whole character, tics, warts, lies, and all. As Teena, she's no stranger to the system. A petty crook (grand theft auto) and locally famous for her masquerades—they almost always get her beaten up or at least threatened with a thumping—she ends up, one drunken evening, in Falls City, down in the southwest corner of the state, one of those mean, scabby towns that most movies usually see as places to leave. For Brandon, here at last is a place to stay.

There, in one of those bars where the cigarette smoke burns your eyes and the C&W hammers your head with its banshee's cries of lost love, dead dogs, and pickups that won't start, and everybody seems strangely angry, she just sort of falls in with a group of young people.

Eventually they reveal themselves to be loosely affiliated with a "mom" of about 35 (Jeannetta Arnette, in another of the movie's brilliant performances) who herself lives on a beer-and-cigarette diet and differs from her daughter and her daughter's friends only in the look of perpetual weariness under her eyes, as if life has worn her out.

I had no luck making out the kinship system here. Are these cousins or siblings or ex-stepchildren or what? It would take an anthropologist to figure it all out; what is clear is only that, against the harshness of an indifferent world and a bitter climate, they've formed a tribal union that gives everybody a sense of belonging.

Mom rules, but only nominally, like an aging queen. The true power rests with two princes of the realm, and the object of everybody's obscure desire is one princess.

The princes are John (Peter Sarsgaard) and his acolyte, sycophant, and shield bearer, Tom (Brendan Sexton III). These are young men stiffed by a society that has very little use for them. They have but one role—other than making Susan Faludi a wealthy woman—which is to not get in the way, which, of course, is exactly where they get.

Someone—presumably director Peirce—has a dead-on eye for rural blue-collar culture. These young men, both ex-cons with time served for petty, hopeless scams, in their hooded sweatshirts and their tight jeans and their spindly nests of well-glopped hair, are seething with anger of a place denied, of their own sense of the world passing them by, of their eternal nothingness. They can face reality and control their impulses toward violence only when well lubricated by beer. They are a fight club waiting to happen, and they could kick Brad Pitt's pretty little rear end all the way to Omaha.

And, of course, they love the Princess. Everybody loves the Princess. The Princess is Mom's daughter. Who wouldn't love her? Lana (Chloë Sevigny) has the lightless eyes of the bored but the face and beauty of a goddess, even if she works in a spinach-canning plant. In hairnet and blue uniform smock, smoking a butt and looking out the window at the far-off horizon, she looks like Botticelli's Venus. To see her is to fall in love; it happened to John and Tom—and it happens to Brandon.

What the movie gets so well is not merely Brandon's attraction to Lana, and hers to her, but also the curious way Brandon's sexual charisma miswires the sexual politics of the situation. For the secret is that, in their way, John and Tom are drawn to Brandon, too. They're picking up on something they don't quite realize is there; they think he's cute and funny, and are forever playing grab-ass and acting on all those strange, incoherent sexual impulses that men cannot articulate and deeply deny but nevertheless randomly feel.

It's a circle of attraction that is extremely unsettling to everybody. And to Brandon's shame, she loves it; you can feel her joy in the deception, even as it's building toward violence. (And you know equally what she cannot: that John and Tom are not the kind of boys to be fooling around with. They won't get the joke. Too many have already been played on them.)

Concealed under its true-crime melodrama, *Boys Don't Cry* contains an argument: that your nature is your nature, and it must be obeyed no matter where it leads. Agree or not, this is a powerful theory of drama that dates back a mere 4,000 years. Character is fate, it says.

So there's something about it that has the inevitability of Greek drama. These people's destiny is rooted in their characters and their hubris; that's what makes them dangerous. And that's what makes them human.

(OCTOBER 22, 1999)

The guiltiest of guilty pleasures at the movies this week is the tough-as-nails *Lockdown*, about bad things happening in the House called Big.

Though bracing and chilling, it's a trip to perdition the faint of heart and queasy of disposition ought to avoid. You need a hard head, a strong stomach, and a willingness to watch the unwatchable. A 2,000-yard stare is a must. If you can't do the time, don't drop that dime.

The movie has two primary if crude virtues: First and best, it has an overwhelming sense of place. This extends to far more than the physical, those bleak corridors, the omnipresence of the cyclone fences, the echoes of footfalls and steel doors, the feel of suppurating institutional melancholy. It also includes the metaphysical aspects of the prison experience. When you saw the old pix—even as brutal as Burt Lancaster's *Brute Force*, probably the most violent of the American forties pictures—you knew somehow that you weren't quite getting the whole story. You can't crowd six hyperaggressive, aberrant men in the space of a closet for ten years without certain things happening.

Some years ago—don't know why, don't know when—the truth began to leak out about those things that happened. The prison was acknowledged for its secret vibration of haunting male fear: It was not only a zone of fisticuffs and gang turf war but, even more horrifying, it was a zone of rape. *Lockdown* gets that elemental reality in all its horror. It ain't pretty.

Second, more like its forebears, *Lockdown* boasts plot patterns, melodramatic story formulas in full bloom and tendril, so reassuring when handled well, as they are well enough here. It follows three young men of varying degrees of involvement in criminal activity through a stretch in one of America's toughest prison systems, that of New Mexico. That's where some years ago the most violent prison riot in history took place, a far worse meltdown than at Attica.

The three are boyz in the 'hood, but each has a different orientation. Avery (Richard T. Jones) is a gifted swimmer, proud father of a son, and is in love with his son's mother. Though a junior college dropout, he's up for an athletic scholarship that will get him up and out.

Dre (De'aundre Bonds) is a transitional figure. He has a job, even if an apparently dead-end one, but he's always looking for a little action. And finally, there's Cashmere (Gabriel Casseus), who's fully into the life. He's a dealer of dynamic demonism, his violent impulses occluded only occasionally by sentimentality toward his friends, particularly Avery. It's Cashmere who is framed by another dealer, but since Dre and Avery were in the car with him and they had discovered and handled a planted gun when the cops make the stop, all three end up convicted.

Though the film turns on a miscarriage of justice, that's not the subject proper of *Lockdown*. It's not a screed against prison or the system or racism; it's about what is, not what can be done about it. It feels like a large hunk of truth, a grueling account of what it takes to get through the long days and the longer nights in a behavioral sinkhole where nobody wants to go, except the people who have a gift for the behavioral sinkhole.

Each young man's cellmate turns out to be his destiny. The lucky Avery finds a wise, compassionate con—he has educated himself by reading Ralph Ellison's great *Invisible Man*—who counsels him on the culture of the prison and how to survive it. Poor Dre is quickly sexually dominated by his cellmate and the whole tattooed crew; he's turned into a—well, it is a term I would prefer not to use because I do enjoy this very fine job. His whole sense of masculine selfhood is traumatized, with tragic consequences. Cash joins the posse of the boss black con, Clean Up (played brilliantly by Master P), which buys him initial survival but bends him further in the direction of crime.

The cast is superb, particularly Casseus as the tormented Cashmere. He has a complex part—a young man pulled toward the criminal life, good at it, driven by a fury of anger and impulse, yet not oblivious to a larger moral responsibility—and he makes that paradoxical personality believable. The young director, John Luessenhop, keeps the story jumping ahead, from atrocity to plot twist to atrocity. Occasionally, a last-minute reprieve or a sudden change of heart will arrive too conveniently and you can feel the strings being pulled clumsily. But what makes the movie memorable is its authenticity. It's not a trip to the multiplex; it's a sentence.

(FEBRUARY 14, 2003)

*T*he French have a deliciously helpful phrase for just about everything, and one of the best is *nostalgie de la boue.*

Nostalgia for the mud, and I'm using it to mean an artist's or a reader's fondness for slime, muck, sewage, degradation, treachery, and perversion. It's a specialty of the comfy bourgeoisie, who yearn for the real and the raw as experienced through the lens of literature or cinema. As far as actually, ick, touching the mud . . . no thank you. But of this set of folks who demand to live life fast, hard, and safe (I proudly count myself), who among us, even the non-French, could not love the new *policier Narc,* which represents *nostalgie de la boue* carried to extremes. It is a veritable *boue*-bath, a *boue*-wrasslin' match, a ghostie that leaps out and goes *boue* in the night.

Clearly, then, its virtues will be the virtues of mud: that is, filth, real and metaphorical, rawness, savagery, the law of the jungle as enacted in the gutter, all in the chilled and grungy city of wintertime Detroit. The weather is cold, the language is profane, the action is hot.

The movie revolves around a single issue: the death of an undercover cop. To solve the apparently unsolvable case six months later, the suits of the Detroit police draw on a certain bad boy, an edge-dwelling under-cover stud named Nick Tellis, whose last bust went sour when he, uh, shot a pregnant woman (*la boue, c'est* Nick!). Even his marriage is mired in the *boue* of broken promises, uncommunication, bleak hopes. Nick is played by the moody looker Jason Patric, whom I would like a lot better if he'd put a *k* on the end of his name and if he weren't so damned seri-ous about being taken seriously all the time. But fortunately, he's not the real story here.

Nick is really just our entryway into the private hell of Henry Oak, played by Ray Liotta at a pitch of psycho fervor it takes a true demon to achieve. Henry is your typical angry white guy chafing against job disap-pointment, lack of respect and too much alcohol—only he has a badge and a gun and an attitude as brutal as a truncheon. He is hellbent on solving the murder of his former partner, but like a sports franchise owner, he wants to do it his way. That involves a lot of yelling, a lot of intimidation, a lot of saliva-dense explosions of spectacular profanity, and even an occasional back of the hand or butt of the gun applied somewhere soft and tender.

You think you've seen this one before? I thought so, too—it had to be the one about the delicate liberal who helps the hate-filled bigot see the light. The best thing about *Narc* is that the only light is the gleam of stag-nant water in the sewer. It turns out that Nick isn't particularly upset at Henry's frequent indelicacies; he's seen too much to take it very seri-ously, and he understands that the world in which they operate is pretty much populated by scum. So he sees Henry's attitude as a kind of extra level of Kevlar.

They interrogate, they investigate, they interview. Little things don't add up, and possibly Henry is trying a little too hard to lead the investi-gation over here when it should really be going over there. And he keeps turning up in the oddest places, like the home of the dead cop's wife, where he's suspiciously familiar. Hmmmm.

But the movie isn't selling plot. What it's selling is *boue*. That's all it sells, that's its only product—a sense of urban life as a firefight inside a battle locked in a campaign, waged by men who have two choices: alpha males or omega corpses. You can get a sense of the milieu that the writer-director Joe Carnahan creates by looking at the names of some of his characters listed in the cast: Strung Out Man, Meth Dealer, Strung Out Woman, Porn Shop Dude, and my favorite, Ruiz's Smoldering Squeeze.

It's a shame such attention to detail wasn't directed at the story. Or maybe the problem is the opposite: Too much attention to detail is directed at the story, and too many times various theories of the death unspool in flashbacks that are rooted in nobody's mind except the writer-director's. It finally more or less implodes on itself, winding up in an unpleasant sequence in which the two white cops speak impolitely to two handcuffed African-American men in tones that could be charitably described as "louder than hell." There's also cursing, spitting, screaming, swearing, cursing, crying, beating and finally, cursing, spitting, cussing, profanity and bad language, as well as a lot of swear words.

One doesn't leave *Narc*; one is finally released from it. You feel beaten down by the film, till no spark of life remains. As I walked out, I felt as though someone had just taken the cuffs off. It's a stunner that sadly grows tiresome at the end.   (JANUARY 10, 2003)

*P*aycheck represents such a professional nadir for each of its principals that you wish better for them in the new year:
For director John Woo: a better script.
For co-star Uma Thurman: a better agent.
For villain Aaron Eckhart: a better lube job for his hair.
For star Ben Affleck: a sensible new career in the insurance industry.
Really, it's miserable, but the saddest spectacle is poor Woo. Here's a man who electrified the film industry in the 1980s with his blend of kinetic violence and macho sentimentality in such Hong Kong gangster classic as *The Killer, Hard-Boiled* and *A Better Tomorrow.* He devised new ways of filming action no one had ever thought of before. Alas, uprooted by Hong Kong's annexation to China, he emigrated to the United States, where he's not quite found his place. He has bumbled into two hits in an otherwise mediocre post-HK career: *Face/Off,* which was pro-

pelled by giant gothic performances from Nicolas Cage and John Travolta, and *Mission: Impossible II,* star-driven by Tom Cruise. His most personal picture, the big-budget *Windtalkers,* flopped.

Why is he doing this film? I have no idea. A job is a job, I guess. But there's nothing in it that's remotely Woovian in tone or texture. When, now and then, he injects a signature touch—the guns-to-heads impasse between antagonists, or the sudden previolence arrival of a slo-mo dove—it seems utterly gratuitous. And he still has pretty much of a tin ear for American performances, so he lets Affleck doze through the starring role. The film feels as if it has no center.

The story, derived (as were *Blade Runner* and *Minority Report*) from a Philip K. Dick narrative, follows a treasured hack sci-fi gimmick: a man whose mind has been "wiped" follows clues left by (eureka!) himself, pre-wipe, to find out why people keep trying to kill or arrest him. Dick may have thought of this first, but Christopher Nolan did it best in *Memento.* And he had good actors!

So Affleck is Michael Jennings, by trade a brilliant reverse engineer. In other words, he deconstructs brilliant technological advances and figures out how they work so that they may be successfully copied. Highly illegal, but profitable. It's usually a three-week project, and the setting being the near future, he normally agrees to a mind-wipe after doing such a job (the movie's conceit is that mind-wipes are possible). His immediate memory—the period of the project—is destroyed, so he has no idea what he's just done, only that he's thousands, possibly millions of dollars richer.

Affleck's character is offered a ton of dough by Jimmy Rethrick, a billionaire greasehead with a body attached—that's Eckhart smirking annoyingly under the petroleum spill—to do a special, dangerous assignment involving a single-word evocation of the future: *Optics.* (Gee, if only the movie had had the wit to say: "plastics"!) Affleck agrees, even though this time it's three years that'll be erased. We see him start, and suddenly he's got the big paycheck and it's over. Except that: (a) the FBI is chasing him; (b) he's in the middle of an affair with Uma Thurman; and (c) Eckhart's henchmen are trying to kill him. But his old self managed to send his new self an envelope with twenty seemingly innocuous objects—bus tickets, keys, hair spray, lighters, that sort of thing—and if he can decipher the message contained by this stuff, possibly he can survive.

Now any red-blooded man in such a situation would simply buy Uma Thurman a big Japanese sword and say, "Go ahead and kill Bill, then kill Jimmy, then everyone else in the world who looks mean and dangerous, and we'll head to Cancún for a fifty-year vacation." But no, again he and the movie lack the wit for such a thing, and Thurman is just used as "the girl," to no consequence one way or the other.

I can't reveal the secret behind "optics," but it's a laugher. Really, a joke. The movie pretty much deflates from that point onward, but Woo soldiers glumly onward, stage-managing action sequences that have by this time become generic. In fact, he's working like a John Woo imitator in all his tricks and stunts.

You can pick this baby apart on a dozen different grounds, but let me choose two: design and star performance. The climax is set on a "campus"—that is, the R&D of a huge computer corporation possibly called Alcom or maybe Alpo—and it's as drearily imagined as Dr. Zarkov's laboratory in the old Flash Gordon serials, with buzzing tendrils of electricity, big display screen, and oddly jagged doors. It's so retro it gives you a headache.

And then there's Genteel Ben. Why is this guy in movies? Really, has he ever given a decent performance? I suppose he was okay in *Reindeer Games* and at his best in *Good Will Hunting*, and he might even have some talent, somewhere, somehow. But he just models his way through this, and his lack of belief in the project is apparent in every single scene.

Paycheck (110 minutes, at area theaters) is rated PG-13 for intense action, violence and language.   (DECEMBER 25, 2003)

*P*oor Janet Leigh never had much luck in motels. In *Psycho*, she was stabbed to death in a motel shower. And in *Touch of Evil*, something much worse happened: She was locked in a motel room, deprived of sleep, and made to listen to bebop music until she cracked.

But if she didn't have much luck in motels, she had great luck in movies set in motels; after all, she was in both *Psycho* and *Touch of Evil*.

The greatness of the former is beyond argument, and now, happily, so is the latter. Orson Welles's mad 1958 candy factory of film noir bonbons and his own sugar-soaked nougat-slathered acting is back, finally re-edited to his specifications after Universal took it from his control and tried to reinvent it as a regular thriller. That was akin to trying to turn one of Liberace's rhinestone-studded jackets into a nice Republican cloth coat. Moreover, it contained what is considered the definitive corporate atrocity against genius: The Universal editors layered the titles over the movie's most flamboyant sequence, a three-minute no-cut tracking shot that set up the premise, introduced the characters, defined the milieu and got the story rolling—just a casual flourish of brilliance that has never ever been matched.

That is the first thing you notice in this restored version, formally titled *The Re-Edit of "Touch of Evil"*: The titles have been removed from the film's opening, and that great gush of genius, at last, is rendered without an interfering scrim. The film's sound editing has also been restored, readmitting Welles's use of overlapping dialogue and impressionistic sound (he served time in radio, after all). And the time scheme has been slightly altered: The original studio release in 1958 recast the narrative into strictly chronological sequences. Welles's own plan was to cross-cut, to suggest that things were happening simultaneously. The new editors, Walter Murch and Rick Schmidlin, have gone to a great deal of trouble to rescue his original concept.

One result, or so it seems to me, is that it seems the long brutalization of Leigh in that motel room has been spread throughout the film; this somehow intensifies it uncomfortably, giving us time to imagine what is going on instead of merely hitting us over the head quickly. That's part of the movie's flirtation, too, with exploitation: It teasingly contrives to get the most curvaceous woman in the world stripped down to one of those fantastic plastic-rubberized gadget-laden undergarment contraptions of the fifties that seem an enterprise of both prurience and world-class elastic-stress engineering. It turns her body into a stylization of art moderne and deco; it weirdly and dangerously eroticizes her ordeal (as, ironically, Hitchcock would do two years later in *Psycho*).

That wasn't the only dangerous thing the ever-adventurous Welles did. He built the film out of taboo oppositions (there are three white-Hispanic couples). That's the touch of evil he was documenting: sexual resentment as it played across racial grounds.

That he approached such ideas is amazing; that he got them into a B-movie in 1958 is truly heroic, particularly when one considers how his career had collapsed since its apogee in 1940, when he flew out to Hollywood to shoot the movie that would become *Citizen Kane* with an unprecedented amount of freedom. By 1958, with one unmitigated commercial failure after another on his résumé, he had achieved an almost unprecedented lack of freedom.

In fact, so unusual is the film's origin that it seems to represent the artist's cynicism at its highest point, his contempt for Hollywood. He agreed to take, almost as a finger exercise, the worst script Universal owned if he could but rewrite it for two weeks (the script was originally adapted from *Badge of Evil*, by Whit Masterson). In this act, one can see his faith in his own powers, his need to subvert the system, and at the same time his desperate need to be loved.

It's probably the most passive-aggressive production start-up ever. He had to know they would take it from him. They always did. But his credo seemed to be: I will make art from crap, because that is what I do; then you will turn it back into crap, because that is what you do.

Permission was ultimately granted when Charlton Heston, then at the peak of his star power on the strength of *The Ten Commandments*, agreed to star, out of his own enthusiasm for Welles's work. Of course, like all good-deed doers, Heston was well rewarded with punishment. His was the thankless role of the straight-arrow good guy amid all the orchids of human evil flourishing in the hothouse atmosphere of what looked like a Mexican border town, but was really Venice, California, about thirty minutes from Welles's beloved Chasen's. And on top of that, Heston had to wear shoe polish on his face and somebody's idea of a Mexican mustache!

The movie really exists in three planes. Its first, the story, is the least interesting: In a corrupt border town, a visiting Mexican police agent named Vargas (Heston) discovers that a legendary American lawman named Hank Quinlan (Welles) is fabricating evidence to convict a Mexican youth of murder. When he presses his objection, the old cop bands with a Mexican crime boss (Akim Tamiroff) to kidnap the agent's wife (Leigh); but the agent rescues his wife, pursues the investigation and ultimately brings the lawman down. Only then—el cheapo ironic denouement—does it become clear that the Mexican youth really was guilty of the crime.

You could write a better story in a morning without coffee. What makes the film extraordinary is its second plane, which is the visual. Using the brilliant cinematographer Russell Metty and shooting in the then largely passé black-and-white, Welles unleashed a torrent of nightmare images that set the piece not in El Robles, or even in Venice, but in his own subconscious. We are strangers in that strange land:

You can pick any of two dozen moments of genius in the film, but to do that, really, is to atomize the totality of it. It is of a piece, one dark rhapsody on the theme of guilt and pride, set in a swirling sewer of a place, peopled with grotesques of such vividness that they linger in your mind like Munch's screamer on the bridge.

The camera itself is almost a character; it glides through the perfectly syncopated action, its grace the only note of beauty in the squalor. It stops now and then to admire a particularly grotesque character, such as Dennis Weaver's craven motel manager, a being so creepy he would give Norman Bates the shakes.

Then there is Marlene Dietrich, under a black fright wig, so incongruous she could have wandered in from the set of *Der Rosenkavalier* next door. This movie even finds room for Zsa Zsa Gabor and, ladies and gentlemen, if we can agree on no other thing, we can agree on this: *Touch of Evil* is the best film Zsa Zsa Gabor ever made.

But the secret thrust of the movie, its third plane, is autobiographical. Amid the perky, pointy Leigh, the noble, suffering Heston, the enigmatic Dietrich, the weirded-out Weaver and the shamelessly submissive Joseph Calleia, as Quinlan's number one guy, there is Welles's Hank Quinlan.

"Honey, you're a mess," says Dietrich, with her gimlet-eyed Teutonic realism. Yes, but what a mess: Quinlan is a great slobbering ruin, his eyes tiny behind the bulging meat sack of his face. He moves slowly, with a bristle of beard, on a game leg, in a suit that's a collection of feed bags and burlap. He has an old lion's eyes, too old to hunt but driven insane by the scent of flesh.

He's a kind of anti-Falstaff, a font not of life but of death, so locked into his way he cannot change. The movie amounts almost to Welles's mea culpa for the waste he's made of his career. Heston's Vargas is the new Hollywood, impatient, disrespectful, morally right but somehow without vision. He is simply dull, and his dullness isn't the flaw of the actor but the design of the piece.

Hank, it is said, always got by on instinct. That is, he knew. He had talent. He could sniff out the guilty. Because he was so powerful he had no need to play by the rules. But now his time is over—brought down by, among other things, technology (Welles makes a great deal of the tape-recording gizmo that is the instrument of Hank's defeat), but more by lack of faith. It's no longer enough simply to feel things, as genius does; you have to analyze them first.

In death, the great Hank floats with the grandeur of an Egyptian pharaoh's barge down the river Styx on a moonless night four thousand years ago, stately, plump, dead. It's really just a fat, corrupt cop, his suit having captured bladders of air, drifting down a river of garbage. Yet what it foretells, tragically, is Welles's own death in a world where genius is never again quite enough.

"He was a man," says Dietrich, offering up an epitaph as aircraft carrier Hank floats away.

But you're thinking: Actually, he was a director.

(SEPTEMBER 22, 1998)

*A*h, scum. Primordial, vicious, cunning, toothless, treacherous, tattooed, unashamed—how much more interesting they make the world. For us yuppie boomers in our senescent prosperity and for our children, the dot-com millionaires, they have one wonderful message: It can all go away in a hurry. They are the whisper of the ax, the whistle of the bullet, a memento mori for the too-comfortable.

They have their day in the all-scum-all-the-time masterwork *The Way of the Gun*, from the dark imagination of the fellow who dreamed up Keyser Soze in *The Usual Suspects*. Christopher McQuarrie won the Oscar for that first movie; his follow-up, which he also directed, shows that he's going to be around for a long time and that the first wasn't a fluke.

This film follows two casually nihilistic boneheads called Longbaugh (Benicio Del Toro) and Parker (Ryan Phillippe), whose names are stolen from the actual names of the men now known to history as the Sundance Kid and Butch Cassidy. That's the point: These aren't romantic fellows out on a gentlemanly lark, all beautiful dreams of chivalry and wit. No. They are the real, hideous thing that lurks beneath—goobers with guns.

The movie begins with a screamingly profane, screamingly comical scene in a movie theater parking lot (McQuarrie worked security at a multiplex for four years) where a snide woman goads her boyfriend into beating them up for sitting on the hood of her car. Okay, guess what they do? You'll never. They kick her butt, a darkly comic improvisation that sets the movie's darkly comic, ridiculously bloody tone.

Looking for a gig, the two idiots—who never pretend to be anything but idiots with too much ammo—come up, at a moment's notice, with a scam: They will kidnap the surrogate mother hired by an extremely wealthy but childless and desperate couple. What they can't guess is that the man (Scott Wilson) is in the life, too, but much higher up the crime food chain, and that he'll go not to the cops but to his own bodyguards (Nicky Katt and Taye Diggs) to get young, pregnant Robin (Juliette Lewis) back. He'll also call in his "facilitator," an old pro named Joe Sarno (James Caan), to supervise the issue.

Can you follow this? I couldn't either, not really. For we're in the noir universe, a betray-o-rama where every seven seconds brings a new lie, deceit, subterfuge, character revelation or hideous moment of violence. So I say to you that if this is not your cup of tea—steeped in slaughter, bone-cracking violence, dark morbidity, and lots of blood—stay far away, and do not call me to complain if you don't. I don't return phone calls anyhow, but I especially won't return those phone calls.

For the rest of us, here's what's good about this film:

McQuarrie has a great skill for the dialect of invective. When these people curse or dis each other, it's like rancid petals of iambic from a mind-poisoned Rimbaud. They rip each other new bodily orifices with the speed of kung fu fighters in a vernacular so toxic it raises the hair on the back of your neck.

He's great at faces. I love the looks on the mugs of the two professionals—Diggs and Katt—when they are first locked gun-on-gun with Longbaugh and Parker: weirdly intense pleasure, a pleased calm. No twitches, no bug eyes, just intense curiosity undercut with pleasure. This is where they want to be. This is what they trained for. This is their moment, come around at last and, doggone it, they will enjoy it.

Gun handling: I happen to know that McQuarrie's brother is a Navy SEAL, and he was on the set telling the guys how to shoot, how to move, how to run the guns fast and efficiently, how to administer a tactical reload, how to reload one-handed when hurt. The movie is an accretion of these little details, some so subtle they don't register, but nevertheless convincing.

The guns themselves: cool. I know they're not supposed to be, not in Bill Clinton's America, but still: cool. There are .45 automatics for the bad-guy heroes, Heckler & Koch submachine guns for the slick bodyguards, old Colt revolvers for Joe Sarno and his boys, plus a scoped Galil assault rifle in .308 for long shots, and pump guns with extended magazines for that close-quarter-battle thing. Remember, you read it here, in *The Washington Post*, first. If you don't get it, you don't get it.

Action: McQuarrie thinks of new ways to stage vigorous physical activity. The first big sequence—the kidnapping—comes up with something original, a kind of slo-mo car chase, where at any moment the cars slow to a crawl, the shooters debark and meander down long alleyways, trying to gain tactical advantage. The last one, a gundown so extravagant it has to be seen to be believed, sets all the players in motion against the backdrop of Sam Peckinpah's scabby Mexican village so that it feels like a crowded ride through the blades of a Cuisinart with people shooting at you. And it has the added attraction: birth by cesarean section in the middle of the battle.

Finally, the fake poetry of tough guys. I love this stuff. It's more beautiful than cowboy poems or Marty Robbins's gunslinger ballads or Barry Sadler's "Ballad of the Green Berets." Phillippe's Parker narrates in a voice so arch and literary it couldn't possibly belong in the head of a guy who shoots so well. It's wonderfully, beautifully fake, mocking the equally flatulent rhythms of Chandler's Marlowe or Hammett's Spade. All this places it squarely in the tradition of that most blasphemed of genres, the intellectual gangster story, which dates back at least as far as Raoul Walsh's *High Sierra* (Ida Lupino to Bogart's Roy Earle: "Gee, Roy, that's poetry") and on through such bleak, black beauties as *The Killers*, *Suddenly*, *Point Blank*, *The Hit*, and finally *Reservoir Dogs* and *The Usual Suspects*. It's good fun for bad boys.   (SEPTEMBER 8, 2000)

*W*ars are always fought between mankind's two oldest and most hate-filled tribes: Us and Them. But suppose, asks Steven Soderbergh's provocative new film *Traffic*, Us is Them?

If Us is Them, then what follows will be extraordinarily complicated. That is why the film itself is complicated; its complexities of plot, its densities of deceit and reversal, its swirls of motive and its growths of malignancy in the soul are the inevitable consequences of a war where the Us/Them dichotomy has gotten whacked.

The movie, adapted from a British television series called *Traffik*, is a kaleidoscopic look at the famous War on Drugs, following its sloppy momentum through any number of lives, destroying or corrupting all that it touches. It examines the war from top to bottom, and watches the drift of battle at the very elitist uppermost layer and at its most squalid base and all the levels in between.

It's set either the day before yesterday or the day after tomorrow—that is, now. At the summit of the structure, a federal judge named Robert Wakefield (Michael Douglas) finds himself appointed commander in chief in the war against happy dust. A law-and-order chap and a distinguished jurist, he gets the Big Washington Job of drug czar. He comes to our town and meets important people and goes to interesting parties and acquires a politically savvy but slippery aide—all the accouterments of success. He never even has to look for parking.

But, he comes to wonder as he gets used to his perks, what's the point of his jetting by government Lear to the El Paso Drug Enforcement Administration HQ and examining interdiction strategies when his own daughter, a straight-A student at an exclusive prep school in Cleveland, is shooting smack in her bedroom? That would seem to suggest the war is already lost.

The judge's melancholy initiation into the realities of the drug war is perhaps the central journey of the film, but far from the only one, as other stories and other characters whirl, touch, mesh, depart, fall apart, climax and trail off with a great deal of energy. *Traffic*, with a script by Simon Moore and Stephen Gaghan, is straining toward a new form: documentary in mode and reportage, dramatic in intimacy and intensity.

At the lowest level of the struggle is Javier Rodriguez, a Tijuana cop played by the splendid actor Benicio Del Toro, who may get the first Oscar nomination for a role played entirely in Spanish. His problems are more intense than the judge's but just as melancholy. First of all, he has to stay alive on a very confusing battlefield, where the difference between colleagues and targets is not always clear. Second, he must stay honest (he is a moral man, to a point), or at least as honest as possible in his highly conditional circumstances.

His basic dilemma is simple, even if its solution is not. Something of a star in his department, he is recruited by a ranking army general, Arturo Salazar (Tomas Milian), as a civilian go-to guy in the general's campaign against a leading drug cartel in Tijuana. It seems like a promotion. But what happens if it turns out that General Salazar is working not for a drug-free world but another cartel? Tricky, tricky, to the point where the cop finds himself standing on the brink of a hole he himself has dug in the desert, and an army lieutenant has a .45 up against the nape of his neck.

More or less at the midpoint of this infected structure is the street-level American enforcement layer, in which a drug mob underling (played by the always effective Miguel Ferrer) is nabbed by two enterprising DEA agents (Don Cheadle and Luis Guzmán) and turned against his powerful boss and cartel frontman (Steven Bauer). When that king of the San Diego suburbs is arrested, his bewildered wife, Helena (Catherine Zeta-Jones), inherits control of his business, his debts, and his enemies. What's an expectant mother to do? After all, she's used to country-club lunches with her tony friends followed by epic shoe-shopping binges.

The surprise is that Helena is a quick study, and that she may, as her career develops, be even more ruthless than her husband. When you hear her screaming into a cell phone "I want him dead, goddammit!" you know you are in strange territory.

Soderbergh—out of, I suppose, pity for the slowest among the audience—encodes the movie with photographic stylizations that help keep the plot lines separate. Sequences set south of the border are blurry with desaturated color to play up the squalor of the Third World; the judge's world—with its fancy houses, its cocktail parties (a variety of Washington heavy hitters play themselves), its hearing rooms—is all cool blue and green in perfect focus, to denote a world where protocol and certainty seem to rule. The *Miami Vice*–like vectors of the DEA agents and their snitch are more straightforwardly portrayed.

The most depressing of the stories follows the tragic downward spiral of the judge's bright and pretty daughter, Caroline (Erika Christensen), who has it all and wants none of it. This is Soderbergh's most disturbing character, and although she feels tragically real, even the director can't explain her. How she goes from straight A's in the 'burbs to turning tricks downtown in cribs above the meanest streets in Ohio is a profound puzzle; who knows the solution? The movie certainly doesn't. It simply concludes that somehow, vaguely, all this effort, all this energy, all this anguish, this huge investment: It feels wrong.

You may agree or not. If the film's bias is liberal, though, and veers away from law-and-order clichés toward a willingness to understand the Usness of Them and the Themness of Us, Soderbergh is at the same time extremely admiring of his agents and cops.

These guys are up against it all day long; they never have a nice day, and all too frequently they don't have a nice night, either, because they are dead. He may disagree with the philosophy that guides them and the policy that pays them, but he gets the most important thing about them: They are heroes.   (JANUARY 5, 2001)

*I*t's far easier to admire *The Pledge* than to enjoy it. In fact the movie actively discourages enjoyment, filled as it is with the mutilation of children, the anguish of grieving parents, and the drunken despair of old cops. Why, it has no mercy at all.

But it has a great deal of integrity. It insists on being a movie in the old-fashioned sense: no fancy editing or camera stunts, no patter, banter, or snippiness, no attitude, no towering propane explosions or computer morphs of monsters that can't be. Instead it's interested in the monsters that can be. And some old values: a tissue of motive (sometimes ambiguous), a corrosive moral dilemma, a languid style of long scenes and slow music, and a great performance.

The author of that performance is Jack Nicholson; what may surprise some is that it's not that typical Nicholson "thing" of, say, *As Good as It Gets*—that cheap manipulation of charm and anger and charisma that destroys the movie while aggrandizing its star. Possibly this is why Nicholson prefers to work with Sean Penn (they also collaborated on *The Crossing Guard* in 1995), who will not permit him to get away with anything. Penn, more famous for his acting than his directing and more famous still for a failed marriage to Madonna, gives him room to work but absolutely will not allow him to be that fabulous creature called "Jack Nicholson."

Nicholson plays Jerry Black, a Reno homicide detective on his way out. His face looks like ten miles of bad road, the fissures fighting the flab for dominance, only the feral eyes still sharp. One look at that mug and you know he's spent too much time in the foul rag-and-bone shop of the human spirit. Retirement is six hours away and Jerry is at his surprise party at a wondrously tacky Tiki-themed restaurant when detectives' pagers start going off all over the place: A body has been found in the snowy mountains, a child's. Jerry must go, even if Penn establishes effectively that the department is now run by younger, smarter, more aggressive men. (Aaron Eckhart is excellent as Jerry's replacement.)

The crime scene is grotesque, again effectively depicted without being sensationalized. A little girl has been raped, murdered, mutilated. Think blood against the snow, the most obscene of tapestries on display in the most pristine of museums. It turns out a witness saw somebody fleeing this macabre scene; that fellow is quickly enough apprehended, confesses, and conveniently commits suicide. That he was clearly a retarded man (played by Benicio Del Toro in one of the movie's many annoying celebrity cameos) bothers no one except Jerry.

Why? One answer is that without Jerry's curiosity, he wouldn't have a movie to star in. Another answer is a pledge he has made to the victim's mother. More probably, the motive is buried in Jerry's mind: He needs something to live for, and so he begins to develop an obsession as a form of self-medication. He can't leave the case alone, continues to investigate, finds traces of other unsolved crimes—in each case, the brutal slaughter of a little girl—seemingly linked to a specific rural area. Soon enough he has invested his retirement egg in a failing gas station and tackle shop that's equidistant to the crime scenes and he begins his slow infiltration of the local culture in search of a monster who, theoretically, is preparing to kill again, if he even exists. Pattern or coincidence? Master detective work or self-indulgent illusion?

Nothing Nicholson does heroicizes or romanticizes Jerry; he's not Dirty Harry with his big .44 Mag, pining to gun down the world's human beasts and save civilization. He's detective as misanthropic loner/obsessive/repulsive: a little man, smart but so focused as to be charmless, digging ever deeper, smoking and drinking too much, eating junk, struggling to keep the business running so that he can keep his investigation running.

But he can't keep his needs quiet, and in small ways he begins to yield to his own humanity. A friendship with a local waitress burgeons into something deeper. Suddenly Lori (Robin Wright Penn, surprisingly effective: harshly lit, behind a chipped tooth and under a lifeless hank of dark hair) has moved in with her little girl, a refugee from an abusive marriage in search of normalcy and security but finding something a little like love.

It's great to see Nicholson doing small things, rather than big things: a man opening up in the stewardship of a child and in the proximity of a woman, a man suddenly finding himself at ease in society, not the outsider a cop will always be, a man with a business and a passion (fishing).

And yet . . . and yet . . . the fascination of the movie, which is derived from a novel by the Swiss author Friedrich Dürrenmatt, is not really in the overarching "detective story" aspects of the plot, though those are powerful enough. Rather it's in Jerry's duality, which Nicholson conveys so well: As he becomes caretaker of this family, is Jerry subconsciously baiting a trap for the killer with his own beloved ersatz-daughter? Is he fishing with the most blasphemous of bait? What are his motives? He cares for the child desperately but, equally desperately, he wants to capture the monster.

This is no Hannibal Lecter film, and there's no heavy breather stalking through the woods at night, diddling with blades and clubs, face unseen to spooky, raspy music. And it does do something that I hate and respect at once: It's so expertly set up, it could have delivered one of the all-time cool pop endings. It could have gone Hollywood big time, and probably made itself a hit.

But Penn and Nicholson won't go there. They walk away, almost contemptuously, toward the bleakness at the end of the tunnel. To make sure everybody's entirely depressed, they conjure up an ending that drives a chilled spike through your heart. I hate it when a movie does that. I also love it.   (JANUARY 19, 2001)

*I*t's not easy being Hannibal Lecter these days. The old fop simply wants to kick back in a café near the Palazzo Vecchio with a nice Chianti and spend the hours fondly remembering the kind of dismembering when death was slow and oh so mellow. But a nasty billionaire who looks like E.T. with leprosy is paying millions to smoke him out and turn him into a Big Mac for three not-so-little pigs.

That's pretty much it for Ridley Scott's *Hannibal*, which suffers from one fundamental flaw it cannot overcome: It is not *The Silence of the Lambs*.

So if you want to see *The Silence of the Lambs* again, the solution to your problem will be found at your local video shoppe. It will not be found in any of the thousand-odd theaters where Anthony Hopkins's elegant, snobbish sociopath is playing an elaborate game of escape and evasion while occasionally testing new recipes.

This movie connects with its predecessor exactly as Thomas Harris's book *Hannibal* did to his *Silence of the Lambs*: It is not bad on its own terms, and it is certainly engrossing, but it comes nowhere near the power and sordid glory of the original.

One must understand from the get-go that *Hannibal* lacks resonance because it is altogether a different type of story from the original. Where *Silence* was rooted in reality and had a detail-rich documentary feel that pushed its creepiness content off the charts while giving it a moral center, *Hannibal* is Gothic opera with black-comic overtones, set in a world utterly disconnected from our own, a world without a center.

Put it another way: In *Silence* they killed us; in *Hannibal*, to paraphrase Bugsy Siegel, they only kill their own kind.

This not just in: Jodie Foster has been replaced by the superb actress Julianne Moore as Clarice Starling, the heroic FBI agent whose presence oddly agitates Hannibal Lecter's inner child. This was a business necessity, based on Foster's decision not to participate in the project. Scott and the producers probably could have done no better than the excellent Moore.

Yet her performance hamstrings the movie. Moore acts, Foster was. Something about Foster's physical being and possibly even her personal history—her tumultuous past, her near-androgyny, her pale radiance, her vulnerability enmeshed with her intelligence, her icy blue eyes (the same color as Lecter's), her strange angelicism—held the movie together. She was fascinating; you could certainly understand how a monstrous anomaly like Lecter could find her enchanting because you yourself found her enchanting.

Moore, by contrast, is all business; it's good business, but it's only business. She plays the older Clarice pretty much as Harris wrote her: a tough street agent, a steady hand in the raid van, but perhaps she's seen too much bloodshed, and feels too close to used up. But that's all. There's nothing resonant or charismatic about her. She's not a paradigm of innocence; she's not a symbolic protector of the lambs. There aren't any lambs in the movie.

The movie is also hamstrung by the structural oddities of the book: It feels at times like the first half of one story and the second half of another. In the first half, set largely in picturesque Florence, Dr. Lecter has emerged under a thin pseudonym as "Dr. Fell," a Renaissance scholar, bon vivant, and epicure, who is campaigning to obtain a chair as curator of an elegant museum in that fabled city.

Why Florence? Well, because Harris likes Florence and spent a lot of time there. No other reason, but it's helpful, because Scott likes it, too, and really lights up the place's lush atmosphere and gleaming cobblestones and enclosed bridges and vaulted, ancient stone buildings. In this picturesque ruin, a rumpled detective named Pazzi (played by the great Euro actor Giancarlo Giannini, whose face has come to resemble Tuscan ceramics cracking in the sun since Roman times) has been alerted to the possibility of Lecter's presence and begun to see through Dr. Fell's false identity. But Pazzi, pressured by a greedy young wife, decides to use his police career as camouflage as he attempts to capture Lecter for the amusement of another recondite sociopath, the fabulously wealthy Mason Verger, back in the States. That will earn Pazzi a $3 million reward, enough to keep his wife in opera tickets and Gucci shoes for years.

And why is Mason Verger so ticked at Lecter? Possibly it has something to do with the fact that Lecter induced him to cut off his own face, and then fed it to the doggies. Arf, arf! This is why Verger now resembles that alien with the skin problem. Seeking revenge, he has conjured up a counterplot: He will feed all of Hannibal to some hungry pigs, feet first. It's not tit for tat, it's feet for face.

Verger, played by an uncredited Gary Oldman under a latex mask, represents the movie's curious transference of values. It finds forgiveness in its heart for Hannibal, because he is so cool and elegant and knows the difference between a '78 Puligny-Montrachet and a '79 Chassagne-Montrachet; this means, of course, it must find a far more repugnant villain. So as it progresses, we watch as Hannibal, despite his adroit handling of the greedy Italian cop (memo to cops stalking Hannibal Lecter: Stay away from high windows and short ropes), ceases to be the true villain and ultimately becomes almost a damsel in distress, while Verger takes over as the prime nasty boy.

It's a tricky transaction, handled deftly for the most part, though the movie makes one small fumble: It locates Verger's evil mostly in his appearance and in the fey, sly decadence that Oldman manages to convey under all that rubber, with only vivid eyes and a voice that seems pickled in pain; yet it fails to display him doing something truly evil. (Harris, in the book, dreamed up some doozies for Mason: Cruelest of all, he enjoyed cocktails made in part from the tears of children, whether shaken or stirred I cannot recall.)

Thus the second half involves a somewhat bizarre plot: The mega-rich Mason uses his political influence to put Agent Starling's career in jeopardy through the offices of a corrupt Justice Department official played by Ray Liotta, who is all wrong for the part. He's too boyish and lacks the gravitas and dead eyes of a true D.C. wonk-careerist. But Mason's psychology is astute: He knows that putting Clarice into danger will attract Lecter to her rescue. His minions succeed in netting the maniac where the now completely irrelevant Italian caper failed.

At that point, the movie gets pretty ordinary, ending finally with a gun-laden, one-gal hostage rescue mission meant to save Hannibal the Cannibal from the swine, which involves some routine gunfighting (Moore never looks as comfortable with guns as Foster did in the final seconds of *Silence*). And yes, the ending has been changed, but just barely. The book left our favorite fun couple together at last, in swank and purely apposite circumstances. Scott and writers David Mamet and Steven Zaillian have cooked up a twist to that deflationary spiral.

Possibly more important, the movie has a talker. By that I mean a scene sure to be the chatter-center of America come Monday at the office. It's *Hannibal*'s dizziest, wittiest, most outlandish scene and also its most ghoulish and not for the faint of heart. This involves—hmm, how can I say this? Possibly it is every Washington journalist's most vivid fantasy: not merely a meal with a spokesman, a common if odious Washington ritual, but a meal of a spokesman!

What keeps *Hannibal* from reaching the heights of intensity is the lack of stakes. Nothing really matters: who lives, who dies, how, why? You are amused by these cold, self-interested but glamorous fish, but they seem to swim in an aquarium sealed off from human life.

(APRIL 2, 2002)

*J*orget Tom Cruise. Forget the first *Mission: Impossible* (if you haven't already). Forget the television show of the sixties with its doodly, infectious musical theme and Peter Graves's gravitas. Forget Thandie Newton and the cross-racial love interest. Forget . . .

Well, forget everything: your mortgage, the things you regret, the times you weren't up to it, the things you never got caught for, the betrayals, deceits, and banal heroisms of everyday life.

Forget them all.

Remember: John Woo.

For *Mission: Impossible II,* which opens today, is such a feast of outlandish pleasures it'll send you home steam-cleaned and shrink-wrapped. It's straight from the hyperfervid brain of the Hong Kong director who has reinvented the action film, and it's so far over the top, there ain't no bottom; you're in outer space, sucking for oxygen. Woo-woo-woo, the man's a pirate, a circus master, a flapdoodle and a necromancer at once, but boy can he make a motion picture!

The plot would be unmemorable save for the fact that it's incomprehensible. Something about an artificially created virus and its artificial cure, meant to be huckstered to the world after the fashion of the dear old Krupp firm of years gone by, which built an armor that no gun could penetrate so everybody had to buy it, and then built a gun that could penetrate it so that everybody had to buy that, too. So it is with Chimera, which turns people to blood sponges, pus sacs, and corpses in thirty hours, and Bellerophon, the magic drug that makes it go away.

It's apparently stolen by a rogue IMF agent named Sean Ambrose (the Scotsman Dougray Scott). Now it's being shopped to the world for billions. Therefore Ethan Hunt (Cruise), who was higher up the IMF alpha-male pecking order than Ambrose, is ordered by Hannibal Lecter to go get it back, in Australia. Why Australia? I would suspect because that's where the best stuntmen live, and Woo's wild and woolly film is a tribute to the guts of professional stuntpeople. And, I suppose, a tribute to Cruise, who appears to do a lot of his own, à la Jackie Chan, including an astonishing opening sequence where he's matching the strength in his fingertips against the ragged glory of the mountains.

And why Hannibal Lecter? Oh, okay, it's an unbilled Anthony Hopkins, but he's clearly playing Hannibal, with that meditative pause between words, that sense of sublimely superior knowledge and that sense of confidence that he can dominate a movie in exactly two scenes.

The subtext here has nothing to do with movies or movie stars: It's almost a dialogue between Woo and his fans. He seems to be saying: I will be the Woo I want to be; then I will be the Woo you want me to be, but I will do that as it suits me, not you. I love a director who makes you crawl like a slug to the good stuff.

Woo opens in a romantic mood. The first part of the film watches as Cruise's Ethan must recruit Newton's Nyah Nordhoff-Hall. She's the key to the caper because she's Ambrose's ex-lover and he misses her tragically. Woo on wooing is something to behold: The camera glides swoonily, lovesick, and capricious, as Ethan stalks Nyah in romantic Spain, where she's gone to steal some jewels, and spots her across a roomful of slo-mo flamenco dancers, their red capes billowing voluptuously as they tappity-tap-tap a *duendo* of love.

Woo loves the big and beautiful, and in these two stars he's found it. Cruise has an art deco face, a stylized icon of male beauty that could be lifted from the hood ornament of a '34 La Salle, all streamline and art moderne. Meanwhile, Newton seems an E.T. from the planet of the small perfect people; her face is exquisite but somehow weirdly untouched by reality. It's as if she were still an embryo floating in her little sac of nourishing fluid.

So Woo takes his time, watching these two tryst the night away, as they find substitutes for actual sex. First is thievery (she's good, he's better); second comes driving, as they flirt at seventy-five miles per through the Spanish Alps, his Boxter nuzzling her Mercedes, as they skid toward oblivion with smiles on their handsome faces. The danger is exhilarating. Soon they're in bed, love, and partnership and he's pitched the deal; re-up with Ambrose and get the virus back, while the IMF team tracks her with a global satellite that reads a microchip in her bloodstream from halfway to the moon.

There follows what might be called the foreplay stage. It has nothing to do with the story, since there's hardly any story to begin with. It has to do with the fans who know Woo waiting for him to get to it, as he holds off with a smile. Wait a little longer, my unruly children, says old papa Woo as the movie just gets drearier and drearier until you are sustained by nothing except love and trust in Woo.

It turns out to be worth it. The last hour of *M:I-2* rocks so hard it rocks its way off the planet. Its one long crescendo after another, as each climax trumps the one before.

You want capers? Woo sends Tom Cruise rappelling down a shaft in the center of a building to land an inch from the glass he must cut through to get into a top-secret lab. You want gunfights? Ten men with MP-5s await him. He seems to have about 20 Berettas. They fired less at Normandy in 24 hours than they fire here in five loud, smoky minutes. You want martial arts? Cruise appears to have mastered enough whirligig flying dragon whipsaw kicks to get by with it (though he's no Jackie Chan). But . . . you ain't seen nothing yet.

The finale is an ecstasy of testosterone-fueled kineticism. Maybe you have to have a taste for this sort of thing or just a single-digit IQ, but the final dust-up, which seems to last an hour, follows Cruise on a racing cycle (which shows up handily enough at just the right moment) to set up a final spasm of vehicular mayhem and ballet that just won't stop. On a red two-wheeler, Cruise darts in and out of the armada of bad-guy Land Rovers, shooting and gymnasticizing as he figure-eights this way and that. Is it believable? Not for a single second. Will you care? Not for a single second. But it's less pure violence than it is pure dance, albeit of men, guns, vehicles, explosions, landscape, and a camera style so aggressive it might be identified as Nureyevian.

We have left the workaday world far behind. We have left much of movie art and culture far behind. We are in some new place, beyond sense and motive, where motion is its own reward and things whirl and fly about with gay abandon, none quite so liberated as your own heart. And you think, as you suck for air, if I get a heart attack, hey, this is a pretty good way to go.

Certain minor flaws must be charted. Besides the fact the plot is incomprehensible, add the following: There is not one recognizable moment of actual human behavior, just as there is not one recognizable human being. Newton and Cruise are employed purely for their iconography. Scott is a little small for his big role, and the rest of the cast—except for the amused Dr. Lecter—are ciphers meant only to swell the story or die on cue. Add in: No one outside the U.S. Army owns as many Berettas as Cruise seems to (where does he hide them and how did he order them from GSA?), and these are the sort that never run out of ammo. Also: When Thandie Newton gets sick unto death, you can tell because she's .000001 percent less beautiful than when she's well.

And finally: Woo has no interest in reality or reasonableness. His view of cinema is as a perpetual motion machine, a circus with fifty rings and a trick in each of them. Like the best of directors and pizza joints, he delivers it piping hot every time.   (MAY 24, 2000)

*C*onspiracy movies can be divided into three parts: small, big, and all gall.

Usually, but not always, quality is inversely proportional to the size: The small movies seem to be good, the big movies are amusing if foolish, and the gallingly gigantic ones are ridiculous.

But taken together they represent something more powerful than a simple audience need to be entertained. Indeed the persistence of the story form is one of its most conspicuous attributes, particularly as the volatile American film industry invents, overuses, recombines, and ultimately abandons genres (like westerns, private-eye films, war movies, and so forth) with almost endless energy. It's not really a genre itself, so much as the content of a dozen or so pulp genres, and can be found in some form or other in any movie universe. Yet like the North Star, conspiracy theories on film are always there to lure us onward.

Now there's even a movie called *Conspiracy Theory*, which has just opened; it's of the middle category, the one in which the conspiracy is grand but not so huge as to topple on account of its own topheaviness. It has some charms—Julia Roberts is splendid, and Patrick Stewart does a fine job imitating the colorless WASP primness of a McGeorge Bundy type—but in the end its inability to explain even the conspiracy around which it is built, much less the many others it invokes, consigns it to irredeemable muddle, a common enough flaw.

But to compare it with films on either side of its classification is instructive. For example, a smaller movie might be a classic like *The Third Man*, while the larger would be the brain-dead *JFK*. In some measure, these three films almost provide a blueprint to the textures, nuances, and pleasures of the conspiracy movie, and how it's changed.

The small-conspiracy film is a staple of forties and fifties film culture; conspiracies mutated into something larger in the seventies and eighties for reasons obvious and not so obvious; and now they are so big there sometimes seem to be more people inside them than outside them, in which case they would have to cease to be theoretical and simply become reality.

The Third Man, directed by Carol Reed in 1949 in the nightmare city of postwar Vienna, is about the most miniature of scams: the theft of penicillin from army hospitals, on the principle that the drug is worth far more on the street than in the systems of children suffering from meningitis. The author of this plot, the ever-beguiling Harry Lime, in the form of calm, qualmless, bacon-fat-smooth Orson Welles, has no problem at all with the consequences. Harry's eyebrows are arched in irony, his sensitive lips pursed with prissy delicacy and his intelligent if slightly thyroid eyes twinkle with merry self-amusement. But his flesh is pallid and chilled; he's like Oscar Wilde with a psychotic streak a yard long and a mile wide.

But that is it exactly: the core of the conspiracy gestalt. A small group of men—or a single, superior man, like Harry—ruthlessly manipulating the masses or the system or the media or something for private profit, political gain, or, in the absence of otherwise knowable motives, for pure kicks. Whatever the scale, the films seem to express the same collective fear: a deep mistrust of elites with inside access and power, long-seeing and cool intellects, obscure protocols and iron will, all applied against that mass of good-hearted losers known colloquially as the Rest of Us, with our mortgages, unruly children, weight problems, and small-beer hopes and fears. We are the tiny dots who may stop moving to advance their celestial agenda.

Of course such a paranoid view is useful outside the movies as well as inside them. Hitler ascended on such a contention, and later, though do not interpret this to suggest moral equivalency, so did Senator Joe McCarthy. A cottage industry has been built on conspiracy theories; in this city, The

Plan is merely the latest example. But for the movies, conspiracies supply the fodder of narrative. They play neatly with mass perceptions as well as mass delusions; they provide platforms for movie-scale emotions like love, hate, and revenge; they let a director blow lots of stuff up.

Of the three films cited, *The Third Man* is the uncontested masterpiece, an example of how much artistic perfection can be achieved in how small a compass. Perhaps its most salient stroke is that at the mechanical level, its conspiracy is really quite simple: A witness is murdered and with the connivance of one or two corrupt officials, his body is identified as the villain's and buried. The villain is thus free to continue his plot, and only the arrival of a naïve old friend who asks silly questions and has a simplistic view of the moral order unravels the thing.

The Third Man has something else to commend it to attention besides brilliant plotting (Graham Greene wrote it) and superb performances. It was not the first but it was surely one of the most sophisticated films to evoke the universe of the conspiracy visually. For to watch it is to feel oneself absorbed into the vortex of plot and counterplot, to be drawn through labyrinths both literal and metaphorical, to enter a world of dappling chiaroscuro where light and shadow marbleize into each other almost effortlessly, like an M.C. Escher print. Reed, possibly influenced by Welles's own great *Citizen Kane*, possibly influenced by the American film noir style that was busily creating fantasies of urban paranoia back in sunlit postwar American, possibly influenced by German expressionism of the twenties (all were connected; that's another story), and possibly influenced by the baroque intricacies of that plum-rotten, history-haunted, pastry-intense city on the Danube, engineered one of the most powerful visual experiences in movie history. In fact, in few films has the sense of conspiracy been so palpably felt: As Reed's camera prowls the sewers and the alleys and watches with ironic detachment as Russian, English, and American occupiers cynically traffic in human souls to advance their historical imperatives, one feels the total power of the shadow to obscure, and one feels the impulse of the conspirators.

So many small conspiracy films seem excellent. It's easy to list them: John Frankenheimer's *The Manchurian Candidate* and *Seven Days in May*, Martin Ritt's splendid, knuckle-cracking version of le Carré's great *Spy Who Came In From the Cold*, even Alan J. Pakula's *All the President's Men*, which, it must be remembered, may have involved gigantic political personalities but, when the conspiracy was penetrated, revealed itself to have been a squalid enterprise more appropriate to the work of Jim Thompson than that of Ian Fleming.

But the conspiracy form mutated in the seventies to the behemoth it's now become. Watergate was one reason; the assassination of JFK and the cottage industry of professional paranoia that grew around it in the years following may have been another; the war in Vietnam, with its embittering toxins of cynicism and frustration still another—all of it adding up to something larger than stolen penicillin: the conceit that history was bunk, and that there was always something underneath it all. Every story has an inside story. Nobody could make a movie like *The Third Man* anymore, at least not in the studio system, because, really, there's so little at stake; now conspiracies have got to be much bigger, to match the scale of our history and our expectations.

This accounts in some way for last year's *The Long Kiss Goodbye*, and for this year's poor *Conspiracy Theory*, which has the outer raiments of conspiracy in spades, to the full extent that major studio backing and big-time movie stars like Mel Gibson and Roberts can provide, but when examined carefully self-destructs like a soap bubble in a hot wind.

It violates the principal rule of conspiracy-as-narrative: It must, in the end, be clear. There must be a moment, totally satisfying, when the pattern at last crystallizes, when we see what all the hubbub has been about. That was easy when the conspiracy involved penicillin; it's somewhat more difficult in *Conspiracy Theory*, when it involves former lives (Gibson's), a seemingly nefarious government agency, a stalwart, idealistic realist, and a gibbering idiot who may be a witness. It doesn't help that key events took place years before and have to be described in a series of static explanations denser than lectures on nuclear physics, while the energy escapes from the film like the air from a punctured balloon.

At the same time, it doesn't take much insight to see that the same roles are present here as in *The Third Man*. Stewart is Harry Lime, the smooth elitist. Roberts is Holly Martins, the naive idealist who begins to ask the questions. Gibson is the femme fatale in whose mind is hidden the key to the mystery—beautiful and mysterious, he just happens to be a guy. But these archetypal characters have been blown out, giganticized. It could be called *The Three Millionth Man*, that's how much bigger it is. It does apparently violate one of the cardinal rules of the conspiracy film, however, which is that if the bad guys have helicopters, they work for the government. They do have helicopters, but unless I've misread the text pathetically (always a possibility), they don't work for Uncle Sam, although they used to.

But the final ingredient is the one that tilts so many conspiracies in movies into absurdity. In the absence of Communist enemies, we've had to develop new ones, and it's usually our own government, or that subset therein, a "rogue agency," ever helpful to desperate screenwriters who can't be bothered to invent villainy but must expropriate from the front page.

It was certainly the Kennedy assassination that gave rise to this fillip. It grew necessarily from a tracking of anomalies in that complex event which, as followed, could be explained only by the utter random nature of the universe or a conspiracy so vast and complex and so beyond the reasonably doable that the only institution with such resources available was the United States government. No one would buy a book about the random nature of the universe, and thus was born the Military-Industrial-Complex-CIA-Army Intelligence-Mafia-KGB-Combined Whole Field Theory of the assassination of our thirty-fifth president.

That led, of course, to Oliver Stone's epic farrago. It too played by the rules of the form despite the mystical quasi-documentary style, but it too blew the form outward gigantically: an idealistic detective with the courage to ask the hardest questions, a villain who was evidently nothing less than the entire culture of official secrecy, and a number of yipping witnesses. To give Stone the filmmaker credit, his jittery camera work, alternating film stocks, and staccato editing rhythms produced a film that was itself a tissue of paranoia. In its confines, nothing seemed sure, nothing stable, anything was possible. Too bad it was such a load.

Why Stone chose the almost comically discredited Jim Garrison as the font of his investigations, driving even the dedicated assassination theorists seriously bonkers, will be known only to God and his psychiatrist. Not even Kevin Costner's earnest pieties could disguise the desperate paucity of the material.

But the impulse toward gigantism does go a long way toward explaining the secret lure of these movies and what the small, bitter stories of the forties have mutated into. Whereas once they offered the pleasures of drama, now they offer the pleasures of religion. Where once they were pointed, specific, resonant, now they are vast, amorphous, spiritual. Where once they were set somewhere, now they seem to be set everywhere, as controlled by systems so vast that their very vastness makes them invisible.

After all, it's no surprise that we call JFK-conspiracy fanatics "zealots," a term steeped in religious fervor. For in some sense, the conviction of conspiracy is an act of faith. The less evidence that can be located, the more intense the belief in its existence. In fact, the very absence of proof in some cases, to some minds, becomes proof itself, much in the way that God's existence must in the end be taken on pure faith.

But more than that, conspiracies now offer many of the pleasures and beliefs of organized religion: I was struck by that particularly in this summer's most conspiracy-dense film, *Waco: The Rules of Engagement*.

For a while the documentary was quite reasonable in its probing of the tragedy of folly, idiocy, bad judgment, and frustration that led to the incineration of eighty-odd men, women, and children on the plains of Waco after an FBI raid on the Branch Davidian sect, the bizarre climax to a bizarre episode in American history. The filmmakers were journalistically solid as they documented the sloppiness of the ATF, the religious seriousness of the Davidians, the cowboy culture of the FBI SWAT teams, and the final tactical mistakes that ultimately spelled conflagration.

But somehow the filmmakers couldn't leave it at that: human stupidity on a grand scale, signifying nothing more than the random brute force of the universe. You put CS gas suspended in a highly flammable carrier into a structure and sooner or later, it's going to ignite, particularly as tanks are grinding through the buildings, spewing hot exhaust. The filmmakers suggest the government was responsible for the ignition, while the FBI has long maintained the Davidians lit the flames intentionally. Both sides are united in this conviction: Someone is to blame. No one seems willing to admit the presence of chance sparks in the world, surely the simplest of all explanations.

No, say the filmmakers: The government wanted to incinerate those people, and the filmmakers even convinced themselves that they had uncovered muzzle flashes on infrared film of FBI shooters driving the fleeing Davidians back into the flames.

In this case, and so many others, the conspiracy theory gives the event meaning that it would otherwise lack. The phenomenon is familiar from the culture of JFK assassination buffs, who cannot abide the squalid possibility that a grim little nobody with stained teeth and rancid breath reached out to twist the shape of history. If that were true, the news is very bad: It means there is nothingness in the universe and that random winds wreck lives and nations on no principle save whimsy.

We who are mere dots used to believe it was God's plan when a dot that was a precious child or spouse ceased moving, and we found some peace and some relief from pain in that. We couldn't know the plan, but our faith told us there was a plan. Now we've subtracted God from the plan, but the plan remains, and lacking clear evidence to the contrary, we take some pleasure from ascribing our misfortune and our tragedy to dark agencies. Thinking of them makes it much easier to abide the dot lifestyle.   (AUGUST 10, 1997)

I don't want to write this but they're making me. Who? Oh, you know. The usual. Them. They. The watchers in the shadows, the manipulators, the hidden persuaders.

They're addressing me through my fillings and telling me, "Go ahead, tell everybody how good *Conspiracy Theory* is! Or be disappeared!"

But, I'm trying to argue, it's not very good.

"That doesn't matter," they insist. "You have our orders."

Well, I answer my fillings, see, this job would be much easier if I could remember one damned thing about it!

For that is the only reality to *Conspiracy Theory*. It is one of those soap bubbles of a film, fleeting, ephemeral, seemingly there when it is not. As you leave the theater, it diminishes with each step, collapsing into shards of imagery and sensations of movement. It's the film that never was.

Only one thing is sure: Director Richard Donner has seen *Taxi Driver* too many times. For as he chronicles the nightly peregrinations of screwball cabdriver Jerry Fletcher (Mel Gibson) through the gritty streets of Gotham, he so faithfully purloins Martin Scorsese's imagery—the sleek yellow cab afire with the reflection of a thousand neon lights as it slides through the wafting steam from underground, negotiating a passage among the carbuncular pimps, whores, gandy dancers, and lost souls who crowd the big hurdy-gurdy—that you're thinking: What is this, Film 101?

When Donner gets around to the story, we finally meet Jerry. Now I may be wrong about this, but who wants to see Mel Gibson in the role Dustin Hoffman was born to play? Mel's Jerry is furtive, twitchy, loquacious, self-important, and tiny. His mind, we learn quickly, is somewhat imperfect, as if Al Capp's old Fearless Fosdick had blown several Swiss cheese-style holes through his cerebellum. Jerry is your Compleat Conspiracy Phreak, who thinks, among other things, the CIA has perfected earthquake control mechanisms. He publishes information of this nature in a newsletter called *Conspiracy Theory*, which has a circulation of five. He has other obsessions that would seem unseemly if only it weren't the beautiful Mel who held them.

One involves a government prosecutor named Alice (Julia Roberts) on whom he spies each night, for reasons that are initially unclear. Sometimes he visits her at her office, screaming that They Are Out to Get Him, which gets him tossed out every time, on the principle that They Don't Give a Hoot About Him. Still, Alice is always kind and clearly has some kind of secret attraction to him, of the sort that is found only in movies.

And something that is found mostly in movies is dark secret agencies with extraordinary resources at their command, just like the one in *Conspiracy Theory*. This one's fronted by Patrick Stewart in McGeorge Bundy's glasses and Adlai Stevenson's haircut and O. J. Simpson's double-breasted suits. To me, the wardrobe director is the key figure in the conspiracy theory behind *Conspiracy Theory*.

The nub of the movie is simple: They Really Are Out to Get Him. That is not the conspiracy theorist's darkest fear, however, but more like his fondest desire. It means he was right, he does count, he's not some marginal lizard scavenging for garbage. But the movie reiterates so many old sequences from the canon that it continues to feel more like Film 101 than anything spontaneously alive. Jerry is kidnapped and tortured by Stewart's ironic doctor (from *Marathon Man*); he and Alice are thrown together and must flee for their lives (from, take your pick, *The 39 Steps* or *North by Northwest*); locked in Jerry's mind are strange memories of government service (*The Long Kiss Goodnight*); and so forth and so on.

The only thing that can be said to provide continual pleasure in the film is the nice chemistry between the two big stars. It's so nice, in fact, and they seem so comfortable in each other's presence, that you wish the movie's theoretical concerns had been with attraction rather than conspiracy.

Donner is slick and shallow, but somewhat off his game here; he never comes close to the intensity of action that marked his original *Lethal Weapon*. It's as if he doesn't really believe in the material. His work is rote, mechanical—as if his mind has been taken over by aliens or Commies or the NRA-CIA-FAA-Martha Stewart combine. Hmm, I wonder if the—siuy;lq cbqu9[3v 9-qu[qc [0vn]q9pjhi!!!

[Editor's note: At 2:44 P.M., Hunter vanished from the office.]

(AUGUST 8, 1997)

*A*ir Force One is a pulse-pounding bull goose of a movie, but more than that, it's a $90 million endorsement of the Great Man theory of history. It's *The Rough Riders* set on a jetliner. It's president as action figure, six feet two of heroic plastic.

This prez kicks butt. He kills. He knows the operating drill on the Heckler & Koch MP5 machine pistol. He gives forthright speeches—and this is really brave!—without clearing them with the staff first! He puts the world on notice that America is back in the saddle again and there's a new sheriff in town.

Harrison Ford, in the role of this righteous galoot, can't really be said to act, because he's not really required to play a character. His President Jim Marshall, lion of the free world, Medal of Honor winner, Big Ten grad, football fan, and beer drinker, is so idealized he makes Barbie's Ken look positively Dostoyevskian. Ford does two things brilliantly: He never bumps into the furniture and he never lets even a whisper of campy self-awareness crack the 100-foot-high Mount Rushmore of his face. *Air Force One* is set in an irony-free zone. Ford's discipline is at its highest as he cleaves to the movie's fundamental proposition: This is not a joke. (It is, of course.)

Naturally, he's the dullest thing in the movie. But that's not bad, that's good. Who wants a neurotic intellectual or an ironist or a policy wonk at the helm when psychotic Russian nationalists have taken over the president's plane on a flight back from Moscow and are busily executing hostages as a ploy to free a demonic nationalist leader recently filched from his despot's den by a joint Spetznaz-Delta team (the movie's fabulous opening sequence)? Much better this sort of leadership: doubtless, fearless, dynamic, clever, aggressive, anachronistic, impossible, and dull. But his dullness clears the way for the movie's showiest special effect: Gary Oldman.

Oldman plays the evil Ivan Korshunov, the terrorist who masterminds the skyjacking of Air Force One and then proceeds to steal not merely the gigantic flying machine itself but another and more important machine: the camera. This actor is never so good as when he is very, very bad, and *Air Force One* provides him with a platform to do a variation on a combination of Boris Godunov and Boris Badenov simultaneously. Throw in some Rasputin and some Alexander Nevsky and even some Ivan Skavinsky Skavar and you've got the whole nine yards. He would eat the furniture if it weren't all plastic and fiberglass.

Director Wolfgang Petersen controls the mayhem with his usual extreme cleverness. Like everybody in the picture, however, he's working miles beneath his head. He once made a great movie about real men in a real war, *Das Boot*, but now he's making straw movies about straw men in a straw war. But you sense the intense level of his engagement. As in his last macho confabulation, *In the Line of Fire*, so much of the cleverness is in the details.

In *Fire*, I loved the way they solved the problem of getting not a ceramic gun but a brass and lead bullet through a metal detector by hiding it in a key chain, which of course would go around the detector in a little plastic tray. In this one, his micro-genius is on display in one sequence where he follows a bad MiG pilot engaging the president's plane and then Air Force F-15s. The actor (Boris Krutonog) has maybe 25 seconds of total screen time, the bottom of his face sealed off in an oxygen mask, the top of his head capped in a plastic helmet. What's left? Eyes. Fabulous, bulging, expressive eyes that radiate the raptor's glee as he looses an air-to-air missile toward the big bird, then utter fear of doom as he watches an F-15's Sidewinder come screaming to erase him in a bright orange blot. Cool movie death!

In fact, one of the pleasant surprises of *Air Force One* is how much of it is an old-fashioned airplane movie. The modern computer morphing does no task better than rendering aircraft in flight. You never for a second tumble to the fact that you are watching electricity concocted by some arrogant kid in a Southern California computer shop: The jets, as they lace through the sky in and around the president's plane, are majestic, and one sequence where a line of F-15s lets fly a phalanx of heat-seekers leaking flame as they streak across the sky has a terrible beauty to it.

But in order to keep the odor of man-sweat, testosterone, and flatulence from becoming too terribly oppressive, Petersen, abetted by scriptwriter Andrew W. Marlowe (of Washington, in fact), provides some female presence. Glenn Close is effectively steely as the vice president who manages to deal with a power play by the secretary of defense while coolly managing the war-room crisis team. She cries only a little bit.

Equally impressive is Wendy Crewson as the first lady. I love her sense of flintiness, too: She upbraids a staff member for not paying attention during a speech, just like the real thing, and she has a commanding presence that never breaks down, even when the guns are pressed against her head. More idealized but also welcome is Liesel Matthews as the teenage first daughter.

In all, *Air Force One* is of a piece. It takes its absurd premise and keeps itself narrowly focused, pushing its heroic cast through obstacle after obstacle. It lacks perhaps a moment of grief for the many warriors who sacrifice their lives for the chief exec, and some of its gambits—a parachute "escape" into where, the Urals?—play well on screen but fray upon application of minimum thoughtfulness. But it's a great ride.

(JULY 25, 1997)

I have seen the future, and it smirks.

I refer to the sardonic grin on the face of the summer's official Next Big Thing, Vin Diesel, a Mr. Clean on steroids who oompahs his way through *xXx* (*Triple X*, or *X* for short), creating mayhem, attitude, and tattoo burnout where'er he goes.

The movie, empathically directed by Rob Cohen, is pretty much a case of new Gatorade in old bottles. It's the superagent deal, in which Our Hero is matched against scurvy *Übermenschen* who seem to want nothing more from the world than its destruction. For some reason these super bad guys are very big on basements, so much of the film takes place in basements.

What makes this superagent different: Instead of sporting a dinner jacket, a small elegant European automatic, and the savoir-faire and sangfroid of an aristo thug, he is big, muscly, wears combat boots and balloony pants, and has Maori warrior designs stenciled on virtually every free patch of non-skull skin. He sounds as though he came down not from Balliol at Oxford but from Morrie's Truck Stop at Newark.

Despite his skin art and gleaming, global pate, bruiser Diesel is a commanding, likable figure. Think of him as a Peterbilt rig with a sense of humor. Or the Rock with talent in places other than his left eyebrow. He should have a big career if he doesn't blow it doing something smarmy. But he is the film, and watching him—he's got a big cat's athletic moves, a New Yorker's smart-guy attitude, and all them skuzzy 'toos—is a lot more fun than staying with the ever-feebler Pierce Brosnan in his decrepit adventures as MGM tries desperately to keep the creaking Bond franchise upright. (Memo to self: Dodge the new Bond coming in the fall; plan on catching a nice cold that week.)

Diesel plays a guy named Xander Cage, and I ask you: Which is the more ridiculous name, Vin Diesel or Xander Cage? Anyhow, Xander is a professional extreme athlete who produces tapes of himself doing stunts of insane bravado, which he then sells via a Web site, presumably Wackjob.com. The movie opens with one: He steals a prissy prosperous guy's red Corvette, leads the cops on a chase, slithering and fishtailing this way and that, then turbo-glides the car over the rail of a very high bridge. End of movie? Are you kidding? It's only Minute 2. He rides the vehicle down like a surfboard sliding on gravity's rainbow, 'chutes off it at the last moment, and lands where his pals await.

It's the first of many great stunts in the film, and although it's a part of the Diesel mystique that he does more of his stunt work than most other stars, you can usually tell when a more lithe, less pumped stunt pro is in the 'chute or on the snowboard or the skateboard or, in one fabulous trick, riding a silver service tray down a banister in Prague. These boys risk life and limb to make the guy a star.

Back in the plot, Xander is recruited roughly—that is, kidnapped—by the National Security Agency's scar-faced Gus Gibbons (Samuel L. Jackson in a ridiculous waste of talent; any competent forty-year-old actor could have played the part as well). The theory is that formally trained agents, with their military backgrounds, are easy for nasty boys to spot. So a new talent pool is needed: extreme athletes, who have developed incredible reflexes for reacting instantly to out-of-control situations. Plus, their tattoos say more interesting things than "Airborne all the way!"

As the best of these, Xander "wins" a dubious series of contests and is rewarded with the assignment of a deathtime: He must infiltrate a Prague-based ex-Soviet military unit, now calling itself "Anarchy 99" and dedicated to orgy and destruction. Or something like that; the motives are never clear. These bad guys want to germ-bomb the world because they're bad guys, and that ought to be enough for anyone.

Xander gets in quickly enough, and starts a love-hate thing with the boss's main squeeze, played by Asia Argento (daughter of the Italian horror-film master Dario Argento). Argento has as much edge as the Diesel man does, and as a pair of snarling would-be lovers and allies they work well together. So do the various Eastern European creeps, by now a genre staple in black leather, greasy hair, shades by Ray-Ban, guns by Heckler & Koch.

The story is nothing you haven't seen a hundred times before, mounted in ways you haven't seen 200 times before. Somehow the movie contrives to put Xander on a parachute tethered to a runaway speedboat called Ahab blazing down the river toward mid-Prague, where it will explode in a poof of nerve gas, killing everyone and ruining Mitteleuropean sex tours for all time. That last might not be such a bad idea, but it wouldn't do much for the no-doubt profitable *xXx* franchise. And I think I'm to be congratulated for not making any porn jokes off the title.

(AUGUST 9, 2002)

Say this for *The Bourne Identity:* It keeps on ticking.

Like the indestructible Timex watch, it just keeps grinding along, oblivious to its own stupidity and to the giant holes in its plot or even the general staleness of its central conceit. It is, if nothing else—and it's not much else—highly professional.

Derived from a novel by Robert Ludlum published more that twenty years ago, it combines a couple of weak-sister pop-fiction story motifs:

amnesia and super-agents. Matt Damon—yeah, that twinky little Harvard kid!—is a . . . super-agent with amnesia!

The movie opens at sea, where cute little Damon is discovered floating near-dead in the Mediterranean by a peasant fishing boat. He's in scuba gear with an inflatable Mae West and a couple of bullets in his back. Fortunately the peasant captain has surgical skills and digs out not only the bullets but one other thing, planted under the skin of his hip: what looks to be a Cracker Jack prize that beams a Swiss bank account number on the wall when you push a button.

Damon has no memory of who he is, but it's clear from the get-go that he is a repository of outstanding if alarming talents. Using the bank number as his first guidepost, he opens a safe-deposit box to learn he is one Jason Bourne, of Paris, France, quite wealthy in cash, with a disturbing number of passports in other names plus a nice SIG-Sauer automatic pistol. Then, suddenly, strange people are trying to kill him.

Meanwhile, back at CIA headquarters (this is the third movie in three weeks with a CIA headquarters segment, and they all look just like the Style section of *The Washington Post*), supervisor Alexander Conklin (Chris Cooper) is taking heat for a rogue operation gone bad, involving the self-same Jason Bourne, whom he now orders terminated to cover up the mess and make it go away.

That is the essential mechanism of the story: Bourne, a man without a memory, being hunted by superkillers from all over Europe as he tries to figure out who he is, how he got that way, and what his destiny is.

As I say: lame, as lame as it was when Richard Chamberlain (!) played the Bourne guy on the tube in 1992. What keeps it from turning into a triple-ZZZ fest, though, is the energy of everybody involved. From Damon downward, they treat this tired old mutt of a tale as if it's the freshest, hottest thing from the freshest, hottest young writer in Hollywood.

Great fights. You wouldn't think of Damon as a tough guy, but he's worked really hard on the physical stuff here and it shows. The best car chase in years—a Mini Cooper being pursued by the Paris cops down alleyways, down stairways, even the wrong way through tunnels, and any stunt man who'll drive in the Paris traffic deserves a medal. Cool gun battles, as in the one where Damon shoots a Beretta upside down—that is, the gun upside down, not the young man. There's even a clever escape from the roof of the U.S. Embassy in Zurich, if only you can accept the fact that the pursuers forget to look behind the building!

Another unexpected treat follows the mold of several hundred other movies: He picks up an innocent chick (Remember that great old *Three Days of the Condor?*) and they fall in love, even as he endangers her. Same thing here, but she's played engagingly by the Franka Potente of *Run Lola, Run* so she's with the run-girl-run deal from the start. More, Potente's so weirdly off center—not your usual Hollywood beauty found at a coffee bar—that the bonding between the two is quite amusing.

But the real engine that drives *The Bourne Identity* is Chris Cooper's CIA supervisor. Always a fine actor (he was so brilliant as the dad in Homer Hickam's *October Sky* as well as in John Sayles's *Lone Star*), Cooper gives his haunted bureaucrat a demonic intensity that drives the plot and the really not terribly dramatic scenes of young analysts staring at computer screens, exactly as this old analyst is staring at the computer screen. But Cooper is standing over them screaming "Do it now!" while the music heats up like Styx on an amphetamine bender. Meanwhile, Oliver Wood's camera is dollying around the room as if someone set the cinematographer's Nikes on fire. How come I never have that much fun at a computer?

When the mystery is finally penetrated and revealed, it's a letdown. How could it not be? It has to do with a botched murder attempt on some vaguely imagined African Idi Amin type, and if it made any sense, I missed it. But even if it did, the idea is so old: It dates from what might be called late Cold War dispirit, when it was given in popular culture that our intelligence services were as murderous and savage as their intelligence services, and either would routinely kill their own men if it proved exigent. Has this ever happened, even in the KGB? Probably not, but it's propelled quite a lot of potboilers.

As for Damon, this may not be a performance so much as an appearance. But he cares so utterly, it works. My daughter said, "You know, that movie was really about only one thing: how cool Matt Damon is." She likes him a lot; I'm indifferent. But she was right: The film was calculated on his earnest toughness and rugged handsomeness—his masculine presence, if you will—and it's a gamble that pays off.　(JUNE 14, 2002)

There are really two movies on the screen in *The Recruit*, the new Al Pacino thriller. The first is the micro-movie: the movie itself, an almost adequate formula picture in which an old movie star barks, a young one yips, cars are chased and battered, and the ending seems completely unconnected to the beginning. It kills time at the expense of IQ points.

The second movie is far more interesting. It's the macro-movie, which clinically illustrates everything wrong with the modern American motion picture.

I'll give you a scene that, in its mundane way, encapsulates the current Hollywood pathology. It's a scene in which Colin Farrell, as a young CIA recruit, leaves by bus for the Farm, a legendary training facility near Williamsburg.

The camera dollies ominously in; the bus rumbles ominously toward the lens, in slo-mo, getting larger and larger and larger, the music throbs and beats and whines, my heart stops going pitty-pat and starts going bumpabumpabumpa and suddenly I remember . . . hey, it's a bus. Leaving the bus stop.

It's not a Peacekeeper missile rising on a dragon's tail of liquid oxygen to end the world in fire. It's not a giant iceberg smashing into the hull of a miracle ship as a way of christening the new century with an act of supreme irrationality. It's not a bridge exploding over a Thai river, cutting off Japanese supplies and changing the course of the war, though at immense, tragic loss.

No, no. It's er, a bus. Pulling out of a government building in suburban Virginia.

Giganticism of effect yoked to smallness of conception to cover staleness of formula. Really, I couldn't have said it better myself: That's Hollywood, U.S.A., in the year 2003.

The film is like a diagnostician's guide to this strain of movie sickness. There is one thing everybody associated with the film wishes to keep you from noticing. These conspirators include the director, Aussie journeyman Roger Donaldson; the stars, Pacino and Farrell; and the screenwriters, Roger Towne and Kurt Wimmer, and the object of their obfuscation is . . . the story.

They know it's old and it's weak and it's been done a thousand times before, as recently as last year's *Training Day*. They know it can't speak for itself, that its devices are threadbare, its characters clichés, that nothing is at stake, that no passion can be found anywhere. So they gin everything else up, until the story all but goes away and you're left with giant faces, star charisma, airbursts of saliva, those crashing cars, a coupla chases and gunfights and all that thumpa-thumpa music. It's edited so fast, it's like the remote is stuck on SEARCH.

Pacino, in his Satanic mode, with a goatee and what looks like an extra-lush hair extender, plays a supposedly legendary CIA recruiter named Walter Burke. He swaggers into Cambridge just after MIT's graduation, and, leaking charm and macho bravado like Errol Flynn after seven but not yet eight gin-and-tonics, seduces young James Clayton (Farrell). James carries a huge load up top (brains in his head and mousse on his hair). Though James is skeptical, he cannot deny the attractiveness of Burke and the life he offers, as opposed to the narratives offered by the cloneheads from Dell. (James is some kind of computer genius, besides being sexy, cute, wiggly, lithe, scruffy, and tattooed.) And when Burke drops the hint that James's mysteriously vanished father might have been a CIA hero, why, James can't say no. Off they go to the Agency for psych testing, and then on to the Farm.

So for its first hour, *The Recruit* is *Training Day* out of *The Devil's Advocate*, tracing a line back as far as *The D.I.* It is every mentor-mentee spatfest in movie history, and while completely unoriginal, the durable structure is at least dynamic and enjoyable, if never quite convincing.

For one thing, there's the training itself. It mainly comprises OSS-type hugger-mugger probably not much practiced by the CIA anymore except by specially recruited operatives with military backgrounds who are already skilled breakers-and-enterers-and-shooters. And when the students aren't breaking and entering and shooting, they're game-playing.

And that is the essence of *The Recruit*, the is-it-live-or-is-it-Memorex? transaction. Will somebody please do a movie along everything-is-exactly-what-it-seems lines? All of us are tired of the old nothing-is-what-it-seems thing.

Soon enough, Clayton has bonded with another agent-in-training, Layla (Bridget Moynahan, a beauty), and mentor Burke delights in pairing them up with or against each other. James cons her, she cons him;

Burke cons both of them. It's the con-con dance. It's "Yes, I Con." It's somebody who read too much David Mamet and took it too seriously.

Then, of course, the movie has to move off the Farm, go operational, and play the games for real. At this point it becomes much weaker, and director Donaldson really earns his money staging hubbub and nonsense. There's a moment where James, disguised as a low-ranking CIA employee who in reality has been assigned by Burke to shadow a suspected mole, retrieves secret instructions that are taped underneath a bench in Georgetown. Hubba-hubba. But, like, why didn't Pacino just, you know, hand the envelope over? The two confer nose to nose just about every day!

The movie ultimately concludes in one of those ever-so-convenient abandoned warehouses on the Georgetown waterfront (where the real estate values really do preclude abandonment), and we can play one more is-it-real game. I should add—I've repressed the memory until now—that a lot of the conning is of the even more tiresome computer variety, so the dramatic possibilities of tappity-tapping at the keyboard and watching the download gauge reach full do not go unnoticed by Donaldson, nor do the laser-dot aiming devices of the sort that have been obsolete for ten years but still appear in movies.

When I see a movie like *The Recruit,* I wonder: Who wanted to make this thing? It's not bad, but it's not good, either. It's nothing but style and noise, threadbare of content, empty of ideas. Is it anything? Not really.

(JANUARY 31, 2003)

For a movie about rich people, *The Thomas Crown Affair* has a radical agenda. It argues with revolutionary zeal that style, jazz, neat clothes, good if aged bodies, and a smart script are still capable of entertaining an audience. People whose synapses have been fried by overexposure to bootleg Internet video from Woodstock '99 won't get it, but anyone who knows the meaning of the word "cool" should have a fine time.

That's because *The Thomas Crown Affair* is very cool.

Note I do not argue that it is good, since cool and good occupy parallel, eternally unconnected universes.

This movie was pretty cool when it starred the original Cool King, Steve McQueen, back in 1968. This time through it stars Pierce Brosnan, who up till now hasn't gotten in the same time zone as cool. As Bond he is not cool or even interesting, but merely pretty.

But in this film, he achieves cool by the Zen of pretending passionately to have not a pretense of passion anywhere in his body. He has devolved to pure style, intellect, and instinct. His heart barely beats, his lungs barely draw oxygen. His suits glide across his svelte body like a second sheath of skin. His Thomas Crown, international financier and Manhattan beautiful person, is gorgeous without seeming to preen. He is smart without seeming to sweat. He never is spotted looking in a mirror, yet his hair is perfect; even when it musses, it musses perfectly.

When Norman Jewison directed Steve McQueen all those years back, the movie itself was a kind of afterthought to McQueen's cool, and Faye Dunaway's, as the insurance investigator more provoked by Crown than offended by him. Mostly it was McQueen posing without seeming to notice the camera, his style radiating outward like a wave of radioactivity. Meanwhile, Dunaway flirted so aggressively she seemed to prematurely age before our eyes.

This time, Dunaway, just as flirty but with a face fortified by enough surgery to hold back the Nile to say nothing of the ravages of time, is still around. But she's not the lead, she's the shrink. (There wasn't a shrink in the original, if memory serves.) More important, the screenwriters, Leslie Dixon & Kurt Wimmer (I don't know what the ampersand means, but I'm sure it's important), and the director, action maestro John McTiernan, have added what seems to be a plot, and it's a definite improvement. The movie isn't just about the animal magnetism of the beautiful; it's also got a twitch of genuine cleverness to it, an actual arc of character movement. Good heavens, it's actually a story! Why, I'm shocked, shocked!

And it's got Rene Russo. At 45. When most at that age have slid unguently into that good night, Russo still had the chops to go sassily topless and make you love her forever. If Brosnan is cool cool, Russo is hot cool. If he's the distant, aloof prey, she's the huntress, all Diana, not so much eager for the kill as for the true hunting pleasure, which is the pleasure of the stalk. Naturally, he loves it when they do that.

The story is fancy yet simple. It stems from the fact that Crown loves art and can afford it. But why buy it? Buying it is not cool. Stealing it:

Now that's cool. A Monet is lifted deftly from the Metropolitan Museum of Art. We know that Crown did it, because we watch him orchestrate the elements, the false attempts that distract the security forces of the institution until they are so hopelessly confused that, like a nimble-fingered pickpocket, he can take possession of the piece.

The cops, led by Denis Leary in a rare likable role (that guy? likable?), are hopelessly outclassed. In strides the insurance investigator as superstar model, just as aware of the power of her beauty as she is of the power of her intellect. Catherine Banning's job is to get the Monet back so that her clients don't have to pay through the nostrils, and she exudes such confidence that she should go into motivational speaking. But this isn't just a triumph of a beauty; it's a triumph of an actress, who is liberated by this role. Through she's been in the talking pictures for a couple of decades now, Russo should be elevated by *Crown* from the one who gets the parts Sarandon turns down to the one who turns down the parts Sarandon gets.

What works best in the movie is the heat of the chemistry on screen between Russo and Brosnan. The movie is actually pretty steamy, and the bodies involved, fatless as only good genes and commitment to some kind of ab machine from Hell can provide, look good, particularly intertwined. It's sex but it's romance, too, because you feel the attraction not merely of the bodies, but of the characters inside the bodies. These two actually like each other.

This is a movie that understands the larger-than-life appeal of the old-fashioned movie star and one of the movies' most primal appeals: beautiful people doing amusing things while talking about them cleverly. It's a pleasure that's almost vanished, but *The Thomas Crown Affair* restores it, gloriously, just this once. (AUGUST 6, 1999)

*N*oir is harsh.
   Noir is bleak.
Noir bites you hard.
That's what's so cool about it.
And that's what's so cool about *The Man Who Wasn't There*, the new Coen brothers film, which is the purest essence of that bitter movie

toxin, distilled from the disappointments and exhaustion of the late 1940s, called film noir. It's the latest and one of the best entries in a genre whose highest philosophical expression is the whiplash realization that the universe doesn't play fair.

And that's what it's about, really: A nebbishy guy reaches for something and for his effort is rewarded with obliteration by a manically laughing universe. But, as my heroine the Wicked Witch of the West counseled in *The Wizard of Oz*, how to do it, hmmm, that's the question. The Coens come up with a dazzling set of moves to get him to the edge.

All this grand doom and crushing of the human spirit takes place, I am happy to report, in a duotone realm not so much of good and evil but of dark and light. Note that I do not say black and white, for it's really everything but: it's the satiny gray of indecision, the off-white of deceit, the gutta-percha of despair, the milky cream of betrayal. So the movie is, among other things, a glorious tribute to the splendors of what should rightfully be called the blackish and whitish movie. It consciously recalls the great film noirs of the past, but particularly Billy Wilder's masterpiece *Double Indemnity*.

The Coens, Ethan and Joel (Ethan directs, Joel produces, they both write) have flirted with noir before and also with its literary forebears, the hard-boiled guys: Their first film, *Blood Simple*, had the sleazy gutter precision of the pulp novelist Jim Thompson, while *Miller's Crossing* was stolen from Dashiell Hammett's *The Glass Key*. In this film, they're completing a trifecta with a story and a sensibility that have to be swiped from the great James M. Cain, who wrote *Double Indemnity* before Wilder put it before the cameras. Cain, a gentle opera buff and old newshound, was as a novelist so hard-boiled he ossified eggs just by reading them a graf or two.

"They threw me off the hay truck at noon," reads the incisive first line in *The Postman Always Rings Twice*, and listen to the squeal as those eggs go internally solid. From those simple declarative words, you know all you need to know about the narrator, a drifter with pretensions and romantic illusions, a man who never surprises as he rides his 140-page roller coaster straight to Hell (whether, on-screen, he's played by John Garfield or Jack Nicholson).

"I'm the barber," says Ed Crane (Billy Bob Thornton) at the opening of *The Man Who Wasn't There*. And that's all we need to know, as Ed goes on his own merry theme-park blast to the same hot destination. "I'm the barber." We laugh. Inconsequential, a prattling voice behind the snipping of scissors and the buzzing of clippers, whose face you only see in the mirror at the end, when it's your hair you're looking at. Who is not there more than a barber?

The place is a small town in northern California. After the austerity of the war and Johnny and his band of brothers have come marching home, everybody's getting his. Except Ed. He's getting nothing. One look at Thornton's real nowhere-man face and you know this chump is a disaster waiting to happen.

And his downfall will be a dame. As were all of Cain's heroes, the Coens' Ed will be lured toward destruction by a female fatale, who's beautiful, cynical, manipulative, whom you worship as she consigns you to doom. The difference is that in Cain she was made of tumultuous flesh (Lana Turner and Barbara Stanwyck were the film archetypes) and in *The Man Who Wasn't There* she is made of an intoxicating idea: She is the bitch goddess Success, that sex siren of all loser dreamers, the dream of counting, of adding up to something. She has ruined more men than any fleshy frail's luscious gams.

Ed wants; he has no way of getting. He's the barber, and his wife is a loudmouthed lush named Doris (Frances McDormand) having a fling with her boss, the department store manager Big Dave (fleshy, powerful James Gandolfini). Ed responds typically—he does nothing. Then opportunity comes to town, in the form of a guy in a hairpiece with a flashy line of chatter (Jon Polito), and Ed tumbles not so much to the chatter but to the possibility it represents: to be independent, to be no longer not there and instead be there.

It's typical of the Coens that they garb this shot at thereness in a wrapping so mundane it's comical (part of the subversive black comedy of the piece). Ed commits to the future this fellow is selling, the "plastics" of the forties, except that it can be expressed only in two words, not one: dry cleaning. Amazing but true: You can wash without water! In 1948, nobody has envisioned such miraculous technology. Next thing you know, radios will have pictures!

Ed needs ten grand to open a dry-cleaning shop. He decides to play a con by blackmailing Big Dave anonymously about the affair, under threat of telling her husband—that is, himself. In a sense, he's using his nothingness as a disguise. Of course the boss figures that it's the dynamic dry-cleaner con man who's the blackmailer—Ed is too invisible and unthreatening to be a suspect. Mistaken identity occurs; complications ensue.

When Ed finally breaks down and acknowledges to Big Dave what's happened—he's not strong enough to keep the secret—Dave, in all that Sopranoesque flesh and fury, goes berserk. In a moment of elegant horror, all the more powerful for its speed and simplicity, Ed jabs Big Dave with a blade. Fortunately, it's a tiny little cut. Unfortunately, it's in the carotid artery.

There you have it: A sucker tries to grab a little something and to break the mold, and the universe retaliates massively so that everything he tries not merely fails, but twists ever more perfectly toward lethal finality. I love the machinelike precision of the trap the Coens have conjured for poor Ed, as each sidestep backfires, and even a late attempt at confession only creates havoc and laughter; you can hear the clank of jaws snapping every few minutes.

Each performance is spectacular, including Polito as the smarmy con man, Michael Badalucco as the barbershop owner (and Doris's brother), and especially Tony Shalhoub as an overbearing defense attorney who seems to think Ben Hecht wrote all his dialogue.

Alas, the confabulation somewhat lessens its grip in the last few minutes, when it just sort of runs out of steam. Possibly a subplot involving Ed's romantic infatuation with a neighbor's daughter (Scarlett Johansson of *Ghost World*) adds an extra level of complexity that doesn't pay off. So the movie feels too long.

Cain never would have let that happen. His characters faced their doom with spare poetry in their mouths and a final acute blast of clarity. They could hear that final snap as doom ensnared them and they faced it unsentimentally, dignified only in the calmness with which they accepted what they had earned. But just when it should be snapping, the Coens' script turns soft and it withers away rather than slams shut.

(NOVEMBER 2, 2001)

*R*oad to Perdition is paved with good intentions. Its ambition is gigantic, its production craft immaculate, a couple of its performances Oscar-worthy. But like so many crusades, it takes a wrong turn—to Chicago, as a matter of fact!—and in the end frustrates more than satisfies.

In its central performance, Tom Hanks, normally America's favorite Mr. Nice Guy, nudges toward the dark side, but not terribly far. He's a gangster, a killer, an enforcer—but still a nice guy. That's a problem with the film, for this most engaging actor never seems quite comfortable with the demands of the role. He's almost too muted.

Pudged up so that his face manifests potatoey comfort in a story set in the scrawny, nutritionless Depression era, Hanks plays Michael Sullivan, right-hand man of avuncular old John Rooney (Paul Newman, brilliant as an Irish pixie), who is the mob ruler of a nameless Illinois town: Kankakee, Rock Island, Waukegan? In some respects, Michael resembles Robert Duvall's Tom Hagen in the *Godfather* saga, a foundling who's been taken in by a crime family; now he labors long and hard for it. But unlike Tom Hagen, he keeps a Thompson submachine gun in the garage, for those late-night business emergencies.

Still, Sullivan loves his own little family of four and is so committed to normality that he shields them from the true nature of his work. With his wife (Jennifer Jason Leigh) and two sons, he lives the life he never had as an orphan: the big house, warm and comfy against the bleak Midwestern winter and the spare scenes of Depression anomie that form the backdrop of the film. Michael belongs; he loves and is loved; he has a place in an otherwise cruel world, and if once in a while he has to unleash the Thompson's fury on Rooney's enemies to pay for it, he's at home with that. It's not as if he had a choice.

But in every Eden, there's a snake. Or in every *Othello*, there's an Iago (the movie begs to be compared with biblical and classic sources). In Whatever-City-It-Is, Illinois, it's Connor Rooney (Daniel Craig), the boss's ambitious, violent and dishonest son. Connor—Craig is dynamic in the role—resents Michael's closeness to his dad, and his own smallness in the organization, and thus plots against both Michael and Dad. The question is: Which of his two boys, the real son or the better, more loyal, honorary son, will Dad choose to love? In other words, what carries more weight in an uncertain world, blood or loyalty?

That's a big question, a classic question, and that *Road to Perdition* asks it speaks loudly of its ambition. The movie is one of those intellectual gangster pix, like the *Godfather* movies or Stephen Frears's *The Hit*, that use the pulp story form to make more universal inquiries. And the responses, from Michael's point of view, are tragic.

By the halfway point, he's fleeing for his life with his eldest son, Michael Jr. (Tyler Hoechlin), leaving behind him a rubbed-out younger son and wife, and everybody in the small city and the big city is gunning for him.

Alas, at this point the screenplay by David Self, from a graphic novel by Max Allan Collins and Richard Piers Rayner, hits the big detour and never quite recovers, leaching the movie of the goodwill and the thunderous momentum it had built up. If you thought, as I did, that it was going toward a state of war between Michael and the Rooneys in which, at great cost, vengeance is slaked and justice achieved, you're only about a third right; he fights that war, but by proxy, in another town, and against other enemies.

A big mistake, I think. We'd invested totally in that city, that place, that dilemma and most important, those characters. The demonic Connor and his leprechaun of a dad all but vanish from the film, the former a particular loss since his anger was the driving force of the narrative.

Instead, we discover other dilemmas. In Chicago, Michael appeals for shelter to the Capone organization, represented by Stanley Tucci as a dapper Frank Nitti. Because of strategic alliances, Capone, through Nitti, says no. Thus Michael wages a surrogate war to acquire leverage over Capone. At the same time, the Capone people hire a disagreeable assassin to track Michael down—one Maguire, in bowler hat, behind teeth that look like rotted corn and fingers that haven't seen the inside of a washbasin in years. It will surprise you to learn that the handsome Jude Law lurks behind those teeth and fingers, and it will surprise you even more to note how weirdly this character develops: He's a sort of combination Weegee and Murder Inc. mechanic—a photographer who likes to shoot first what he then photographs. (Like the Capone mob couldn't do better than this?)

Very odd that Maguire gets so much screen time, so little dialogue, and so much less character evolution. It's hard to care about him when the more interesting drama languishes down- or upstate. And at the same time, Michael has begun a campaign of robbing mob-affiliated banks of their dirty money, effectively holding the cash hostage until he can convince the Capone people to help him in his crusade against the Rooneys. But again, this is largely uninvolving; he's doing things to people we don't know for reasons we can't figure out. And the following basic question is never answered: How does he know which banks to hit?

Perhaps as devastating to the film is the dreary relationship between Sullivans *père et fils*. As I've said, Hanks has been better; I hope Tyler Hoechlin has too. This central dynamic just doesn't work; you never enter into it, and it seems numb and dead while by contrast the pain and love between Rooney and his son is brilliantly evoked.

Clichés arrive in swarms: People find each other with astonishing ease (several times), kindly farmers take in wounded gangsters without a question or a line of dialogue, and a wounded gangster who has murdered a cop and a colleague and is last seen collapsed with half his face blown away after a bloody hotel room shootout somehow escapes to reappear at a key moment.

More damaging still, the end of the movie gives the weird impression of having been filmed through the wrong end of the telescope. It seems small, muted, played out in the most anti-dramatic method available to its talented young director, Sam Mendes, who really hit the big moments out of the park in *American Beauty*.

All in all, *Road to Perdition* is more in love with strangeness than excellence.   (JULY 12, 2002)

*B*ad Boys II might be considered three action sequences and four comedy routines in search of a story. Failing to locate one, the film diverts to Plan B: the invasion of Cuba.

That was tried, with even less success, in 1961, not that anyone associated with *Bad Boys II* was alive then or has any passing acquaintance with history. As it plays out here, it's simply a final idiocy. In the iron logic of summer movies, filmmakers are locked into a big-bang theory. The bang at the end has got to be bigger and badder than any previous bangs, so hot-dog director Michael Bay, who's already engineered a fabulous car chase in which Chevy Malibus drop off an auto carrier and bounce along the roadway like pumpkins to dissuade our heroes in pursuit, has to find the bigger bang. He overreaches badly.

Up till then the movie has simply been frenzy, 'tude, violence and good, clean, stupid American fun. It's actually pretty funny: Bad boy Miami cops Marcus Burnett (Martin Lawrence) and Mike Lowrey (Will Smith) have as much rapport as they had in the original eight years ago. Much of what the two do together seems improvised, and it's always pretty amusing.

The relationship is built along Mel Gibson–Danny Glover lines: Lawrence's Marcus is a family man, nervous, trying to deal with his anger, career-conscious, conscientious, troubled. Meanwhile, Smith's Mike is a true bad boy, a wild card: He's reckless, quick-tongued, a banterer's banterer, insanely self-confident. He's always pushing out, Marcus is always pulling back. Put it another way: Mike wants to go clubbin', Marcus wants to pay the mortgage. So these two battle each other like the Bickersons across the landscape of south Florida while bullets, cars, and bodies fly their way, which they barely notice because each is trying so hard to outquip the other.

Though the film boasts ten actual screenwriters and story authors, I suspect the script was assembled in the following way: Extra pages from *2 Fast 2 Furious* were mixed in with old scripts randomly selected from the long-sealed files of the *Miami Vice* TV show. All those pages were tossed in the air over a staircase, then collected from the bottom up. Then, just for the wacky fun of it, the climax from one of G. Gordon Liddy's unproduced screenplays was tacked on. No one ever read any of it, of course, so each day on the set was a new adventure.

The director is Michael Bay, and you have to say, this guy has chops as an action master. In his last film he blew up Pearl Harbor more thoroughly than the Japanese did, and my ears are still ringing. He blew up an asteroid in his film before that, the Zen-moron masterpiece *Armageddon*, which closed on an image of Bruce Willis weeping crocodile glycerin tears as he pushed the button that blew himself and 10 billion tons of deep-space pig iron to bits before it could cueball the Earth into the sun. And he was the director of record on the original *Bad Boys* in 1995.

So when Bay gets revved up, there's no calming him down, It so happens that his is the third variation this summer on the somewhat arcane theme of cars-chasing-trucks-and trucks-counterchasing-cars-on-a-freeway. The first two were in *The Matrix Reloaded* (anybody remember?) and just two weeks back in *Terminator 3*, but it's Bay's stroke of genius to add a fleet of Rasta-men with AK-47s to the carnival of wreckage, so besides dozens of bouncing cars you have thousands of whizzing bullets. The air is alive with the sound of metal ripping.

The problem is, this sequence, staggering though it is, happens too early. There's no place left to go, and the movie still has an hour or so to run (at two and a half hours, it's way too long, by the way). So the plot—stop me if you've heard this one before: A scurvy yet glamorous Latin chap who shaves with a spoon is importing drugs into Miami and our boys have got to stop him, but the DEA is also on the case—runs out of steam. Well, that's an exaggeration: since there was no plot, there was no steam. Best to say, the plot just quits on the movie.

So what eats up the time? Comedy and gunfights. The former is by far the better time-waster. In one sequence sure to be remembered, Lawrence and Smith do a number on a poor young man who has come by to court Lawrence's daughter; Smith impersonates a somewhat incoherent ex-con, to extraordinary levels of dead-eyed craziness. In another, Lawrence, the better physical comedian, has accidentally taken two Ecstasy pills and is in a different universe when they go to visit the captain (the redoubtable, ubiquitous Joe Pantoliano) to secure his backing for a subpoena. While Smith, in the foreground, tries to stay focused and professional, Lawrence, in the background, is imitating an octopus stoned on mescaline and patio sealant.

Another time-filler: subplots. But, you ask, how can there be subplots if there is no plot? I don't know the answer, only that they do it somehow in this movie. One involves Smith's attraction to Syd (Gabrielle Union), an undercover DEA agent who happens to be Lawrence's baby sister. Peter Stormare shows up at odd moments as a Russian mafia member being squeezed by the bad guys, to utterly no detectable consequence.

The movie really loses its mind in its concluding commando junket. You can stay with most of the film because it's operating in a zone of summer movie hyperbole, and it demands you trade logic for simple pleasure. Okay, that's the summer bargain. But you can't stay with this: It's simply preposterous that the Miami Police Department would invade Cuba with more firepower than the 101st Airborne hauled into Iraq.

Who gave the okay? Oh, I get it: Condi Rice wasn't available, so they called Sonny Crockett and he said it was fine by him.   (JULY 18, 2003)

*9*t is a truism that if you've seen one con man movie you've seen them all, and *Matchstick Men* probably won't challenge the truth of that truism.

Flimflammers, grifters, double-talkers, sting operators, it's all pretty much the same: you set the mark up by appealing to his greed and thereby taking him out of his right mind, you arrange a theatrical presentation of unusual circumstances, all aimed to get him to look over there while you take his dough over here.

And while the over there/over here dichotomy runs through *Matchstick Men* in ways that sophisticated moviegoers will get in a second (I'm telling you, I figured it out too early), there's still a good deal to enjoy. First, there's Nicolas Cage, twitching like a Jell-O sculpture in a big breeze as a severely phobic con genius named Roy, slick, successful, but so riddled with guilt his muscles are in rebellion against his face. He has a whole medicine cabinet full of annoying behaviors: He's also an anal-retentive housekeeper (he vacuums every hour on the hour, eats only tuna fish from a can, which he throws out instantly), keeps his money hoarded in a porcelain dog (no taxes that way), and everything else wrapped in plastic, including his psyche.

But to watch him operate against a background of unglamorous suburban Los Angeles is to watch a pro at the top of his game. Tic-free in operation, seductive, shrewd, so very very fast, he can outmaneuver his poor marks without giving it—or them—a second thought. In fact, one of the deep pleasures of the movie is the subversive thrill of the kill: watching the con tweak cash from the pockets of his marks, and identifying with his cruel manipulations. When Roy and partner Frank (oleaginous Sam Rockwell) take down an elderly couple, it's a thing of beauty and you, like the two crooks, don't seem to feel a twitch of pain for the hurt they are causing.

That's Roy at his best. Roy at his worst is falling apart, or falling through. He's a nineteenth nervous breakdown waiting to happen. So he finally takes Frank's advice, or maybe it's Tony Soprano's, and goes to see a shrink, Dr. Klein (Bruce Altman). It comes out soon enough that Roy is consumed with guilt, but his original sin is a broken marriage and the possibility of a lost child. The doctor urges him to pursue this possibility, and before you can say "the magic power of therapy" three times fast, Roy has met with his fourteen-year-old daughter, Angela, played by the superb young actress Alison Lohman (she was the big news in last year's *White Oleander*).

The heart of the story is the relationship between Roy and his newly acquired daughter. It's a terrific duet between two extremely gifted practitioners: She's fascinated, vulnerable, critical, and blasé; he's unsure, desperately addicted to the redemption of new fatherhood, trying to find that right place between overbearing and undernourishing. As his daughter, she's got many of his dubious gifts: a sense for weakness, a pleasure taken in manipulation, an eye on the prize. When the two of them work a game just for a taste of it, it turns out to be more fun than either has had in years.

Besides the theme of the new father discovering his new daughter, two other thrusts are powering the story, and the director, old pro Ridley Scott, who usually works on a more spectacular scale (*Alien, Gladiator*), keeps all the forward momentum in synchronization. First there's Roy's continuing therapy as he comes to rely on wise, compassionate Dr. Klein for guidance; and then there's a scam that Roy and Frank are running against a particularly loathsome rich guy (played by the ever dependable Bruce McGill). And of course the three story lines play against and ultimately into each other, so that Roy must decide whether to take Angela into his shady little world, and once he does, how to rescue her from the chaos and even danger that he had engineered for profit. Meanwhile, we want him to take money—as long as it's not our money, but only a guy who drives a Boxter's.

The movie will work best for you if you don't fight it and try not to put too much thought into certain anomalies that crop up along the way. Let it swindle you; it's part of the fun. In fact, it's all of the fun.

(SEPTEMBER 12, 2003)

Three

WAR

The problem with war isn't the army stuff, the camping out, all the calisthenics you have to do at 0-dark-thirty, or even the sergeants who call you a maggot.

It's the battles.

Bummer.

You could get killed in a battle.

That's what's so terrifying about the just-opened *Black Hawk Down*: It puts causes, politics, and policies aside, and just inserts you into the heart of combat. Dead people everywhere. Smoke, awesome noise, percussive explosions, fear the size of a mountain, all playing against some theoretical necessity not just to survive but to do what must be done and finish a job that someone says is important. Oh, and don't forget: Your IQ is now 7 and your pulse rate is 244; and someone is trying to kill you.

The movie persuades you absolutely that anybody can die at any time, and that awful whimsy hangs in the air, smirking in the smoke. Why one guy gets it in the neck and the other in the collar .002 inches to the left of the neck is never dealt with as a philosophical proposition, because it transcends philosophy. As Hoot, the heroic Delta Force operator in this gritty re-creation of the Somalia firefight in 1993 that left 18 Americans and possibly 1,000 Somalis dead, says to his new Ranger chum Sergeant Eversmann, "That's just war."

He meant, of course, "That's just combat. That's just battle. It's irreducible and defies meaning."

It's a crucial moment. Eversmann, the young man seeing his first combat, still clings to an absurdly poignant human notion of such meaning, a sense that things are parceled out fairly by some rational belief system, so that you get what you deserve, the good and beautiful die old, and no one with cheekbones like his (or Josh Hartnett's, who plays him) can catch a bullet through them. Hoot, the old pro with lots of trigger time, has seen through all that; he knows there is no meaning, not for the warriors, there is only the us and the them part of it, and for us to survive the next few hours, we've got to kill a lot of them.

And that's why *Black Hawk Down* isn't really a war movie, it's a battle movie, and that's why it joins a very small list of films that leave the larger questions unasked and instead concentrate on the bitter reality.

Battle movies tend to be dense with frenzy and confusion, and very messy. After a while, when the boys' faces dirty up with muck and sweat and blood, you can't tell anybody apart. They're set in a very small compass—hell in a very small space, as Bernard Fall described Dien Bien Phu—and the ground upon which the action transpires is well defined. We here. They there. They want come here. We want stay here. Hello, let's fight.

Battle movies usually eschew history. They ignore hindsight, larger meanings, the reality of armies as social institutions, the higher interpretations of policies, the wisdom or foolishness of the elderly who have decreed such a bloodfest into existence in the first place. They just put you in the thick and fast and try to answer a single question: What's it like?

This question has fascinated writers for years, back to Homer, whose descriptions of the hand-to-hand nature of Bronze Age warfare are stunningly vivid to the point of delineating what a spear point does to teeth during its rush to the cranial cavity. Even Stephen Crane pondered it, and wrote a classic though he'd never whiffed a sniff of powder. But only recently has the subject interested historians much.

Ever read any standard battle history of just a few years ago? I tried, and never got very far. Headache city. It's full of sentences like "The Third Regiment of the 45th Brigade moved at the oblique to a ridgeline about a quarter of a mile to its left salient, pivoted and met the Quarkist attack with massed musketry until they were overwhelmed." Next to it was a series of maps explaining the fate of the 3/45th at the hands of the Quarkists: It seems that 350 men who lived, breathed, and fought in the ranks of the doomed 3/45th were reduced to an oblong block, which followed a series of arrows across an indecipherable topographical grid, until the Quarkists, represented by smaller blocks, followed smaller arrows from a variety of angles, and then the large block of the 3/45th simply disappeared.

Helpful, one supposes, to the experts, but of no aid at all in conjuring the desperation of the 3/45th as the wily Quarkists overwhelmed them with stones/clubs/spears/arrows/Mausers/AK-47s.

It fell to a British historian named John Keegan to change that in *The Face of Battle* (1976), which insisted that the history of war was too important to be left to the historians, that battle was a fearsome thing, that it was more important as a human experience than as an abstraction of unit-blocks manipulated until other unit-blocks destroyed them upon a featureless map. Other historians have followed suit, and now history is as clotted with vivid narrative as it is with trapezoids moving across maps. That's a good thing.

The movies were a little faster than the historians into this because, after all, they deal with drama, not history; they always made things personal. But for oh so many years they took their tones and signs from those official battle paintings that hang in every museum.

I'm no art expert, but one painter alone seems to have gotten it right; that was Goya in his series of etchings *Disasters of War*. Terrible stuff, shorn of the heroically posed, the picturesque, the beautiful, the symmetrical: instead, bodies as meat impaled, or hanging limp, so terribly, totally dead-weight that you know they're finished.

And ever so occasionally, the movies have gotten it right. The only masterpiece in the battle-movie genre is Cy Endfield's 1964 mind-boggler, *Zulu*. You can say what you want about the evils of British imperialism as it turned the world and its diverse peoples into barely glimpsed figures lost in the shadow of the Union Jack, but what a small group of British infantrymen did at a mission station called Rorke's Drift in 1879 was pretty spectacular. A paltry 150 of them stopped a 4,000-man Zulu army that was highly motivated not merely by their own fierce warrior tradition but also by the news of a Zulu conquest of a much larger British force at Isandlwana. The Brits did it the hard way, too; no air support, no automatic weapons, no Puff the Magic Dragons: just bayonets and single-shot rifles.

Endfield's movie—it stars the young Michael Caine and Stanley Baker as Bromhead and Chard, the two officers—captures completely the iffy quality of the fight. At no point does he allow an audience to believe in the inevitability of the British victory; the battle is too fierce. It's what might be called a typical Western battle in the Third World: the Brits in their squares, locked in a kind of survival discipline, against warriors who rejected such tactics as cowardly and longed to get in close for the thrill of the kill.

The issue was weirdly similar to the issue in Mogadishu in 1993: Will they tire of dying before we run out of ammunition? If it's the former, we win; if it's the latter, they do. Hundreds of Zulus died as they rushed through the rifle fire, and even when they breached the line, they could not stand against the determination of the well-trained British bayonet fighters who found that four feet of Martini-Henry rifle tipped with twelve inches of steel was just as effective a close-quarter weapon as the assegai, the Zulu stabbing spear.

Endfield also finds a quality missing from all too many battle sequences in millions of movies: that is, the utter physical labor of battle. It's very hard work to fight, which is why the young are so much better at it. His troopers emerge like footballers after an overtime—exhausted men, drained and emotionally flattened, smeared with dirt and blood, beyond the need to do anything but sleep for days. Almost no other film captures that soul-deep weariness.

To be sure, Endfield mythologizes somewhat. It's a wonderful shot at the end when the Zulu warriors salute the Brits as their fellow braves, particularly as Endfield draws on the majesty of the landscape of South Africa—but it never happened. The Zulus, at least according to a debunking Rorke's Drift Web site, saw a British relief column and took off, leaving 350 dead at the barricades and countless wounded. The British then bayoneted the wounded, presumably to save ammunition.

You would think a great American battle movie would have been made about the Civil War, but only *Gettysburg* comes to mind; in its lengthy running time, there's one extraordinary sequence, in which Joshua Chamberlain leads a Maine regiment in holding the Union position at Little Round Top. It's a small, intense and utterly gripping American *Iliad* in an otherwise rambling, incoherent film, and that's exactly representative of the kind of incoherence that afflicts so many other would-be battle films. *The Longest Day* suffers from gigantism, as does

A Bridge Too Far, about the Arnheim campaign: too many stars running around doing too many movie-star-phony things.

The British, with a more vivid imperial history than ours, seemed to get it more right more often. Another extremely interesting battle film is *Culloden,* made by the documentary filmmaker Peter Watkins. Freed of the concerns of drama, he simply set out to re-create, in nonfiction fashion, the last battle fought on British soil, in 1746. It was an enormous undertaking, and as he prowled among his costumed volunteers, somehow their irritation and fatigue became utterly real on film.

But generally movies dedicated to a single battle are rare. Dino De Laurentiis hired the Russian mass-movement expert Sergei Bondarchuk, hot off the heels of his world success in a gigantic production of *War and Peace,* to do a big number called *Waterloo* in 1970. Christopher Plummer was okay as Wellington, but who the hell was that Noo Yawk guy as Napoleon? It can't have been Rod Steiger! But it was.

That idiocy aside, the movie, which employed the whole of some Slavic country's rent-an-army, actually did a good job creating the nexus of the battle: a war of constant collision between French cavalry and British infantry. It was the worst kind of war—like a rugby scrum against 1,200-pound players in acrid fog with death the penalty for losing a yard. And the poor horses!

World War II produced a lot of generic war movies—biographies, mission stories, unit tributes, personal dramas, but very few pure battle movies. The one classic was William Wellman's *Battleground,* about the 101st Airborne at Bastogne. This was a film that inspired Steven Spielberg in *Saving Private Ryan,* for its lack of posing and prettiness. It doesn't view battle as an opportunity for glory or a linchpin in the nation's destiny, but as an ordeal to be survived. The movie has surprisingly little fighting in it, and the one foggy firefight it does chronicle isn't at all the Hollywood stuff; it's rather more like an epic of camping out, where the true enemy is the terrible winter cold that assails the underdressed paratroopers, along with little sleep or hot food. The heroes at the end don't leave on a note of pious superiority but, under the command of a tough bird of a sergeant played by James Whitmore (who seemed old even in 1949!), simple, quiet professionalism. They form up and march out in step, saying to their replacements and the world at large not "we are heroes" but "we are soldiers."

Korea produced few enough great moments and fewer great movies. Its primary battle movie was *Pork Chop Hill,* the 1959 account of a holding action taken in the last days of the war by one dog-tired company. Here the key was irony; as Gregory Peck and his weary boys first took and then held the chunk of Korea shaped like Mom's favorite serving, a few miles away the brass hats from both the American and North Korean armies yapped about peace proposals.

The man who made that film had a more than passing acquaintance with war: Lewis Milestone had already made *All Quiet on the Western Front* (1930), but he'd also done less rigorous works: *Edge of Darkness* and *The North Star* (1943), *A Walk in the Sun* (1945) and *Halls of Montezuma* (1951). In an odd way, the severe and bleak *Pork Chop Hill* represents a repudiation of the romanticization and the melodrama that filled those more conventional pictures and returned him to the severity of the 1930 masterpiece.

Vietnam produced its share of movie claptrap, but the one battle film that lingers after so much is John Irvin's *Hamburger Hill* (1987). It has the strengths and weaknesses of the battle picture: It was hard to tell the boys apart (more paratroopers from the 101st), and the visuals of the repeated assaults—the fight was ten days long in 1969—simply grew numbing. The movie was in some sense an attempt to reclaim the war for the right, a kind of response to Oliver Stone's leftward *Platoon* of a year earlier. Politics isn't my beat, so I don't care; what does matter is that in spite of its many weaknesses, Irvin's film captures the numbness of battle. It was just an over-and-over thing, a here-we-go-again thing. There was no glory in it at all, and it was fought for a country that didn't care.

What you get from a battle movie, as flawed as the genre might be, is something you don't get from a war movie. In fact, all the battle movies have the same meaning: that the young soldiers are always better men than the politicians who sent them there. And it's that anybody who's been there and done that has done something spectacular. The British schoolchildren in the nineteenth century said it best: "If you were at Waterloo, if you were at Waterloo, makes no difference what you do, if you were at Waterloo."   (JANUARY 20, 2002)

*D*on't turn to Ridley Scott's stunning *Black Hawk Down* for lectures on geopolitics, the tarnished Clinton foreign-policy legacy, or theories of terrorist conspiracy. The movie reflects not a public intellectual's view of the world, but Sgt. "Hoot" Gibson's. Hoot's the guy with the M-16 who doesn't make decisions but only tries to survive them.

The movie, then, may disappoint pundits and op-ed cowboys and all the men in gray suits and black shoes who so self-confidently throng this city's streets over the lunch hour. It teaches stuff they don't know, only the smallest and most bitter of lessons: that ammunition is more important than water, that cover is more important than concealment, and that the good die young.

Black Hawk Down re-creates war at the micro level, as experienced by Army Rangers and Delta Force commandos on the ground in Mogadishu, Somalia, October 3, 1993. On that day, a routine if dangerous mission slated to last an hour fell apart in the worst possible way. The young soldiers found themselves the targets of what can only be described as a citywide homicidal rage, in which every angry Somali with a Soviet-bloc assault rifle or a rocket-propelled grenade launcher petitioned his grievance in lead and warheads.

The soldiers, initially deployed to represent their country's humanitarian instincts toward famine relief, had by this time become policemen, hunting a powerful warlord who usurped United Nations food supply efforts. Now they found themselves in a pitched battle. For fifteen hours they sheltered in the ruins of the city, scampered to consolidate, rescue their wounded, and collect their dead, shot at everything that was shooting at them, and prayed for deliverance.

When it finally arrived early the next morning, eighteen Americans and an estimated 1,000 Somalis were dead and the city had been turned into a warscape resembling Stalingrad. It was the worst single day of combat for American soldiers since the Vietnam War, and even if the job the young men had been sent to do was accomplished, that achievement—in the way these things always seem to go—turned out to be largely meaningless.

You may be impelled to ask: What was the point? But you probably won't have time while the film is onscreen. The movie doesn't moralize, and its political meanings may be arrived at only by laborious inference. It's too intense to let the rational part of your brain gear up; instead, you are simply there, scurrying, ducking, wishing you had more ammunition, luck, or courage, and wishing the whole thing would end. You come out shaking and weak.

Shot in Morocco with an unusual amount of Pentagon cooperation, *Black Hawk Down* re-creates the events of that day with the full technical resources of modern cinematic technique. It helps to have a few Black Hawk helicopters to play with, of course, and a $90 million budget, a Pico Boulevard clubful of hot young actors and, in the role of the Somali militia, the Royal Moroccan Army. But it's still possible to have all that and screw it up; Scott, an experienced big-movie maker (*Gladiator*, for example, wasn't too shabby in the size department), tries to keep the phony movie moments to a minimum and the sense of frantic professionalism to a maximum. It works.

Task Force Ranger's mission—to arrest two men said to be the warlord's lieutenants in a building in a teeming market district—seemed to go well enough at the start. As planned, the Delta commandos, choppered in by small helicopters, assaulted the building and "extracted" the men; the Rangers, arriving minutes later in heavier Black Hawk helicopters, fast-roped down and set up a perimeter. Meanwhile a lightly armored convoy headed through the city to rendezvous with them and take everybody back to base three miles away.

But—spontaneously, it seems—the city's militia rallied and began to bring fire on the hated Americans; the whole thing went south when one, then another, of the big Ranger helicopters were shot down, and troops had to be diverted to the crash sites. Each one became an Alamo or a Little Round Top as the Americans took up defensive positions while rescue convoys attempted to reach them.

So focused on the experience of the fighting is *Black Hawk Down* that it doesn't bother much with context or with character, something that could never be said of reporter Mark Bowden's original book. Bowden took the time to explain not merely the politics involved but, more important, the culture of the new, volunteer army.

There's not a whiff of Vietnam-era sullenness and resentment; these aren't draftees but volunteers, in it for the fun, travel, and adventure. They aspire to be, or are, solid professionals; they don't see themselves as victims but as warriors. They are gung-ho, Number One, and RA (regular army) all the way.

But they weren't interchangeable; there were essentially two American military cultures on the streets of the Mog that day, and while Scott evokes them visually, he never explains them. The Rangers are shock infantry, basically conventional in all military respects; their hair is trimmed or shaved, their ranks low, their ages young (most are in their first enlistment). An institutional vanity requires that they bark "HOOOO-AGH!" in place of "Yes, sir" or "Yes, Sergeant." Most "want action" or joined to fight; they're full of the bravado of a JV football team on its first road trip.

The Deltas, or D-boys, are all senior noncommissioned officers, heavily trained and armed, who've seen a lot of action in our little wars of recent note. They are in their late twenties and early thirties. They are not just Special Forces but the elite of the already elite Special Forces; so they are stars, and used to being treated like stars. They have a lot of little perks, too, and like so many gifted men, they know their talent buys them extra latitude even in a bureaucratic empire as chronically anal as the American military. They wear their hair long, they dispense with conventional military courtesy, they have customized weapons, and they wear plastic bike helmets instead of the Kevlar pots of the Rangers. And in action they are, by training and instinct, very, very aggressive.

It's the strategy of Scott (and the several screenwriters who toiled on the script, including Bowden) to play up that big brother/little brother relationship between men of each unit; it provides an emotional subtext to what otherwise might be simple chaos, spectacle, and things blowing up. Each grown-up Delta will "adopt" a baby Ranger, and nurse him through the conflict with words of encouragement or chastisement. Each boy will try to please his big brother, and in the end, that, more than any exhortations to duty and country, is what gets them through the night.

As an exercise in star charisma, the movie is fascinating. All the guys end up with dirty faces and big moments, but only a few of them connect with the audience. Josh Hartnett plays an earnest young Ranger staff sergeant named Matt Eversmann, and he's essentially the sensitive one, in whose burning, tender eyes the full horrors of the conflagration are mirrored. He's not bad, and Hartnett may in fact become the big star everyone expects.

Still, others register far more powerfully, and some people disappear altogether. Eric Bana, the Australian actor of last year's *Chopper*, will probably be promoted from Sergeant First Class "Hoot" Gibson to full-fledged movie star. Affecting a believable Southern accent, he's Hartnett's big brother; but he's so cool in his swagger, toughness, and professionalism—and he has all the good lines—that he's the one you'll remember.

Meanwhile, William Fichtner, who's been a yeoman for years, has a great role as another Delta pro, Master Sergeant Jeff Sanderson, more or less based on Paul Howe (Bowden's primary source on Delta operations for the book). Fichtner is really good: tough and smart and gritty. But his little brother, Ewan McGregor, as a company clerk elevated to assistant machine-gunner at the last moment, all but vaporizes. You forget McGregor—no less than Obi Wan Kenobi!—is even in the movie until the end, and then you realize he's actually been in most of the scenes.

The stunner is Tom Sizemore. Sizemore, who always appears as working-class stalwarts with doughy faces, dead eyes, and imperturbable psychology, plays a Ranger colonel in charge of the rescue convoy. His calm dignity and endless well of courage are breathtaking. When a boy says to him, "Sir, I've been wounded," he replies quietly, "Son, we've all been wounded." It's as if he's still the platoon sergeant, Mike Horvath, from *Saving Private Ryan*, commissioned, grown older and wiser.

There are some disappointments. The two Delta snipers Randy Shughart and Gary Gordon, both posthumously awarded the Medal of Honor for their sacrifice (they set up security around one of the downed Black Hawks and stood off hundreds of militiamen until eventually overwhelmed) are only seen in their brilliant action. They are not established as characters in the early going, and we have no sense of them as men, so we don't feel the pang of their loss as much as we should.

And while Scott largely resists Hollywoodifying the material, he doesn't do so entirely. I didn't care for the way two of the Somali generals were personalized by their shades and gangsta outfits, and the way the camera delivered up their eventual demise with a sense of melodramatic payback. Take that, sucka! It seems beneath the movie. One of them even lectures a downed helicopter pilot in rhetoric that sounds like something Richard Loo would have said as an evil Japanese colonel to John Garfield in a 1943 Warner Bros. morale-booster.

But those cavils aside, *Black Hawk Down* is the next worst thing to being there. That's how real it feels.   (JANUARY 18, 2002)

G. I. *Jane* watches with admiration and not a little sadism as a female SEAL recon team candidate takes a whipping and keeps on kicking—butt, that is. She also shoots, kills, and blows things up. Is this a great country or what?

The director of this stylized quasi-feminist mayhem is Ridley Scott, who has a thing for armed women (*Thelma & Louise*, don't you know, as well as Sigourney Weaver's Ripley in *Alien*). A legendary visual stylist, Scott doesn't tell a story so much as attach electrodes to your brain and zap it into your central nervous system at high voltage. That tingle you feel as you leave the theater is merely the onset of post-combat stress syndrome, as amplified by oxygen debt.

All this is not to say the film is good, merely that it's effective. It's so jazzily cut and so driven by music that it's not much more than *Flash-dance* with machine guns. It doesn't even take its own argument too seriously. In fact, it can't really be said to be agitprop for full sexual integration of the combat forces as much as an anecdote about the potential of one exceptional woman who takes her crusade so seriously that she skips on the gender-norming adjustments that a politically correct military allows in physical performance standards for female trainees. In that way, *G.I. Jane* is brilliantly packaged to embrace all and alienate none of the perspectives on this thorny issue.

Demi Moore, buff and ripped as Xena but with some actual electrical energy behind her eyes signifying mental activity, is a career naval intelligence officer thwarted by her gender as she seeks to climb the ladder. Lacking combat experience, she'll never run with the big dogs. When an obstreperous senator (Anne Bancroft) pressures the navy into integrating a woman into the testosterone-crazed SEAL teams, Moore's Jordan O'Neil is chosen to head to a naval special warfare installation and begin the intense training.

This, it should be noted, isn't straight SEAL training, but even further up the elite pyramid of special operations culture: la crème de la crème, the CRT—combined reconnaissance team. But according to Scott's take, what it seems to specialize in isn't recon of the sea, air, or land, but recon of the soul, achieved by acquainting the trainees with the textures of despair, pain, fatigue, and their own infernal nothingness. The candidates must be destroyed before they can be re-formed in the image of the compleat SEAL: resourceful, cunning, impervious to pain, committed to mission, and a master of close-quarter battle.

In nine and a half weeks, O'Neil is tied, beaten, held underwater, soaked in mud, PTed, tongue-lashed, and finally cursed halfway to hell and back. She not only perseveres but becomes almost radiant in her suffering; her hair self-shorn to sexless fuzz, her face a purple tapestry of welts and bruises, she seems as though she should be strapped to a cross, not an M-249 automatic weapon. There's something a little creepy in the way the movie dishes it out and seems to celebrate the visuals of the agony traced in hemorrhage and abrasion on her skin.

You've seen this before. You saw it when it starred John Wayne as Sergeant Stryker in *Sands of Iwo Jima*. You saw it when it starred Jack Webb and it was called *The D.I.* You saw it when it was called *An Officer and a Gentleman*, and starred Louis Gossett Jr.

But *G.I. Jane* does add a new element. Now, instead of the world simply being composed of *Über-* and *Untermenschen*, there're the powerful, disorienting pheromones of sex in the air. She is woman, hear her roar; try not to notice her boobs. The closed men's locker room rife with the stench of sweat, gun lube, and bourbon has been penetrated by the one thing to which it is vulnerable.

The representative of that cult is a masculine phantasmagoria named Command Master Chief Jack Urgayle, played behind pale killer's eyes, hawklike cheekbones, and a fallen intellectual's Faustian fury by Viggo Mortensen.

The relationship between Mortensen's chief and Moore's first lieutenant is the fascinating core of the movie. One feels the sexual electricity between them: He hates what she represents even as he admires who she is, and she appreciates the blood and pain and courage he spent in gaining his wisdom, but fears his cruelty, his virility, and his willingness to commit violence. It's impossible, of course, but they both want each other; as fellow alphas, they own genes coded to interbreed.

Getting by the issue of sexual attraction is the lieutenant's triumph. She is willing entirely to play by men's rules and to survive or falter by them. She never destroys them by laughing at the stupidity of their games or playing her own games; she plays by their rules, to win, as when, after a particularly brutal hand-to-hand encounter with the chief, she's able to signify her ultimate acceptance of their view of themselves by unleashing the deepest of male insults. It's a great, satisfying audience moment, but on the way home you may be ashamed at yourself for hooting so hard. After all, the movie is arguing: If you can't beat them, become them.

Unfortunately, you can guess where it's all headed; plot originality is not *G.I. Jane*'s strong suit. After some nasty D.C.-style down-and-dirty infighting, its last, lamest move is to contrive to turn a training mission into the real thing and actually insert the newly minted SEAL into a hokey job on the Libyan mainland. Thin, thin, thin.

This, of course, signifies the last stage in O'Neil's development and her passage into that most exclusive of masculine worlds, the most jealously guarded of all the kinds of man's work: killing. But Scott takes from her the ultimate test of that—the close-in business with a knife on the sentry that is the commando's most brutal skill. And his later vision of a hot, dirty firefight in the Libyan arroyos is the most generic thing in a movie that has heretofore found astonishing visual poetry in the most banal of military subject matter. It's about on a level with any routine episode of *Combat* from the sixties. Scott should have looked at Bernhard Wicki's terrifyingly intimate account of infantry battle in *The Bridge* or Phil Karlson's in *Hell to Eternity*. Those guys knew how to put you in it; Ridley Scott can only show you how it looked on TV thirty years ago.

(AUGUST 22, 1997)

*M*aybe it's the monuments.
        After all, as film objects they are naturally fascinating and naturally loaded with meaning. If all the Joes and Janes from Oshkosh can't stop pulling out the Instamatics, who can blame the directors for yielding to the same temptation?

In olden times, the monuments were used literally. They were celebrations in stone and marble of great men but also of great ideas and a great culture: of a form of government and a national purpose and a proud heritage. They stood for purity of moral vision, for the most shining idealism imaginable, and their presence lent a special air of dignity to the city, even in times of trial. They were profoundly inspirational: To look upon them was to look upon the altar of the cathedral of democracy, and to be stirred and motivated.

For example, it's to Lincoln's memorial that Jimmy Stewart's Jeff Smith retires on the cusp of his crisis in Frank Capra's great *Mr. Smith Goes to Washington*, and it is from the marble visage of our heroic sixteenth president that Jeff draws the strength to resume the fight, by way of a one-man filibuster that ultimately overturns the nasty Taylor machine. The monument and what it symbolizes energize him; they improve him.

But contrast that to the monuments as they're presented in *G.I. Jane*, Ridley Scott's account of the adventures of the first female Navy SEAL: We come upon them in the early moments in what seems to be a predawn helo assault. We skim across the pewter waters low, under the radar, and then pop up to rocket-and-minigun attack altitude, and there they are before us, like obstacles or dragon's teeth fortifying a strong point. The whole city is low and dark, not a marble citadel so much as an objective to be taken at great cost. It is really an enemy city.

What I mean to discuss is that concept, now so dear to American film culture: Washington as the enemy city. But I mean not to do it in plot terms or in story terms or in anything having much to do with the spoken word. Rather, what interests me is the unspoken visual nature of the condemnation, the way filmmakers express their ideas not merely in ways beyond words, but in ways far more eloquent than words. That is the track from *Mr. Smith Goes to Washington* to *G.I. Jane*. Another way of thinking of it is as the track from monument to smoke-filled room to empty parking lot to the Washington party scene.

Consider again *Mr. Smith Goes to Washington* of 1939. Lanky Jimmy Stewart, with a basketball center's body and Huckleberry Finn's face, is appointed senator after the death of a party hack. His prime attribute: He's an idiot. He's cornball, easily manipulated, he's an idealist. In fact, he's really an object of pity, put in office to facilitate the Taylor machine's latest graft scheme, the building of an unnecessary dam on land that it secretly owns. Fronting for the scheme is an ostensibly great senator, who's really a party hack behind his phony cosmopolitan ways.

How corny is Smith? Smith is so corny that on his first day in Washington, he wanders out of Union Station and gets aboard a tour bus, where he sits wide-eyed and dreamy as he's hauled around to all the monuments. Capra uses the monuments as a way of defining Stewart's uncomplicated patriotism. That's what distinguishes Jeff Smith from the old-timers, the caustic journalists and smart-aleck Hill staffers: He actually sees the statues and the stones, where they see nothing except possibilities for opportunity. They know how it works; he knows nothing.

For Capra, the monuments are palpable symbols of democracy, of, if you will, the system. For in its way, *Mr. Smith Goes to Washington* isn't cynical at all; rather, like the monuments it so adores, it believes in the system. Capra makes the point that the source of corruption isn't this city at all but the mythical Western state back home; that's where Taylor's boys are, where he runs the newspapers and the factories and has constructed a machine whose sole purpose is to perpetuate itself and earn tons of dough by scamming the feds.

But what destroys the corruption is the system itself, or at least as Smith uses it by turning on a one-man filibuster that convinces the nation that he's pure and the machine is rotten. In fact, Capra envisions the Senate floor as a huge marble arena, well-lit and supervised by a cowboy icon (that's Harry Carey as the president of the Senate, one of the most famous of movie cowpokes in a series of John Ford silents a few years earlier, looking on benignly as Jeff wages his battle). The system, he is saying, is as stable as these marble walls and solid wooden benches and desks (Jeff sits at Daniel Webster's); it merely requires the persistence of a good man to prompt it into action.

By 1962, the monuments had almost disappeared. In Otto Preminger's *Advise and Consent*, based on the Pulitzer Prize–winning novel by Allen Drury, the city has become dark, almost a blur, and not yet threatening. It's hardly seen because those twin demons career and duty are truly the focus of the culture it invokes; the architecture, the houses, the fine public buildings and the great sculptured spaces never come into focus. The city has become entirely a professional political arena, the city of the workplace, an indoor city. Preminger's is a Washington of offices and clubs, where men get together and work things out amiably among themselves. The reigning value isn't patriotism or purity at all, and not even pragmatism, but the lubrication of pragmatism: civility. It's about working within the system, not challenging it, and its villain is a senator whose crime is that he's too loud, too crude, too ambitious, and too strident. Fred Van Ackerman (played by George Grizzard) is something even worse by the political standards of 1962: He is an unregenerate peacemonger!

The film, which looks consciously back on the Hiss-Chambers brouhaha and unconsciously forward to the Weld-Helms brouhaha, is a chronicle of ordeal by appointment, a uniquely Washington circus. It watches as an aging president tries to appoint Robert Leffingwell, a left-leaning pointy-head (it's Henry Fonda; think Adlai Stevenson with better posture), as secretary of state. It falls to the Senate majority leader, Bob Munson (ever-dapper Walter Pidgeon), to guide this appointment through the thickets of the Senate, a bramble of ego, grudge, self-inflation, obedience, self-doubt, and opportunism, even though he's not sure he believes in the man himself.

Here the key design element is that symbol of the white-collar worker in those times: the cigarette. Do these guys ever smoke or what? The cigarette is clearly used as an allusion to the symbolic memory and the authentic presence of the smoke-filled room, the back chamber where the deals are really cut, but it has another meaning here, too. It's almost ceremonial, as if to say, if men can smoke together, they can, somehow, work together. As Bob maneuvers, draws on favors, smokes, tries to put out brush fires, and smokes, he's aware that old Senator Seab Cooley (Charles Laughton in his last great role) has put in motion a plot to quash the Leffingwell appointment, because he hates and distrusts Leffingwell (they're in the same party, but that doesn't really matter, then or now, as with Helms-Weld). But he's not aware that the duplicitous Van Ackerman, who's so far outside he doesn't even get that he's outside, schemes to advance the appointment by blackmailing young Senator Brig Anderson (ever-innocent Don Murray) into supporting Leffingwell under threat of revealing a homosexual episode in all-American boy Brig's past. (Preminger's vision of gay culture in New York—complete with demon jazz!—is pretty damned funny.)

The scheme isn't held against Van Ackerman nearly so much as his refusal to get with the rules of the club. He doesn't understand that you have to go along to get along: That's how the system works, that's its strength. He's uncomfortably ideological and inflexible in an environment that demands cooperation as its highest value; he doesn't even smoke, the priss!

Come 1976 and we are outside again, but in a Washington never before seen. This is Alan J. Pakula's fabulous film version of Bob Woodward and Carl Bernstein's *All the President's Men,* easily as interesting a piece of visual design as it is a narrative. We are outside, but we are all alone.

Pakula tells the story of the now-legendary *Post* reporters' lonely penetration of Richard Nixon's unconstitutional tendencies as they asserted themselves in the 1972 election in brisk, pared-down, minimalist terms, at least dramatically. The movie plays out as a brilliantly understated, terse examination of the journalistic process. Pakula was smart enough, however, to let the visuals of the movie express the meanings.

For example there's a constant visual contrast between the *Post* newsroom—a bright communal place of endless hubbub, where the chattering classes chatter their brains out—and Nixon's empty, scary Washington. When Robert Redford's Woodward goes to meet Deep Throat, he's always a lonely little man in the middle of hollow darkness. The movie, when it moves away from the communal processes of journalism, almost moves into a film noir universe, where shadow dominates light and the sound of footsteps echoing out into the darkness suggests an existential quest.

The visual signature of the film is the extreme long shot of Redford, reduced to tiny silhouette, isolated in some vast, usually shadowy space. Here's Washington as Conspiratorial City, with unseen phantasms lurking in the darkness, and a sense, always, of being watched. As the film is constructed, the reporters' courage is symbolized not by anything said or acted upon—that would be too obvious and self-serving—but rather by their willingness to go alone into this huge darkness, to run the lonely risks to get their story. At no time could the actors turn to the camera or each other and proclaim, "We are the forces of light penetrating the dark world," but Pakula's design of the film, aided by Gordon Willis's superb cinematography, makes that point more vividly than words ever could.

Since then, movies bashing Washington have become so common they are almost no longer worth commenting upon. This summer, for example, has seen an unusual crop of them, from *Contact,* with its emphasis on political back-stabbers interfering with the heroics of true science, to *Air Force One,* where a staunch vice president has to fight off what amounts to a coup even while the president is snuffing terrorists with a machine pistol aboard his big jet.

But even with that in the background, *G.I. Jane* really takes the cake.

The movie is pretty simple in its attempts to bundle hostilities into neat little packages and pander to as many groups as possible, frequently at cross-purposes: It panders to feminists by showing an incredibly strong woman, to the old military by showing a woman who sneers at the idea of making things easy for women, to Washington-haters for displaying the duplicity of the Cabinet and the media, to sadists who like seeing women humiliated and tortured, and to those who like it when a lot of neat guns get fired. Now is that great marketing or what?

It follows Demi Moore as a naval intelligence officer. Somewhat like Mr. Smith, she's chosen for a great honor—first female SEAL candidate—because everyone assumes she'll fail. Like Mr. Smith, she turns out to have more guts and stamina than anybody could imagine; then it turns out that her sponsor, a powerful female senator, is willing to sell her out to keep some bases open in Texas, so she's on her own. The movie is built upon a contrast between the soft and decadent life here in Compromise City and the rigors of SEAL hell-week, where the wannabes are brutally weeded out from the can-do's.

But for a kind of visual emblem of how it sees Washington, the film settles on the party. Ridley Scott, who directed, is of course one of the great visual technicians of the age, as *Blade Runner* and *Alien*, among so many others, make abundantly clear. So when Ridley throws a party, it's a beaut.

I loved the brief, vivid Washington party scene in this film, meant to contrast with the heroics of the SEAL trainees crawling through the muck under the machine gun fire down in Florida. These are parties that Caligula would have enjoyed and could have thrown. They lack only dancing girls doing the hootchie-kootchie to qualify them for the A-list in suburban Sodom, circa 1800 B.C. or so. You keep waiting for Michael Eisner to show up with Tiffany Mynx on his arm or for Cecil B. DeMille to end it with a blast of cosmic lightning.

Such opulence. Such decadence. Such rotted flesh and bunches of bulging grapes and chunks of cheese, such cleavage amid the rich silk gowns, so much wine and hard stuff, so many parade-dressed, effete officers quaffing bubbly beverages from so many thin-stemmed crystal goblets. How come I never get invited to parties like this?

Why the depiction of Washington shifted is not so clear as it seems.

One may ascribe it to post-Watergate, post-Vietnam, current-Clinton cynicism. But one must also realize that something deeper is operating: that is how useful as a dramatic platform the concept of Washington as enemy city is, and how universal not merely to our own body politic but to all body politics.

For if Washington is anything, it is headquarters. Anybody who has ever served in the military, the government, private industry, journalism, or a family (and that would seem to include everyone except the boy in the bubble) agrees on one thing as a universal of the workplace: Headquarters never knows what's going on, that's what's so awful about headquarters.

Call it Battalion, call it Management, call it the North Wall, call it the Brass, call it the CEO, call it the Staff, call it Washington, D.C., it's the same: They're stupid. They don't know what we're going through. They don't understand us and how hard we work and what we're dealing with. Wahhhhhhhhhhhhh! That's the real meaning under the anti-Washington movement. It's really nothing personal.

But it is baffling to anyone in workaday Washington, hustling, sweating, bustling, looking for a good hot dog cart and a good parking place. We have become Byzantium, Dodge City, St. Petersburg, Paris in the 1780s, Berlin in the twenties, Bangkok in the seventies, Hollywood in the teens, twenties, thirties, forties, fifties, sixties, seventies, eighties and nineties, all the voluptuary's prized burgs rolled into one.

So we as Washingtonians must therefore ask: If we are the damned, how come we ain't having any fun?   (AUGUST 17, 1997)

*I*f you lived through them, chances are you'll never forget the thirteen days of the Cuban missile crisis. I remember cowering before my bedroom window, transfixed by an image in the imagination: a radiant and weirdly beautiful mushroom cloud erupting over Chicago in majestic blasphemy, its shock wave still thirty seconds away before, out in the suburbs, I would be obliterated, then incinerated, then atomized, and finally folded, spindled, and vaporized.

But—I hate to give away a surprise ending—the world didn't end in 1962, and the film *Thirteen Days* does a pretty good job of explaining why.

It's no kind of great film, and sometimes it's a little ridiculous. When Adlai Stevenson (portrayed as the comical house weenie at the Kennedy frat party) finally stands up to the Russkies in the United Nations—"I'm prepared to wait until hell freezes over, Mr. Ambassador!"—it is supposed to play like Rocky's KO of Apollo Creed. Everybody back in the war room cheers and yelps and jumps. Did this really happen? Possibly, maybe even probably. But somehow the moment feels false and cheap and more connected to showbiz formulas of redemptive reversal than to anything real.

Generally, though, the movie skips the hysterics and concentrates on a certain species of American narrative, derived from *Dragnet* and, before that, Dashiell Hammett: clipped, brisk, rigidly controlled, slightly stylized but not overstylized. Its title is also its structure: It takes you through the thirteen big ones one at a time, from start to finish, snapping around the world, from the crisis room in the White House to JFK's office to the cockpit of a camera-packing Crusader jet hurtling over the Red missile sites through a dangerous sleet of Commie ack-ack to the bridges of the blockading men o' war.

Of course, all this is punctuated by that movie trope of escalating global tension, the dit-dit-dash of a telegraphic subtitle reading something like: "USS Arleigh Burke, 233 nautical miles off Cuba, 1133 Hrs Zulu." Dit-da-dit, dash-da-dit, it's fast fast fast and believable believable believable and ritualistic ritualistic ritualistic.

You can laugh at this, but I never will, because I once wrote a dit-da-dit-dit book starring the end of the world in fire, and made a hatful of dough from it. As I proved and this movie proves, dit-da-dit-dit always gets 'em squirming in the front row.

Anyhow, the vantage point is that of JFK's close adviser, Kenny O'Donnell, played by Kevin Costner (who also co-produced and was presumably the guy who got the project greenlighted by New Line). O'Donnell, it says in David Self's script, was a brusque political pro, an expert at chewing people out and protecting the boss's best interests. In the movie's first seconds, when you hear Costner's blatant Boston accent, your heart sinks, and you think, "Oh, God, three hours of Kevin Costner doing a bad Vaughn Meader impression."

But let me, er, say this about that: You get used to Costner right away. Before he became a star, he was an actor, however briefly, and in this movie he's trying desperately to regain his actor's reputation, a crusade that's generally successful. It's not a vain, hammy performance, and he doesn't seem to hog the camera or get the best lines. He comes across as a very tough guy, a bully and a brute in service to his lord and master. And when you see that a guy this willing to wrestle anybody on any floor in any gym in the world is scared, you know the stakes are high.

And they were: Our U-2s snapped photos of Soviet missiles being installed in Cuba, in violation of treaties and our own public policies. We raised a stink, and ultimately erected a naval blockade by which we turned back Russian ships bringing more of the weapons to the island. Meanwhile, even as he struck macho poses for the cameras and relied on his oratorical brilliance, Kennedy maneuvered for time and leverage in a number of backstage arenas, ultimately reaching an agreement that kept the silo hatches shut and the big bombers on their runways in Omaha and Smolensk.

Kids who have only heard vaguely of these days will probably get with the film right away, and it won't do them a bit of harm; the little buggers should know why they're still alive to invent dot-coms and drive Porsches. They won't have to fight the ghosts who, unbidden, hop through their fathers' and mothers' brains.

For us geezers, growing used to the movie will take a bit of time. At first I felt as though I was in some kind of hideous waxworks of Disney animatronic figures gone berserk, with such lesser lights as Dylan Baker and Bill Smitrovich pretending to be actual historical grown-ups like Robert McNamara and Maxwell Taylor; Michael Fairman somewhat loopy as Stevenson; and Kevin Conway chewing a whole pig's worth of Virginia ham as the movie's bête noire, General Curtis LeMay, whose very eyebrows, wild and curly bosques beyond discipline, signify untrammeled aggression.

But what saves the film are two central performances—Bruce Greenwood as John F. Kennedy and Steven Culp as Robert F. Kennedy—and director Roger Donaldson's insistence on letting the story tell itself, quickly and for the most part without flamboyant overdramatization.

Greenwood, a yeoman's yeoman who usually plays vapid pretty boys, quickly transcends Kennedy's quirks and graces. It's a performance, not an imitation, and you feel the character's intellectual and emotional submersion in his terrible dilemma, as well as the crunching weight of history upon his shoulders. He's never macho in the blustery style of movie heroics, but a reserved man, his arms usually folded as if he's worried about his own frailties and his nation's in a hostile world.

He and Culp play together well, particularly in communicating the ways brothers interact: So much is unsaid, only felt, in their empathy to each other. (Costner also conveys this sense of empathy among men close as or even closer than brothers.)

Historically, the film is mildly revisionistic. Though the Cuban missile crisis has entered popular history as an American triumph and an example of how through matchless leadership the savvy, gutty Americans forced the Soviets to blink, the movie tells a gentler story.

In this version, the Russians are only half the problem; the other half is LeMay, portrayed here as a nut case who wants to go straight to Defcon 5 and start pushing buttons and heading for the bomb shelters. He's one of the enemies Kennedy must defeat. (Speaking of LeMay, I do note that, while he has become the prototypical cigar-chomping nuclear boogeyman of our collective memory, nobody was making fun of him when he was leading combat missions over Europe and Japan, directing the Berlin Airlift, or forging the Strategic Air Command.)

In this film, we see actions taken that seem reasonable one by one, but which together take on a frightful momentum, producing consequences no one imagined or wanted. That's exactly how World War I marshaled itself into existence, in the aftermath of an essentially meaningless shooting in a part of the world of which few had even heard.

This JFK is smart enough to know history, to have read Barbara Tuchman (*The Guns of August* had just been published) and to prevent the march of folly toward the missiles of October. He will permit no such thing, and the movie portrays him almost as a secret dove; once he'd stormed into this mad crisis and the world stood on the brink of Armageddon, he and his brother and his counselors worked like hell to find a way to back off.

The answer was a backdoor deal with Chairman Khrushchev in the Kremlin: The Russians would back down on Cuba (not that it mattered, anyhow; they had subs packed with nuke warheads parked in Long Island Sound and probably the Potomac basin, right near the Jefferson Memorial, as well), and we would quietly remove some of our birds from an air force base in Turkey.

At least 6,000 people have said that those who forget history are condemned to relive it. On the other hand, those who don't forget it have this one pleasure: They can go see movies about it, and marvel at the pleasures and the miracle of their survival.   (JANUARY 12, 2001)

*C*ommandos *Strike at Dawn* was both the title and the operating principle of the first commando movie in history, way back in 1942. Paul Muni led British raiders against his Nazi-occupied Norwegian fishing village at the crack of first light.

They don't strike at dawn anymore. Now they strike well before, to take advantage of their night-vision gear. And sometimes they don't even strike at all: They just get real close and laser-designate the target, so the air force's genius-bombs can ride that beam down from four miles out, find the right window, go down the hall, turn left, pass the bathrooms and the vending machines, and blow up in the case officers' bullpen.

But if commandoing isn't what it used to be, commandos will always be with us, and maybe always have been. Genghis Khan's right-hand man said it best: "With forty picked men, I can change history in a single night." Much before that even, weren't Ulysses's Ithacans the first Delta Force? They hid in that horse and sneaked out after the revelry had passed into drunkenness for a night of Trojan throat-slitting and city-burning.

As it appears we are about to begin a commando war where our lives and our fortunes are riding on the stealth and guts of our trained night killers, perhaps we ought to look at what our movies have made of commandos over the years.

Here's the answer in a nutshell: a lot. The movies love commandos. One can see readily why the commando—the highly skilled, elusive practitioner of deadly close-quarters combat talents—is so attractive. He is, in his own way, a star to begin with: an elite fellow, honed and trained to murderous spinosity, able to do things others haven't the strength or skill or will to do. Moreover, he represents something uniquely individual, the one area where show business culture and military culture intersect. He is fundamentally a soldier of the imagination: He sees things that the run-of-the-mill military mind cannot accommodate and is unsure of—

possibilities, long shots, fabulous opportunities. For this reason, until quite recently, commando units have always been mistrusted by their orthodox comrades in arms, who feel that unpicked men, in the thousands, the hundreds of thousands, the millions, are the way to vanquish an enemy.

Best of all, he is dynamic, and the camera loves dynamism. Not for him the dreary sludge of waiting in fixed positions for an attack that may never come, while nerves fray and uniforms turn sodden. Not for him the endless trudging of the infantry experience, the lineups for chow, the four-holers behind the tents, the hundred squabbles and flare-ups of the garrison life. He's a mover, a shaker, a doer. He kills a lot of bad guys.

The commando has other advantages for moviemakers. He moves in small teams, so it's easy to keep track of the characters. Along these same lines, he is better dressed, by far: You don't see him in a steel pot, one of hundreds of like-dressed, dirty-faced helmeted automatons, again hard to sort out. (As brilliant as *Band of Brothers* is, don't you get the fellows all mixed up when they're in action? And that's always the case, even as far back as *All Quiet on the Western Front* in 1930.)

But the commando usually wears black, like most Hollywood types; he rarely wears a hat, and when he does, it's a floppy, insouciant job that can be personalized, or a *très* chic beret; he's not one for the anonymous steel pot. He carries more and better weapons, most of them fully automatic, all of them sleek, black, sexy, many of them wearing outlandish optical amplification systems. He also has knives, handguns, ropes, flashlights, goggles, and other cool tactical gear. He looks as though he stepped out of an REI store after a buying spree.

As far as the movies go, there is at least one actual commando work of art, though the film in question is hardly ever thought of that way. Among other things, it identified the formula of the typical ideal commando film and fulfilled it perfectly. That is David Lean's brilliant disquisition on the necessary insanity of war called *The Bridge on the River Kwai*, of 1957.

This movie follows a British team—actually not commandos, which in World War II were special raiding units used mainly in coastal encounters like Dieppe, but members of one of the British intelligence establishment's more heroically berserk units, called the Special Operations Executive, who did the true behind-the-lines commando stuff—as it penetrates a Burmese jungle to blow up a key Japanese bridge. The bridge has been built (brilliantly) by a stubborn British colonel who thinks he is defying the Japanese but actually has sold out to them.

The movie is an examination of the phenomenon of heroic leadership; the contrasts are between Alec Guinness's Colonel Nicholson, Jack Hawkins's Major Warden, and the Japanese prison camp commander, Colonel Saito (Sessue Hayakawa), all essentially the same man, duty-haunted, obsessive, and self-destructive; and American William Holden, an opportunist and sensualist who has no larger commitment than the self and considers both the British and Japanese officers crazed.

The ironic ending, of course, recounts how that cynic, forced to choose between his own survival and the necessity for a sacrifice, chooses the latter. He turns out to be just another damned hero. The last words in the film, spoken by James Donald as a doctor observing the final convulsion, are "Madness. Madness." But note that he does not say, and Lean does not endorse the idea of, futility. The point has been that the madness was necessary, not wasteful.

Its deeper themes aside, the movie perfectly establishes the commando movie formula, its quintessential narrative and its subtexts: the identification of mission, the evocation of rigorous training, the doubts of a younger man as to whether he can kill with the ruthlessness that his officers demand, the initial recon, the cleverness of the plan, the improvisation when it goes awry, the rally, the splendid, murderous triumph, and the exultant withdrawal. (Of course Americans, when they later reinvented the form in the eighties, modified the last image: the ceremonial beer-can opening. Ah, Miller time: the taste of triumph!)

Most World War II commando movies followed these steps in a number of greater or more usually lesser keys. The Brits, as might be guessed, were best at it. Two fabulous "special operations" movies were *Cockleshell Heroes* (1955), about commandos in kayaks who planted bombs on the hulls of harbored ships, and *The Dam Busters* (1954), a commando movie in spirit even though it took place above the ground instead of upon it: The movie was about low-altitude heavy bombers that literally bounced spherical bombs into German dams in the Ruhr valley.

Even when the Americans tried it, they paid homage to their British masters, adapting a British novel with a British director into the most popular commando movie ever made, *The Guns of Navarone* (1961). It was lots of fun watching Gregory Peck and Anthony Quinn as they Vesu-viusized a German artillery installation in the Aegean, even if you always knew you were looking at Yanks hiding behind bad accents. It was a well-made, big-budget Hollywood film.

Others followed without distinction: *The Devil's Brigade* (1968) put Holden back in the commando business, as the commander of the first American special forces unit in World War II, but it was pretty generic stuff, as was *Tobruk* (1967), when a behind-the-lines mission was led by—good God!—Rock Hudson and George Peppard.

Commandos are part of the larger picture in *The Longest Day* (1962), which examines the American Ranger assault on the cliffs of Pointe du Hoc in Normandy, and a French commando operation against a German-occupied casino. The most cynical of the World War II commando movies was 1967's brutal *Dirty Dozen,* which turned the "elite" image of the commando on its ear by collecting a crew of condemned men for a special operation on the eve of D-Day; it featured American soldiers burning German general officers to death in a bunker.

Ironically, one of the best commando movies came late in this cycle: It was John Irvin's 1980 version of the Frederick Forsyth novel *The Dogs of War.* The dogs of the title weren't state-sanctioned killer elites but freelancers—mercenaries, that is. The little corner of hell they were let slip upon was an African dictatorship of utter corruption, and the spon-sor for their mission was a multinational industrial conglomerate. Very late twentieth century, no? But the movie really got the grittiness of raid warfare as waged by professionals addicted to the adrenaline rush.

In its strange way, it captured something few more conventional movies ever get, which is the desperate aggression and will to violence of the very few (but verifiably extant) alpha males who do this stuff for a living. They aren't wannabes, like the mall commando in cammies you see hanging out at Sunny's Surplus, but the real hard-core McCoy. Irvin gets something so ferociously real that it's scary: their need to get in close and unleash maximum violence in minimum amount of time, to destroy everything in their path without a second thought.

And this may have been the movie that made yet more vivid that spectral phenomenon known as Christopher Walken: A sensuously physical specimen with cheekbones like Viking spear tips and eyes the color of blue death, Walken gave his mercenary leader a catlike grace and fury. There was nothing consciously glamorous about him; he just got the job done unconsciously by applying automatic-weapons fire to all his problems and burying them in a sleet of lead. It is probably the truest evocation of the commando psychology on record.

But the rise of the commando as a movie hero can be linked especially to the rise of the modern terrorist. Before the Palestinian operation at the Munich Olympics of 1972, hardly any Western armies had specific anti-terrorist commando units, with the one exception of the British Special Air Service regiment, which has subsequently acted as a godfather of all free-world commando teams. One can look at the recent documentary *One Day in September* for an invocation of the world before special operations teams became a necessity: A ruthlessly accurate account of that grotesque event, it watches as the West German government struggled to deal with a situation it had not even imagined, and responded with such clumsiness and passive-aggression that the tragic outcome was all but foreordained.

The first American commando movies post-Munich were pretty miserable. Chuck Norris kicked A-rab butt in the unconvincing *Delta Force* films that came out of the Golan-Globus film factory. The films bore as little resemblance to actual military operations as did Norris himself to an actual actor. You'll forgive me, I know, for leaving out the three *Rambo* movies, which I cannot bear to contemplate; nor can I spare more than a few typestrokes for *Commando* (1985), an oafish Arnold Schwarzenegger thing of no importance whatsoever, or even John Wayne's brain-dead *Green Berets* of 1968. All were set in fantasyland.

Indeed, only a few films seem to have caught the intricate intensity of anti-terror special operations. The best of these is from George Roy Hill, off a text by the great John Le Carré. *The Little Drummer Girl* (1984) is about the wilderness in which special operators must function. It follows an extremely proficient Israeli team as it tracks a ruthless terrorist across Europe. The book, and the excellent movie made from it (flawed only by the late-thirties Diane Keaton in a role written for a young-twenties British actress, a concession to Hollywood practices) showed something we may not want to hear right now: how devilishly hard this work is. The Israelis track their man with extraordinary thoroughness, and the key to the operation is building a legend of a phantom lover to the martyred brother of the terrorist, knowing that the man will ultimately contact her and therefore make himself, however briefly, vulnerable. Anyone who thinks that manhunting just involves Green Berets scuttling through Afghan caves ought to look at this film for some indication of the complexity of the business.

Special-operations sequences—that is, the narrative of the pure commando raid—show up effectively here and there, always good to goose the flagging energy of a film actually about something else (SWAT teams, the civilian equivalent, serve the same function in too many films). In the weirded-out *Alien* rip-off *Predator* (1987), there's an extremely neat sequence—it has nothing to do with the gist of the movie—where Schwarzenegger's special ops team takes out a Central American guerrilla unit. In the recent *Proof of Life*, otherwise nondescript, the final assault on a guerrilla camp holding hostages by an ad hoc team of British and American former special operations people is terrifyingly authentic about the nature of the business.

The big American disappointment in the movies is the utterly programmatic *Navy SEALS* (1990), which reduced that extremely proficient special operations team to a rather generic war movie status. Why do I feel that actors on the level of Charlie Sheen and Michael Biehn aren't really good enough to play Navy SEALs? Then there's *G.I. Jane*, misnamed because GIs were, in the understood vernacular, army; in this one, though, Demi Moore plays the first female SEAL, but again the movie is ridiculously pro forma.

The best news on the movie commando front is that Ridley Scott is off filming Mark Bowden's brilliant book *Black Hawk Down*, an almost clinical examination of a special-operations disaster as it recounts the unfortunate adventures (18 men killed) of the Army's Delta Force and a Ranger battalion in urban combat in Somalia in 1993. Let's hope that by the time that account of a special operation gone wrong reaches the screen, we've seen accounts of special operations gone right on the television.

(OCTOBER 7, 2001)

*I*t is not known whether, as one of his most famous characters did, the director Francis Ford Coppola loved the smell of napalm in the morning. However, this much is clear: He loved the spell of napalm.

He loved to watch it blossom in slo-mo, a rolling crescendo of oxidizing jellied gasoline, devouring as it sped through jungle and village, its silky orange undulations combining poetry and hideous destruction. There was something so Vietnam about it, so Vietnam that he could not deny himself the pleasures of spreading it all through his great if flawed *Apocalypse Now* (1979) as a symbol of American arrogance, vanity, and cruelty. In fact, the movie opens with a rupture of the flaming stuff spewing across the landscape, one of the most unsettling film images of the last century.

If you loved the film or hated it, this week your duty is clear: You must get yourself to *Apocalypse Now Redux*, the restored three-and-a-half-hour version of the film, which opens Friday at the Cineplex Odeon Cinema on Wisconsin Avenue.

First off, the movie offers one of the great lost pleasures, one we so seldom encounter at the Bijou anymore. You watch this monster unreeling in its splendid vitality, its absurd ambition, its wobbly tone, its beauty, its stupidity, its immaturity, its tragedy, its grandeur, and before you know it, close to four hours have blasted by. And when you leave, you seize whoever is up close to you—friend or foe, stranger or lover—and begin to talk. You have opinions. You must express yourself. You must be heard.

Alas, that other person also must be heard. The point is that a great movie like this—great in its goodness, great in its badness, but never, for a single second, banal—gooses the yakking centers of the brain. It might even cause an actual thought to tumble forth, though this has become quite rare in America.

The movie was controversial from the get-go. Its "shoot," to use the professional term as if I know what I'm talking about, was a famous farrago of disaster. One star quit and had to be replaced by another; the new star (Martin Sheen) promptly had a heart attack. Coppola, then the hottest director in America after his triumphs with the first two *Godfather* movies and *The Conversation* in between, struggled to keep costs down while his cast sweltered in a Philippine location that stood in for the real thing and became so intense it felt like the real thing. Coppola struggled with a marriage that was coming apart. Then he struggled with the editing, chopping the film down to a sub-three-hour release time and trying desperately to solve the problem of an ending, which he didn't then and still hasn't been able to. (All this is covered in a brilliant 1991 documentary called *Hearts of Darkness*.)

Apocalypse finally opened, years behind schedule, to mediocre reviews and dismal business. But over the years its reputation expanded and expanded; it moved up the food chain from failure to mere disappointment to cult classic to pure classic. This *Redux* restoration adds 49 minutes of deleted material. The additions have the effect of magnifying the movie: It is still magnificent, only more so; it is still maddening, only more so; it is still imperfect, only more so.

The movie's literary ambition is epic. It takes the story structure of Joseph Conrad's great *Heart of Darkness* and imposes it upon Vietnam, which it locates as an American heart of darkness. In Conrad's tale, a narrator named Marlow, a professional seaman, recalls traveling up the Congo in search of a lost "great man" named Kurtz, who was supposedly "civilizing" the natives in the name of good King Leopold of Belgium, while at the same time removing their ivory. After an arduous trek up the dark torrent, Marlow arrives to find the man deathly ill, ravaged by his experiences, possibly insane; but evidence of his corruption is everywhere. For he has not civilized the natives; they have savagized him. Kurtz's remedy: "Exterminate all the brutes!" (a chilling 1902 forecast of what was to become a genocidal threnody in the upcoming century).

But what Mr. Kurtz provides memorably to readers is a glimpse of the savage within the human heart, which another great writer, Yeats, phrased succinctly as "the rag and bone shop of the human spirit." That's Conrad's conclusion, too: "The horror! the horror!" Marlow reports as Kurtz's last words, implying that he had seen his own heart of darkness, which was, in its metaphoric way, our own.

In Coppola's retelling, from a story by the writer-director John Milius, Marlow has become a young Army paratroop officer, a Captain Willard (Sheen in a brilliantly controlled if Winston-fueled performance), who's obviously seen a lot of hairy stuff and is known for his expertise operating alone. Like Marlow, he is sent up a dark river to find a lost "great man" who is named Kurtz, but who in the film is a Green Beret colonel. Captain Willard's job is not to rescue the man but to terminate him with extreme prejudice, which is the term of art for assassination.

What exactly is Kurtz's crime? That is the crux of the matter. Even Willard sees it's not a reversion to savagery; that's already a condition of the war, as the movie demonstrates over and over. Perhaps it's that Kurtz has achieved a clarity that the army cannot permit: He understands the nature of the war (or of war itself), and in an odd way, his solution is terrifying to the corporation that is the establishment. He wants an army of committed guerrillas, as fanatic as the North Vietnamese Army and the Viet Cong, and as willing to die for its mission; he cannot tolerate the fat, sluggish, violently sloppy way the Americans make a war they somehow don't really intend to win. But he is winning, even as he sinks into debauchery. For this apostasy he must be silenced forcefully.

But first Willard must get there, which is the true magnificence of *Apocalypse Now* and even more so of *Redux*. Willard's journey up the river is really a journey through an epoch. Some of the added materials make this point even more inescapable, and supply incidents that seem to be visits to most of the iconographic moments of our least favorite war. All of them attest to squalor, brutality and futility. We see the failure and sometimes disappearance of leadership, the accidental but inevitable tragedies that ensue when teenage boys are turned loose on the world with machine guns, the boundless suffering of the Vietnamese people.

But it must be said of Coppola that he is fair: His villagers aren't all innocents caught in the whirlwind, and his soldiers aren't all beasts hell-bent on slaughtering anything that moves in the free-fire zone. Even a wacko like Colonel Kilgore (Robert Duvall), who loves the smell of napalm in the morning, has his grace moments, as when he commandeers a helicopter to deliver a wounded mother and child to a field hospital after the famous helicopter assault on her village.

Willard is an expert observer because he's so unshockable: He watches but hardly ever reacts. A total cynic, he is surprised by nothing. His passivity is a kind of weird mirror image to our shock.

Where does this vision of the war come from? Well, it's pretty much the house style of Vietnam movies, up until Oliver Stone's *Platoon*. It's essentially an outsider's, a journalist's view. It comes out of the work of Michael Herr, who covered the war for *Esquire* and made his reputation on a series of brilliant, bitter mood pieces that saw the Nam through a glass darkly: His pieces emphasized the surrealism of the war, the disconnect between the five o'clock follies of Saigon (the press briefings) and the ugliness in the field. Herr collaborated on *Apocalypse Now* and on a later epic movie that shares its same satiric, absurdist tone, *Full*

Metal Jacket, for Stanley Kubrick. So what we are seeing, it seems to me, is Herr's Vietnam: from the vantage point of a sensitive, educated writer with a connoisseur's nose for irony and paradox.

Stone changed all that: He was no tourist but an infantryman, and he didn't have time to note the literary themes and conceits of the experience or find archetypes; he just killed people and tried not to get killed. That's why I think *Platoon* is the best of the Vietnam movies from a GI's perspective: it's brutal, harsh, without literary artifice, a stunning overload of sensation and crushing reality.

That's not to say that *Apocalypse,* in this version or the original, is a failure. You cannot see this movie without mourning the expenditure of a nation's will and the heroism of a generation of professional soldiers on something that seems ill-conceived from the beginning and wasteful to the end.

The newly added material amplifies this. One sequence plays up Willard's arrival—he's traveling upriver on a patrol boat with a reluctant navy crew—at a base where nobody's in charge, nobody's doing anything. They just want to rotate back to the world and they ain't going nowhere until that magic DEROS day comes and their trip on the Big Freedom Bird arrives.

Then there's the *Playboy* incident. In the original, we saw bunnies doing the frug and driving sex-deprived soldiers mad to the point of rioting. *Redux* supplies a melancholy coda, in which the patrol boat crew discovers the downed bunnies at a rainy base camp somewhere up the river. The clever and resourceful Willard trades diesel fuel (odd: The helicopters that transport the bunnies wouldn't use diesel) to the bunnyboss (Bill Graham, the rock impresario) in exchange for some bunny intimacy. Some of the guys get a few minutes in paradise with the young women, who are revealed to be empty, drugged-out narcissists, as clueless as the generals running the war. Does this extended scene add anything, other than underscoring the already powerful sense of surrealism and moral squalor? I don't think so.

The worst addition is the long, talky business with the French. If I read the film correctly, this may even not be literal action, but a head trip for the too-intelligent Willard—a nighttime reverie of a professional soldier on a mission that may kill him. It begins and ends in fog, movie code for "fantasy." The boat comes ashore on the edges of a magnificent plantation. The sailors magically drop away until only Willard is left; he attends a formal dinner in the great house where various Frenchmen, dressed in the elegant fashions of 1954, lecture him. In this case Coppola's ambition seems to include history: He wants us to know where the war came from, see how we were essentially fighting the same war the French had already lost in 1954.

But it's the least dynamic sequence in the film: stilted, slow, talky. Moreover, Coppola, that most American of directors, has no imagination for the French: They seem like clichés, parodies of the French, where his American characters have always crackled with the eccentricity of life and individuality. In my ideal restoration, the French sequence would have remained on the cutting room floor.

Finally we reach the enigmatic climax of the film, which is still its most problematic point. Famously, an immense Marlon Brando plays Kurtz and it's a somewhat muddled performance: He's a dying king, immense, introspective, curious, consumed with contempt. He knows Willard is here to kill him but he seems ready to die, for the world holds no pleasures for him and he has no desire to return to it.

This ending really doesn't come from Conrad and it doesn't even come from Vietnam; it comes from James Frazer's epic of comparative mythology called *The Golden Bough* (the book, which also inspired T. S. Eliot, whom Colonel Kurtz quotes, is portrayed on the colonel's bedside). In his introduction to the book, which argues for a commonality of myth in all societies (somewhat like his successor Joseph Campbell), Frazer conjures up the sacred grove at Nemi, in antiquarian Italy, where a priest-king held uncomfortable sway, aware that at any moment another priest would spring on him to slay him and take over as king. King of what? Well, king of nothing: That was the ritual aspect of it, the valuelessness of the throne in comparison with the fatal seriousness of the conflict. Come to think of it, that's a viable metaphor for Vietnam, is it not?

We were the old priest-king, in our arrogance and power. We went to the sacred grove, Vietnam, confident of our rightness. But we were ambushed and after a terrible fight, we were slain. We have never recovered, not really; or at least the generation that either fought the war or fought against the war has never recovered, and that is why now, so many years later, it still matters so much to us.

In this elongated version, the death of Kurtz feels even more stately, which is the essence of its dramatic inefficiency. It's not a climax in the dramatic sense, something that satisfies the emotions that have been aroused by the journey to reach it. It has the feeling of a ceremonial sacrifice, spectacular in its imagery but inert in its emotional communication. It's not a fight, it's a slaughter. A victor emerges, but he's a victor who has won nothing and who has stolen away in the night with no prize except his own shame. As elliptical as it seems, that's what seems so right all these years later. But it still doesn't quite feel right.

(AUGUST 5, 2001)

earl Harbor is definitely about December 7, 1941, but it is not of December 7, 1941. It's not even really of our age, either. It has more of the feel of a film from, roughly, midwar.

That's because it's not just a generic World War II movie, but a specific kind. In tone and mood, it does not belong to the first wave of bitter agitprop, those encomiums to genocide like *Bataan* and *Air Force* in which the Japanese were a monkey-race to be exterminated without mercy. But neither is it a post-Bulge, post-Iwo late-war movie, exhausted, sacrifice-numbed, and confidence-shattered so that the war was no longer a crusade but had become an ordeal.

Rather, it's from that weird midwar period where romantic idealization was still possible, but tempered by an awareness of the depth and breadth of the struggle. The movies were no longer furious and racist; they had become passionate examinations of the emotional conflict between love and duty. The greatest of these films, of course, was *Casablanca*, whose low-tech plot is subtly echoed underneath all the high-tech frenzy of *Pearl Harbor*. And that is one reason why, until a disappointing tailspin in the last hour (of three), *Pearl Harbor* is the best piece of popular entertainment to come along in years, for my money a much better heartbreaker, thrillmaker, and tear-tweaker than *Titanic*.

Some people—most of them professional moviegoers—will argue that it's corny and predictable. I would counter-argue: That's the point. The movie's greatest accomplishment, after its extraordinary re-creation of the Day of Infamy, is the brilliance with which it understands and integrates forties movie tropes. You've seen 'em before; you'll see 'em again here: the noble woman, the two heroes who love her, the end of a beautiful friendship, the big battle, the reconciliation under fire, and the last sacrifice. It's the same old story, but not a fight for love and glory: It's a fight between love and glory, really. Yeah, okay, it was better with Bogart and Bergman, but everything was better with Bogart and Bergman.

Our heroes have nice forties names and cheekbones: Rafe McCawley (Ben Affleck, the seasoned one) and Danny Walker (Josh Hartnett, the beautiful one). Both look good in the forties flyboy duds, with leather A-2 jackets over khakis and Ray-Ban aviators and a cap scrunched nearly flat under earphones. Best pals from a hardscrabble Tennessee childhood, they're now hot young Air Corps studs, P-40 Warhawk jocks out of a Long Island air base where they regularly play mock-chicken at 350 miles an hour 35 feet above the ground, to the delight and admiration of the rest of the squadron.

Remember the meet-cute of forties movies? For *Pearl Harbor*, some-one—presumably screenwriter Randall (*Braveheart*) Wallace—came up with a lulu of a gag for this old-time ritual. Handsome Rafe meets beautiful naval nurse Evelyn Johnson (Kate Beckinsale, who has the classic face of a forties screen goddess) over the point of a hypodermic needle. He is not, at that moment, exactly putting his best face forward. She really gets his attention when she gives him three inches of booster shot where it's always pasty white. Since, it turns out, he has already had that same shot and only came around again to meet her, he promptly passes out from the double dose. Heck, even I could get a girl that way.

But though they have a magic night in the New York City of early 1941 (swing rules, as do brassy nightclubs and bottles of bubbly), and though love is absolute and instant (as it always was in forties movies), duty beckons. He's already volunteered to go to England for a tour with the Eagle Squadron, the Yank volunteer unit with the Royal Air Force in the Battle of Britain. Danny remains in the States, and by the miracle of the motion picture's capacity to abbreviate time, Rafe is swiftly in the cockpit of a slightly used Spitfire, jousting with the Hun Messerschmidts over the White Cliffs. He brings down the ace's handful: five. But the sixth smokes him, and we see him sliding under the waves of the Channel.

Is he dead? Was Victor Laszlo dead in *Casablanca*? Am I giving away a secret? Yes, if you're a moron.

Meanwhile, the movie widens. It flirts with, but never commits to, documentary style as it flits among a number of more or less historically accurate plot strands. The Japanese genius admiral and Harvard grad Isoroku Yamamoto (the great Formosan actor Mako, turned into a leathery, wizened Yoda of naval warfare) plots the attack on Pearl Harbor. In Washington, code breakers led by ex-ghostbuster Dan Aykroyd attempt to crack the numeric jive of Japan's secret radio chatter. President Franklin D. Roosevelt (brilliantly played by an unrecognizable Jon Voight) worries about the Pacific and Japanese intentions. Back at Pearl Harbor, a black mess steward named Dorie Miller (Cuba Gooding Jr.) hates the fact that he's relegated to the galley of his battle wagon.

In the main story, meanwhile, both Evelyn's nurse unit and Danny's fighter squadron are transferred to Pearl and the easy living in that peaceful paradise under blue skies and green palms and on white sandy beaches. Evelyn and Danny are so noble it will make you sick unless you once dreamed of Ingrid Bergman—so close, so far away, as you lit a butt and cursed the fact that of all the gin joints in the world, she picked yours. Evelyn and Danny, mourning Rafe and made hesitant by their guilt over what they're feeling, wait three full months before going goo-goo-eyed over each other. Here, the movie gets moony and slack, and many of you will be saying, "Send in the Zeros!"

Of course Rafe, miraculously rescued from the dead, arrives in Pearl twenty-four hours before the Japanese, and in that brief time the movie shunts through sequences of romantic betrayal, jealousy, anger, anguish, and all those High Emotions from *Casablanca*. But there's a subtle rearrangement of the materials: It's Rafe, the Victor Laszlo substitute, who gets to show Rick's rage and bitterness and cynicism. Rafe is crushed at what he views as treachery; Danny wanly tries to rationalize what really wasn't his fault, after all; and Evelyn tries to decide which hunk is more to her taste, a situation made more urgent by the bun in her oven.

Just when you think all of this would play better in black-and-white, the Japanese arrive to bring you back to the movie's title. What follows is certainly the most spectacular hour of American film since the Normandy sequence in *Ryan*.

Of course what you're seeing was not created in the actual world, not quite like this; we're looking at some computerized constructions mated magically to a few big props in a big Baja tank. But not for a second can you believe it's not real: The Japanese planes swarm like insects, buzzing low to the ground, spewing tracers—they ping-ping-ping when they hit the ships—and dumping torpedoes and bombs. The camera in cyberspace conjures up some fantastic rides: We cling to the tail fin of a Japanese 500-pounder sailing down toward the *Arizona*, its silly little propeller fuse spinning loose like a child's toy as it rushes closer and closer to the big gray target below. We strafe with the fighters and watch their tracers arc out into space before us and rip their targets. The gigantic ships roll over like dying dinosaurs on the day of the big meteor, spilling sailors by the hundreds into the boiling waters. Astonishing.

And the movie, bless its heart, is quite decent to our opponents in that conflict, the Japanese. You can feel restraint all the way through, and if this is certainly market-driven, the gentleness is still worthy of appreciation: The Japanese are never personified in the old style, and there's no money shot of grinning Oriental fiends, cackling with raptor's glee as they machine-gun sailors, and there's no sense of Americans then paying them back in vengeful lead. Yet at the same time the unlovely word "Jap" is uttered promiscuously during the attack, as it must have been in the real thing. So there's an effective balance between '01 decency and '41 accuracy.

Director Michael Bay focuses on small moments of heroism to give focus to the slaughter: That black mess steward ends up on a 20mm AA gun and splashes a bomber. Everybody behaves with a great deal of nobility and courage, and in the hospital, in a scorching, searing scene, those forties-doll nurses get with the program and become dirty-faced heroines who live up to the terror inflicted upon them, like the gals in *So Proudly We Hail* (1943).

Of course even as the carnage continues in the harbor, fighter pilots and former best buddies Rafe and Danny struggle through strafing runs to a satellite airfield and, hung over and bleary-eyed in half-buttoned aloha shirts, still in high-spat mode over the Evelyn issue, manage to get aloft for a touch of retribution, P-40 style. The movie really delivers this sortie with satisfying dramatic crunch: The big Yank pursuit ships rumble through the air like forces of industrial might after the more agile but flimsier Japanese craft. What they hit, they kill.

This sequence reflects the actual flights that morning of two genuine American heroes, George Welch and Ken Taylor, who brought down seven Japanese planes, exactly the number ascribed to Danny and Rafe.

Alas, the movie quickly squanders much of the goodwill it has accumulated in an unnecessary and unnecessarily protracted denouement, where you have no choice but to rescind its poetic license.

It's feeble but forgivable that Rafe could go from P-40s to Spitfires back to P-40s again without missing a beat because, after all, both were low-winged, high-performance fighter planes. But somehow fighter jock Rafe, as well as pal Danny and the rest of the squadron from Pearl, end up flying B-25s off the aircraft carrier *Hornet* in a hurried version of Jimmy Doolittle's reprisal raid on Tokyo and several other Japanese cities in April 1942.

This seems to be where *Pearl Harbor* abandons the forties and leaps headlong into our own dismal century. You could say the hammer has fallen, or is it the Bruckheimer, after producer and vulgarian Jerry Bruckheimer, perpetrator of such monstrosities as *Armageddon* and *The Rock* (both of which Bay also directed, quite loudly). It's not merely the nauseating spectacle of a paunchy, double-chinned liberal blowhard like Alec Baldwin playing the rock-solid, cueball-bald conservative war hero Doolittle, it's that the Bruckheimer spirit of giganticism has to be indulged.

The raid on Tokyo was a fabulous uplift for a beleaguered nation. But guess what, folks: They dropped about sixteen bombs and blew up a few outhouses. The old chestnut *Thirty Seconds Over Tokyo* (1944) does a much more fair version of the raid; in the overexaggerated stylizations of '01, the bombs rain down on Tokyo and devastate blocks and blocks of factories.

Then, as all the Tokyo raiders did, Rafe and Danny, in separate bombers, crash-land in China and immediately begin a ridiculous gunfight with Japanese soldiers. Suddenly it's *The Wild Bunch*, with .45s blazing away and grenades blowing up and men dying like flies and the problem between Danny and Rafe solved in the most cowardly way possible, a way Bogie never would have countenanced.

As long as *Pearl Harbor* stays in the past, it's perfect; when it wretchedly changes gears in the late going, it becomes the wrong kind of same old story: Hollywood stupidity and callowness, writ large across the sky.　　　(MAY 25, 2001)

*W*ar is so much better on the big screen than on the small.

On the big one, DreamWorks movie stars dash improbably through heavy enemy fire, lob grenades, blow the enemy away, and if they're exhausted by the ordeal, their fatigue is somehow beautiful. Everybody has a quip. You always know: Somebody wrote this, somebody designed it.

On the small screen, kids—ours, that is; actual young Americans—cower and flinch under enemy fire and are inarticulate about what they're doing there. They look as if they're about to puke. The settings are always squalid and fly-infested places like Kuwait or Sarajevo, and callow young officers say things that will not get them in trouble with their superiors, while the generals, with CEO haircuts, announce the geopolitical thrust of the operation, its cosmic significance.

This disconnect between big and small reflects the eternal tussle between entertainment and news cultures, between drama and reality, a secret game of influence and anti-influence that underlies a lot of movie material. That game seems in full sway now: No war bodes blackly on the horizon. No moms are getting those sad little telegrams. It's all long ago, far away. So, suddenly war seems fabulously adventurous once again, as it always does if you haven't been shot at in a while or you don't know anybody who has.

This is one reason why we seem now to be in a mini-boomlet—not quite a trend, but more than a blip—for the Big War Movie, particularly if it is set in World War II. In fact, the fourth big World War II movie of the past few years is fast approaching. It arrives on Memorial Day weekend from the folks who brought you *Armageddon*: producer Jerry Bruckheimer and director Michael Bay.

That would be the multi-zillion-dollar re-creation of America's most pathetic day of infamy, called *Pearl Harbor*, in which Ben Affleck in his P-40 Warhawk takes on the Japanese Zeroes, Vals, and Kates that sank the Pacific fleet in an hour's worth of great combat flying on December 7, 1941.

I would track the initiation of this trendlet not to *Saving Private Ryan* (1998), which represents the artistic ne plus ultra of the genre, but to *The English Patient*. That 1996 film featured no combat or missions, and was moreover a postmodernist document with difficulties of meaning and narrative comprehensibility. Nevertheless it had the effect of restoring the Second World War to imaginative importance and underscoring the spectacle, the bigness, of the thing. It taught an otherwise historically unlettered generation just exactly how great a deal that war had been, and why their grandpas still went all somber when it was invoked.

But the yin-yang that makes war either fascinating or unwatchable, depending on whether your own countrymen are dying in one, is not the only reason for the film industry's rediscovery of boom-boom as subject matter and the public's evident revival of interest in it as well, if the anticipation of *Pearl Harbor* is any indicator.

The movie even now is probably unassembled while thousands of techies try to get it cleaned up for release. But the previews certainly suggest something about the reasons for the movie: airplanes.

For the other movies, similar reasons. With *Ryan* it wasn't airplanes but a sense of land warfare. With the clunky, old-fashioned *U-571*, it was subs. With *Enemy at the Gates* it was actually airplanes again. And cities. (I omit the disappointing *Thin Red Line* for many reasons, but mainly because it failed to suggest battle with the ferocity and reality of the others.)

A technical breakthrough in the past twenty years, refined exquisitely in the past five, makes it possible to visualize on screen things that before had to be re-created literally, or in miniature. Beginning with stories set in a generic future (the *Star Wars* films), filmmakers gradually mastered the computerization of the moving image. It has even been argued elsewhere that we are no longer watching "movies" but rather some new techno-form with little connection to the great films of the past, which were photographic documents, bound by the limits of photography.

The computers give animators the freedom to specify not only the precision of a shape (machines are much easier to do than human forms) but the integrity of that shape as it is manipulated to mimic movement; the computer can trace movements from point to point. This means that anything may be replicated on a hard drive, and by some alchemy then transferred to film, where it has the palpable density of the actual.

With one exception—a deliberate throwback—each of the new war movies made extensive use of this technology.

It's further helpful that each of these war movies, except the highly original *Patient*, has a kind of predecessor by which this point may be illustrated. And it turns out, with that one exception, that today's war movies are further refinements of the last big cycle of war movies. Those fell into an odd category that might be called the pseudo-documentary, in which famous events from World War II were re-created, with stars in cameo roles as true-life heroic personalities.

Private Ryan, of course, harks back to Darryl F. Zanuck's *The Longest Day*, of 1962, which began the earlier cycle with its own restaging of the Normandy invasion. There's no artistic comparison between the pictures, of course, given the clunky, straightforward quality of Zanuck's mock-doc vs. the deeper drama of character, motive, and duty in Spielberg's far greater film. But Spielberg's picture also excels at the technical level, because with the digital process he can reach into his frame and make corrections.

Spielberg could create an impression of combat so realistic that—true story—the World War II historian Stephen Ambrose, thirty minutes into his first viewing of *Private Ryan*, had to go outside to recover emotionally from the chaos on the beach.

This new verisimilitude may be ascribed to several elements. One, certainly, is that Spielberg had studied the seven extant photographs taken at Omaha Beach by the great war photographer Robert Capa, whose smeary, blurry images captured the true horror of the experience. The director was able to bring that smeary, blurry quality to the film with its desaturated color and its clumsiness of men moving awkwardly through fire. It also helped that he was Steven Spielberg, that he had the industry clout to make real his desire to convey the physical carnage of death in battle as never before.

But the computerization was key as well, because by using it, Spielberg was able to "paint in" tracer bullets coursing savagely among the men. (Robert Zemeckis did the same thing in the Vietnam battle sequence in *Forrest Gump*, to equally spectacular effect.) Thus we see something we've never seen, the palpable presence in the air of enemy ordnance; it supplies three-dimensionality to accounts of combat that no previous generation of moviemakers could manage.

Zanuck's production was state-of-the-art for 1962; it's just that there was no art. Everything had to be done literally and, involving human beings, imperfectly. His movie is about moving large numbers of actors, most of them reluctant (they were U.S. Army troops stationed in

Europe), through fake explosions on Mediterranean beaches standing in for Normandy's. The camera had to stay far away—although in one of the memorable gaffes in that film, you can see its shadow on a drifting screen of smoke as it cranes its way up the beach.

Put it this way: Zanuck gives you a producer's view of the war, something full of spectacle and bravado but somehow not entered. He's God on high, looking through a series of backward telescopes. We see hubbub, we see frenzy, we see blooming orchids of hot gas, but it's all from a bloodless distance and it looks like a rugby scrum with explosions.

Spielberg gives us the war photographer's view—down close in the sand. He makes us feel the grit; the bullets, flying past our ears, throwing up geysers of sand or banging loudly off steel obstacles, are like insects, buzzing everywhere, chewing the flesh where they happen to alight.

Though both *The Longest Day* and *Ryan* are artifices, they carry opposite metaphorical meanings: The Zanuck version has to do with control and mass movement, while the Spielberg version suggests chaos, slaughter, irrationality. The former has the sense of an official view of the war, with our soldiers as noble and self-sacrificing. In the latter, a counterargument, almost a backlash, is pushed: Our soldiers are cynical, squabble among themselves, doubt their mission, and are capable of the same kind of cruelty toward the enemy that the enemy is toward them, particularly in the shooting of prisoners.

Among the new crop, *U-571* is clearly the lamest variation. Yet technically it's pretty spectacular, though in its case computer animation appears not to have played much of a part, except to amplify some explosions on the dark sea. In fact, its charm is retro; it re-creates, almost literally, the clunky pleasures of the old Warner Bros. studio movies, and that famous Burbank Big Tank where so many marine sequences were shot (the Warner war films are very big on shipwrecks).

But *U-571* trumps this with its pièce de résistance: a literal seagoing copy of a German sub built to scale, so the filmmakers could put men and cameras aboard it without resorting to special-effects trickery. They built a fiberglass hull and mounted it on a tug; Matthew McConaughey could actually be seen shouting instructions from the conning tower.

This movie's earlier counterpart would probably be the equally hokey old *Crash Dive*, from 1943, with Tyrone Power and Dana Andrews raiding a secret German base in the North Atlantic while squabbling over Anne Baxter back in New London. In that film, a B-product of the midwar period, fatigue and honesty had yet to set in; it's still a gung-ho exhortation, full of gags and fisticuffs and colorful character actors distributed unconvincingly around archival footage of real subs at sea, clearly distinguishable from the more polished studio product and mock-ups of the conning towers in the studio tank.

I actually happen to prefer *Crash Dive* to *U-571*, purely for its for-mulaic earnestness. It was a movie made as part of the war effort, while the later film with its much bigger fake sub and its rather indiscreet pur-loining of one of the biggest English successes of the war—retrieving an Enigma code machine from a German U-boat—is somewhat indecent. But it reconfirms the general principle that at least occasionally, the war can be boffo BO.

Then there's the insanely ambitious *Enemy at the Gates,* still in area theaters. This one is a computer festival. Indeed, the movie's most pow-erful attribute is its ability to give us vistas and machines that could never have been seen on film before.

Though it's a story of ground warfare (German sniper vs. Russian sniper at Stalingrad, late 1942–early '43), *Enemy at the Gates* really shines in its evocation of the Big Picture. It also demonstrates how the computer, as a filmmaking resource, can be superior to reality. In the movie's most astonishing sequence—right at the beginning—*Enemy* de-picts Russian reinforcements crossing the river to the ruined, contested city on the far shore. At the halfway point of the journey a fleet of German Stukas drops from the sky, screaming down to dive-bomb and strafe the Russians, who respond with typical totalitarian brutality. Secu-rity troops begin shooting all soldiers who flee.

The spectacle is extraordinary, but more important, it could be mounted in no other way. To begin with, there are almost no flyable Stukas left. The gull-winged German dive-bomber, with its predatory sil-houette (that underslung radiator and those droopy wings gave it a par-ticularly aggressive profile), was an icon of Nazism, particularly as it devastated the Low Countries and France.

Even if such planes did exist, there are things that couldn't be done with them. You can't crash them. You can't maneuver them. You can't order them into the near vertical as they vector in, then pull out and watch their released bombs continue to arc downward toward the barges, some of which explode and some of which don't. This scene simply could not exist without the computer, nor could the vistas that follow: the vast, smoky ruin of a city, spreading to the horizon.

Not many English-speaking films set on the Eastern Front exist. The trashy *North Star* of 1943 would be one, and Sam Peckinpah's absurd *Cross of Iron* (the Germans are the good guys!) another. But in larger terms, the one earlier film that *Enemy at the Gates* comes closest to resembling would be *Is Paris Burning?* That's also an account of a great contest for a city and the various forces converging upon it that will decree its survival or destruction. It too turns on the spectacle of the city, and the importance of the city to culture, indeed to civilization. It made the point that cities are worth dying for.

Is Paris Burning?, however, told the opposite story; it turned on a German general who decided not to turn Paris into Stalingrad. But the city, like the city of Stalingrad in *Enemy at the Gates*, was the heroic presence in the film, not the men who scurried about it.

As for *Pearl Harbor*, there's no doubt that its antecedent is the thumpingly literal *Tora! Tora! Tora!* of 1970. That film came at the end of the quasi-doc cycle, and in fact may have killed them off. Again, it's based on a nonfiction account, in which stars played cameos of true-life figures, and the gist of the film was re-creation, not dramatization. *Pearl Harbor*, like the other films of this new cycle, is fiction, giving its characters private lives, although I understand it will depict some famous heroics of that day, such as the two army pilots who shot down seven Japanese aircraft between them.

Tora! Tora! Tora!, like its predecessors, was utterly hamstrung by its literalism. The producers realized that model planes on strings just wouldn't get it done, and indeed, in that time period, it was still possible to assemble a surprisingly authentic fleet of Japanese war planes to re-enact the attack. You would think: This makes it realistic. In fact, this doesn't make it realistic.

Flying airplanes is a tricky business, especially when the ground is close at hand. So the planes that filled the air in *Tora* were flown gingerly; somehow the eye could perceive that the pilots were more interested in landing at day's end for a beer and a burger than in burying a bomb in the smokestack of the *Arizona* for the glory of the emperor and the Greater East Asia Co-Prosperity Sphere. So this film has a certain awkwardness to it: lots of airplanes, lots of propane explosions, but it lacks the instinctive reality of war; it certainly doesn't match up with archival film, which discloses that in aerial combat, the pilots get close, then closer, before they kill their opponents.

What I like about what I've seen of *Pearl Harbor* is, damn, those airplanes may be fake, but they certainly seem real. They seem more real than real planes, because, duplicated in cyberspace, they can display the controlled aggression of combat flying in ways that are remarkable.

In fact, the trailers alone may be better than the movie. (Bay is not known for his character subtlety.) But the trailers show the Japanese planes roaring over the island in flocks, fifty feet above the ground, and one feels the throbbing reality of piston-driven aircraft, the roar of the engines, the incredible blast of heat and power from the things, the way the pilots are always making adjustments to keep them in trim, the subtle ways the planes relate to each other and to the ground. Indeed, that shot of a bomb being released from a dive bomber and sailing down, down, down to a rapidly giganticizing American ship may be an image as powerful (and profitable) as the shadow of the alien ship blotting out the Mall.

Whatever else it may or may not be, *Pearl Harbor* certainly looks as if it will be an airplane lover's fondest dream, one that will recapture the power and glory of those old warbirds as no movie has. But it's only possible because Hollywood has mastered the hard drive.

(APRIL 22, 2001)

Some wars are tragic, but some are holy. Of the latter category we have fought but three, the most recent against the Germans and the Japanese, before that against ourselves, and before that against our British masters.

Of the three, the Revolutionary War hasn't produced many great movies. Maybe it is because the men wore buckles on their shoes, wigs on their heads, and wooden teeth in their mouths. Who knows? But one thing is clear. With *The Patriot* it can now be said: The American Revolution still hasn't produced a great movie.

Written by Robert Rodat, who authored *Saving Private Ryan*, starring the grave and mature Mel (*Braveheart*) Gibson, and directed by

Roland Emmerich, the mad German genius of *Independence Day*, the movie is a strange combination of cartoon and diorama. It means to be simple and pure, but it is simplistic and pureed.

Of the three main personalities, it would seem to be Emmerich's that prevails: The movie turns the Brits into voracious space aliens and it builds, like *Independence Day*, toward Big Visual Moments that are, nevertheless, somehow inert. It's a movie of things to see, not things to feel.

I don't mind being instructed to hate the British. They are so adored in our Anglo-obsessed media that maybe it's their turn to endure a few slings and arrows. And anything that upsets Tina Brown—as this movie is sure to do—is okay by me.

But still, did Lieutenant Colonel Tavington, the movie's thinly fictionalized version of the British cad Banastre Tarleton, have to crowd women and children into a church and burn them? I know the war was bloody, brutal, and felt endless, that hostages were hanged, that prisoners were murdered, towns put to the torch, yes—but were little girls really wantonly burned alive in churches?

Anyhow, the movie roughly traces the unknown part of the war. This is good; the war of the Revolution played out over a vast theater, but we tend to think of it as centered in two neighborhoods in Boston where fops and wits exchanged quips along with cannonballs. No. Huge battles were fought in the Carolinas and won with bayonet work, and down there, the war was at its most brutal and total. *The Patriot* follows in general outline the year 1781, climaxing in a version of the Battle of the Cowpens, in North Carolina, which some regard as the turning point in the southern campaign and possibly the war. There's a coda at Yorktown and the final surrender.

It plays with two authentic figures: Francis Marion, an American partisan who roamed the Carolinas harassing and annoying the British, and "Bloody Ban" Tarleton, a brilliant if savage cavalry officer who was memorialized by the mocking phrase "Tarleton's Quarter," which was no quarter at all. He specialized in killing prisoners.

Marion is disguised as Benjamin Martin (Gibson), an idealized portrait of someone who was probably a very tough guy. As the movie has it, Martin is the perfect single dad, a kind of Ward Cleaver with a ponytail, living in a kind of idyllic serenity on a beautiful but oh so conveniently slave-free plantation in South Carolina, near the Santee River, with a tribe of kids. A veteran (he served in the French and Indian War of twenty years earlier), he is a reluctant patriot, loath to get involved in his radical neighbors' revolutionary fervor. But his sons—he has four—are children of their time, and the oldest (played by hunky Heath Ledger) is pining to join the rebels, finally doing so without his father's permission.

Meanwhile the savage Tavington (played by British actor Jason Isaacs, a fellow with the dead, glittery eyes of a very dangerous snake) is roaming the land with his horsemen, laying waste wherever he can. Circumstances bring Tavington to Martin's plantation, where the oldest son is recuperating from a wound. He orders that the boy be hanged; another of Martin's sons tries to intercede and is shot by Tavington.

The next sequence elevates the movie to a status of "talker." Everybody will have a position on it. Mine is that in time of war, people do what they have to—by the lights of their times, and not by ours. But even saying that, I didn't quite believe it. Martin grabs a brace of flintlock rifles from his burning mansion and takes his youngest boys—roughly ten and twelve—on a quick ambush mission to intercept the British squad and free the oldest son. Do you not like to see children with guns shooting people? Put more generally, do kids and guns make you think of the teenagers of Columbine or the teenagers of Iwo Jima? Your answer will almost certainly determine your policy. (I do note, however, that the movie doesn't focus on the guns, turning them into fetish items or objects of romantic worship; it sees them strictly as tools.)

After that bloody episode, Martin recruits troops, obtains a commission and begins his guerrilla war, and the movie becomes a chronicle of missions, ambushes, counterambushes, ruses, and traps, in which the clever Swamp Fox (as Marion was called) continually outthinks the Brits, who are represented by Tom Wilkinson (of *The Full Monty*) as a Cornwallis so arch and prissy you doubt he got out of that wig even to sleep.

The Brits offer irony and musketry, the American counter with earnestness and riflery. We shoot straighter (the important revolution was the revolution of the ball in the barrel). It goes on and on and on, for nearly three hours, epic in length but somehow not in content.

At last, frustrated, General Cornwallis looses Tavington to "do it his way," which seems to prefigure the SS Totenkopf Division's anti-partisan activities near Demyansk in 1942: He simply kills everybody and burns everything.

The film is therefore contrived as a lot of tit-for-tat nastiness between Martin and Tavington; clearly, for these two, it's not about politics. This has its downside. In the Cowpens battle (a battle that, for the record, the real Tarleton commanded and, ha ha, lost) a Hollywood cliché occurs: The two opponents find each other in the busy battlefield and have a nice personal duel amid the more general slaughter. All troops cooperate by clearing an empty space in the middle of the long day's dying. It's that sense of Hollywood artifice that continually robs the film of vigor and sucks the juice from what should be the world's greatest story of empowerment.

And so much of it is—no other word will do—corny.

Gibson melts his dead son's lead soldiers into balls for his pistols. Oh, please. At a key battle—Cowpens again—he pulls out the flag another dead son was mending ("building the nation"—duh! I get it!) to rally the troops and the camera turns him into a heroic statue, a painting hanging in a state house, a stamp.

It's not that patriotism is the last refuge of the scoundrel and the overrated director. It's that for this primal impulse to apply, you somehow have to believe. It has to come from inside, which is the one part of the war *The Patriot* studiously avoids. There's no majesty, no tragedy, no feeling here; it's all FX and costuming and casting directors.

Michael Mann's *The Last of the Mohicans* still strikes me in every way as a better film of roughly the same period. Besides being somehow more authentic, it has something that *The Patriot* doesn't.

That is the sense that as brutal and violent as the course was, for these people in this time, freedom was worth dying for. It was worth being massacred for, losing your children for, being tortured for. To earn it, they had to soak the land in blood, largely their own. But in *The Patriot*, freedom's just another word. (JUNE 28, 2000)

*W*hose war is it, anyway?

Who owns the American Revolution or, more significantly, its latest cinematic iteration in the form of *The Patriot*, a saga of a fightin' family in South Carolina as it struggles against dastardly British invaders?

The issue remains up for grabs. In one of those mini-tiffs that break out during the silly season in the professional typing industry, pundits of left and right have been yakking away on the Mel Gibson film, trying to sort it out.

Many conservatives would like to believe that it's a great film, that liberals hate it because, after all, they are liberals—and that anybody who is against it is somehow against America. James Pinkerton, a former Reagan and Bush aide, writing in *Newsday*, scoffs: "What might explain the critics' particular hostility to *The Patriot*? Could politics enter into their assessment?" To him, the movie seems like a loyalty oath: If you won't sign up for it, you're one of Them.

Then there's Richard Poe, writing for David Horowitz's Front-pagemag.com. "Every scene is vibrant with passion and manhood," says Poe, adding with a snarl, "qualities as alien to leftwing scribblers as patriotism itself."

There is a problem with these two comments. They are wrong. The truth is, not all liberals hated it and not all conservatives loved it.

One need look no further than *The American Spectator*, where James Bowman writes: "It is only to be expected that Mel Gibson takes on and defeats the entire British army, virtually single-handedly . . . but you would have thought that at least the film would have had something to say about what, from the point of view of the historian, the Revolutionary War was actually fought about." He gave it ze-nada-zilch-ro stars.

Rich Lowry, editor of *The National Review*'s Web site, wittily observes that the film suffers from a "terminal lack of seriousness" and reports that it sags "of its own cartoonish weight."

Finally, I myself had the experience of being a piñata on Ollie North's national radio show because I had expressed doubts about the film. The colonel yelled at me, and if memory serves, I yelled back. We fought for control of the microphone; we didn't listen; we were rude. It was fun. And here's what I should have said . . . Well, never mind. But the joke was, see, he thought I was a liberal.

Except that I'm not. (Don't tell anybody; maybe they haven't noticed yet.) But I still didn't care for *The Patriot* and now, after having seen it a second time, care for it even a little less.

I would like to offer the following radical argument: Not only is *The Patriot* a fairly lousy movie, it is a fairly lousy conservative movie.

Let's summarize what's good about it. It's about the American Revolution. It re-creates, primer-style, some forgotten campaigns, and it generally reacquaints today's history-stupid Americans with the immense quantities of blood that got them their precious, if taken-for-granted, freedom. It's handsome, it lets a sly British actor named Tom Wilkinson steal the show as a slightly perturbed Earl of Cornwallis, and it shows what cannonballs do to ranks of men unfortunate enough to stand in their way. Alas, that's about it.

Some conservatives see it differently. Horowitz, an energetic and amusing popper of left-wing balloons (he used to inflate them when he was a radical peacenik in the sixties), had already checked in on the subject in a tone so breathless that it sounded as if he were blowing up a dirigible: "*The Patriot* restores all the elements of our national legend—the heritage that arouses the better angels of our nature—to a state of invigorating wholeness."

One can almost see why they think so, the way the film manipulates core conservative values. It waves a lot of flags. It hopelessly sentimentalizes "family." It regards the Nation's Past through a lens of uncritical triumphalism. It mythologizes a militia, armed citizens ready to leap to the defense of the community. It trashes the Brits not only for their imperial arrogance but for their holier-than-thou, prissier-than-thou style.

But, see, here's the problem. None of those things has anything to do with the film's value as drama; none addresses the fact that it's pretty primitive. And none of them has anything to do with its political ideas— or lack of same.

The movie's greatest artistic sin is crudeness. It has the same us/them crudeness that marked director Roland Emmerich's previous great hit, *Independence Day*, and its unerring accuracy in hitting movie clichés dead center, a rare anti-gift indeed. Aside from some well-done battle scenes—though not as well done as those in dozens of other films—it's stale.

It's assembled from the clumsiest possible materials, made as simplistic as possible, and is manipulative in ways that subvert whatever passions its invocation of the War for Independence unleashes. The sum total of these defects is that it somehow misses the point of the American Revolution and its ideas. It waves flags but has no idea what those flags symbolize. The last thing it knows anything about is patriotism.

And it's weird, also, in certain details. For one thing—I can't remember another movie like this—it's built out of tiny objects that are charged with meaning and are meant to stand for the emotions that the film otherwise is not subtle or fluent enough to evoke. I've never seen a film that fetishizes so many little things, among them a Cherokee tomahawk that Gibson carries, the lead toy soldiers he melts to form pistol balls with which to kill British soldiers, a flag picked up by his son and slowly mended over the course of the film, and, finally, a piece of jewelry that belonged to his wife and is given to his daughter-in-law, and then is discovered in the ashes of the burned church where she perishes.

Emmerich's camera lavishes attention on these objects, and the music swells when they are observed. Each has a meaning in the story, which Robert Rodat's screenplay is otherwise unable to suggest. The tomahawk stands for Gibson's character's sociopathology, his insistence on fighting as a berserker, and his own guilt about it. The melting lead soldiers reiterate the theme of his dead sons and stand for the spirit of righteous vengeance. The flag, slowly repaired and then unfurled at a key point in the battle, serves as the cheapest kind of patriotism: the patriotism not of ideas or commitment to family, community, and culture but to hoary symbols. And finally, the jewelry is emblematic of romantic love, presumably that which the evil Brits insist upon traducing with sneers upon their faces.

Note what is lacking: freedom.

Freedom is one thing never discussed meaningfully in *The Patriot*. There's a little subplot in which a slave, signed up to fight on the side of the Americans, learns that he has served enough time to qualify for freedom. But he stays anyway, and at the battle of Cowpens, fights heroically and is told by a white Southerner that it's a privilege to share the battlefield with him. Corny but very nice, the one authentic emotional moment in the film—even if, as has been pointed out time and again, it was the British who offered slaves freedom, not the Americans.

But what about the film as politics? Is this the conservative film in ways other than its flag-waving and fife-and-drum-playing, that we cons have been yearning for, lo these many years?

Far from it. In fact, the film has been milled toward the generic, the politically correct, and away from provocative conservative issues. Much has been written already about its pitifully PC look at race relations, so I won't be going there. Let's instead look at the key conservative issues that the movie, in spite of its reputation, runs away from posthaste.

Guns. On that issue, it's a particular letdown. In Boston in April of 1775, the British weren't after leaders or property or flank security; they were after guns. As the British General Thomas Gage ordered his troop commander on the paper that started the war, according to Mark Boatner's vivid *Encyclopedia of the American Revolution*—"Sir, a quantity of Ammunition and Provision together as cannon and small Arms having been collected at Concord for the avowed Purpose of asserting a Rebellion against His Magesty's Government, you will march with the Corps of Grenadiers and Light Infantry put under your command with the utmost expedition and secrecy to Concord where you will seize and destroy all the Artillery and Ammunition . . ."

Of course, they got the small arms, all right—bullets first, in the form of the shots heard 'round the world.

The movie makes nothing of the gun as guarantor of freedom, which is exactly what a true conservative document would feel obliged to do. Its most troubling scene dramatizes Colonel Benjamin Martin's use of rifles—which the British hadn't even bothered to confiscate!—to save one son from soldiers by instructing his two younger sons to shoot and kill British officers.

It pays lip service to, but in truth makes nothing meaningful of, the affiliated concept of the "militia," that troubling phrase from the Second Amendment. Martin's men are all militiamen, drawn from the general population as opposed to the professionals of the Colonial Army. They have guns because they had them as civilians, but the movie never notices this. It treats the men more as a ragtag ad hoc guerrilla force than as an official state-sanctioned armed force. They're like hillbilly hobos, not skilled civilian partisans.

In fact, more generally, I think *The Patriot* makes a pretty lame selection in choosing the South Carolina campaigns of 1781 (climaxing in North Carolina at Cowpens) as its fulcrum. From the conservative point of view, a far more illustrative film could have been made from the battle of Kings Mountain in 1780, where the overmountain boys—these were Tennesseans, true militiamen under no real command save their own elected leaders—responded to threats by the British officer Patrick Ferguson that they "desist from their opposition to the British arms and take protection under his standard" or else he would "march his army over the mountains, hang their leaders and lay their country waste with fire and sword."

Bad career move, Pat. They came after his butt, found it at Kings Mountain, and there kicked it royally, along with 300 of his Tory troopers. Er, not to put too fine a point on it, but no prisoners were taken.

That's the classic conservative version of the Revolutionary War: a spontaneous, self-armed civilian army arising from the forests and glens and destroying a usurper who has threatened them with execution and destruction of homes. Moreover, the overmountain boys in 1780 made the professional Continentals of 1781 at Cowpens possible, which in turn made Cornwallis's surrender at Yorktown inevitable a few months later.

Farmers, guns, guys who wouldn't be pushed around by the most sophisticated military on the face of the earth, who outfought it brilliantly. Now there's a story! If screenwriter Robert Rodat wanted to be a conservative, and not just another summer moviemaker, why didn't he tell us that one?

Then there's the issue of taxes, and within it the key conservative conceit that freedom must be economic as well as political, as the Englishman John Hampden made clear in 1605 when he wrote the words that would, a century and three-quarters later, become the slogan of the Revolution: "Taxation without representation is tyranny." In the first few seconds, *The Patriot* raises this issue, but its own Patriot, Gibson's Benjamin Martin, is totally unswerved by it. He hardly notices it.

The impact of onerous taxes on an American population is never dramatized; the Brits are too busy burning churches full of women and kids for that. Yet the distrust of taxes—ever increasing and funding the growth of an ever more intrusive government—remains key conservative dogma. What a missed opportunity.   (JULY 30, 2000)

*W*hatever its merits or demerits, *Rules of Engagement*, like the service it celebrates, certainly isn't afraid of a fight. In fact, so pugnacious is this film, so defiantly does it threaten to coldcock anybody who moves against it, it's refreshing.

But not surprising. Basically the film decodes into a cri de coeur from the United States Marine Corps; it seems a gyrene-pure scream: "Don't tread on me, blankety-blank civilian."

Here are some of the fights it picks: with the left in general, with soft, career-concerned security liberals in particular, with those who aren't siblings in the brotherhood of battle who would nevertheless judge those who are, with those who don't listen to G. Gordon Liddy and do read *The Washington* [bleep], with holier-than-thou demonstrators who would spit on the uniform, with cowards, slackers, deviationists, nonabsolutists, and those who don't get this fundamental element of the Semper Fi creed: that every drop of marine blood is sacred.

The movie, from an original story by the old Washington hand James Webb, who is an Annapolis grad, a highly decorated Vietnam vet, former secretary of the navy turned best-selling novelist (the classic *Fields of Fire*, among others), seems assembled from a meltdown of recent military fiascos. It contains a body count that recalls the USS *Vincennes*'s missile launch against an incoming plane that turned out to be a 747 full of Muslim pilgrims, and an intelligence breakdown that recalls the marine aviators whose Intruder tail fin snipped a cable car wire in Italy, sending sixteen skiers to their deaths.

According to Webb's scenario (the screenplay itself was written by Stephen Gaghan), a marine fast-reaction team is choppered to the U.S. Embassy in Yemen, which is under ferocious siege by demonstrators. Commanded by an able thirty-year veteran, Colonel Terry Childers (Samuel L. Jackson), the men find the embassy under hostile fire, and the ambassador (Ben Kingsley) a sniveling, cowardly wreck, hiding under his desk while the flag is being used for target practice (it's his professional responsibility to secure it from such indignities). The ambassador and wife and child—and even that bullet-ripped flag—are evacuated, but then the marines begin taking casualties; when three are KIA and several more hit, Colonel Childers orders them to return fire, which they do with weapons set on full automatic. They kill eighty-three people, many of them women and children.

An enraged world, driven by an enraged media, demands justice for the baby killers. An administration of professional appeasers (no names, please) demands that Childers take the sole blame. Childers is court-martialed and put on trial for murder. He chooses as his attorney another colonel, Hayes Hodges (that supremely weary, wary old pro Tommy Lee

Jones), who warns him up front that he's a weak lawyer and he'd be much better with "someone like Bob Bennett." But Childers knows that Hodges won't let him down; they shared the same mud and the same blood thirty years back, in a stink-hole glade in the 'Nam, where Childers saved Hodges's life, even if the act of mercy concealed an act of murder.

The director is another old, old pro: William Friedkin, who years ago directed *The Exorcist* and *The French Connection*. He's great at the action stuff, particularly the way he uses sound to compensate for the budgetary limits placed on the film's production; his visions of battle in Vietnam and Yemen are quite convincing (Dale Dye, an ex-marine officer who's made a career advising Hollywood films, was involved in the production and appears as a general officer).

But the film, ultimately, is about ideas, which are encrypted into the court case that takes up the majority of the running time, so that the film is sort of *A Few Good Men* retold from Jack Nicholson's point of view. The marines would call it *A Few Good Men*, too, but without the sniggering irony in the inflection.

The initially inept Hodges finds himself up against a noncombat hotshot major (Guy Pearce, hiding his Aussie accent behind a New York one), and heavy hitters from the administration (represented by Bruce Greenwood as the national security adviser); key evidence of exoneration is destroyed. Witnesses are coerced into lying, or lie out of self-preservation. The machine clicks into fifth gear: You know the drill—spin, cover-up, selective leak.

Conservative politics aside, is it a brilliant courtroom drama? Not really. Does it ever reach the incendiary pitch of the mano a mano between Tom Cruise and Jack Nicholson in *A Few Good Men*? Not even close. But it does do one bullheaded thing that took a great deal of Marine Corps guts: It speaks the truth that Nicholson's colonel didn't believe the rest of us could handle.

It's an icky, unpleasant belief. That melancholy truth: The marines' job isn't just to die for their country. Sometimes it's to kill for their country.

The movie says: If you send men into battle expecting tidy, "surgical" responses, that's fine. But battle, particularly the kind of close-quarter urban mayhem in which the marines must prevail, can't always be kept tidy and surgical. Things happen. Men die. Panic sets in. Pain and blood fog clear thinking. Us or Them becomes the organization of the universe. When the command to open fire is given, people will die tragically, many of them innocent. It's called collateral damage when the air force does it; it's called dead babies when the marines do it. Live with it, the movie says, accept it; but if you haven't been there, don't you dare judge it.

Does *Rules of Engagement* play fair? Of course not. It's about as tilted to the right as the average Hollywood film is tilted to the left. Instead of stock villains like napalm sniffers and kill-crazed snipers, its stock villains are parodies of liberal excess: The Greenwood character, slick and ruthless, charming and manipulative, could be a stand-in for a certain president. The Kingsley character represents the secret conservative belief that liberalism is really a mask for physical cowardice, an oh-so-convenient way for men who cannot fight to argue that fighting is wrong and "never solves anything."

It probably doesn't even play fair in the technical sense. I'm not sure why men on a roof (as the marines are) would be in so much danger from men on the ground (as the shooters in the crowd are). The advantage always lies with elevation. I'm not sure why the marines don't have snipers, who could have neutralized armed opposition with that beloved surgical precision. I'm not sure why an after-action analysis of bullet impacts wouldn't have revealed the origin of ground-based fire.

It cheats. But it makes its case hard and it dares you to argue with it, rare enough these days. (APRIL 7, 2000)

*A*mong the liberal yakking classes, admiration for *Saving Private Ryan*, Steven Spielberg's graphic war movie in which a small group of soldiers crosses Normandy to rescue a single man, has been almost universal. The acclaim has crept out of the entertainment sections and onto the op-ed pages. What few demurrals exist have come from the right.

I've seen two pieces purporting to attack the film—Richard Grenier in *The Washington Times* and John Podhoretz in *The Weekly Standard*. There's also been an artistically dismissive review by John Simon in *The*

National Review. (Simon, affecting his usual voice of the Duke of Marlborough addressing a conclave of fish peddlers on the subject of the new carp tax, considers the violence of this war movie "gratuitous." What planet is this man from?)

Both Grenier and Podhoretz are somewhat baffled by military affairs—one thinks Tom Hanks's eight-man unit is a company (about 120 men) and the other a brigade (several thousand men!). It's a squad. But then neither piece is serious: Both are more ad hominem attacks than analysis. They simply don't like Spielberg. Given the politics of the writers, one can certainly see why. Spielberg, after all, is one of the most famous public liberals in the country.

When the president and the missus go money-grubbing in the Hamptons, it's at Spielberg's much-publicized ten-acre estate that they park themselves. In interviews, Spielberg presents himself as the high priest of liberal orthodoxy. Name a piety of political correctness, and he's its champion. Example: He, who owns a fleet of the finest European shotguns that lots of money can buy and has posed for the cover of *GunGames* magazine, is in favor of forbidding the citizenry (that is, those who can't afford the armed guards that lurk outside his hotel room and home) access to semiautomatic pistols. It seems not to have occurred to him that the day after my .45s are banned his Perazzis will be, too.

He claims that he wants women in combat arms. He's pro-choice, pro-feminist, pro-Clinton. You'd have to look hard to find a more orthodox liberal in captivity.

But that's the public Spielberg, the Hollywood Spielberg. At the artistic level, all this vanishes. Whether he's reflexively, unconsciously different when he creates and doesn't even recognize it, or whether he consciously divides himself into two people, a citizen and a filmmaker, or whether it's all done cynically, the fact remains: As a moviemaker, he's as conservative as John Wayne, and *Saving Private Ryan* is probably the most conservative film of the decade.

For one thing, it refuses to view the Second World War through the prism of Vietnam and turn it into a symbol of futility, command stupidity, immoral use of power, and the full exercise of evil by the state. Rather, it looks on the war as duty. The movie, in its broadest strokes, is an examination of character, which finds that duty, commitment to a higher cause, is the defining attribute of nobility. It's saying something quite different from the usual left-progressive cliché, which maintains that war is a hell so total it should be avoided whenever possible. *Saving Private Ryan* is saying that war is hell, but it can be a necessary hell and we should salute, respect, adore, and remember those who fought it in our name. It's about conservatism at its most absolute level: conserving the past, and respecting it.

The movie is, literally, about doing and dying, but not without knowing why. These guys know why, and that's the source of their strength. They've made a conscious decision to walk into the guns and to take up the mantle of killer and sacrifice some considerable portion of their humanity in order to destroy an enemy of the nation and the civilization. When the film evokes the flag, it does so without irony or sarcasm.

Central to the movie's politics is the issue of compassion and its opposite, force. Liberals love compassion, hate force; conservatives hate compassion, love force. Liberals spread compassion magnanimously all over the universe, conservatives hoard it dearly for their own kind, and sometimes won't spend it even then. Liberals want you to obey them because they feel your pain, have negotiated you to their position, and have enlightened you with their higher morality. Conservatives want you to obey them or they'll beat you up.

In *Saving Private Ryan*, compassion takes it in the face. In fact no less than twice does Spielberg produce anecdotes that might be considered parables on the dangers of promiscuous compassion. In one, an infantryman yields to his better instincts and attempts to save a French child from a combat zone. He is rewarded with a bullet in the diaphragm from a German sniper, and bleeds out pitifully in the mud. He's Christ in the rainy muck, crucified on a cross of compassion.

Force, on the other hand, is something the film extols: It reserves its one moment of uncharacteristic movie glamorization for the squad gun nut, a Southern Baptist who slithers into the downpour, shrewdly changes to his long-range scope, and puts a Springfield bullet through the enemy's optical tube, eye, brain, and skull. (By the way, this replicates a well-known anecdote from gun culture, a shot that the marine sniper Carlos Hatchock reportedly made on a North Vietnamese countersniper; it's almost a communication in a secret language that hundreds of thousands of conservative gun people will recognize.)

The second parable of compassion is even more pointed: The squad members capture a single German survivor, immediately in the aftermath of the death of one of their most beloved. They intend to execute him, as was occasionally done, if little talked about afterward. The German begs hysterically for mercy but there's precious little of that in the company of a dead, blood-soaked GI. Force seems to prevail. Until, that is, the new boy (Jeremy Davies as Corporal Upham), an intellectual who quotes Emerson and Wants to Write, argues loudly for the higher morality of life over death. His stridency—plus the captain's bone-deep weariness—carries the day, and the pathetic little German is permitted to wander away, blathering with fear.

Surprise of surprises, when next we see him, he's in the camouflage smock of the Waffen SS and is a tough, resilient, powerful soldier. He kills and kills and kills, finally snuffing the most precious of all lives the movie has evoked.*

In *Saving Private Ryan*, compassion is equated with catastrophe, with the softness that intensifies, rather than solves, problems. Force ends issues, settles them permanently and rightly. And this particular dramatic gambit also leads to another profoundly conservative and anti-liberal prejudice of the film: its mistrust of intellectuals, of the refined and morally superior.

Spielberg's Upham is a smart guy with a quote for everything who, when the chips are down, fails completely. So much for education, so much for a higher order of intelligence. While portraying Upham as a coward and worthless soldier—he can kill only when it's too late, and utterly meaningless except in some kind of prissy intellectual's way—Spielberg loves the inarticulate, the instinctive, the strong.

Much has been written about Hanks's portrayal of Captain Miller, a CO of great courage and an ideal American Everyman. But the movie is equally admiring of the character played by Tom Sizemore, Sergeant Horvath. Horvath is a tough working-class city kid with a slack face and the wit of a toilet seat. His eyes are devoid of feeling, as opposed to Upham's, which brim with indignation when they're not clouded with tears. Horvath is bereft of irony, has never had an original thought in his

---

*Wrong, wrong, wrong. The SS trooper is another guy. The captured German soldier shows up at the end, is the one who shoots Captain Miller (Tom Hanks), and is in turn murdered by Upham.

life, and is utterly inarticulate. And, of course, he's worth ten or a thousand Uphams, because he's loyal, incredibly brave and the absolute facilitator of the unit. He believes in hierarchy and obedience; he doesn't care how you feel or what's bothering you. He cares about getting the job done, and wars are won by him, although the novels and the movies that follow are written by the Uphams. (Upham's craven survival is a reminder of this truth.)

And that leads to a third conservative element in the film, which is its belief in the benevolence of authority. Much has been made, in the critical press, of the foolishness of the mission that Hanks and his Rangers are sent upon—to save Private Ryan, the sole surviving son of an Iowa widow—but it's clear that Spielberg doesn't mean this as an indictment of "the brass." He doesn't represent the mission as cynical, stupid, self-serving. The mission represents the decision of authority and the film's— and Spielberg's—motto might be: "Never question authority." And as the story plays out, indeed authority is right.

In the context of the film, authority is vested in the army chief of staff, the beloved George C. Marshall (Harve Presnell), who orders the mission out of profound moral commitment to the mothers of America. At several points in the film, these orders are questioned by squad members (notably, Edward Burns's acerbic automatic rifleman Reiben) and it's Hanks's character who delivers Spielberg's verdict: Those are the orders you follow the most loyally. He himself doesn't see the point; but because it's an order, it has to be done.

And it works out. If Hanks's Ranger unit hadn't shown up when it did, clearly the bridge would have fallen into German hands and the beach breakout—which is dramatized by the arrival of 29th Infantry troops at the movie's climax—would have been postponed for several hours, days, or even weeks. Hundreds, maybe thousands, more men would have died; the Thousand-Year Reich would have lasted twelve years and seven months, as opposed to twelve years and five months. Perhaps the Soviets would have gotten deeper into Europe, so far that NATO would never stand; with a Communist Germany, a Communist France would have followed; the Cold War would have been very different. But none of that happened, and it all stems from six tired and inarticulate men following an order they didn't agree with and ending up on a little bridge in a French town. That's what he's dramatizing—how the

West was won, how civilization was saved, and has been time and time again, by little squads of witless men at bridges who had nothing to offer but their lives: Ask the Persians at Thermopylae—they learned that lesson the hard way.

This is an idealization of a practical principle that remains forever cloudy to those who reflexively despise the military: In any war, all kinds of anecdotal evidence can be produced of command foul-ups, cynicism, self-aggrandizement, arrogance, all of it stupid. And you say: How pointless, how evil.

But Spielberg chose an opposite interpretation. His view of Captain Miller's mission could have led to doubt, revisionism, self-contempt, and the general feeling that we are no better than they, which is the heart of relativism. Instead it led to faith and respect for history and the men who made it in our name. He argues, without smugness and with great passion and precision, that, like courage, there was plenty of nobility to go around.   (AUGUST 9, 1998)

There are movies and then there are movies.
      And then there is Steven Spielberg's *Saving Private Ryan*.
   Searing, heartbreaking, so intense it turns your body into a single tube of clenched muscle, this is simply the greatest war movie ever made, and one of the great American movies. In one stroke, it makes everything that came before—with the exception of two or three obscure European variants on the same theme—seem dated and unwatchable. And it redefines the way we look at war.

Generically, it could be called the last example of that vanished category, the unit tribute film. But this unit is not the 2nd Ranger Battalion or the 101st Airborne. Rather, it is a generation: those men born in the late 1910s and early twenties, who, when asked, simply put aside their tools and settled the great issue of the century, determining who would administer the industrial revolution, dictatorship, or democracy. They did this without complaint, bitterness, anger, or remorse. Then they came home and picked up their tools again. To this day, few will talk about what they saw and did, and Spielberg shows us why.

In the first seconds you understand you are in a place different from any you've ever been in before, unless you survived the Normandy invasion. You're in a Higgins boat in the gray dawn of June 6, 1944, wet and cold and already exhausted, scudding through the sloppy surf, and all around you men are puking. The noise is astonishing. Your hands tremble; your breath comes in dry, hurtful spurts.

Then the landing gate falls and in the very first instant, zeroed German machine gun fire spits through the boat. At this moment you'll wish you were elsewhere, as did surely every man in the real thing. In Spielberg's terrifying version, the bullets seems somehow angry—they pierce the air, trailing a whine or a streak of neon illumination, and when they strike sand or steel, they kick up big, vicious geysers; and there are so many of them, and they come so fastfastfast. But when they strike flesh, they strike it with a thudding finality that reduces a man to maimed meat in a sixth of a second, and takes it all away from him, so that he falls forward obedient only to gravity. He dies like a sack of potatoes falling off a shelf.

Spielberg's ability to capture the palpable madness of all this borders on the incredible. The first twenty-five minutes of the film—a re-creation of Omaha Beach from the point of view of an all-too-human Ranger captain, who's been here and done this, but not at this level of violence—is surely one of the great tours de force of world cinema. From the spillage of viscera, the shearing of limbs, the gushing of blood, and the psychotic whimsy of the bullets, to a final kind of fog of panic and soul-deep fear, he makes you glad it was your daddy's job, and not yours.

But Spielberg also understands war's deepest reality, which is that being there is not enough, and being willing to die for your country is also not enough; you have to be willing to kill for your country. So much of the battle carnage pictured in *Saving Private Ryan* is based on the craft of close-quarter, small-unit combat: It's watching men maneuver across terrain for geometrical superiority, hunting for a position to vector fire in on the enemy. He who shoots from the best position and brings the most fire to bear, he's the winner. The thermodynamics of infantry combat: Shoot well, shoot fast, shoot often.

Where does this unprecedented version of war come from? It may come out of a few other movies, ironically all of them German. I think of *Die Brücke* (*The Bridge*), *The Winter War* (actually Finnish, about the short brutal Russo-Finnish war of 1940), or *Stalingrad* or even *Das*

Boot—all movies that portrayed unflinchingly the iron randomness of war. But more vividly, it has clearly been informed by a close study of as much archival footage of The Real Thing as can be had. In this sense, it's ersatz documentary, with desaturated forties color, jittery, terrified camera movement (you feel the cameraman's fear of getting hit) and the sensation of overwhelming chaos.

It's mean, terrifying, exhausting, and quipless. There's no spunk and very little humor. Morale is nonexistent. It's a grinding, debasing job carried out in physical misery in an environment—mud, rain, cold—that is itself an enemy. It's Bill Mauldin's Willie and Joe without the punch lines, but with a lot of dead GIs and a crushing melancholy hanging over everything like smoke.

But this will become evident only in time. Initially, we are in such a fog from the intensity of the invasion sequence that fatigue is the only response: A few survivors eat K-rations and try to decompress from the pressurized brutality they've both suffered and dealt. Word comes: a mission.

Here the movie broadens somewhat, for just a moment: Two Ryan brothers have died in the invasion and a third has just perished in New Guinea. Mrs. Ryan, of Every Farm, U.S.A., will get three letters on the same day. But it seems there's a fourth Ryan, James (Matt Damon), the youngest, somewhere with the advance units of the 101st Airborne in the small French towns that cover the approach to the beaches. No less a personage than George C. Marshall himself, the chief of staff (played by Harve Presnell with a less kitschy quality than might be expected), orders that a unit be sent out to pluck this boy from battle and return him to the farm. It's typical of Spielberg that this position is not treated glibly, as another bit of idiocy by "the brass." In a spirit of decency and in accordance with what seems to be his career-long recognition of benevolent authority, he makes us see on what basis Marshall makes his decision, and that, no matter how it plays out, it represents the best of the American spirit, not the worst.

Eight men—that heroic captain, John Miller (Tom Hanks in another of his quietly brilliant Everyman roles), a sergeant (Tom Sizemore), a Browning Automatic Rifleman (Edward Burns), a sniper (Barry Pepper), a medic (Giovanni Ribisi), two riflemen (Vin Diesel and Adam Goldberg), and an interpreter (Jeremy Davies)—are charged to cross the dangerous ground between the beachhead and the town, locate Private Ryan and bring him back alive. Or bring back his dog tags.

As pure story, the movie has a swiftness to it that goes far beyond the sheer fidelity of the battle sequences. The narrative has been expertly configured; it moves us through a variety of experiences—squad assault, town battle, sniper duel, a final stand against armored units—while at the same time keeping precise track of the overall story situation. Simultaneously, the personalities of the men are expressing themselves, in small ways. Even Damon's Ryan, who could be the font of sentimentality, turns out to be just another kid, low-key and quietly, furiously decent. (Damon, like all the actors, is excellent in this lesser role.) But it's no flashback-o-rama, in the fashion of *The Naked and the Dead*, where each man's life is summed up in a banal recollection. Rather—this is a point Spielberg makes over and over—these men have essentially given up on their civilian personalities—with the exception of the unit intellectual, the interpreter played by Davies—for the duration. They know the drill. They know what to do. They can hold it together. They've become, in Stephen Ambrose's wonderful term, complete Citizen Soldiers.

In this way, the film approaches its true subject, which isn't heroism, but duty, which is to say, repression. It's about men who make a conscious decision that the self does not matter; the personality is irrelevant; feelings are dangerous. Thus they become what they must, to survive, to kill and to win: sealed-off beings locked away, hoarding their emotions, giving vent only to rage. They let nothing hang out because hanging out can get you killed. And Spielberg dramatizes this point twice, explicitly, in episodes where two soldiers yield to compassion. In this cruelest of worlds, the result is catastrophe. This movie is about a generation that put its heart on the shelf, dialed its minds down into a small, cold tunnel, and fought with its brains.

All the way through you can feel Spielberg flirting with cliché, almost daring us to recognize it and then at the last moment pulling it away from us and leaving us open-mouthed. But the biggest cliché that the movie assaults is the very conceit upon which war movies have been eternally built: It is the idea that somehow, combat is cool. There's always been an athletic grace to battle as the movies have portrayed it, a kind of photogenic sportiness. Even in the most violent of battle sequences, a little boy in you thought, "Hey, that's kinda neat." You know, dropping grenades on the German high command trapped underground in *The Dirty Dozen* or spray-painting Nazis red with your Thompson in *The Longest Day*. And there was that Hollywood thing where the hero ran through blizzards of fire and somehow was never touched, because, after all, he was the hero.

That's all gone here. Not merely because of its gore but far more because of its cruelty, the war here will inspire no enlistees and no one will relive it in private later. It's flat-out terrifying, and the emotion it finally produces in you is more than any other film has gotten, but about one-thousandth of what the infantrymen of 1944 must have felt after one day on the line: utter exhaustion. You feel bled out, and at least emotionally, you have been.

So in the end, this one is for the boys of Pointe-du-Hoc, and also the boys of Utah and Omaha, Salerno, Monte Cassino, Iwo, the boys who took the long walk ashore at Tarawa through the Japanese fire, the boys whose last moments were spent in a flaming Fortress over Schweinfurt, or whatever, wherever, between the years 1941 and 1945. Take a bow, little guy, it says to them.

And to us, their inheritors, it says: Hey, look what your daddies did, what they went through, what they survived or didn't survive—and be proud. And it also asks us the hardest of all questions: Are we worthy of them?   (JULY 24, 1998)

*D*espite reports to the contrary, Terrence Malick's *The Thin Red Line* isn't set on Guadalcanal in 1942. It's set instead in some strange internalized zone between now and Zen.

Infernally contemplative and self-absorbed, it's only briefly a war movie in any conventional sense. It is far more a philosophical inquiry into the nature of . . . well, everything. And the nature of everything turns out to be opaque and poetic, rich in questions and impoverished in answers. Where does this evil come from, a man wonders. Why is love so perishable, another asks the sky. Would a giant find you if you hid, asks still a third (a joke, but just barely).

The movie loves birds and flowers and beauty and lean young men who look too much alike and too much like Montgomery Clift. Most of these young men are either taken up in the business of killing or the business of posing dramatically against an empurpled sunset while muttering precious little insights that come closer to Jack Handey's *Deep Thoughts* than to Rimbaud. Malick, a famous maverick in film culture who with this movie ends a self-imposed twenty-year exile (*Days of Heaven*, 1978, was his last, following on his only other film, *Badlands*, 1973), never met a story he could tell, an idea he could resist, or a sunset he could ignore.

The result is a big, fat, gorgeous, mesmerizing mess, in a variety of tones and colors with a variety of obscure goals and moments of high kitsch. It plays like a brain-damaged combination of Eugene O'Neill's wacky *Strange Interlude* and Phil Karlson's gritty Okinawa war story *Hell to Eternity*. Then there's a weird strain that could only be called *The Longest Day: Part 2*.

Derived (just barely) from James Jones's great but crude portrait of an infantry company in combat on Guadalcanal, the film isn't quite brave enough to depart from the platoon-as-microcosm structure that undergirds so many war pictures, while at the same time its penetration of deeper issues seems jejune. A lot of it is just artsy photography; it's like looking at postcards with an eyeful of Murine.

As I say, frequently the overall inspiration of the film seems not at all to be Jones but rather O'Neill's *Strange Interlude*, where the action stopped onstage while the characters delivered long monologues describing their inner thoughts. This happens in *The Thin Red Line* all the time, but not nearly as intelligently.

It's extremely difficult to tell the monologuists apart because they all speak the same generic, prettified ersatz poetry in the same generic, prettified ersatz Southern accent. Did it not occur to the great auteur Malick to give them different voices and different perspectives, and by that way to track the changes in (fewer) characters over the ordeal of the campaign? But worse, the film simply dies during these moody, passive passages, turning into nothing more than guns and poses and bad poetry.

There's a small, good movie lost in the middle of all this; it runs about an hour and it's certainly worth seeing. This involves C-for-Charlie's adventures taking a grassy knoll called Hill 210 at the top of which is not a lone gunman, but hundreds of them, in the khaki of the Japanese army.

Cleverly, Malick does not show us the enemy for the longest time: instead, they are represented merely by their effects—streaks of tracer spurting off the ridge line, the random squall of mortar rounds incoming, the relentless body-piercings of the machine guns.

The episode offers *The Thin Red Line* what little narrative spine it has, and it allows a few members of a too-huge cast to define themselves through action, not passive soliloquy. Most important, it constructs a story to illustrate the essential dilemma of warfare in any age, which is the calculus by which commanders figure the worth of an objective vs. the lives of their men.

The battalion commander, a lieutenant colonel named Tall (played with apoplectic intensity by Nick Nolte, spewing spit with each utterance), wants to move inland, but between him and his goal there lurks the lovely Hill 210. Alas, because of flanking cliffs and impenetrable jungle, it can only be assaulted frontally. It falls to Captain Staros's Charlie Company to make that attack. Staros (Elias Koteas) has bonded so tightly with his men that he cannot bear to send them into machine gun fire. To make it more interesting, Tall is a martinet, a blowhard and, damn his soul, right; Staros is a sweetheart, a truly wonderful human being and, bless his heart, wrong. The men, feeling this disunity in goal, perform poorly and are chopped up in the high grass.

The next day, Tall sends his protégé, Capt. Gaff (John Cusack), to lead a smaller, less wasteful attack. Using stealth, more automatic weapons, and sheer grit, they get up close and get the job done in a withering blast of firepower and grenades. The key question—was it worth it?—goes unanswered, as it always must. Then Tall replaces Staros, who seems relieved, and we're left to wonder if he did so out of compassion or ruthlessness. It's a brilliant chunk of narrative filmmaking in the middle of an ocean of self-indulgence. It's also a salute to Jones, who among all American novelists of his generation seemed to understand the dynamics of the army best of all.

But at that point, the movie is over. Unfortunately nobody told the director: It runs another hour and a half.

Stealing a technique from the highest kitsch item of World War II, Darryl Zanuck's stupefying *The Longest Day*, this film inserts celebs in ridiculous cameos. One hopes there's a longer director's cut somewhere that would justify the famous faces, but in this iteration, some of the appearances just seem pointless. John Travolta, in a Smilin' Jack mustache and a hat that's too small, seems preposterous as a general in his one scene. Cusack barely registers. Why is John C. Reilly in this movie if he has only one line of dialogue? Adrien Brody, ballyhooed in national magazines, has even less. They ain't doughboys, they're duh-boys. Then Woody Harrelson and George Clooney appear in meaninglessly brief vignettes, one as a sergeant who literally pulls the grenade and throws the pin (ouch!), the other who drops by to give a Zig Ziglar motivational talk at the end. Travolta, at least, has the good sense to disappear early.

The main character is really the company itself, but two or three actors manage to connect. Jim Caviezel plays a GI named Witt, a stubborn, mule-proud Kentuckian who will make many recall the character Prewitt in Jones's earlier novel *From Here to Eternity*; Malick himself seems to get this, for Caviezel greatly resembles Montgomery Clift, who played Prewitt in the movie. Ben Chaplin does a nice turn on the love-struck GI whose "Dear John" letter is just waiting to happen. Sean Penn plays the company's first sergeant—it's a continuation of Burt Lancaster's first sergeant in *From Here to Eternity*—but it's curiously muted and undynamic. But far too many of the actors simply merge into a geek chorus, buried under tin pots and two-day beards.

It's pointless to compare or contrast *The Thin Red Line* with Steven Spielberg's *Saving Private Ryan*, because their intentions are so vastly different. With *Ryan*, a kind of generational tribute, Spielberg's ambition was to commemorate the men who won the war. Malick's seems to be to photograph as many parrots as possible. Polly want a movie?

(JANUARY 8, 1999)

Tears of the Sun offers one of the greatest never-happened-but-should-have moments in movie history. An African death squad is in the process of destroying a village for the crime of belonging to the wrong tribe. They are shooting the men, raping and mutilating the women, and getting rid of the kids any way that's convenient. They're laughing, they're drunk, they're having the time of their lives. But then they run into one very teed-off U.S. Navy SEAL team.

The pleasure of that moment is profound if subversive: Even you highly evolved, postnational pacifists out there will probably enjoy the spectacle of highly trained American commandos with suppressed weapons moving through the glades and lanes with the grace and purpose of athletes and—pffft! pffft! pffft!—serving up justice in 9mm portions, hot and steamy.

But the movie has other pleasures, less subversive but just as profound. One of them is the glee it takes in expertise, special operations variety, as it chronicles this tough, laconic crew's odyssey across a fictitious Nigerian civil war. The film is a strictly no-bull proposition: Bruce Willis, who never met a quip he didn't like, has been enjoined to keep his yap shut and play his team leader's role with wary grace and almost pure silence. I don't think he cracks wise even once. He just looks, as soldiers do and are, really tired most of the time. He doesn't even kiss the girl, and since the girl is Monica Bellucci, that gives you some idea of his discipline!

The technical adviser behind *Tears of the Sun* is Harry Humphries, who spent sixteen years as a SEAL, including time in Vietnam. He would seem to know what he is talking about. He has given the movie a quiet, confident, almost documentary feel, as well as getting so many of the little things right—the proper guns, for example, and the SEAL penchant, unique in the service, for going into battle with scarves wrapped tightly around the head. There's no speechifying, and when the guys go to the radio, the militarese they spout has the terse poetics of the actual stuff. (Humphries was also the military adviser on *Black Hawk Down*, where he achieved a similar sense of verisimilitude.)

The story might be called classic or trite, take your choice. It has been used as recently as 1999's *Three Kings*, set during the Gulf War, and at least as far back as *The Magnificent Seven* (1960), which I suppose in turn tracks to *The Seven Samurai* (1954). All of these plots turn on the honor of professional soldiers of the highest alpha-classification when they are faced with something that is not in their own best interest but clearly moral in meaning. Do they stay and fight, or do they run? Well, we all know that if they run, there's not much of a movie, right?

In this brilliant variation from director Antoine Fuqua, a SEAL team is sent to the interior of Nigeria to rescue an American missionary doctor (Bellucci, whose citizenship by marriage explains her Italian accent). Her jungle hospital lies in the way of a rebel army column. When the commandos get there, she refuses to leave without "her people." It's part of the romanticism of the piece that the team commander, El Tee Waters ("El Tee" being military speak for Lieutenant, i.e., Lt.) tries to swindle her into going, then kidnaps her, but finally has a change of heart—knowing that those he leaves behind will become bayonet dummies for the pursuing soldiers—and waves off the air evacuation. With his team and the seventy refugees, they go for a little walk in the warm African sun.

Bellucci's presence in the center of a holocaust seems quite unlikely. Would the SEALs have stayed behind if the doctor were played by, say, Linda Hunt? Maybe not, whereas just about anybody would have stayed for Monica. But then Fuqua never plays up her beauty, and she's one of those performers with what might be called life force: You feel her belief in her cause, which is the mainspring of the plot. Equally, you admire her for willing to get with the gunky work of action pix, which is to get grimy, sweaty, bloody, and have a mother of a bad hair day.

The movie wisely never gives us too much: Each commando has a face, a personality, a set of quirks, but no backstory. Not even Waters is grounded in a past: He's just a bullet-headed war hound interested in mission and little else. The guys are wonderful but never campy, and Fuqua—a great director of actors, who helped Denzel Washington win his Oscar in *Training Day*—makes them more than men with dirty faces and identical kits; he never stereotypes them along comic *Dirty Dozen* lines. These seem like the real deal, especially Atkins (Cole Hauser) as the team medic.

Fuqua also recognizes the weird beauty of soldiers. Whether this is homoerotic or just erotic, I am not sure, but it's something artists have responded to for thousands of years (look at the Greek hoplite statues if you doubt me). This film offers up a good portfolio of what might be called commando calendar art: It's full of dirty, haggard men in sweaty camouflage battle dress, festooned with ammo belts and tattoos, laboring under a load of automatic weapons that would break a donkey's back, who look simply gorgeous.

The politics—both of the movie and of the moment—are interesting. I infer that Fuqua, who is black, brings such passion and precision to the project because he's furious that the United States did nothing during the genocide in Rwanda, very like the genocide portrayed here. This movie seems to have a fever-dream quality to it, as if he wants desperately to rewrite what happened then, to substitute a scenario in which SEALs, backed by F-16s, came to the rescue of hundreds, if not thousands.

But *Tears of the Sun* launches at the height of another crisis, with Rwanda long forgotten. It seems to be an endorsement of the American right of intervention, just when most of Hollywood, led by commandos like George Clooney and Janeane Garofalo, is in the opposition. When the film ends with Burke's famous line "All that is necessary for the triumph of evil is that good men do nothing," one wonders who is listening.

(MARCH 7, 2003)

*H*ere's a not-so-divine secret of the ya-ya brotherhood: We boys like war movies.

We like it when stuff gets blown up, enemies get mowed down by heroes with tommy guns, and at the end, that's our flag flying up there. I don't know, it's just so . . . cool. So sue us.

And here's the warriest of all war movies to come along since *Saving Private Ryan,* called *Windtalkers,* John Woo's story of the not-famous-enough Navajo combat encoders. It's like one of those big fifties jobs with huge battle scenes, emotions painted in bold primaries (love! loyalty! sadness!), a core of truth and heroism, and a kind of technicolor grandeur.

So why don't we like it so much?

The answer is that despite a cast of thousands, a budget estimated at $118 million, and a re-creation of the Pacific battles that rivals any before, the movie's stylizations—for which, of course, Woo is justly famous and without which he could not or would not have made the film—seem singularly wrong.

I am always amazed at actual combat footage: The soldiers appear so informal and undramatic. They never seem to be in any heroic poses; their minds, if you can infer from their body postures, are concerned with very small things, like "Let's get over there" or "Let's get down" or "Gosh, I wish I wasn't here." They are beyond rhetoric or exhortation. They look sad and weary, not charged with blood lust. They look like the homeless, and in a sense they are, for who ever would be at home on a battlefield?

That's not how Woo sees war. For him it's almost an opera, declamatory and dramatic, and the body language has more to do with dance than actuality. It's highly theatricalized and to a certain extent martial-articized. Of course he's developing his war not from any actual experience but from the aesthetic he devised for the Hong Kong gangster movies like *The Killer* or *Hard-Boiled,* which combined the grace of martial arts with semi-automatic pistols.

It worked better there—where it could be intimate and acrobatic—than here, where it is blown out beyond all scale. The postures, the grace of the marines, the musical crescendo of the editing, all this distances us from the horror of the actual and the horror of our feelings. When Nicolas Cage's tough sarge Joe Enders drops a satchel charge in a pillbox, is scampering away when it goes off, and is picked up (digitally) from the radiant heart of the blast and hurled at the camera, eyes wide, arms swimming against the concussion, you think: How did they do that? The image has more to do with images than with war. John Wayne blew a pillbox in *The Fighting Seabees*, and the black-and-white photography and sense of an actual man rolling through the dust kicked up by the machine guns seemed truer, at least in its connection to documentary film.

As for the brutality and heroism of the marine war in the Pacific, I still much prefer Phil Karlson's 1960 *Hell to Eternity*, a forgotten classic. In *Windtalkers*, which makes many of the same points that Karlson's movie does, though much more flamboyantly, race is the subtext. *Windtalkers* is obsessed, in the center of a war between two races, with finding out how different—and how similar—we are and if men of different races can love one another. The vessel for this investigation is Cage's Marine Sergeant Enders, who just barely survived the fighting on Guadalcanal. Now, a year later, he is recovered and, perhaps driven by survivor's remorse, pines to get back into action and face again the enemy that wiped out his squad. (One thing: Too many times in the film is Cage an "only survivor.")

He's assigned to an intelligence and communications platoon. His job is to babysit one Private Ben Yahzee, a handsome, even peppy (and almost preppy) Navajo code talker whose language is impenetrable to the Japanese. What Joe knows that his charge doesn't is that he has been ordered to protect the integrity of the code, not the integrity of the private. In other words, he cannot allow Ben to be taken alive; his job may become Killing Private Yahzee.

Many think such a policy existed. And those who might suspect that the world was too naïve in 1944 to give such a cynical order should recall that in 1946's *13 Rue Madeleine* U.S. fliers are ordered to bomb a Gestapo headquarters because an American (Jimmy Cagney, terrific) who knows the invasion date has been captured. The difference is that Cagney laughs as the bombs that will kill him begin to land, because he knows he's won and it is, after all, a war in which people do die; Adam Beach's Private Yahzee, who also figures it out, gives no such evidence of getting with the program.

The film, after evoking briefly Enders's nasty experiences on Guadalcanal and Yahzee's recruitment and training, unites the two men uneasily and follows them across the bloody battle of Saipan, June 15 to July 8, 1944. What ensues is equal part savagery and sentimentality. Of the first, there is no doubt that in his stylized way, Woo is a master.

In four major battle scenes, the camera dances and swoops, and watches hundreds of men, like dance troops, move against each other and mingle. The movie is bloody but weirdly beautiful, sometimes along what seems like naively stereotypical lines. Everyone knows Indians are knife fighters, right? So when the Japanese close in on Yahzee or his close friend Charlie Whitehorse, each private pulls an Indian knife—the deer foot as grip, available in the Wisconsin Dells or on the Internet for only $12.95— from his buckskin boot sheath and dances with blades, as they whirl and dodge and slice and spin. I cannot say the primitive kid who will not leave my head didn't like this stuff; at the same time I cannot say the occasional grown-up who occupies the same space believed it for a second.

When these gyrenes aren't fighting, they're loving it up, guy-style (nothing, er, suspicious going on here, no, sir! These are United States Marines, for God's sake!). The movie is set up to contrast the love-hate between two white-Navajo couples. Cage and Beach have a stormy time because the knowledge of his mission occludes Joe's mind, as well as the pain of his former combat experiences and his hunger to kill Japanese. He cannot open up to the youngster. (Wayne had the same problem in *Sands of Iwo Jima*.) But a sunnier time is had between Ox Henderson (Christian Slater) and Whitehorse (Roger Willie) when Henderson just realizes he isn't going to kill his pard even if the Japanese take him, and that's that. With impossible crudity, Woo gives us a scene so bloated with gaggy symbolism it boggles the mind: The two literally play beautiful music together!

At least as it concentrates on Cage's Joe and Beach's Ben, the movie tracks the old liberal feel-good things so familiar from the original *Lethal Weapon*, back through *Cry Freedom* and all the way to *The Defiant Ones*. It is the obligation of the "other" of color to rescue the twisted white man from his own nihilism and inner torment. The weird thing is that Beach's Yahzee accomplishes this not with love but with hate. Embittered after realizing the true nature of Enders's assignment (he had truly respected and adored the sergeant), he becomes a killing machine without mercy and without fear. It's as if his death wish is now bigger than Joe's, and that's what draws Joe back from the edge.

The performances are adequate though utterly without subtlety. Cage and Beach manage what little is demanded of them, the first to go from nihilism to love, the second to go from love to nihilism. Slater is irrepressible as always and seems too contemporary, even to his haircut; he's more 90210 than 1944. Then weird touches of reality mingle with complete absurdity. For example, in the Guadalcanal sequences, the men have the appropriate 16-inch-long bayonets of late 1942 issue; someone actually bothered to consult the records and bring that to the film. But at the same time, this appears to be a Marine Corps without officers—only two appear, inconsequentially—and even the intelligence and communication platoon is commanded, ludicrously, by a Swedish sergeant-major (Peter Stormare) who gives all the rousing speeches usually uttered by the new lieutenant.

In all, *Windtalkers* feels slightly off-key, out of focus. Its style keeps getting in the way of the action and the emotion. Woo hasn't caught on that it's World War I where they went over the top.

(JUNE 14, 2002)

Four

COSTUMES!

*I*t may be worth nine bucks to see the great young British actress Keira Knightley as a kill-crazed, blood-drenched pagan Tinker Bell, a pixie sprite with a battle ax chopping and hewing left and right. She bends it like Beckham with several pounds of cold steel and you think: Hmmm, that's a young lady with spunk!

But if Knightley's warrior Guinevere is absolutely the best thing in *King Arthur*, it's not the only delight. The film boasts all the hallmarks of the fifties historic epic save the presence of Tony Curtis: battles galore, tons of rolling mist standing for the vapors of myth, cool castles, gross Germanic villains, nobility, sacrifice, mud, sweat, tears, and death, with less gore than one might expect, as the movie has been engineered to a PG-13 rating.

And the film has a gimmick. This isn't your father's Knights of the Round Table song resung for the umpteenth time but a whole new tack into the material. The conceit is to locate the authentic Arthur, not the Lerner-Loewe Welshman yakkety-yakking *Camelot* to Julie Andrews amid the sunlight of a suspiciously over-illuminated Dark Ages. No Lancelot-Arthur-Guin triangle, no sword in stone, no Merlin the Magician, no Mordred the bad boy.

Instead the production is located in the 500s, when a crumbling, shrinking Roman Empire is retreating from its farthest flung outposts, leaving chaos and carnage in its wake. One of the farthest flung of those outposts is Hadrian's Wall, separating Roman Britannia from pagan Britannia. There, a noble Romano-Brit officer named Arthur (Clive Owen, kingly and powerful) attempts to deal with the coming madness, made all the more threatening by the approach of yet a third antagonist, the forces of Saxony, blond, brutish invaders from Germany who threaten to overcome the island and turn it, er, Anglo-Saxon.

So one point the movie makes almost incidentally is that nobody comes from where they are, and that everybody comes from somewhere else. Many of us are slavish admirers of what's called Anglo-Saxon culture as if it were the indigenous culture of Britain and the West, but it wasn't. The Saxons were just another, earlier wave of invaders, and like all invaders their weapons were terror and rape. Stellan Skarsgård, playing the Saxon king Cerdic, looks like Yosemite Sam with a serious case of constipation.

Anyhow, in the fight to repel the invaders, Arthur has his knights. But Lancelot, Gawain, Tristan, and so forth are not fair-haired Etonians in search of Christian purity. They are Sarmatians—that is, Central European mercenaries who have been compelled by the Romans to put in fifteen years' service. Their enlistment is about up, and a return to the steppes is haunting their imaginations, as is the pleasure of at last giving up the perpetual state of war in Britannia in which they've lived. In the language of today's army, they're short.

In other words, the movie offers what might be called the Arthurian Urtext: a vision of the original reality, now long-forgot and all but irrecoverable, that was later gilded by more romantic tellers from other times and traditions, until it became so glamorized it had lost all contact with the harsh brutality of the real.

That's the theory. In practice, *King Arthur* basically encompasses two stories, somewhat awkwardly conjoined. The first is of a rescue mission that Arthur and his knights must partake, even though all have been promised release from obligation, to rescue a Roman nobleman living beyond Hadrian's Wall and thought to be in danger. As always, politics intrudes. The big shots in Rome don't care about this fellow but about his son, a favorite of the pope (who at this time is more powerful than the emperor). This initial story almost feels like a reprise of director Antoine Fuqua's last film, the underrated *Tears of the Sun*, in which a U.S. Navy SEAL team was inserted into a civil war (in Africa) to extract a vulnerable citizen. In *King Arthur*, the knights are the SEALs of A.D. 550, elite warriors with highly refined combat skills. It's on that mission that they encounter the teenage Guinevere, who has been captured by the Roman nobleman. She's the daughter, it turns out, of the tribal leader Merlin, a longtime antagonist of Arthur.

But he sees that the pagans—they're called Woads here—and the Romans can make common cause against the encroaching Saxons. And indeed, it is thought that the one true Arthur did such a thing: He unified Roman and Celtic troops and faced the Saxons 12 times, finally at the Battle of Badon Hill, where he turned them back and won for "civilized" Britain a forty-year respite, which might be seen as the antecedent of the storied peace and justice of Camelot, however brief it was.

In any event, as Fuqua tells the tale, the second half of the film is much stronger. Arthur must put away his blood enmity with the Woads and form an alliance with them to fight the Saxons, even as the perfidious Romans (personified by a smarmy bishop) are fleeing for their lives.

As he has proved many a time, Fuqua is a superb action director, and he always finds an unseen spectacle around which to build his big action set pieces. One recalls the famous Battle on the Ice of Sergei Eisenstein's *Alexander Nevsky* as the knights—plus Guinevere, a gifted archer—face a mass of Teutons charging across a frozen river. I'm as sick of computer imagery as you are, but the legerdemain by which the ice cracks and sends the proto-Nazis to a cold, watery grave is masterful. The final fight pitches the fire and strength of the combined Arthurian-Woad alliance against the Germanic throngs. It's beautifully filmed as the skies fill with fire arrows, like SAMs rising against our jets over Baghdad in the recent fracas, and the forces close and clash, and the delicate Knightley goes all samurai on her opponents, while atop their horses the surviving knights function like M-1 tanks raking through the battlefield.

You might fault the eternal cliché by which, in the middle of thousands of fighters, the two kings locate each other and settle their differences steel on steel, as the minions around them cooperate by clearing a nice little free space. On the other hand, you might as well just sit back and enjoy the fight.

Fuqua has a real weakness for calendar art compositions, and I would argue that this was kitsch, except that I have the same loathsome weakness. So a lot of *King Arthur* is a kind of macho battle porn of posture, weapon, and uniform: The knights are forever rearing up their steeds before charging, pennants flapping behind them, long swords drawn and glistening, armor alight with the illumination of the battle fires, all this in rapturous slo-mo, all of it framed and romanticized even further by the ghostly layers of mist floating everywhere. If this is the sort of thing you like, you're really going to like it here.

I wish the film were technically—oh, what's the word?—"better." We don't really get much sense of personality beyond archetype, and for a movie that pretends to a high realism, it's still plenty jammed up with macho bluster and romanticism. Guinevere and Arthur? Well, not a love story for the ages, as they're both so busy slashing and bashing they don't have much time to relate. Knightley is probably too good an actress for this sort of thing, though she makes a great battle faerie. Ioan Gruffudd, who plays Lancelot, the smartest and most loyal of the knights but also the most conflicted, really doesn't feature in the workings of the story. He's just there, and more attention goes to the sexy beast Ray Winstone as someone named Bors, more man-mountain than cavalry trooper, who gets most of the best lines.   (JULY 7, 2004)

*I*f you played a word-association game with *Alexander the Great*, you'd probably come up with "conqueror," "king," "warrior," "legend," "despot," "wastrel," or "killer." Unfortunately, Oliver Stone has chosen to build his epic of the Macedonian military genius around a word highly unlikely to make the list: "crybaby."

In Stone's view, this is a highly neurotic young man whose emotions, far from being repressed or disciplined as one would expect of a great soldier of the fourth century B.C., are worn on his sleeve, except, of course, that he doesn't have sleeves, the shirt still being two millennia down the road. So he wears them on his wrist—and it's a limp one.

That's the weirdest aspect of the extremely weird, if absurdly expensive, movie. Stone gives himself much credit of "telling the truth" about Alexander's bisexuality as if it's some progressive badge of honor, but at the same time he can't get away from the cruelest, least imaginative stereotyping: His Alexander, as expressed through the weepy histrionics of Colin Farrell, is more like a desperate housewife than a soldier. He's always crying, his voice trembles, his eyes fill with tears. He's much less interesting, except as a basket case, than Richard Burton's Alexander of far less enlightened times—1956—in Robert Rossen's *Alexander the*

Great. Burton got Alexander's dissipation, but also his martial spirit; this was, after all, one of the great light-cavalry commanders of all time and a general who fought by leading his troops, sword in hand, not directing them from some safe hill. But in this one you think: Teri Hatcher could kick this twerp's butt.

In many ways the movie feels fifty years old already. It offers the standard 1950s melodramatic theory of Alexander's sexual orientation: the scheming, sexualized, domineering mother, and the distant, uncaring father. So much for today's theories of genetic predetermination. Yet at the same time, it fails to account for what was remarkable about Alexander, rather than what was not.

His bisexuality, after all, is fairly commonplace in the world of this movie, while his will to conquer, and his skill in actually bringing it off, are not. But we never see what drives him. He never projects much in the way of ambition or vision; his fixation is always emotional, and the occasional attempts to match his motives to his accomplishments don't resonate. Equally, we never sense his animal magnetism—Farrell showed more on Letterman on Monday night than he does in three hours of world conquest—or his leader's charisma. He seems to motivate by pouting or holding his breath.

The movie lacks any convincing ideas about Alexander. Stone advances but one, the notion that Alexander was an early multiculturalist, who wanted to "unify" the globe. He seems not to recognize this as a standard agitprop of the totalitarian mind-set, always repulsive, but more so here in a movie that glosses over the boy-king's frequent massacres. Conquerors always want "unity," Stalin a unity of Russia without kulaks, Hitler a Europe without Jews, Mao a China without deviationists and wreckers. All of these boys loved to wax lyrical about unity while they were breaking human eggs in the millions, and so it was with Alexander, who wanted world unity without Persians, Egyptians, Sumerians, Turks, and Indians.

It has the same biopic failings as any MGM product of the mid-thirties, in that it rushes from high point to high point, it synopsizes (he fought dozens of battles; it dramatizes only two) and it whitewashes truth (Alexander's ruinous retreat from India gets about four seconds). The mechanism of the plot is trite: Ptolemy, one of A-team's leading generals, now grown august and stentorian as only Anthony Hopkins can project august stentorianism, recalls the days of Alex as he dictates his memoirs. Yak yak yak, blah blah blah. Hopkins's Ptolemy is a wordy old geezer, and his prose style, as crafted by Stone himself and co-writers Christopher Kyle and Laeta Kalogridis, has that kind of purple glaze Hollywood has always used to signify "in olden times." Other trite old-timey signifiers include too much Maybelline eyeliner (and I'm talking about the guys!), too many subtitles in a font that might be called Greco-Roman 36-point Bodoni, with V's for U's, and thunderous bad battle music that seems to have been composed only for trumpet and trombone.

As a director of performance, Stone is hopeless. For one thing, Farrell so overacts with the wah-wah-wahs gushing that none of the other young Greek and Macedonian generals makes an impression. Since all these young men are stunningly handsome, in shaggy hair and cool clothes, it's sort of like hanging out with a rock band. Musicians, however, don't have to have personalities, while characters do.

Alexander's great love was said to be Hephaistion, who is played in the film by Jared Leto, but unless you know Jared Leto by face, even late in the movie you'll have no idea which one he was. I thought he was this other guy, equally handsome, equally vapid, equally unmemorable, whom Alexander prongs with a spear in a drunken rage late in the movie. But that was some other guy.

Then comes the moment when we Meet the Parents. Brother, talk about Christmas with the cranks! Dad—the Macedonian king Philip, from whom Alexander inherited the tiny empire he was to build into a gigantic one—is played by Val Kilmer in hearty barbarian mode. He seems to have wandered in from a remake of *The Vikings*, shooting in the next Moroccan village down the coastline. Loved the one-eyed thing, which appears to be a Stone fetish. The movie is full to brimming with one-eyed men, which demonstrates two things: The Greek battle helmets had eye slots, and there was extra money in the makeup budget for putty. Then there's Angelina Jolie as Mom. Really, words fail me here. But let's try: Give this young woman the hands-down award for best impression of Bela Lugosi while hampered by a 38-inch bustline. Though everyone else in the picture speaks in some variation of a British accent, poor Jolie has been given the Transylvanian throat-sucker's throaty, sibilant vowels, as well as a wardrobe of snakes. She represents the spirit of kitsch that fills the movie, and with all her crazed posturing and slinking, it's more of a silent movie performance than one from the sound era. Theda Bara, call your agent.

And finally, the battles. Hollywood should realize that these big tiff things aren't nearly as impressive as they once were, particularly in the aftermath of three years of Iron Age combat apotheosized in the great *Lord of the Rings* pictures; when you've seen Orcs and hobbits fighting for the future of the world, it's a little hard to get excited about Persians and Greeks fighting over someone's imperial hubris 2,300 years ago. To be fair, the film does a pretty good job of explaining and dramatizing the tactics of Gaugamela (thought to be near Mosul, Iraq, today), where the clever Alexander, with 40,000 men, outthought and outfought Darius III's 200,000, including a daring cavalry strike (which Alexander himself led) that drove Darius from the field.

But there's nothing singular here. When you see what the Chinese are doing with action (in the upcoming *House of Flying Daggers*) and even what younger and more inventive American directors are doing, these fights seem very much a part of the rest of the movie. It's the same-old, same-old of charging into battle from half a century ago.

Even amplified by CGI, which can multiply a thousand extras into 40,000, nothing in the war-making feels unique. We don't learn anything new about this kind of fighting, and the imagery—bigger in scale but not bigger in vision from the past—feels stale. The one fresh image, that of Alexander on horseback rearing at an enemy pasha on elephantback, has been diluted of its power by overexposure on television ads. Like every other second of more than 10,000 seconds in *Alexander*, it doesn't engage in the least.   (NOVEMBER 24, 2004)

*A*fter all these years, it's still the same old story:
    Iceberg 1.
Titanic 0.

But at least James Cameron's retelling of the haunting catastrophe of April 14 and 15, 1912, has the grace and decency to sound a few new notes even as it derives much of its power from that old mainstay: bad things happening to other people. It's rich with the secret pleasure of watching a small, posh floating city turn into a gigantic iron coffin and slide headfirst into the deep, taking with it 1,500 of the innocent and not nearly enough of the guilty.

You sit there horrified and yet an ugly worm deep in your brain whispers: Better them than me.

Titanophiles should have plenty to celebrate and plenty to complain about. On the positive side, Cameron expensively re-creates the sinking of the ship in accordance with the latest and best theory, informed by high-tech exploration of the wreck. Thus in this film, unlike *Titanic* of 1953 or *A Night to Remember* of 1958, the ship is not shudderingly gashed by the berg but merely penetrated by a stiletto of ice, spreading twelve square feet of damage over three hundred feet of hull. Thus, too, the big baby, as she goes down prow first and elevates her stern to the stars—almost as if displaying a cosmic middle finger to the God who doomed her—does in fact break in two as her brittle, frozen steel shatters, perishing not with a whimper but a bang.

Still, in his urge to simplify, fictionalize and mythologize, Cameron ignores many of the fascinations of the doomed voyage and its gallant crew and passengers. The heroic, indefatigable Second Officer Charles Herbert Lightoller, who emerged as the tragedy's hero, is nowhere to be seen, though he was everywhere that night and the last man plucked from the sea the next morning. No credit is given to the stalwart Captain Arthur Henry Rostron of the *Carpathia*, who, by dashing through the ice to the site of the disaster, probably saved more lives than any other human agent. Nor is the dastardly rascal Sir Cosmo Duff-Gordon, who may have bribed his way into the boats, on hand. And where is the deeply annoying Henry Sleeper Harper, who escaped with his wife, his manservant, and his Pekingese while fifty-two children in steerage drowned? It's partially this tapestry of character weak and strong, of angels and devils in attendance, that has locked the disaster into our imaginations.

Though Cameron glimpses the actual—heroine Molly Brown, villain J. Bruce Ismay, head of the White Star Line—mostly he replaces it with a thin, nearly inane melodrama that at least feels appropriate to the era. It's as if the film were written by a scriptwriter in 1912 fresh from reading stories in *Woman's Home Companion*—but completely unversed in the psychological complexities of Mr. James and Mr. Dreiser. The dialogue is so primitive it would play as well on title cards. This overlay of fiction pursues an unlikely Romeo-and-Juliet coupling in which poor starving artist Jack Dawson (Leonardo DiCaprio, forever blowing a hank of hair out of his eyes) falls in love with society slave Rose Bukater (Kate Winslet, alabaster yet radiant), much to her delight and the disgust and ultimate fury of her fiancé, Cal Hockley (Billy Zane). The Zane character—a Pittsburgh steel heir—inherits some of Duff-Gordon's least attractive characteristics, but he's so broadly imagined a portrait of aristocratic knavery that he comes to seem almost a cartoon figure, like a William F. Buckley with hemorrhoids.

The whole framing story is a cartoon, so much so that it seems another element of doomed hubris: Cameron is a guy who thinks he can improve the story of the *Titanic*! He's like the producer in a famous L.A. writer's joke who knows how to make everything better. But this stroke does yield a meager benefit or two: One is a chase sequence set in the unstable bowels of the very wet ship as the witching hour of 2:20 A.M. approaches. As a device for taking a tour not only of the death of a ship but also the end of an era, it's quite efficient; as drama it's ludicrous. Moreover, Dawson is the mildest, the least threatening of rebels. He's no Wobbly or Red, not even an arty radical like Edward Steichen, just a kid who might someday sell covers to *Boys' Life*. Winslet's Rose is Cameron's one anachronism, a Thwarted Woman of our age thrust backward in time to represent Heroic Feminism in wild ways, such as smoking in public. Their love story is strictly for the puppies and the guppies.

It does yield a couple of amusing scenes, however: One is a kiss at the westernmost point of the ship—its very proboscis—as it steams toward New York. The clever camera captures their love and the hugeness of the structure behind them in one breathtaking shot. The other is an intellectual trope: Progressivized by her time in Europe, Rose has become a champion of the avant-garde; her newfound respect for the works of a fellow named Picasso and a chap named Freud signify her willingness to acknowledge the irrational in the universe. The manly men across the table from her—not merely Zane but also *Titanic* designer Thomas Andrews (Victor Garber), Ismay (Jonathan Hyde), and Capt. E. J. Smith (Bernard Hill), head man of the ship itself, a true rogues' gallery of macho hubris—stand for that late-nineteenth-century belief that nature is tamable, that man is master, that a ship could be unsinkable. They scoff, unaware that they are about to get a tutorial from God in the form of 10,000 tons of ice.

It need not be added that the movie is very long, since everything is long this year, including the line at the restrooms. It is, in fact, about forty minutes longer than the actual sinking (which lasted 2 hours 40 minutes vs. 3 hours 20 minutes) and quite possibly more expensive. It should be added that, despite a slow start, the thing still goes from first point to last faster than any movie in the marketplace. Once that big ol' thang begins her last swoon—about an hour into it—you ain't looking no place else and you ain't going no place else.

This is Cameron at his best. Always thin in the imagination when it comes to conceiving the tissue of character and motive (typical Cameron motive, from his first hit, *Terminator*: "He kills—that's all he does"), he's the apogee of techno-nerd filmmaker. Thus the movie's central wonder is that it puts you aboard the sinking ship, palpably and as never before.

In the early going Cameron foreshadows his narrative strategy when, in a not-so-interesting setup involving greedy high-tech grave robbers visiting the *Titanic*'s resting place 12,500 feet beneath the waves, we see a computer-animated scenario of the sinking. The rhythms of that event will be the rhythms of the movie that follows, almost exactly: a long, seemingly dead time in the water as the first three compartments of the lower hull invisibly fill; the slow tip forward as, almost imperceptibly, the bow begins to settle, then disappears; the contrapuntal stately climb of the stern amid an increasing shrapnel of falling furniture, flying glass, and tumbling bodies; and the final, cataclysmic death spasm as the triple-screwed stern juts straight up, like a white whale hellbent on showing the floundering, drowning Ahabs the futility of their puny humanity, and then roars downward toward seventy-three long years of undisturbed silence, leaving a sea full of frozen dead and a fleet of half-empty lifeboats.

Yet in all this spectacle, the scariest element isn't the crushing power of the water and its ability to bend, drown, and twist, but its creepy insistence. Watching it trickle upward (actually the boat is trickling downward), almost a teacup at a time, a thin, clear gruel of death, almost no more than you'd leave on the bathroom floor if you forgot to tuck in the shower curtain, is somehow more unsettling than watching a bulkhead go and a dozen anonymous steerage victims being swept away.

Cameron captures the majesty, the tragedy, the fury, and the futility of the event in a way that supersedes his trivial attempts to melodramatize it. I didn't give a damn about cutie-pies Leonardo and Kate, much less their vapid characters or the predictable Hollywood Ten social "issues" they represent, but I left with an ache for those lost 1,500, rich and poor alike, for the big ship in ruins, and for the inescapable meaning in it all.

It is the same old story: Pride goeth before the fall, even when the fall is through 12,500 feet of black, icy water.   (DECEMBER 19, 1997)

*L*et us now damn famous movies. Let us now deconstruct American icons. Let us now make thousands angry and hundreds psychotic.

Let us now tell an unpleasant but finally necessary truth: *Gone With the Wind* isn't very good.

Long, stupid, ugly and, alas, back for the sixth time (in theaters; innumerable television showings have preceded this rerelease), it is probably the most beloved bad movie of all time, as its adjusted box office gross of $5 billion makes clear. If you love it, that is fine; but don't confuse its gooeyness, its spiritual ugliness, its solemn self-importance, with either art or craft, for it boasts none of the former and only a bit of the latter. It is one of the least remarkable films of that most remarkable of American movie years, 1939. In fact, far from being one of the greatest American films ever made, I make it merely the twenty-eighth best film of 1939! It may not even have been the best movie that opened on December 15, 1939! It is overrated, overlong and overdue for oblivion.

Gone With the Wind, how I hate thee. Let me count the ways.

1. Miz Scarlett, she's uppity. It's profoundly misogynistic. Admittedly, this is not my best issue. I'm not on Gloria Steinem's list of evolved males and I'll never win the Martin Abzug Man of the Year award, but even someone as Neanderthal as I can figure out that the secret pleasure of the film is watching striving Scarlett O'Hara being punished for the sin of selfhood. The movie delights in her crucifixion, even to the point of conjuring the death of a child as apt punishment for her ambitions. Her sin, really, is the male sin: the pride which goeth before the fall.

2. Mistuh Wilkes, he's dithery. Ashley Wilkes, played by the ever so delicate Leslie Howard, must be the most misbegotten male ever to appear on screen. Howard was a great actor and a brave man, who raced home to join his unit when World War II broke out, thereby missing the famous December Atlanta premiere. He was killed in 1943 when the Nazis shot down a plane he was in. Let us lament him as we lament all the men who gave their lives to stop that evil. That said, the truth remains that on screen, he was a feathery creature, best cast as the foil to Bogart's brutish Duke Mantee in *The Petrified Forest*, where his patrician features, porcelain nose, and cathedral-abutment cheekbones gave him the look of an alabaster saint in the wall of an Italian church. But he was about as believable as a sexual object as he would have been as Duke Mantee. How could Scarlett O'Hara fall for him? (Not how could Vivien Leigh fall for him; after all, she did fall for Laurence Olivier!) Much better idea: cast Errol Flynn—less actor, more sex object—as Ashley, and then the movie's central tension, Scarlett's attraction to Ashley and her contempt for Rhett, at least makes some sense.

3. Miz Melanie, she's gittin' on my nerves! Ouch and damn! Yikes and yuck! Ulp and urp. The wondrous Olivia de Havilland was an actress of spunk and pizazz, and she gave as good as she got, even across from such hammy scene stealers as her longtime costar Flynn. But she, too, is trashed by *Gone With the Wind* as sugary Melanie Wilkes, a character of such selfless sweetness she could give Santa Claus a toothache. Are all good girls so interminably boring? I guess they are, but none of them is as boring as poor Ms. de Havilland in her petticoats and politeness. Only once does she stir beyond archetype into some kind of life, and that's in the agonizing childbirth sequence, probably the film's strongest.

4. Too much spectacle, not enough action. David O. Selznick, who produced the film and rode it to immortality, didn't understand the difference between the two. Thus the film has a fabulous but inert look to it; the story is rarely expressed in action but only in diorama-like scenes. It is curiously flat and unexciting. Even the burning of Atlanta lacks dynamism and danger; it's just a dapple of flickering

orange filling the screen, without the power and hunger of a real fire.
And the movie's most famous shot—the camera pulling back to
reveal Scarlett in a rail yard of thousands of bleeding, tattered Confederate soldiers—makes exactly the wrong point. It seems to be
suggesting that Scarlett has begun to understand that the war is
much bigger than she is. And yet she never changes. The shot means
nothing in terms of character; it's an editorial aside that really mis-
leads us.

5. The South, it warn't like that. No, it wasn't. From its opening credits,
   which characterize the South as a lost land of lords and ladies, to its
   final images of Tara nestling among the Georgia dogwoods, the movie
   buys into a myth that completely robs the region of its truth. Love it
   or hate it, it's a land (as Faulkner knew) in which the nobility of its
   heroism lived side by side with the ugliness of its Original Sin: slavery. I'm not attacking the South here, just Margaret Mitchell and
   Selznick's version of it.

   Other movies of 1939 were beginning to find the courage to express some subtle ideas. One of them was John Ford's *Young Mr. Lincoln*, where Henry Fonda's rube lawyer takes a stand for justice in the
   rough Illinois of the 1840s, a test of character that would serve him
   well when he became the sixteenth president.

6. 1939, what a year! We will never see anything like it, and the stunning thing about *Gone With the Wind* is how out of touch it was with
   the brilliance of the American film at the peak of the Hollywood
   studio system: These were fast, zippy, coolly professional jobs that
   took themselves fairly lightly, and demonstrated such craft that it
   was almost art. By contrast, *Gone With the Wind* mistakes its source
   for literature and itself for art, and plods along self-importantly—
   miswired, sluggish and dreary. I found 797 titles from the year 1939,
   had seen fewer than a tenth of them, and even on that small list there
   were 27 that struck me as fundamentally better than *Gone With the
   Wind*, movies that I would watch again with utter delight. They are:
   *Allegheny Uprising, Another Thin Man, Babes in Arms, Beau Geste,
   Confessions of a Nazi Spy, Dark Victory, Dodge City, Drums Along
   the Mohawk, Golden Boy, Gunga Din, Juarez, The Light That Failed,*

Made for Each Other, Mr. Smith Goes to Washington, Ninotchka, Of Mice and Men, The Private Lives of Elizabeth and Essex, The Real Glory, The Roaring Twenties, Stagecoach, The Story of Alexander Graham Bell, The Three Musketeers, Union Pacific, The Wizard of Oz, The Women, Wuthering Heights, and *Young Mr. Lincoln*.

Dammit, my dear, I'm just being frank. (JUNE 28, 1998)

*I*n *The Mask of Zorro*, you see a figure with hot flashing eyes, the lightning-quick moves of a panther, a deftly flicking sword arm that could inscribe *The New York Times* crossword on a button, and a passion that reaches out of the screen and grabs you by the lapels.

And that's the girl!

This would be the big news in the film: Catherine Zeta-Jones, instant star, the new Rita Hayworth, as in, yes, I say again, yes yes yesyesyes. Zeta-Jones plays—well, the plot is somewhat garbled, as if modeled on a piece of wrought iron from the balconies of Barcelona—but let us just say, she's the girl. Zorro likes her. The Spanish governor Montero likes her. Zorro's mentor likes her, because he used to be Zorro and he is in fact her papa. The American mercenary renegade likes her. The peasants like her. I like her. Everybody likes her. There's something about Elena.

As for the rest of the thing, it can be summed up as follow: I went to a sword fight the other night, and a movie broke out.

The Mask of Zorro is entertaining without being exhilarating. It's fun at about 62 percent of the level that the old Errol Flynn swashbucklers hit in the late thirties. As Zorro movies go, it's pretty good. As movies go, it's a little bit better than okay.

Zorro, which means "fox" in Spanish, has been around since a crime reporter with a lurid imagination and a leaden pen made him up in 1919. Usually played by grinning gringos of the Tom Dewey–mustache variety, like a Fairbanks, a Power, or a Guy Williams, he is here played by a gentleman for the first time both authentically Hispanic and authentically mustacheless, Antonio Banderas.

The accent, therefore, may be accurate, but the moves are nevertheless predictable, though to be fair, they still enchant. Zorro, after all, is the original man in black as well as the original masked man, and Banderas gets all the moves right; more important, he looks good in tight pants. I also like a man with a graduate degree in bullwhip gymnastics and improvised field evacuation techniques. He finds the usual astonishing number of trees, flagpoles, castle battlements and, oh yes, flagpoles, to snap that lash around and then zip himself out of trouble as though he's got one of those James Bond space rocket dealies on his back.

Plot? A lot. In fact, too much. It seems stolen from one of the lost episodes of *The Wild, Wild West,* the old western that tried to stick secret agent conspiracy shenanigans in among the sagebrush and the arroyos. As *Mask* has it, the old Zorro—Anthony Hopkins, bringing Hamlet's moody gravitas to a movie that in no other way deserves or matches it— escapes from prison after twenty years of growing a beard and nurturing a steely glare. Evil despotism having returned to old California, he recruits a new Zorro, a young thief, to wage war on a Spanish governor who is enslaving peasants to mine the gold from El Dorado to buy California from Mexico (it's roughly 1841); the movie could also be called *Indiana Zorro and the Lost Gold Mine.* There's even a beachboy-looking blond American named Love (Matt Letscher) around to bedevil everyone and die of close encounters of the sword kind.

Stuart Wilson, who specializes in villainy (as in *Lethal Weapon 3*), plays the vicious, hypocritical Governor Montero. He seems to get these parts when other, more charismatic actors turn them down. What a nasty Montero Basil Rathbone would have made; what a nasty one Sean Bean or Steven Berkoff would make. But Wilson's chap is dour, bland, grouchy, unmemorable, a serious flaw in the movie's melodramatic calculations.

The Mask of Zorro really strikes sparks only twice; once is a dance scene between those hot-blooded kids, Banderas and Zeta-Jones, and another is an erotically charged duel scene, in which they cross blades, wills and, ultimately, tongues. He's great; she's fabulous. Watch her face light up with passion and exhilaration and pure alpha-being joy. Watch her quickness. Watch her beauty.

Finally, watch her career. It's probably the fastest-moving flying object in the summer skies. In this version of the film, the letter Z again takes on huge significance—but it's the Z that stands for Zeta-Jones.

(JULY 17, 1998)

hink of *The 13th Warrior* as Akira Kurosawa's *The Seven Samurai* jacked on amphetamines.

This crazed Iron Age battle rhapsody is so overripe that its flies probably have flies, but that's not bad; it's good. It's why the film qualifies as the summer's primo guilty pleasure. It's red meat for the soul.

What I love most about it is its utter syntheticity: It hasn't a genuine bone in its body. Everyone in it or attached to it is imitating someone or something else. The director, John McTiernan (two *Die Hard*s, the original *Predator* and the new *Thomas Crown Affair*) is imitating Kurosawa, except when he's imitating Sergei Eisenstein's *Alexander Nevsky*. The composer, Jerry Goldsmith, is imitating Carl Orff's *Carmina Burana*. Michael Crichton, who wrote the original novel (*Eaters of the Dead*), was imitating literature.

As a whole, the first twelve warriors are imitating an outlaw biker gang. More specifically, one of them, Dennis Storhøi, is imitating Errol Flynn. Another, Vladimir Kulich, is imitating Klaus Kinski in *Aguirre, the Wrath of God*, and the biggest star, Antonio Banderas, is imitating Omar Sharif, which is the easiest imitation of all: He just had to look across the campfire because there's Sharif himself, in the role of the Wise Sidekick.

And folks, can't we agree on one thing: Any movie with four separate beheadings is pretty darned good entertainment.

Banderas, at once both charming and squirrelly, plays Ahmed Ibn Fahdlan, a tenth-century Arab diplomat-poet exiled from Baghdad in retaliation for his attraction to a powerful noble's wife. Interesting fact about the tenth century: They didn't have toothpaste or, for that matter, many teeth, but they did have Maybelline eyeliner, which turns Banderas into Cher in the early going.

Somewhere in Central Asia, he runs across a very dirty dozen mercenaries, largely Viking in character but with a Scot, a Spaniard, and what appears to be a Tasmanian (this is the Errol Flynn imitator) along for diversity. Ibn is contemptuous, maybe because they gargle from the same pot, which they also drink from, wash in and blow their noses into, and maybe because their names are so dopey: Herger the Joyous, Edgtho the Silent, Rethel the Archer, Weath the Musician, and so forth. Steve the Critic was thinking: This is pretty goofy.

But there's a fjord in everybody's future. Word reaches them that back home, up some mythical, frosty, foggy crack of water, the folks are being assailed by legions of creepy beings who come out of the mists. The heroes are recalled from their careers in freebootery to deal with this crisis. But when a soothsayer—every screenwriter should be issued a soothsayer to get out of those tight plot corners—decrees that War Dog No. 13 must not be a Northman, they acquire the reluctant services of Ibn the Eyeliner Wearer.

Thus, as the only rational man among a group of yakky, laughing, death-loving, kill-counting, hygiene-disadvantaged, largely blond proto–Green Berets, Banderas's thirteenth guy is the hero. For them, courage is second nature, fearlessness first nature, and head-crunching a nice hobby. Before battle, they nap; after battle, they party. During battle, they persevere or they die, and it makes little difference to them. For him, it's an effort. He's had sex with women who bathe at least once a month, so he knows the pleasures of civilization.

But the movie's real hero is its fourteenth warrior: This would be Mc-Tierman's camera, which roams with supple athleticism through the carnage. McTiernan loves to penetrate the melee and find grace moments, odd details, new kinds of wounds, peculiar angles for arrows to pierce flesh, that sort of thing, then send the camera roaring upward to watch not only the struggle from on high but to contrast it with the beautiful mountains of Denmark, played by the beautiful mountains of British Columbia.

The movie pretty much follows the template of *The Seven Samurai,* including the final battle in the rain to slow things down for slo-mo and turn the jagged spurts of jellied blood into exploding Lava Lamps. But it's the same progression: fortification, bonding, fraternizing with the village gals, early assault, counterassault, and final wet encounter. Not only did Kurosawa do it do it first; he did it better.

Kurosawa—this also applies to other great battle movies, like *Zulu, Braveheart,* and even *Saving Private Ryan*—found time to explain the strategic and topographical nature of the battle, so it made sense and we could understand its ebb and flow. McTiernan's melees, though bloody and energetic as all get-out, seem completely arbitrary, without regard to topography. The Bad Guys run at the Good Guys, and more of them die. The pedant in me wants to see the principle of creativity applied to the situation; I want to see them outthink, not merely outfight, the enemy.

There are other annoyances, the most irksome of which is anthropo-
logical. The enemy is revealed to be a race of beings—I think I give nothing too crucial away by acknowledging that they are not werewolves or
bearmen—who live in caves and are sustained by an agricultural system
that might be called human husbandry. They eat people. Yet, at the same
time, they are able to field a bold, savvy, and courageous cavalry unit,
easily the rivals of the Sioux or the nineteenth-century Hussars. How do
an underground people come up with horses, saddles, stirrups; where do
they graze and train the animals? And, gee, wouldn't someone notice?
Or am I taking this a little too seriously?

Of course, as you have probably guessed, there's a literary template
under the movie template, which gives the movie the odd daily double of
being the season's most violent, and also most literate, film. It's actually
a certain lit class ordeal reimagined from the viewpoint of an outsider
with access to an $80 million budget.

In other words, it pretends to dramatize authentic events, which, we
understand, would acquire in the retelling over the generations a crust of
legend, a polish of style through songs and tale-tellers and shamans of
the night, and emerge a thousand-odd years later in all our sophomore
years as *Beowulf*.

When hero Buliwyf (Kulich) finally faces the Wendol Mother, a
mud-faced, snake-bejeweled, finger-fang-wearing harridan definitely in
need of a dental plan, we're not just witnessing a fight to the death between ancient enemies (civilization and chaos) but something else: the
birth of the narrative tradition. That is, the novel. Go Beowulf-Buliwyf!
Odin be with you! Kill Wendol-Grendel's mother! America's hacks
thank you to this day!   (AUGUST 27, 1999)

*L*adies and gentlemen, as mature adults, can we not agree that revenge is infantile, pointless, antisocial and, above all, really cool?

Ah, revenge! So impractical in the real world, so much fun in the fantasy one! Frustrate me and suffer, fool! Feel the lash of my scorn, the
heel of my boot, the tip of my sword! Die sniveling, dog, knowing of
your inferiority! And I'm only talking about editors! I haven't even
started on you readers!

But if the stuff of revenge is fuel for countless popular fictions as well as popular fantasies, it has never been delivered more expertly than by Alexandre Dumas the elder and his riveting tale of Edmond Dantes, the chump who became a champ as he whacked all those who had done him wrong. Plus, he got the girl. One might call it the revenger's urtext; what has followed has been mere reiteration.

That tale gets a first-class Hallmark Hall of Fame treatment in Kevin Reynolds's swaggering *The Count of Monte Cristo*, which is old-form moviemaking at its best. It's full of sword fights, ripped bodices, rippling cleavage, witty ripostes delivered under curled upper lips, an aristocrat's sangfroid, a commoner's passion. It plays by the rules not of history but of genre, which hold that an English accent connotes a foreign language, anybody in a funny hat gets skewered, and a foofy shirt doesn't necessarily mean you're a wuss. You may be a duke.

However skilled Dumas was, he was also, happily and abidingly, a hack, and this is hackwork at its most inspired. It's an almost perfectly structured story, which puts it miles beyond modern moviemaking. It actually has—kids, don't panic, you can handle this!—a plot. Lots of plot. Lots and lots of plot. Each character has a complex set of motives, often contradictory but never incoherent; it stays on track, while conjuring up magnificent surprises; its climax is in perfect synchronization with what has built up to it. It is a powerfully expensive vintage of cheap melodrama.

Reynolds, whose hit was *Robin Hood: Prince of Thieves*, whose best picture was *The Beast* and whose Waterloo was *Waterworld*, appears to have just the right temperament for the project. He doesn't imagine he can improve on Dumas; he has clearly defined his role, and the actors', as bringing the old warhorse to fabulous life, not to show off his Style and Sensibility. It's so refreshing to be in the hands of professionals who are too busy for kitsch, camp, or irony.

The story, like all the great ones, is a dramatic examination of an idea. That idea is the genuineness of the natural nobility of character and the artificiality of an imposed nobility of blood—that is, an aristocracy. The novel is built on the contrast and conflict between two Frenchmen, one noble by character, the other by birth. The second uses the entire mechanism of the state, as well as his own capacity for evil, to destroy the first; but he only makes his adversary stronger and assures his own so-picturesque doom in the process.

A duke's son, Mondego (Guy Pearce), loves a clerk's son, Edmond (Jim Caviezel), for his grace, his goodness, his toughness, his bravery, but he hates him too, for the same reasons. And Edmond has the love of the beautiful Mercedes (Dagmara Dominczyk), whom Mondego covets grievously.

The setting is Marseilles near the end of the Napoleonic era. When the innocent Edmond (a ship's second mate) puts ashore at Elba, meets the Great Man out on a constitutional and naively agrees to carry a message to Bonaparte's supporters, the jealous Mondego leverages that into Edmond's downfall.

Arrested by a corrupt judge on a charge of treason and sentenced to life imprisonment without trial, Edmond is shipped to a cruel Mediterranean prison to live out his life in solitary confinement, while Mondego marries the beautiful Mercedes. When his father dies, Mondego becomes the duke and moves to a grand house in Paris.

But fate is with Edmond: One day, the floor to his chamber suddenly ruptures, and through the rubble crawls the Priest (Richard Harris). Ex-cavalry officer, ex-university student, ex-rich man's secretary, who took a wrong turn in his tunnel to the outer wall (I hate it when that happens), he has been incarcerated for refusing to give up his employer's hidden fortune to Napoleon. (That Edmond got thrown in jail on suspicion of helping Napoleon and the priest for hindering him simply points up the delirium of early nineteenth-century French politics.)

Now the Priest has a new project, much more fun than a tunnel. He will rebuild a new Edmond. He teaches him writing, philosophy, sophistication, the cosmopolitan way; he teaches him the way of the blade; he teaches him cunning. And he gives him freedom. And a map.

Escaping in the priest's own body bag when that worthy helpfully dies at just the right moment (it's melodrama, remember, not tragedy; things can happen when they're supposed to!), Edmond claims the fortune. Now he can go to Paris a billionaire and toy with not only Mondego and Mercedes, but the magistrate and other conspirators against him from those many years ago. He will eat them all, slowly and deliciously, in a dish served cold.

How cool is this? Dumas has brilliantly calculated it to play on human vanities and insecurities, the secret truth that none of us is as powerful or talented as we dream. Wouldn't it be great if some wise old man took us under his wing and taught us all the fabulous stuff we'd otherwise never learn; and even better if he made us tough and brave and strong in the bargain? That's a dream of empowerment that beats at the dark place of most *Homo sapiens* brains.

Initially, it's Pearce's caddish, soigné Mondego who dominates, in the best George Sanders fashion; he shows us the emerald envy behind the blue eyes that always makes an Iago so compelling.

Caviezel, a handsome man who is waiting to become a star after *The Thin Red Line, Angel Eyes,* and *Frequency* failed to make him one, is meanwhile rather bland, with his blue eyes so wide shut that he can't see what's being set up for him. But he ripens as he ages, becoming ultimately quite masterful and even satanic in the totality of his obsession. Like Edmond, Caviezel seems to grow in strength, determination, and competence.

Dumas's novel and Reynolds's vivid version of it ask an eternal question: What profiteth a man to gain his revenge but give up his soul? And it answers: It profiteth him not a farthing, but boy, it sure feels good.

(JANUARY 25, 2002)

There's very little mystery why the first five film versions of *The Four Feathers* were made. Drawn from a novel by the poor man's Kipling, A.E.W. Mason, the story is a sturdy Victorian melodrama full of noble sacrifice, heroics, love lost and found, and, best of all, slaughter. When it's all over, the survivors sit around a damask-covered table, drink port, smoke cigars, and laugh. That's why there'll always be a British Empire.

Oops. There is no more British Empire. It done gone away.

Then why a sixth *Four Feathers?*

That's a question the director Shekhar Kapur, something of a specialist on the pathologies of the tight little island (as he demonstrated in *Elizabeth*), can't answer. The result is a movie that lacks the jingoistic bravura of earlier editions (though movies with jingoistic bravura are unmakable these days) but hasn't replaced it with meaningful historical revisionism appropriate to our post-colonial age. It's neither there (the past) nor here (the present); it's nowhere.

Mason may have been a hack, but he was an inspired one. The reason that this among all his novels (they have titles like *Miranda of the Balcony* and *Musk and Amber*) has lasted is that wonderful business with the feathers themselves, the savagery with which they are delivered, the insouciance with which they are, many miles, deaths, battles, journeys and ironies later, returned.

The setup is brilliant: A group of hotshot aristo infantry officers are ginned up on testosterone and adrenaline because it's the 1890s and they are going to go off to the Sudan and close with the dervishes, avenge Gordon at Khartoum (if you don't know, read a book, idiot!) and win glory, fame, a knighthood, and, gee, maybe get to have tea with the queen's third cousin's footman.

But one of them has seen through it, it being what a later Brit poet called "the old lie, dulce et decorum est pro patria mori"—'tis sweet and proper to die for one's country—though it didn't save that poor bastard's life, as poor Wilfred Owen took a Hun bullet in the head on November 4, 1918. Anyway, the lad, one Harry Faversham of an old military family, son of a general, engaged to a general's creamy daughter and best pal of the fellows, resigns his commission.

Go get skewered in the midday sun so Queen Vicky can add a few more quid to her Barclay's account? He would prefer not to. The widow at Windsor can do without. For this tasteless apostasy, of course, he is drummed out of the company of fit people, three of his closest friends each give him a feather with a card attached, as a formal way of calling him a coward and beginning the shunning; and then his fiancée adds the fourth. He is shamed and humiliated.

He sets off to regain his honor by going in mufti to the Sudan, passing for native, infiltrating the battle zone, and managing to save each friend's life with a series of increasingly heroic stunts. At certain points—here's the genius part!—he gives the particular fellow the feather back, so that he can see how wrong he's been. See how this connects with universal human need to face all those people we've disappointed, offer them a gentle smile, and crush them into nothingness with the information that, hello, I am better than you. That's a pleasure that the earlier filmmakers, particularly the brothers Korda (Alexander produced, Zoltan directed and Vincent art-directed), served up in spades in the nearly perfect imperial encomium of 1939.

The new filmmakers have done a little, but not much, to update the story. Teen heartthrob Heath Ledger plays the earnest Harry, though Kapur, following on Michael Schiffer's screenplay, has seen fit to deprive the character of the elaborate childhood prologue that established his motivation. This is no improvement at all; it makes Harry's decision seem arbitrary when the Kordas, following from Mason, rooted it solidly in psychology.

Ledger is cute but just okay. Wes Bentley, of *American Beauty*, as his best friend and most hurtful betrayer Jack Durrance, is about a tenth as good as the great Ralph Richardson was, even given the fat chance to play the second half of the movie in both blind and noble modalities. Talk about a soft floater at the net! Yet Bentley is largely unremarkable. As for Kate Hudson as Ethne, the betrothed, the beautiful, the bewitching, despite her Aubrey Beardsley ringlets, she is so unremarkable it makes me wonder why you people voted her a movie star. You certainly didn't have my permission, and you still don't.

Pointless little changes are made, to be followed by pointless big changes. In the original, Jack Durrance is one of the feather-givers; in this version he is not, though utterly by chance. That effectively removes from this movie the old movie's most powerful scene, where Richardson's Durrance, now blind, pulls out an envelope given him by his silent savior in the desert, and the feather falls out. All at the dinner table know exactly what it means, but Durrance prattles on, oblivious. It's a great movie moment, and it showed that Mason and the Kordas and the other directors embraced the melodramatic cheesiness of the feather gimmick, and bled it for all it was worth.

But Kapur does not. He seems embarrassed about it. He never comes up with its equivalent. He's tentative, as if the movie were named *The, uh, you know, Four, um, Feathers*.

The bigger changes are threefold, all in the spirit of political correctness. First, a man of color has been added as Harry's mentor, warrior-father and heroic example. Why is it that the elegant Djimon Hounsou, as Abou Fatma, swears loyalty to Harry and guides him through many adventures while himself embodying the spirit of humanity and the virtue of manliness? Well, no reason is given. It happens because it's a movie, that's why.

Second, the dervishes are given credit for a tactical subtlety that they lacked in the original. They aren't just peasants hell-bent on a trip to the seventy-six virgins of paradise; no, they are smart guys who create a clever plan to ensnare Durrance's troops that's as well thought out as Ulysses' cunning horse trick on the fields outside Troy. In fact, this *Four Feathers* is at its best on the battlefield, as it re-creates the smoke and fury of a nineteenth-century colonial war.

And third, Kapur has removed the movie from history. It takes place in a generic nineteenth century in a generic Sudan in the generic year of 18somethingsomething. The book and all the movies after it were based around and celebrated the British victory of 1898 at Omdurman, which settled some radical Islamic hash for a good fifty years. Alas, ever since John Ellis published *The Social History of the Machine Gun* in 1975, that battle has picked up a bit of a stench. Ellis pointed out that it was far from a glorious engagement: Men on horseback charged men with automatic weapons, with predictable results. When the buzzguns stopped buzzing, the dervishes stopped whirling. Final body count: 11,000 dervishes, 28 British soldiers. Is that a battle or an industrialized execution? The acerbic British poet Hilaire Belloc summed it up ever so brightly: "Whatever happens we have got/The Maxim gun and they have not."

Kapur steers away from this carnage. He cuts the final battle altogether, and Omdurman, though named, is simply the site of a prison, which Harry penetrates in order to liberate two feather-givers who have been captured in an earlier, nonhistorical engagement. After the Kordas, Kapur builds his prison horror around the notion of crowding, conjuring a hell so packed with flesh that the thousands must sleep upright; to fall is to be crushed. That is powerful and unsettling, but at the same time it signifies the movie's deeper problem and its primary disappointment: its unwillingness to deal directly with the issue of colonialism.

The earlier films did, for good or evil; they believed in colonialism, without doubts. Thus it was all well and good, in those versions, for the heroes to live as natives and experience Empire from the boot-end of its exploited masses, and then settle back in among the privileged without a whisper of a doubt. Nobody had any doubts.

But that same obdurateness seems misplaced in this version. Doesn't Ledger's Harry learn anything being kicked in the arse, whipped and bludgeoned by the British, or anything from Abou's heroism? He just fits back in, happily, unhaunted by his experiences, unchanged by his acquaintanceship, among the people who deserted him. Even Kipling saw through it (as did Orwell, the Stracheys, the Bloomsbury set, and hundreds and hundreds of others) when he gave voice to a soldier recognizing that Gunga Din was the better man. Harry never gets this, because Mason never got it. The Kordas didn't get it. Not even Shekhar Kapur gets it. For them all, it's just a case of Gunga who?

(SEPTEMBER 20, 2002)

*W*hat is a movie? That's a question Martin Scorsese, as great a director as he is, really can't answer clearly in *Gangs of New York*. Such confusion is at the middle of this muddle.

For if a movie is a time machine, a trip to another epoch, a realization of looks and sounds and sights not seen in 140 years, then *Gangs of New York* is a great movie.

It has the genius of thereness to it. You are there when two tough crews named the Dead Rabbits and the Natives meet at Five Points, a raggedy intersection of streets in Lower Manhattan in the 1840s, back when Gotham was essentially a slum built on a cesspool in a swamp. You are there as these two deadly armies clash with flail and blade and club. You are there when they fight in top hats and spats and sashes and mustaches that curl up like the tips of a caliph's slippers, and the battle looks more like Culloden—Scots vs. English, 1746—than anything else.

And you are there when the Natives—long-settled old stock who've forgotten their own immigrant origins—vanquish, then banish the Dead Rabbits, the Irish. You are there when folks think the name "Dead Rabbits" is cool and dangerous.

So if the idea expressed by the word "movie" is some sort of meta-museum of history that shows you exhibits, then *Gangs of New York* cannot be missed. Scope, vision, power, immaculate filmcraft, sense of wondrous newness, sense of history's melancholy vapors, sense of the bloody ground that is this country of ours. Friend, is that your idea of "movie"? Then be my guest, sit back, enjoy, learn, stretch, expand, be morally improved.

Unfortunately, if your idea of movie comprises one word and that word is "story," you're going to be disappointed. For under its scope and reach and passion, *Gangs of New York* is pretty ordinary stuff. You've seen it before at least a hundred times, and it's extremely dispiriting that a director of Scorsese's power and experience didn't choose something more complex.

It's as if he preferred to concentrate on the production—the building of the sets, the sweeping moves of the cameras, the depth and detail of the compositions, the montage of furious battle action—rather than on the dramatic issues and, oh yeah, taking up the rear, the human beings who live them. It's just the old revenge melodrama, the one about the son seeking payback for the murder of his father. When, after exile, he returns to the arena, he is so gifted that his father's murderer, a powerful man by virtue of that murder, is attracted to him, and invites him into the gang. So Our Hero is tempted: success or vengeance? Wouldn't be a movie if he chose success, right? You already know that, so you already know everything.

It begins with that street battle, but the point of view is that of the young Amsterdam Vallon. His father, Priest Vallon (Liam Neeson), leads his Irish boys against the nativist Natives—a mob of guys terrified then (as now) by the new waves of immigrants, who they know must be kept down or they and their little private world will be overwhelmed.

The fight, at Minute 3 and lasting through Minute 9, is pretty much the high point of the movie. Scorsese has always had a genius for depicting violence (*Taxi Driver, Raging Bull*), and here he really outdoes himself, with an evocation of the racing fear and exhilaration of close-quarters combat that leaves you shaken. But some of the blood in the snow comes from Priest, who is defeated by the Native leader, a fiery galoot named Bill the Butcher (played with screaming bravado by Daniel Day-Lewis).

So the boy Amsterdam watches his father die, particularly the coup de grâce issued by Bill to put the writhing man out of his pain. But the plucky Amsterdam steals that knife and runs off with it, and the camera stays with him as he penetrates the multitiered Dead Rabbits' command structure (which I never quite understood) and manages to bury the knife, which he will recover when he turns into Leonardo DiCaprio and then . . .

And then nothing. That's a suggestion of the story's lack of narrative savvy: The whole first act of the movie is about the theft and hiding of that knife, and its recovery sixteen years later, in 1863, in a move heavily freighted with symbolic foreshadowing. All from Storytelling 101. And then the knife just disappears. So what was the point of dramatizing this knife above all others in a universe of knives? That question is left hanging.

Continually, Scorsese's impulse to inform overwhelms his instinct to dramatize. He is so proud of his mastery of the source material, a pulpy, anecdotal true-crime volume published in 1927. A whole sequence, for example, involves the beautiful Jenny Everdeane (Cameron Diaz), professionally a Five Points pickpocket, who goes on an uptown foray to crash mansions in a maid's outfit and steal the places blind. This, we are informed, is so specific a crime, its practitioner has a colorful old-timey name: she's a "turtledove." But so what? Everdeane as turtledove never again figures into the plot; she just becomes, generically, "the girl" in a predictable triangle with Snively Whiplash—Bill the Butcher, that is— and Amsterdam.

As for DiCaprio, he's certainly the weakest performer up there. He's cast as a deadly, beautiful street youth, with a quick cunning and a will to do battle and seek revenge. Well, you believe the beautiful part. But somehow he never projects the city-rat toughness of a young slum champ. Remember John Garfield fighting his way out of the mean city back in *Body and Soul*? No, you don't? Well, then try this: DiCaprio is never feral and edgy like, say, the young Robert De Niro in Scorsese's *Mean Streets* so many years ago. Still a blank? All right, let's go here: He's never as tough and believable a city kid on the hustle as Eminem is in *8 Mile*. He's way too uptown. He should be wearing a black turtleneck and Italian director glasses and Prada shoes.

A whole middle hour (of three) follows plot twitches of little consequence, such as Amsterdam's friendship with another street kid grown too handsome (Henry Thomas), the interplay between Bill the Butcher and Boss Tweed (Jim Broadbent), and the most important of all, will the Dead Rabbits' hallowed symbol of identity (yes, that would be a dead rabbit) be hoisted downtown again. The facts are fascinating: Are you aware that firemen in the 1860s were essentially gang-controlled looters whose main job was to steal the valuables of the house before it turned to ash? Interesting, but it has nothing to do with the story.

But it finally seems that the movie itself has nothing to do with the story: Scorsese pretty much forgets about it in the end. It's clear he wanted to say something about the New York draft riots of 1863, an ancient holocaust that has all but vanished from memory as it was so overshadowed by contemporary slaughters at Antietam and Gettysburg. He just has nothing to say about it.

It's a shameful episode, a spasm of urban bloodletting in which, among other things, more African-Americans were slain than in any other single event in American history. Yet Scorsese's treatment of it is distressing. In the first place, it blows into town like a hurricane, presented almost as a natural occurrence, and it all but obliterates the nominal climax toward which the film has clearly been building, the return match between Squashed Bunnies and Native natives; even the last meeting of the Butcher and Amsterdam is muted, as if obscured in a fog or a squall.

In the second place, it has an extremely curious and debilitating effect: It takes the New York draft riots completely out of a moral context. The movie fails to make the point that even a little research convinces you of—that these folks, who were refusing to go to war to end slavery and save the Union, were hardly victims; they were essentially in open, murderous rebellion against, er, America and were committing violent treason. And that's before they started lynching black people. Considered in that light, the arrival of the army hardly feels like the neutral tragedy of Scorsese's imagination. You want to rape, burn, pillage and tear down, and murder any black person you can get your hands on? Then say hello to the Fifth Pennsylvania Infantry with its bayonets fixed and fingers on the trigger. Then as now, there are always consequences.

(DECEMBER 20, 2002)

Someone once described a particularly beautiful thoroughbred as being "nothing but run." I thought of that during *Seabiscuit*, because that wondrous animal was everything but run.

Biscuit, as he was called, was small, kind of ugly, temperamental, lazy, and compared with the other steeds of his time and place, pretty pitiful. The only thing he could do was beat the hell out of them just about all the time, to the delight of an American public stressed out by the Depression.

That fabulous story is re-created—well, distilled—from Laura Hillenbrand's brilliant book in a movie that, although nowhere near the class of its equine hero, is quite a satisfying ride. In places, it looks a little too much like a high-gloss car commercial—I kept expecting someone to say "rich Corinthian leather"—and maybe we could use fewer slo-mo trumpet-driven struts across the finish line. It comes to resemble a *Chariots of Fire* for quadrupeds.

Oh, let's get all the snottiness out of the way while we're on a roll. Writer-director Gary Ross (*Pleasantville* was his breakthrough) imagines the story as a kind of populist fable, as if he's Frank Capra and the horse is the angel Clarence sent down by Joseph not only to win match races but also to give hope to poor souls. He ain't a horse, he's a salvation machine. There's also an implication that in political terms, he was the New Deal, a kind of surrogate for FDR.

This is okay for a while, but I think Ross takes it too far. After all, racing then, as racing now, is a sport of kings and car dealers. And Seabiscuit's owner, Charles Howard (big, buoyant Jeff Bridges), whom the movie presents as a little guy taking on the big guys, was a much bigger guy than the movie pretends. He was way rich, even in the Depression; he'd landed the West Coast's Buick franchise back in the teens. And, though he arrived in San Francisco with 21 cents in his pocket, he actually hailed from wealthy stock (his father was a Canadian millionaire). He had grown up in military schools and had unusual entrepreneurial and marketing skills. And he was no outsider: The movie forgets to mention (but Hillenbrand didn't) that he was one of the founding partners of the Santa Anita racetrack, and he hung out with a best pal, a fellow horse enthusiast and Santa Anita investor named Bing Crosby. So he was hardly a scruffy Capra dreamer-hero.

As for Seabiscuit himself, he was, after all, still a thoroughbred, whose lineage was noble (by Hard Tack, by Man o'War; out of Swing On, by Whisk Broom II). It's not as if he was pulling a milk wagon in Cincinnati or on the way to the glue factory when discovered by accident. He was where most racehorses are when they are seen by their ultimate owners and trainers: at the racetrack. Though smaller and spindly, his blood was as blue as, say, his ace opponent War Admiral's. He was more a fallen prince (his early career had been disastrous) than a plucky, talented working-class guy.

Still, as narrative recipe, this willed misreading of the truth works. It's as if Howard and his ragtag crew of retreads, never-weres, and walking wounded were challenging the money and the power of the plump, truffle-eating snobs and debauchees of the tainted Babylon of the thirties. That's how Ross imagines Baltimore, home of Pimlico and the Maryland Club, those unstormed Bastilles of privilege and pampering. Even Pimlico's stud muffin, War Admiral, is presented as a villain of the upper classes! Hey, he was Seabiscuit's uncle (both were descended from Man o'War, though in different generations).

Oh well. On it goes, handsome, thin, and compelling. As Ross simplifies it, the humane Howard is shattered because of the loss of his only son (he actually had a batch of children) and the subsequent desertion of his wife. He goes to Tijuana, where he meets a beautiful young society woman. (The movie leaves out the somewhat unusual fact that she was the older sister of the wife of his oldest son!) She was a horsewoman (they met at a rodeo, actually, not a racetrack, as the movie has it). To save himself, to woo her, he gives himself over to horses—that is, to racing.

He begins to acquire oddball geniuses. He's attracted to an old trainer named Tom Smith (well played by Chris Cooper) with almost silent ways and unusual empathy for horses, sometimes called the first horse whisperer. And a scrappy li'l rider named Red Pollard. Here again the movie goes slightly awry. Tobey Maguire plays the role, because (a) he's red-hot and (b) he's thin and short enough to just barely pass as jockey-size and (c) he has a relationship with Ross from *Pleasantville.*

But if you read Hillenbrand's book, the Red Pollard you'll see in your mind's eye is as tough as brass bushings, and could chew up and spit out any twenty sensitive young Tobey Maguires. Maguire is to this story almost as Leonardo DiCaprio was to *Gangs of New York*—too pretty to fight. Ross and Maguire play Red's off-again, on-again boxing career as a kind of joke, with the boy always getting comically knocked out. Ha ha ha, except that you don't get in the ring to be knocked out, you get in the ring with a serious aggression fixation and you want the savage joy of sending the other guy to the canvas, blank-eyed and bloody. There's no warrior in Maguire's Red, whereas Hillenbrand's Red was all warrior, a guy literally bred for combat, with a pain threshold off the charts—he was thrown from more horses than any other jockey of his time, but he always got back on.

The last member of the team is Seabiscuit, and here again I wish the movie had been more successful at evoking the horse's personality. We see it only through the eyes of others; the animal himself seems to have no permanent character. We never make true eye contact and feel his presence as a sentient being. (Possibly this is because ten horses, each trained to perform a certain action, depicted the Biscuit on the set.) It's just the horse, in the way that movies used to always have "the girl." And, speaking of that, Elizabeth Banks, as Howard's wife, Marcela, is pretty much "the girl."

Where *Seabiscuit* excels and thrills is in its evocation of the races themselves. Horse-racing movies are rare enough, but the few that have been made always see the race from the bettor's point of view and track the progress by his reactions. Not so here: Ross cares not about bettors, but about jockeys (a dozen worked on the production, including hall-of-famer Gary Stevens in a big role as the Biscuit's alternate rider). Ross takes us inside the frenzy, the thunder, the danger of these affrays. They feel more like cavalry action, a charge of the slight brigade. The horses shudder and shoulder together as this jock or that searches for the hole that will let him spurt through and take the lead, though it may be open only for a fraction of a second. The ground, roaring by beneath, is hard and treacherous and seems to yearn to crush your body; the other horses feel immense and violent. Dust and noise clot reality, sweat stings eyes, the wind whips, the action blurs. It takes a cool head, great strength and stamina, and a spider monkey's tiny body to master this world. *Seabiscuit* puts you in the middle of it.

And the reality itself is terrific. Seabiscuit just kept on winning and soon was on the trail of War Admiral, then the most famous horse in America (he'd won the 1937 Triple Crown). A shrewd marketer, Howard personalized the conflict between the horses and campaigned for a match race—that is, a two-horse showdown—against the bigger, more powerful animal. He actually took Seabiscuit on a cross-country barnstorming tour, holding news conferences in every state. National radio, the dominant medium of the day, played a big part in the campaign, too. Howard finally got the Admiral's owner, Samuel Riddle (played by Eddie Jones as if he's got a case of the gout from too much duck à l'orange and terrapin soup at the Maryland Club), to agree to a one-on-one at Pimlico in 1938. It has been called the greatest horse race ever run.

Of course, reality isn't always story editor. How nice to end the story on that excellent adventure; instead, however, the Biscuit was shortly thereafter injured (jockey Pollard had been injured before the race, and didn't ride that one), and the movie has to account for a last drama, as the injured horse and the injured man heal each other for a race they'd never been able to win, the Santa Anita Handicap. Maybe by that time, you'll be just a little fatigued of horse racing.

But generally, *Seabiscuit* is a winner. Like its eponymous hero, it runs and runs and runs.   (JULY 25, 2003)

A good rule of thumb is, avoid movies with colons in the title. A colon connotes equal weight for both halves of the entity surrounding it. In other words, someone, namely the author, hasn't been able to make up his mind which half is more important. He hasn't discriminated—and that, after all, is his job.

And thus the much ballyhooed and ultra-handsome *Master and Commander: The Far Side of the World* suffers from what might be called colonitis. It comprises too many equal parts, and they tangle each other up. Everything is important, which comes to mean that nothing is important. Derived from two novels in the famed Patrick O'Brian series set aboard a British man-of-war during the Napoleonic era, it also pulls in snatches from other O'Brian books and additions from the imaginations of director Peter Weir and his co-scenarist John Collee. Lots of material, but nobody has done much discriminating.

Thus the thing feels weirdly overstuffed, as stories keep stumbling into and over one another or are buried beneath the arrival of other stories. The worst example is the film's narrative framework—a long cat-and-mouse sea hunt between the British ship HMS *Surprise* and a faster, meaner, bigger Frenchy called the *Acheron* that is presented in the early going as a matter of utmost, almost overwhelming importance. But if it's so important, why does Weir keep shunting it aside, even losing contact with it as other, lesser stories take precedence? He even puts the hunt for the devious *Acheron* on pause to make room for a bird-watching expedition! Only when the bird-watcher stumbles upon the *Acheron* at harbor does Weir remember what the movie is about.

The center of the O'Brian novels is the relationship between two men, the indomitable man of war Captain Jack Aubrey (Russell Crowe) and his ship's surgeon, amateur naturalist and, in the books at least, intelligence agent Stephen Maturin (Paul Bettany). So in sync are the two very different minds—Jack's is action-oriented, direct, noble; Stephen's is subtle, ironic, witty—that they make beautiful music together on the *Surprise*'s afterdeck.

But as beautiful as the music is, and as experienced as the actors are with each other (they related brilliantly in *A Beautiful Mind*), the truth here is that neither shows particularly well. Crowe is outsize in the old movie-star fashion, a stern face, a stout body, a formidable presence, but the movie idealizes Jack Aubrey to a somewhat irritating degree: Not only is he brilliant, brave, and inspirational, but he's also inspirational, brilliant, and brave. Plus, he plays a mean fiddle, gives great speeches, and is handy with a sword. But on the downside, he's—oops, they left the downside out of the film (but not out of the books, where Aubrey frequently displays an importunate randy streak, expressed on the wives of various Brit officials in ports of call). The movie makes him into a Sergeant Rock of the Royal Navy, though I suppose that would make him Captain Rock. So the character isn't nearly as persuasive as a more subtly shaded, darker evocation might have been.

As for Bettany, this was to be the picture that would make him a star, and it won't. The movie is so pitched to Crowe that Bettany doesn't imprint with any singularity, and certainly not with anything like the power and charm he brought to both *A Beautiful Mind* and his first widely seen film, *A Knight's Tale*, where he so amusingly played the publicity agent and wrytyr Geoff Chaucer.

As it wanders about the globe, windblown and drifty, the movie does find a good subplot now and then. The best of these has to do with the presence of young men—very young—on these ships as midshipmen preparing for a life at sea. The precocious among them are given yet more onerous responsibility, which leads to certain astonishments. The hero-boy of the *Surprise* ends up one-armed and, at the tender age of 13, leading wizened, tattooed sailors in hand-to-hand combat when the *Surprise* finally does surprise the *Acheron*. The young actor Max Pirkis, who plays Midshipman Lord Blakeney, is terrific in the part, easily the master and commander of his elders.

Then there's the ship itself. As has been well publicized, the movie company actually built a replica and floated it in a famous Mexican movie tank (where both *The Abyss* and *Titanic* were shot). So one thing *Master and Commander: etc. etc.* is long on is a sense of shipboard life in the early nineteenth century and, hey, if that's what you want, then this is where you go. It's a maze of chambers and byways, of dense riggings (there's a whole universe of rope to be mastered) and canvas walls, of creaking and grinding and groaning slats. The *Surprise* feels as much like a living thing as any of its crew.

And then there's war. The movie begins with battle and closes with battle. It's a shame the first one is so powerful and the last one so generic; it ought to be the other way around. But that first fight, when the *Acheron* opens fire from a fog bank—loved the sudden flashes breaking out of the white wall of vapor—and the French heavy ball tears into the *Surprise*'s wooden hull and what it strikes it converts by shot's deadly alchemy into shrapnel, is immediate and terrifying. Suddenly we're in a wooden Verdun where the very air seems alive with death. Wow: It has to be the best naval battle sequence ever gotten onto film, and totally as terrifying as Weir's brilliant re-creation of the crucible of *Gallipoli*.

Alas, the last engagement lacks the immediacy and the singularity of the first. If you've seen any of the great swashbucklers of the Errol Flynn era, such as *Captain Blood* or *The Sea Hawk*, it will feel as good as, but no better than, any of them. It's familiar stuff, not made particularly raw or real: the grappling hooks, the clank of sabers and cutlasses, the weirdly unloud poofs of the muskets. I didn't hear "Shiver me timbers" or a "Yo-ho-ho," but if I had, it wouldn't have seemed out of place. I kept waiting for Johnny Depp to swing over on a yardarm.

In the end, *Master and Commander: The Far Side of the World* seems fated to disappoint everyone except the slick magazines that put it on their covers. The cognoscenti who have memorized the O'Brian novels will pull out their hair at the liberties taken, the plots and incidents meshed together haphazardly. The Aubrey-innocent, who don't know the difference between a topgallant and a preventer backstay, will just wonder what the fuss is about. (NOVEMBER 14, 2003)

*H*as any man in history had a Christmas morning like the one the novelist Charles Frazier is having this very second? He opens up the big present under his tree and finds a first-class, literate, moving and sure-to-be-mega-successful movie adaptation of his bestseller *Cold Mountain.*

Oh, that's right: He's a writer. Probably found something to grouse about already!

But here's the best part: It's a present for the rest of us as well.

Cold Mountain, directed by the subtly spectacular craftsman Anthony Minghella, is one of those films that might be called "complete." It has everything, in the best possible way, but most important, it has a coherent, if tragic, view of life and society. It builds a world, takes you into it, makes you feel it; it tells a story, makes you love the characters, and pulls you through life, love, and death. It's funny, it's heartbreaking, it's scary, and it's exhilarating. It's got love stuff and lots of laughs and cool gunfights. It's really long and it feels like it's over in fifteen minutes. It does something so few movies do these days: It satisfies.

Frazier's story, famously, was a fusion of classical sources—*The Odyssey* in particular—and family history. Where one stopped and the other started remains open to doubt, and Frazier isn't talking. But from Homer comes the prime image: a warrior-king in love, who's been at war too long, who is sick of slaughter, who yearns to return to an Ithaca. And in Ithaca there waits, patient and loyal but beleaguered, the noble Penelope. She is beset by problems and suitors, her only armor against an increasingly chaotic world her love of the man.

The trip here, of course, isn't from Troy to Ithaca but from Petersburg, Virginia, to Cold Mountain, North Carolina, in the cold winter of 1864. Our Odysseus is one of those naturally noble southern yeomen who charged at Gettysburg and held firm at the Marne and the Bulge and Pork Chop and Dak To and Tikrit. Inman (Jude Law) is scrawny and tough, good in a fight, good with guns, all in all a most capable man. But he's touched with a kind of special grace and kindness. He's something of a mystery to his buddies, except the one thing they know about him is he'll be there when they need him, and he is, until they all are dead. As the movie opens, he is at the terrible crater in Petersburg, that awesome Union snafu where a bold tactical stroke—a potentially siege-busting mineshaft filled with explosives under the Confederate lines—resulted in tragedy when the assaulting troops became trapped in their own crater and were slaughtered like cattle. This wasn't much fun for them, but it wasn't for their killers, either.

Wounded, the war lost, Inman lies abed with the flies gathering at his blown-open neck. All his friends are dead. There arrives a letter from Ada Monroe (luminous Nicole Kidman), declaring her distress, wishing him home, confessing her adoration.

Here's the delirious stroke of genius from Frazier, left pristine by Minghella. Ada and Inman, Inman and Ada: They're in love to the level of souls, but it is, after all, the century before the century before this one, and things were different then. Love is ethereal and passionate and possibly more forceful because it doesn't involve sex until the words "I do" are spoken before the parson. In fact, the two have looked longingly at each other at Sunday meeting, have shared a few mumbled words (he's not exactly glib by nature) and exactly one kiss when Johnny went marching off to war, hurrah, hurrah. This love is all the more powerful for remaining unconsummated, uncontaminated by lust, an expression of feeling, not a jingle in the glands.

The movie thus follows, and cuts vividly (as did Homer, first master of the contrapuntal narrative) between the two stories: Inman gives himself an honorable discharge and hits the road, roaming across the dangerous world of a war, where he will be hunted not only by Yankees but also by homegrown "Home Guard," men who did not fight but have filled the power vacuum by decreeing themselves a militia with discretionary powers of search, seizure, and execution.

The other story is Ada's. She's utterly of the century that spawned her, a delicate flower who can play frilly etudes on the piano and discuss Mr. Thoreau's disagreements with Mr. Emerson, but can't plant a bean to save her life. She was brought to Cold Mountain—a kind of piney sanctuary high in the Blue Ridge—from the more hospitable climes of Charleston by her pappy (Donald Sutherland), the reverend, who then up and died. So she's alone and languishing pitifully until the arrival of Ruby Thewes (Renée Zellweger).

There's no Ruby in *The Odyssey*, but there sure is a feminist mythology and there sure is in *Cold Mountain*. She's all grit and practicality and stubborn savvy, who don't take no sass from no man, nor woman nor child. Ruby is the spirit of reality, of what must be done to get through the night, and Zellweger all but steals the movie as this bundle of furious energy and concentration. She's not just admirable in her determination, but funny in it as well.

In fact, Minghella has gotten a sublime trio of performances from his stars, including his beautiful ones. People this gifted by their genetic mandates frequently just pose their way through life, but both Law and Kidman think hard about character and are willing to give up on being beautiful to be real. And, of course, that's the magic of movies: The more real they are, the more beautiful they seem.

I had trouble with the book because so many of Inman's adventures led nowhere and just ate up pages until he got home. I know, a minority view. Still, that problem seems muted in the more immediate experience of film production, and such interludes as the one with the promiscuous minister Veasey (Philip Seymour Hoffman), the goat lady (Eileen Atkins), and the lonely widow woman (Natalie Portman) feel of a piece with the picaresque, not arbitrary at all. And the general view of the ruined South as a ruined paradise, still rich in beauty (Romania stands in for a North Carolina, now too rich in Mickey Dees to do a filmmaker any good) but blighted by hate and violence that stand against the love and nobility that was there already, is utterly convincing.

All in all, *Cold Mountain* is everything you could ask for. It's a great old-fashioned wallow of a time at the movies.   (DECEMBER 25, 2003)

*T*he great fabulist Jorge Luis Borges has a story called "Pierre Menard, Author of 'Don Quixote.' " It's about a French critic who so loves the great Spanish novel that he wants to write it. Not copy it, not rewrite it; no, to make an empathetic connection with Cervantes to such a degree that he is actually writing anew a novel that was written 400 years earlier.

Borges, ever so niftily, is getting at a basic but often unacknowledged circumstance of creation: Younger artists are so taken with a certain established work that they have to, in some fashion, make it their own. This seems to be the mechanism that underlies the Tom Cruise film *The Last Samurai*, in which the director, Edward Zwick, of *Glory* glory and

Legends of the Fall legend, desperately aspires to become, by some weird transformative process of yearning and hoping, Akira Kurosawa, and to make a great Kurosawa movie.

And that explains also why, under its beauty, its lush production values, and its superficial spell of enchantment, the basic product feels lame and thin, wan and stale. It's wannabeism on a multimillion-dollar scale, with an icon of Japanese culture somehow crudely penetrated by an interloper and turned inside out. Movies set in Japanese history should not be about handsome white people. It just feels wrong and, in the end, leaves in your mouth the taste of desecration.

If you're not a fan of the great director Kurosawa and don't care a whisker for Japanese film, you most likely won't give a damn. What's up there is, at least at that immediate level, engrossing. Endless yen have been spent on swords and armor and horses and costumes—Zwick adores the flag-helmets so beloved by Kurosawa—and New Zealand, which has made a pretty good Middle Earth, turns out to make a pretty good 1870s Japan, all shire and hill for battleground. Those battles are reasonable well staged, and lots of people die. There's some cool sword-fighting. But still, it's junk.

Basically what Zwick has done is to take Kevin Costner's *Dances With Wolves* and insert it into the Satsuma Rebellion of 1877, with a samurai clan in the role of an Indian tribe. Hmmm, I don't think so. Costner evoked all of Native American culture; the survival of a whole people was at peril. It was a culture war, not a class war. But the samurai, after all, were but a small part of Japan; they represented, by the nineteenth century, obstructivist, regressive values. They really can't, or shouldn't, be sentimentalized.

That doesn't stop Zwick. Nothing stops Zwick. He's like General MacArthur returning. He marches through everything, immune to subtlety, nuance, sense of appropriateness. So he's got Tom Cruise, as earnest and hopeless as the day is long, as both Toshiro Mifune and Kevin Costner. And to make this travesty worse, you can feel the handsome little guy "acting" with every fiber of his being. It's kind of unsettling. He resembles Sean Penn in *I Am Sam*, except he seems to be shouting "I am Samurai." His face is a perpetual mask of scorn, his body a knot of anxiety, his eyes cranked down to laser glare. He's a poster boy for the concept of trying too hard. He's not a hero, he's the guy at the party who's so intense you want him to stay away.

Cruise plays an American cavalry officer named Captain Nathan Algren, a hero of both the Civil and Indian wars. But we find him sunk in bitterness, soaked in alcoholism. He's shilling for a gun company at some kind of industrial exposition, and haunted by guilt over a Wounded Knee-style massacre in which he was forced to participate. Pay no attention to this anachronistic conceit: No professional military officer of the era could have conceived of war against Native Americans as unjust or genocidal; there wasn't even a vocabulary by which, given mass cultural commitments to manifest destiny, such a thought could be expressed.

After a showy tantrum onstage to dramatize his discontent, Algren gets an offer from a Japanese industrialist to come to that country and use his vaunted skills to train an army for deployment in a campaign against samurai who are violently resisting the industrialization, and by implication the Americanization, of Japan. Algren accepts: It's the only war he's got.

Almost instantly you can see the agenda. First, Zwick insists on stale stereotyping that all but destroys the film. He expresses Algren's moral contamination by associating him with a hated modern institution, a gun company. But at the time, Connecticut's gun valley was something like today's Silicon Valley, part of that holy dream of manifest destiny. The opprobrium that visited the gun business didn't arrive until well into the next century.

Then there's that Japanese industrialist, very much the movie's bad guy. His villainy is expressed in terms of his Americanization: He's a cigar-smoking, derby- and waistcoat-wearing capitalist, and we're supposed to respond to him as representing the morally wrong course for Japan to take, while the old ways are without any rigor sentimentalized as superior.

What happens next is both inevitable and far-fetched, a series of improbabilities out of old Hollywood dumbbell tradition. Cruise's Algren trains his soldiers—they are, of course, depicted as hopeless rural peasantry, unable to master such implements as the musket—and leads them in battle. He is overwhelmed by the near-mythical samurai, who ride out of the fog as if from *The Seven Samurai*, and only Algren survives the battle. Because he matches exactly a symbolic dream that we've seen in the head of the rebel samurai lord Katsumoto (Ken Watanabe), that warlord decides not only to spare his life, but also to move him in with his own widowed sister. (It was Algren who made the woman a widow, but that, strangely, is not a factor in the drama.) Oh, and Katsumoto happens to be the rare nineteenth-century Japanese warlord who somehow has picked up English, so Algren doesn't even have to learn the language.

Katsumoto is clearly a movie version of the perplexing Japanese hero Saigo Takamori, who led the Satsuma (clan) rebellion. The major difference here, of course, is his sentimental indulgence of Captain Algren, who would have, in the real world, symbolized everything the warlord hated and waged war to destroy: industrialization, Westernization, lack of respect for Japanese custom, the democratization of force when common soldiers with muskets could bring down the elegant, armored, mounted, and skillful samurai. By what twisted theory of human personality would Zwick build a movie based on such a zealous professional warrior's love for that which the record showed indisputably that he hated? It simply makes no sense, but without it—and Cruise's art-moderne profile—there's not a bankable movie.

What makes even less sense is Zwick's sentimentalization of Saigo—through the vessel of the fictional Katsumoto—and the code of Bushido that animated him. To Zwick, the way of the samurai is akin to the way of purity: It stands for nobility, service, self-sacrifice, denial of ego, tradition. It did, of course, but only for a small number of the elite who enjoyed its fruits; for the general population, it was simply feudalism, in which a small band of hereditary aristocrats controlled society by force and looted its profits to sustain themselves in castles and enjoy blood sport.

It was a simple, brutal system of exploitation, in which the anonymous millions lived and died to provide sustenance for a few. In the West, we call that "the Dark Ages," and we invented something to end it, called a "government"; Zwick calls it paradise and has constructed a movie that asks us to endorse it. It's the first, and I hope last, pro-warlord movie! This is something Kurosawa, by the way, never did: He understood that the warlord's way was the way of chaos and war and endless slaughter; his rogues and scalawags stood against that, not for it.

In any event, after placing his tight little white guy at Katsumoto's right hand, Zwick more or less sticks to chronology, with a few annoying flourishes. One is an attack by ninjas upon Katsumoto's headquarters, in which Cruise figures mightily, his flashing blade (Algren has learned the Japanese sword with stupefying ease) slashing this way and that at buzz-saw speed. The ninja thing just seemed cheap and crummy to me, simply a way of letting Cruise show off his newly acquired sword skills in a fanciful sequence that more or less violates the consistency of tone of the rest of the film.

In the end, Katsumoto, with Algren by his side, faces a battle with newly industrialized forces. This is set up to showcase the uniquely Japanese value called "The Nobility of Failure," to quote the title of Ivan Morris's book on the subject, evidently an inspiration to Zwick. In the last battle of *The Last Samurai*, Katsumoto, Algren, and a few hundred others ride into Gatling guns. We're supposed to feel, I don't know, sorry for them, because their little con game is over, because Japan is achieving a central government and a unification under national leadership, along with other little things included in the bargain like education, medicine, and so forth.

This movie thinks that's terrible; it yearns for a medieval country to remain medieval. What sane person could buy into such absurdity? *The Last Samurai* stands for the Banality of Failure.

(DECEMBER 5, 2003)

Five

YUKS

*T*he nerve of some people. The makers of *There's Something About Mary*, for example, believe it is enough for a comedy to be funny.

Talk about arrogance! Talk about self-importance! Talk about the vanity of corporate greed-heads!

Nothing makes me sicker than to report that the theater in which I saw this film was actually filled with people crumpled up with laughter! These benighted fools actually appeared to believe that "feeling good" is appropriate in a world so filled with human tragedy and economic injustice. What is this thing called "humor" anyway but the sound of the bourgeoisie enjoying its ill-gotten gains and of filmmakers refusing to acknowledge their responsibility to enlighten the masses? These times are too troubled for mere "comedy." There are much higher values to be defended, such as compassion, social and political correctness, liberal piety, progress toward a more just society and, of course, redistribution of the wealth, as advanced by those of us anointed to the media elite.

And compared with such heroic responsibilities, how pale and disturbing seem the middlebrow conventions known as "hilarity," "happiness," "the giggles," and "foam-flecked, mucus-spewing gasps powered by intense oxygen debt," which is what this dreadfully anti-humanist document produces. The movie invites us to revel in man at his most elemental as an issuer of fluids, odors, and orifice-valved noises. What a cloud of gas is man, these profit-driven jackals insist!

But far more disturbing, they provoke us to chuckle when man—yes, the same "man" who was in the forest with Bambi's mother!—actually contrives to feed a harmless puppy narcotics. We are then invited to laugh at this victimized creature's tribulations, included certifiable brain death, resuscitation by electrotherapy (in the form of a cord plucked from a lamp), advanced catatonia, chemically induced aggression, and finally an immense agglomeration of broken bones.

Sir, as the sainted Joseph Welch said to the Antichrist Senator Joe McCarthy, have you no shame?

Even the "story" is infantilizing of our responsibilities to our fellow creatures on spaceship Earth. It follows from the crush a high school nerd ("nerd" is a classist term for "ungainly, awkward, pimply fellow") develops for a high school dish ("dish," in the language of sexist society, would refer to a young woman of uncommon comeliness of feature, purely by the random distribution of genetic information). When he takes her to the "prom" (disgusting bourgeois celebration of liberation from the consciousness-raising responsibilities of public education), terrible events take place, namely he gets his "thing" caught in his zipper.

Is this funny? They call the fire department, the police department, the news media and this is . . . funny? Methinks not, gentle reader.

Years later, the young man, Ted (played by Ben Stiller), hires a private investigator, Pat (played by Matt Dillon), to find the girl, Mary (played by Cameron Diaz). Alas, the private investigator falls in love with Mary, and he seeks to take her for himself. In fact, she seems to inspire stalkers, as several others show up and pitch woo in her direction, like Penelope's suitors.

No doubt, Diaz is the best member of the cast, the rest of whom, all male, are asked to act as if compassion, fair play, brotherhood, and human love had no place in the universe in their quest to win the hand of Mary, now a Miami surgeon.

There is no respect for privacy in this movie! Don't they realize that privacy is the government's business! There's no respect for women, the tanned, the four-legged, the forlorn, the uncool, and the unfunny!

Why, one would actually think the point of the enterprise was to be funny and not advance, as all movies must, a social agenda of brotherhood as decreed by us of the media elite.

It should come as no surprise to anyone that this movie is directed by the Farrelly brothers, Peter and Bobby, who once did a film called *Dumb and Dumber*. This one is dumbest. And funniest, as if that matters even a little bit!

(JULY 15, 1998)

*G*o on. Admit it. It's okay. It'll be good for you. Back in high school, you hated the student council president.

He or she was a little icky gob of simpering perfection, a cloying, suck-up fascist with a taste for self-aggrandizement, high grades, and a lengthy extracurricular résumé. The narrow self-interest of this obsequious smiler and glad-hander made you sick, particularly as it sequestered behind giant clouds of cosmic flatulence entitled "School Spirit." He or she had a delusional insistence on self-importance, a rigidity of spirit and intellect, an almost total lack of either irony or self-awareness.

And while there is a special room in hell for these horrible people, until they die, the most pain they'll have to face is *Election*, a wonderful, piercing, and hilarious examination of high school politics and how bitter and ruinous it can become. Urge them to see it and suffer.

To encounter Tracy Flick (Reese Witherspoon), the iron mistress of Carver High school in Omaha, is to hate and fear her. There's something in the prim set of her jaw and the steely gray of her eyes that shows through when she thinks she's not being watched. She is pretty, perfect, perky, and given totally to the accomplishment of her goals. She's not lazy. She gets to school early, edits the yearbook, has a high GPA, and always has her hand raised highest and first in class. Her life is consumed in petty ambition. If you get in her way, she will stomp you to pulp and, like Hannibal Lecter, her pulse will never rise above 85. At least that's how Jim McAllister, better known as Mr. M, sees her. Jim (ever friendly, ever rumply Matthew Broderick) is a familiar figure to most grads of suburban high schools: He's a kind of teacher as celebrity, who is everywhere, sponsors everything, and has donated his body, soul, and ego to the school. He actually knows the words to the school song. He may even believe them. Everybody thinks he's so nice. And he is nice. But at the same time, you slightly suspect his motives: Like, doesn't this adult man have a life?

Of course he does, and the movie is complex enough to see that although he's its nominal hero, it's not much of a life. He has a loveless marriage with a doughy spouse whom he seems unable to stimulate, much less satisfy, and a transparent need to punish Tracy in the real world of the high school to pay her back for the sexual heat she inspires in him in the unreal world of his head.

That's pretty much *Election*. It sees through everybody. Nothing impresses it. All ideology is hollow self-aggrandizement, all causes bogus, the good are always punished, and the bad always triumph. It's misanthropic, cruel (so cruel it draws laughs from a vice-presidential nominee in a wheelchair, and I defy you not to laugh), and dead on. It's got the best faces on screen in years. Everybody looks exactly like who they are, particularly the school's clueless administrators with their open Midwestern mugs and gray crew cuts, or the hard-set eyes and too much makeup of Tracy's paralegal and very litigious mother (Colleen Camp). Seeing it is like standing in line to get the crusty macaroni and a milk or lemonade carton and still having no place to sit in the lunch hall, that cruelest of all arenas.

The main technique underlying this joyous celebration of human weakness is an obscure trick of the storytelling trade called "the unreliable narrator." Tracy and Mr. M take turns telling the story of the election in which they were essentially opponents, and both lie blandly to us as they speak, in clear contradiction to the behavior we witness on the screen. Both claim virtue as their cause and shield; both reveal the lowest kind of base human greed or envy as their motive.

The director, Alexander Payne, displays the same equanimity of contempt he showed in his previous film, *Citizen Ruth*, where both liberals and conservatives were bashed with gusto. That realpolitik obtains here as well, as perky pretty perfect Tracy, with her foursquare bromides, stands for conservatism in its insipid claims to moral purity and higher patriotism, and Mr. M is liberalism, propelled into deviousness by its own notions of superiority, quite willing and able to subvert democracy to achieve its supposedly high ends. It offers a pox on both their houses.

It's Mr. M who cadges the decent jock Paul Metzler (refreshing Chris Klein) to stand against the unopposed Tracy, but the race isn't thrown into turmoil until Paul's sister Tammy (Jessica Campbell) also enters the race, out of frantic sibling rivalry and frustrated sexual longings (a long story, best left for the movie to tell).

The movie watches as the conflict between Tracy and Mr. M, though sublimated into secret stratagems and small, insincere gestures, intensifies to the point of hysteria. It's not hard to see the folkways behind a certain semi-square city on the Maryland side of the Potomac in all this. The true battles are battles of spin and combat by proxy, under a veneer of sniveling genteelness, only occasionally giving vent to pure hatred. Ultimately one of the contenders becomes so wrought up in the conflict that he or she stupidly destroys him or herself.

Of course *Election* illustrates a famous adage usually ascribed to faculties or newsrooms: The fight is so bitter because the stakes are so small. But the laughs are so big.   (MAY 7, 1999)

*E*ndearing if slight, *Superstar* at least knows what it's doing the whole way, which is more than can be said for many movies lately and most movies derived from *Saturday Night Live* skits ever.

Catholic schoolgirl Mary Katherine Gallagher is the poster child of the walking wounded. The poor thing, horse-faced and -hipped, as yet unkissed and unloved, lethally self-loathing and yet achingly swollen with yearnings, has been a staple of the show since 1995, under the stewardship of Molly Shannon. Now as it happens, Shannon, a mature and even voluptuous woman, looks about as much like 17 as I do like 25. But realism was never and still isn't the point: The character works because Shannon so precisely gets the dank weirdness of the truly alone. And also because she shows her underpants a lot.

I do not mean that in the erotic sense. Rather, it's Shannon's absolutism, the way she breaks down all barriers between the self and the character and when, in a whirling dance of Mary Katherine's thwarted eros and selfhood, she loses all control and crashes like a fallen gymnast amid the folded chairs, her legs askew, her too-tiny schoolgirl kilt aflutter and the little white delta of her panties flapping before the world, we sense someone profoundly disturbed yet poignant at the same time.

Similarly, the movie understands the fine line between Mary Katherine's neediness, which attracts us, and her repulsiveness, which doesn't. It keeps her in this odd zone as a kind of sacred monster and it keeps her in a universe where sacred monstrosity is appropriate. It's set in an extended-sketch universe of primary colors, unlikely occurrences, cartoony opposites and complete improbabilities. The movie isn't like a sketch, it is a sketch, though an eighty-two-minute one.

Thus its sensibility is never really conventionally narrative or even very coherent; it's anarchistic, surrealist, set in an upscale parochial school called St. Monica's that no Catholic school graduate will recognize. It's a fabulist environment in which Jesus can be a New Agey hipster who hopes to win Mary over with the Hi-I'm-Jason sincerity of a La Jolla waiter; Sky (Will Ferrell, who also plays Jesus) can be a self-satisfied parody of fifties narcissism, whom Mary Katherine adores even as we see he's not worthy; Evian (Elaine Hendrix) will be Mary Katherine's nemesis because she has a cute butt, blond hair, and those eyebrows that are kind of hinged in the middle, giving her a look of wanton cruelty. The fact that all these people seem about thirty-five skews the thing even further into craziness.

The plot is a whisper of a murmur of a twitch, not meant to be taken seriously. When it isn't bothering to parody Brian De Palma's *Carrie*, it follows as Mary Katherine, total outsider relegated to special ed (with other unusual students, like a kid who pretends to be high), aches to enter the *Catholic Teen* magazine "Let's Fight Venereal Disease" Talent Contest, which, if she wins, will make her a superstar and ultimately get her kissed, preferably by Sky (meanwhile, she practices on trees and lampposts).

Of course her overprotective grandmother (Glynis Johns) won't permit it, hoping to spare Mary the fate of her parents, who were stomped to death by Irish step dancers. And the cool kids at school think it's gross that such an armpit-sniffing crazo of Mary Katherine's addled intensity should even consider such a thing. The administrators advise Ritalin. But Mary Katherine slogs onward like a Christian soldier.

The story is basically a pretext for inspired riffs and numbers so bad they're good and for Mary's signature ritual of self-deconstruction, taking the immediate environment with her. And the fact that Shannon, a gifted comedian, isn't much of a dancer and an even worse singer just gins the sense of the absurd up to a higher pitch.

Mary Katherine will never be confused with Madame Bovary or the French Lieutenant's Woman, but when she's disrupting the cosmos with her insistence that it notice her, she expresses a universal attribute that proclaims simply: I exist! The cosmos, of course, answers: Huh?

(OCTOBER 8, 1999)

*B*ut first, a quiz. Which of the following doesn't belong?

    a. Clark Gable.
    b. Gary Cooper.
    c. Jimmy Stewart.
    d. Adam Sandler.

If you guessed A, B, or C, please leave the article right now.

Next: Which of these doesn't belong?

    a. *It Happened One Night.*
    b. *Mr. Deeds Goes to Town.*
    c. *Mr. Smith Goes to Washington.*
    d. *Mr. Deeds.*

Folks, this isn't rocket science.

And neither is *Mr. Deeds*, the lame Adam Sandler remake of Frank Capra's classic 1936 piece of Americana, which starred the great Coop as Longfellow Deeds, a hick from French Lick—actually, Mandrake Falls, just down the road from Bedford Falls—who brought small-town practicality, compassion, and civic spirit to the blighted burg of New York and of course was put on trial for his sanity.

In the current film, directed incoherently by Mr. Nobody, Steven Brill, Sandler is in the Gary Cooper role &%$#*DOESNOTCOMPUTE DOESNOTCOMPUTEDOESNOTCOMPUTEDOESNOTCOMPUTE DOESN—

Sorry, folks, I had a hard time getting that one by my computer. Sheesh, everyone's a critic these days.

But the clicking box has a point. It does not compute that Adam Sandler is the new Gary Cooper, as he lacks the common majesty, the grace, the stoicism, the dignity of that towering figure. What he has, I suppose, is feisty childishness and narcissistic shamelessness. At the least he's not Pauly Shore.

But pairing him with Winona Ryder is a disaster. Ryder, who plays Babe Bennett aka Pam Dawson, the reporter who worms her way into Deeds's confidence in order to betray him, but ends up falling in love with him, seems a bit intense. Get this woman a Prozac prescription. Her delicate, dark-eyed, wren-boned beauty and vibrations of meltdown make you want to hold her close and whisper, "There, there" into her ear. The last thing you want to see is her laying a lip lock on the mullet-headed Sandler.

In any case, when Capra gave the role to go-getting, raspy-throated, saw-blade-tough Jean Arthur, he struck movie magic, and made Arthur a star. No such luck with neurotic Ryder, who already is a star, at least for a little longer, but has zero chemistry with Sandler. Again, the best that can be said is that she isn't Helena Bonham Carter.

And the modernization of the old text is a completely spotty effort. In the original, Deeds inherits an opera house, which brings him chockablock against ironic swells and sophisticates. When they snicker at him, he beats them up. Sandler's Deeds inherits a giant media empire, apropos 2002, but he still seems to hail from 1935's version of Mandrake Falls, a Brigadoon if ever there was one. Don't Brill and Sandler get it that in most small towns they have this new modern invention called "television"? Deeds's naïveté makes him seem not charming but mentally ill.

And his propensity for violence—he beats up several older, weaker men, and only one younger, stronger one—seems not like foursquare masculine bravado, à la Cooper in the less psychotic thirties, but again, crazy, ugly, and scary. In fact, a sense of the grotesque runs through the film; an extended joke about Sandler's black, dead foot (from frostbite as a kid) borders on something you find in John Waters.

Of plot, there's not a lot. Indeed, the few pleasures in *Mr. Deeds* are entirely incidental to star and plot. One is John Turturro (aside: Adam Sandler ought to be a comic sidekick in John Turturro movies, not the other way around) as a Spanish butler, one of Turturro's effortless zany turns, and the only thing in the film up to 1935 standards. Then Peter Gallagher, always a reliable manufacturer of industrial-grade unction, manufactures industrial-grade unction as Chuck Cedar, the CEO of the company that plots smarmily against Deeds.

And finally, yes, I must admit, it is enjoyable to watch ironic sophisticates get beaten up in fancy restaurants.

But all in all, this baby makes you ever more eternally grateful for AMC and TCM on the cable. That's where the real movies have gone to hide.   (JUNE 28, 2002)

*A*ustin Powers in Goldmember is puerile, pitiful, grotesque, offensive, immature, repulsive and, of course, extremely funny.

Possibly it helps to be twelve and pretty much unsocialized. Perhaps it helps to believe passionately that jokes involving orifices and their work-product are hilarious. Perhaps it helps if you like Mike Myers so much you don't really care if he's gotten larger and larger, like a runaway zeppelin, while his co-stars get smaller and smaller. Look quick and you'll note Robert Wagner, behind his Hathaway-man eye patch, as No. 2, but mostly he just stands there, looking bored. Michael Caine is also in the film, in the role of Powers's father, Nigel, but I can recollect nothing of his performance.

The plot is the usual meltdown of story situations from the James Bond oeuvre blown out to imbecile proportions and completely disconnected from any cause-effect theory of reality. I suppose the antecedent is *Goldfinger*, the excellent Bond film from 1964, in which the superb German actor Gert Frobe played a gold-obsessed sociopath whose plan was to nuke the gold reserve at Fort Knox so as to increase the value of his own holdings. His best line came when Sean Connery's Bond, splayed on a table and about to be eviscerated by a laser, asked Goldfinger if he expected him to talk: "No, Mr. Bond, I expect you to die."

There's no line as smart or memorable as that in *Goldmember*, but then Bond didn't crack nearly as many flatulence jokes.

This variant replaces the bomb with an asteroid, which Dr. Evil (Myers), the Dutch psychopath Goldmember (Myers—and, boys and girls, can you figure out why they call him "Goldmember"?) and the Scottish bully Fat Bastard (Myers) draw into collision with Earth to disastrous consequences. Why do they want to do this? I must have missed that part.

Anyhow, they are opposed in this effort by swingin' sixties Brit secret agent Austin (Myers), in Carnaby Street colors, with bad teeth, froufrou shirts and Edwardian jackets in shades of paisley and plaid unseen this side of a bad LSD experience. The only key part that Myers doesn't play is Mini-Me (Verne Troyer), the pint-size clone of Evil. But he's probably working on a way to do that next time.

That would be a shame. Troyer, alone among the regulars, gets a real showcase. He has developed into a skillful film performer, at least within the narrow confines of the *Austin Powers* series. He plays extremely well off Myers in whatever role Myers happens to be occupying at the time; I loved to watch the flow of bafflement and illumination on that tiny face of his. He's the one actor who can stand against the Myers juggernaut and walk away unscathed.

Even token beauty Beyoncé Knowles, of Destiny's Child, registers dimly as Foxxy Cleopatra, a seventies-style jive-talking FBI agent who gets into the picture via time travel, probably the series's weakest stroke.

But the level of inventiveness remains high. Another reliable source of comedy is the appearance of various uptown movie celebs, who are obviously delighted to be included in the fun. You'd be surprised how high-powered some of these folks are. I'd tell you who they are, but I'd be killed shortly thereafter, so best leave it at that.

Of course what really drives the film is Myers. The brazenness of his ego is dwarfed only by the size of his talent, and in this one, he really lets rip. The core of it is the true narcissist's shamelessness: He has no repression holding him back, and you can't embarrass him. Thus all his characters, with the exception of Fat B. (rather diminished in this film), have a sublimely unique way of moving, slightly effeminate, a projection of softness and decadence. It's not that they're gay, it's just that they're in that zone of sexual androgyny whose most salient aspect is a lack of connection to either sex. Their swishiness expresses nothing except the idea that swishiness is funny; it is original unto itself. (Martin Short, another fabulous Canadian talent who graduated from *Saturday Night Live*, has the same powerful vibration.)

This is only amplified when, as he frequently does in a variety of guises, Myers is moved to dance. He's a very bad dancer, yet his utter lack of fear and shame is the fuel that drives the charming power of his rottenness. The world has entirely too many excellent dancers; it needs more bad ones. (JULY 26, 2002)

*T*he most sincere thing about *Down with Love* is its deep insincerity. Nominally, it's a romantic comedy set at the high-water mark of the empire of repression—1962, to be exact—when not only didn't things all hang out, but nothing hung and there was no out. Nobody seemed to be getting any, although babies arrived in the millions, possibly by virgin birth. The movie ticks off the icons of the era; primary colors, pillbox hats, slick magazines, mind-altering drugs known quaintly as "cocktails," filter cigarettes, and the fabulous isle of Manhattan. The high art form of the period was the double-entendre-driven s-x comedy, where nothing was named (much less shown) but everything was hinted. Some people liked it better that way, and they will love this picture.

So *Down with Love* is really an extended parody of the Rock Hudson/Doris Day films of that era—*Pillow Talk* was the best and most famous—but the term "extended parody" describes exactly its greatest flaw: the strain of sustaining the artifice over the long haul. It's like a *Saturday Night Live* sketch on a $60 million budget.

The stars trying to bring this off are Ewan McGregor, essentially playing Rock Hudson playing someone, and Renée Zellweger as Doris, similarly playing someone. The script follows the formula so religiously that Rock even has a neurotic sidekick. In the original, this was Tony Randall, so you could say that David Hyde Pierce has the Tony Randall role. The only problem is that Tony Randall is in the film, though not in the Tony Randall role; he's in the Dean Jagger role.

Anyway, as Eve Ahlert and Dennis Drake's script has it, McGregor, his hair dyed black, his body fat reduced to 0.00001 percent, his wardrobe cool-bachelor dark, plays one Catcher Block, man about town. A famous reporter for *Know* magazine (a clear analogue to *Esquire*), Catcher—debonair, suave, slick, manipulative—is the one guy who seems to have figured it all out. His life is a chick-o-rama, primarily with the highest fantasy class of early-sixties chick, the international stewardess, usually Swedish, German, or French, in the tailored blue uniform, the tightly coiffed blond hair (she looks like a plastic blond mushroom) and the airborne freedom from stuffy moral laws.

Meanwhile, the new girl in town is Barbara Novak (Zellweger), authoress of the new bestseller *Down with Love*. It postulates, astonishingly, that women have as much right to sexual enjoyment as men, and that women should put off marriage and have their own season of flings, meanwhile striving to become successful in the workplace.

Such heresy must be obliterated. So the fabulous Catcher, after ducking out on an assigned interview with the new celeb, decides to woo and seduce her, get her to fall in love with him, and thereby prove that women really want to be married with kids. All this liberation stuff is just a phase they're passing through, and he means to end it right here and now, plus get a sensational exposé for *Know*. Thus he invents a phony personality, meets cute with her at a dry cleaner, and begins to romance her as Zip Martin, astronaut and straight arrow.

One odd effect of the film: It makes anyone with a long memory see how good an actor Rock Hudson was. I mean that quite sincerely; to get anywhere near Hudson's ebullience, confidence, and sexual magnetism, poor li'l Ewan must work overtime. You never saw a face so busy: He's continually arching an eyebrow, pursing his lips, sucking in his cheeks, dilating his eyes up for warmth or down for cunning, concentrating on his timing. He's doing every Brit-actor thing he can think of, huffing and puffing. You just want him to cut the twinkle factor down to nil and relax a little.

Hudson—big, slow, phony, a poseur, and a fake—did all this so effortlessly you never saw him break a sweat. Maybe it was the joy he took in the giant trick he was playing on the straight public; maybe he was just a natural-born con man; maybe he was too thick to think it through, thus liberating his instincts to trump his thought processes. But he was brilliantly spontaneous, warm, sexy, and magnetic in those films. McGregor doesn't hold a candle to him.

As for Zellweger, she seems a little more comfortable and appears to enjoy aping the goofy stylings of the period, when actresses didn't just walk into a room, they entered it, model-style, with a pirouette to show off Edith Head's latest knockoff in nuke-blast yellow. The truth, though, is that the twitchy Hyde Pierce steals the camera every time he's on it; and in the end, you care more about his thwarted affair with the editor played by Sarah Paulson than the phony bond between Rock and Doris—that is, Catcher and Barbara.

The movie's better tricks are the filmmakers' flourishes, from the scrambled Manhattan geography in the opening sequence (Barbara gets off the train at Grand Central Terminal, crosses the street to the United Nations and climbs into a cab that runs three blocks down First Avenue to the Empire State Building) to the swank "modern" apartments with the latest in with-it hi-fi and sofa-bed equipment. Director Peyton Reed loves the stylizations of the period, doting particularly on the ancient male custom of never entering a room without first pouring a nice brown liquid into a big glass. Now where did that one go?

But best of all is a scene-you-never-thought-you'd-see riff, right out of Mad magazine. In the old films, Day and Hudson could appear in the same frame in a quasi-naked state (in the bath behind strategically arranged suds, or in a robe) only if they were in separate geographical locations, via a split screen. Someone here has come up with the brilliant idea of using the split-screen technique again—but placing the actors in positions that evoke a number of sexual practices that could not even be alluded to in the early sixties. It's a grand device to suggest what the movie tries for more than an hour and a half to, but can't quite, express: How different then is from now.   (MAY 16, 2003)

*U*nder its title, *Lost in Translation* begins by displaying an image that is itself lost in translation: a beautiful woman's rear end in repose, lightly sheathed in gossamer knickers.

Hoo boy, you think (if you're emotionally about seventeen), is that ever in the Esperanto of sexual possibility.

But that very image is misunderstood. Scarlett Johansson's lyrical caboose decodes not as sex, but as something related yet utterly distinct: intimacy. For if you see a woman in her skivvies, that doesn't always mean sex is about to happen. (If you're married, it means sex is probably not about to happen.) But it does signify that between the two of you there's a feeling of trust, of togetherness, of wholeness against a world full of idiots and morons and schemers. And that's exactly the subject of *Lost in Translation*.

Directed with grace and dexterity (but no great need to be done in a hurry) by Sofia Coppola, it's the story of an unlikely alliance between an aging movie star and the young wife of a photographer when the two find themselves abandoned in a Tokyo hotel for a few days, while other people all around them do seemingly necessary and important things. Although the basis of their confederation is their mutual conviction that these necessary and important things are pretty much bull-flop.

Bill Murray, in his most complete performance since *Groundhog Day*, plays Bob Harris, the star, a lion in . . . if not winter, possibly edging toward autumn. Bob's fatigue shows in his tone, his body language. Murray reminds me of Jerry Lewis's great performance in Martin Scorsese's *King of Comedy,* in that it seems as if gravity has singled him out for special punishment, pulling his flesh down, closer and closer to the earth. His Bob is in Japan to shoot a sublimely ridiculous whiskey commercial for a sublimely ridiculous fee. (It's a poorly kept secret that many stars, like Harrison Ford and Sean Connery, have shown the yen for easy yen.) Two million bucks to look sophisticated and say, "Suntory Whiskey—it's smooth and relaxing," or something like that. Bob is a pro and he soldiers on, even if dealing in Japan with the Japanese is a bafflement wrapped inside an enigma inserted into a sushi maki.

In the same hotel, the Park Hyatt Tokyo—Coppola gets a great sense of place from this noplace, 211 caverns and halls and streamlined Japanese rooms without character or tone—stays Charlotte, with the loose, dull face of the utterly disengaged. Charlotte's husband, John, who photographs rock musicians, is played at full-tilt narcissistic abandon by Giovanni Ribisi. In fact, all of Coppola's pocket portraits of entertainment figures—agents, publicists, photographers, and particularly a grotesque young American actress—are dead-on and hilarious. She's got the satirist's gift for killing swiftly without a lot of blood and screaming.

But Charlotte isn't hilarious, and it's another vivid example of Coppola's gift how quickly the young director evokes the dynamic of a marriage gone stale. Charlotte is a smart, beautiful Yalie, and she was obviously taken with John's glamour. But he's the kind of person who, in getting it, doesn't get it. He's too career-obsessed to notice how trivial his career is. And he has begun to dislike the fact that she sees through his shallowness and the dreariness of his friends, and that she can't focus on his passionate discussions of his interpretations of the looks of various artists he photographs. It's not stated, but clearly the issue in play is: Can this marriage be saved?

Probably not. So it is that John disappears for a bit, and Charlotte and Bob meet in the hotel's swanky bar and immediately begin to hit it off in subtle, secret ways. Clearly, they are agreed on the fatuousness of much of the world and the infertility of the rest of it. And they both hate someone passionately: themselves.

What unspools is essentially two separate movies, one very funny in a Bill Murray kind of way, the other very poignant in a Sofia Coppola kind of way. The technical difficulty is that each movie requires a different Bill Murray and, try as I might, I can come up with no coherent theory of Bob Harris's psychology.

One movie chronicles the adventures of an American movie star with a career in deep hemorrhage trying to get through a financially necessary ordeal in Japan. Murray certainly doesn't overdo it, but with that prehensile face, and its weird ability to project not just broad-stroke attitudes like "irony" but substates like "58 percent irony/40 percent fatigue/2 percent responsibility," he's very funny. Coppola keeps throwing up things for him to react to: a masseuse who may be a prostitute lying on her back on the floor riding an imaginary bicycle and screaming incomprehensibly in Japanese while he just sits there, that magnificent instrument of a face generating various shades of sub- and sub-substate; or his inability to stay focused during a commercial shoot that is utterly chaotic, because his translator speaks worse English than he speaks Japanese—and he speaks no Japanese.

The other movie is about a lonely, sad older man, who seems as completely un-movie-star as you could imagine (he seems more like a CEO), who meets an equally lonely, sad younger woman in a hotel, and finds her magically simpatico. You know the sensation: It's not love, but it's some immediate awareness that the two of you may have been separated at birth, your minds operate alike, your synapses fire in the same pattern, you recognize the same enemies (many) and the same allies (few). It's you and she against the world, and boy, is it ever fun.

Sex, somehow, doesn't come into it. Sex, somehow, would ruin it. You can get sex anywhere. (And Bob does.) From this one, you want that precious process that E. M. Forster so wisely described as "only connect." So Bob and Charlotte connect and proceed through a number of adventures in Japan, and discover that their equal bafflement at all things Japanese is somehow a part of their bond.

That's really the magic of the movie, which is, in the end, wonderfully nice. It gets at something exquisitely human, so human that even movie stars feel it.   (SEPTEMBER 12, 2003)

Six

MONSTERS AND SCI-FI

What is the number of the beast?

If you said 666, you said wrong.

It's actually something like 207, give or take a few creatures at the margins of beasthood.

The number comes from the ever-helpful *VideoHound's Golden Movie Retriever* of 1997; it's the number of entries in sub-agate type under *Monsters, General,* running from *The Astounding She-Monster* to *Zarkorr! The Invader,* for a total of 204. Then I added *Jurassic Park, Anaconda,* and, of course, today's *The Lost World: Jurassic Park.*

The point to be made from this little adventure in subatomic type sizes is that, as a genre, the monster movie has been with us a long time—dating from at least 1917—and has acquired a classic structure, a set of traditions and an abundance of variations.

Also, it's been pretty lousy. The editors at VideoHound thoughtfully put little black triangles next to outstanding entries, and they only spend 11 of them over their 204 listings.

But their own list is rather suspect: They don't include such classics as *King Kong, The Beast from 20,000 Fathoms, It Came from Beneath the Sea* and the great *Them!* although curiously enough they do have the last of the fabulous Ray Harryhausen stop-motion masterpieces, *20 Million Miles to Earth* (1957). That's the one where the Air Force officer (Hedda Hopper's son Bill) bazookas the creatures from Venus off the wall of the Colosseum in Rome. That was really cool. (Bazookas were big in the world of fifties monster movies: better living through rocketry.)

Two questions immediately arise: (a) What is their enduring appeal? and (b) Don't we spoil all the fun if we take them too seriously?

The first attraction of the monster movie is simple preadolescent power fantasy. You look at something big, something civilized, something ancient and dignified and you think: Wouldn't it be fun to smash it to smithereens?

Of course, as a small, weak child, you could never do such a thing, so you reinvent your urge to crush the world in the form of a large, hideous but very neat beast. It's from the past or from space—reptile, insect, alien, or mollusk (*The Monster That Challenged the World*, 1957; big snails). Still, its real source is your own id. Though it might be radioactive isotoped to death, it can never be spanked, yelled at or sent to its room.

You love to imagine the crunch of the bricks as they tumble, the taste of policemen, the anger of the military, the irritations of scientists and principals, the pleasures of pulping the city.

But there's more than the child's rage at being in a world misrun by adults. Underlying every monster movie there does seem to be the same argument—man vs. nature.

Does man have a right to exploit nature or even the nature of the universe? If so, won't nature retaliate in the form of a big bad thing that squishes everything?

Put another way, is some knowledge forbidden by God? That's what wise scientist Edmund Gwenn says at the end of *Them!* after large, carnivorous ants have munched their way through the sewers of Los Angeles.

This stems from a subtler premise yet: that man and nature are somewhat separate. There is man, there is nature. We, it. We are not of nature, having removed ourselves via the jalopy known as Original Sin. Thus, it is possible to contaminate our own planet, to spread our sin to it. Therefore, we will be punished.

In some form, monster movies are an account of nature's punishment on mankind. In that way, they are sagas of purification through retribution. Hurt us, we scream. Love to, the beast answers, smashing buildings, snapping up human hors d'oeuvres. And in *The Lost World: Jurassic Park*, we are in an hors d'oeuvre-rich environment.

And thus it is that the classic monster's demise always aches with sadness. He dies, we survive, and we know that somehow, this is not good for the world. We have not been cleansed by the blood of the really big, mean lamb; we have killed him and will go back to our merry rape.

All this began—well, it began in the Bible or with Gilgamesh and was later refined by Mary Shelley and Sigmund Freud et al.—but it began in the movies in the head of a tragic little fellow named Obie; he was the first to let us see the nature of the beast—both what he had done to us and what we had done to him. Obie was Willie O'Brien, a visionary special-effects guy who animated a dinosaur as early as 1915 in a film titled *The Dinosaur and the Missing Link*.

The technique, which was to build a miniature, flexible model and move it with infinite patience, was called stop-motion. In Dr. Franken-stein's memorable phrase: It's alive! It's alive!

Obie was involved in the production of two monster masterpieces, the original *Lost World* of 1925; and of course the mighty *King Kong* of 1933. The first of these, adapted from a story by Sir Arthur Conan Doyle, re-flected the idea that the exploration of nature was heroic. In it, an expedi-tion ventures to a plateau in South America. The attitude of the day was this world was "lost" because white people didn't know where it was. It is a majestic playpen for the Western mind and only exists to amuse its pene-trators. In the end, ravaged by a volcano, it is, like Eden, snatched from "us."

In the great *Kong*, the issue is clearly race. The order being violated isn't the scientific order. (There's no science at all in *King Kong*.) It's the more fundamental moral order of the universe. Next to *Birth of a Nation*, *King Kong* is probably one of the most embarrassing masterpieces ever made. To see it today is to enjoy it for its vigor and cringe at its ugliness. It's doubtless unfair to judge the efforts of 1933 by the standards of 1997, but such things should be nevertheless talked about.

Kong, a sixty-foot-tall ape, rules a forgotten jungle island, even able to defeat the mighty T. rex in single combat (a great sequence). Moviemak-ers, led by the adventurous Carl Denham (blowhard Robert Armstrong), go to film him. Instead they capture him, seeing him as a great attraction. Brought to New York, and chained for the pleasure of his viewers, he breaks loose and bounds through the city. Ultimately, he climbs that great monument to Western man, the Empire State Building, and is brought down by a fleet of pursuit ships, as fighter planes were cutely called in those days.

Kong is a pure metaphor, though possibly unconscious, for the slave. He's huge, robust, muscular, captured in a jungle, brought in chains across the sea by people of another race who are unable to imaginatively enter his mind or share his pain or recognize his tragedy. He is exploited cruelly, even his heart is trifled with, though his tormentors believe him to be inflamed by sexual desires. He is ultimately destroyed by them. Then, of course, it's all his fault. "It wasn't the airplanes," says Carl Denham at the end, "it was beauty slayed the beast."

Er, no, Carl. See, it was white people who slayed the beast.

The genius of *Kong* is O'Brien's ability to personalize the beast in ways that his exploiters never got but which admitted the audience to his sympathies. We feel a pain for Kong that the cops, the pursuit-ship pilots, the massively moronic Carl Denham never do. O'Brien built a head for close-ups and understood how important the eyes were; Kong's glitter with pain and confusion and love. Think how subversive: The slave has feelings, too. The slave can love, too. Perhaps even more than its then-awesome spectacle, that's what lingers about *King Kong*: the suspicion that its great ape was the most human thing in the film.

By the fifties, O'Brien acolyte Ray Harryhausen had commandeered the monster market. He made a number of superb monster movies, trashing Washington (*Earth vs. the Flying Saucers*). But I'll take Manhattan. This would be his great *The Beast from 20,000 Fathoms*, of 1953, probably the best pure monster movie ever made. I happened to see it again recently on AMC; it stands up pretty well after all these years.

By the fifties, of course, science meant something. It meant The Bomb. Therefore, not surprisingly, the man vs. nature argument was couched in the terms of Armageddon. The endless slew of monsters who advanced from the sea, the Arctic, or underground to menace us were the bomb's swollen, mutant children, nurtured on poisoned breezes and sent to punish us for our hubris.

In *Beast*, the creature was a gigantic dinosaur called a rhedosaurus, liberated from natural cryogenic storage at the North Pole by an atomic bomb test. Yes: We decided to test an atom bomb at the North Pole and to hell with Santa Claus! Imagine a sixty-foot-tall puma with scales and that's pretty much Mr. R. Harryhausen was known for his "realism," by which is meant his infinite patience. Harryhausen, after O'Brien, worked with small models, a movie at a time; his beasts were far more graceful than the twitchy Kong, but still a far cry from the fast movers of the Spielberg ilk.

But he really tapped into something with the spooky imagery of his monster tripping the light fantastic on the sidewalks of New York. And through them, as well. Roaming the canyons of the city, impervious to bullets or New York rudeness (City to Monster: Drop Dead), Mr. R is The Bomb, the destroyer of cities, given flesh and attitude and set to work. He punishes us for our sins in inventing the technology that liberated him in the first place.

The monster movie died everywhere late in the fifties except in the minds of the kids who'd been transfixed by it. Cheap, cheesy Japanese imitations like *Godzilla* and *Rodan* (big flying lizard, went "Caw, caw," you could see the strings) glutted the market.

Harryhausen, after turning to a series of mythological retellings, retired grumpily a few years back, grousing about how the "anti-hero" had killed the business he loved so.

He may have been right; but the one place the monsters still thrived was in the brain of Steven Spielberg, who got near their primordial power in *Jaws* and has now returned with a vengeance in the two *Jurassic Park* movies.

Spielberg is clearly a connoisseur of the genre, and his films are chock-full of warm references. Like many fifty-year-old moviegoers, he must cherish memories of that big Mr. Rhedosaurus going out on the town. He's cared enough to construct the films once again as arguments over men and science. Now it's not the atom, it's the specter of genetic engineering—that is, rewiring the very juice of life, DNA, to create the bad old boys for corporate greed.

The science in the Spielberg films is totally up to date, in more ways than bioengineering. The model for the creatures is no longer the hulking thunder-lizards: These boys are fast, supple, smart, and mean, birds of prey who happen to be land-bound, though they can leap yards at a time.

But for all of that, they wage the same argument: They represent the notion of science gone too far, taking man into forbidden areas, and offering up a spectacle of retribution for this blasphemy. What is different is the sense of human responsibility.

In the old movies, the death of the beast was never an issue. But it's clear that Spielberg, his screenwriters, and even original novelist Michael Crichton understand that the creatures cannot be killed without remorse. Thus, though they are homicidal in the extreme, the idea of actually putting them down is never faced frontally: In a new eco-conscious age, the life of the beast is far more valuable than the life of the man.

The answer has to do with the nature of our concept of nature and redemption. First we're lost; now we're saved. Nature, we suddenly realized, won't last unless we make it last. In the early days—really until quite recently—we had a vision of the world as infinite. Everything was replenishable; our appetites knew no bounds, and we had the right to slay anything that wandered in front of our gun sights, especially if it threatened us. Now we've learned of the secret of the universe, which is that the gap between us and it isn't nearly what we thought it would be. If we slay him, we somehow slay ourselves.   (MAY 23, 1997)

*W*e thought it was dead.

We were wrong.

It walks among us, crushing cities, laughing at our delusions of might, leaving a wake of destruction, challenging our fundamental notions of superiority.

It cannot be reasoned with, bought off or destroyed. It just keeps on coming. That's what it does. That's all it does.

Godzilla?

Er, no, not really. What I happen to be talking about is something far more troubling than a thunder lizard doing the monster mash on Wall Street.

I'm talking about . . . the fifties.

The fifties—in style, to some extent, but in ideas to a more important extent—seem to form a kind of collective unconscious of eighties and nineties popular culture. Though prime fifties forms like war movies, westerns, musicals, and costume drama have all but died out, to be replaced with banter-driven, motive- and irony-free engines of computer-morphed spectacle, if you look closely enough you can still usually feel the thrill of that last antediluvian age and its notions of supremacy and entitlement.

That is especially true of *Godzilla,* possibly the most fifties-haunted film to come along since, well, *Independence Day,* which by no coincidence at all was assembled by the same team. In fact, what is most impressive about *Godzilla* goes beyond any pure movie pleasures, guilty or otherwise, and into the realm of design: It's how shrewdly director Roland Emmerich and producer Dean Devlin have managed to conceal the core fifties-ness of their film behind a comforting screen of more politically correct nineties-ness, while at the same time reveling in that fifties-ness in all its savage horror.

Godzilla is pure reincarnation of another vanished fifties movie type, the monster movie, just as *Independence Day* reincarnated the invasion-from-space opus. In fact, so pure a monster movie is *Godzilla* that it really has very little to do with its namesake, the kitschy Japanese film of 1956, which itself was a rip-off and crudely incorporated the heroic Raymond Burr in scenes inserted for importation to give American audiences a recognizable face and rooting interest.

Rather, this *Godzilla* seems at first to be an almost shot-by-shot remake of a much better film, *The Beast from 20,000 Fathoms*, a big American hit from 1953, which also featured a thunder lizard taking a 24-hour liberty on the town, ripping the Bronx up, tearing the Battery down. It repeats almost the same sequence of shots, as scientists try to decipher a series of marine and coastal catastrophes that reveal not merely the existence but ultimately the destination of a large, predatory underwater reptile that has somehow been liberated by nuclear testing. Only the locales of origin have changed, to accuse the guilty: In 1953, the movie postulates, the air force was detonating the scions of Little Boy and Fat Man up at the Pole; now, we've moved to the South Pacific, and it's French tests, which allow a rather bizarre (but necessary, as I will explain) subplot.

Emmerich even includes a number of homages to the magic genius of Ray Harryhausen, who animated that fifties proto-beast and many others. For one, he lets us glimpse a scene, in a looted video store, of Harryhausen's *It Came from Beneath the Sea* on a tilted tube; a giant squid wrestles with the Golden Gate Bridge. And he exactly duplicates a close-up of a bewildered New York cop as he first spots a 120-foot-tall felon coming his way. And for still a third, the creature itself seems far more similar to the athletic, lithe, muscular monster of Harryhausen's *20 Million Miles to Earth* than to either the Japanese guy in the rubber suit or his own crudely animated "rhedosaurus" from *Beast*.

At about the halfway point, *Godzilla* mutates; the plot morphs into a duplicate of another fifties monster movie, Gordon Douglas's great insect-noir, *Them!*, about giant ants hiding in the sewers of Los Angeles. *Them!* turned into a dark, terrifying and bunnyless egg hunt, as the FBI and the army looked for a queen ant's chambers, where her progeny were about to erupt from larvae and begin a biological progression that would replace *Homo sapiens* at the tip of the pyramid of life. As in *Them!*, so does *Godzilla* build to a baby-roast, though it's more discreet than the one in *Them!*, which nakedly invited its human audiences to cheer as the flame-throwers churned out cleansing flame to assure a man-dominated planet.

Finally, the movie returns to *Beast* for its last ten minutes (though to be fair, it also replicates the chase scene in the first *Jurassic Park*, with the big liz leaping after a speeding carful of squealing humans). But it takes us to a bridge, where our jets can finally get that fabled clear shot (key plot moves in *Beast* and *It Came from Beneath the Sea*, too), and the movie ends as *Beast* did, not with the creature driven back to the sea—as was the earlier *Godzilla*—but speared by a Harpoon-class missile from an F-18, to die in twisted, operatic poignancy, its yellow eyes fading to black, all its beautiful wickedness melting, melting, melting.

The movie's true athleticism isn't in its bounding, leaping, burrowing monster, it's in the brilliant juggler's way it keeps ideas from the fifties in play with ideas of the nineties. In fact, so diagrammatic is this that each fifties idea seems to have a corresponding nineties version, a sort of corrective correlative.

First of all, *Godzilla* is entranced with a key fifties idea: air power. The fifties was the decade of air power. The decade before we had used it to smash the Nazi and send all the Japanese ships to Iron Bottom Sound; now our bombers protected us with the ability to deliver nukes into the heart of Redland. Emmerich knows this; he loves it, in fact. In some ways, both *Independence Day* and *Godzilla* are most fabulously airplane movies: He loves the heroic iconography of planes and loves the way that in formation they relate to each other, in arrays that recall the old V-for-Victory posters of World War II, or those archival scenes of vast fleets of B-17s heading toward Berlin, or Avengers scudding out of the skies amid a black-blossoming spring of Japanese flak as they veered toward the flat-tops.

In this film, the Apache attack helicopters are the real stars, next to the monster itself. In the movie's best sequence, they hunt that bad boy through the canyons of New York, sending out arcs of tracers to bring him down. Mostly, they miss, providing us with shivers of pleasure as the tracers keep flying and whack down some of Trump's towers in the background; ah, destruction! It so amuses the secret adolescent in us all, possibly the true monster of monster movies. But the planes are seen as mankind's last best hope, and Emmerich dotes on the techno-jingle of pilot babble, the radar screens resolving the fury of beast-missile combat into neon-lit computer representations, but most of all the sheer energy of the tiny craft vectoring in to take the big guy down.

But here's the countervailing nineties idea—the marginalization of the military. In the fifties film, there was always a soldier standing by, ready to shout orders. He was almost always played by a red-headed Irish pug named Kenneth Tobey (in *The Thing, Beast,* and *It Came from Beneath the Sea*) who had the command thing down to perfection. Tobey's colonel or commander—usually named "Chuck," if memory serves— made up his mind in an instant, was never wrong, and had a spine of cold hard steel. He was American military might at its best, dadgummit.

Now, he's been pushed from the center. The officer in the film is played by a fat potatoey guy (Kevin Dunn) who screams too much, and makes wrong decision after wrong decision. He is assisted by a dunderheaded sergeant who always looks as if he's about to throw up. One other officer has a speaking part: a general who displays his stupidity by his Southern accent. The macho part has been ceded to Jean Reno, as a French secret service agent, whose presence is justified by the French atomic tests. This is a brilliant stroke, for it gets the same business done, but without retrograde bluster. Reno is much less intimidating, with a beard, a hulking gentleness, a comic yen for French coffee that the Big Apple cannot service; the film, which endorses the use of military force wholeheartedly at the visual level, backs away from it at the dramatic level.

Meanwhile, the liberal scientist, another fifties cliché, has moved from the edges to the center. Matthew Broderick is the film's nominal hero, a fuzzy-wuzzy green type known affectionately to his team as "the worm guy." He presents the humanistic point of view, that the big Zil is an animal, we made him, we are responsible for him. At no point will Broderick exult, and when he confronts the dying beast he looks upon it with such sadness that you feel his widdle bunny wabbit has died. Waaaaaahhhhhh!

But Broderick also sets up a harsh, ugly fifties idea: that women can't be trusted. In its subplot, *Godzilla* manufactures a tepid workplace drama in which Broderick's ex-girlfriend, played by the childlike Maria Pitillo, tries to advance in the world. A frustrated TV researcher who wants to be a reporter, she reestablishes contact with Broderick, then steals classified tapes from him, to make herself a star. That's straight out of fifties film noir: she's the femme fatale, the woman as black widow spider, who will do anything to achieve her means.

But here's the nineties twist: It's not that she's evil, it's not that she's ambitious, it's certainly not that the First Amendment guarantees the public a right to know about such things as 4 million tons of out-of-towner painting the town red. No, it's something far more profound. She is thwarted in her quest for stardom by the movie's clearest villain: a middle-aged white man. Harry Shearer plays an unctuous, sexually manipulative anchorman who commits the gravest of crimes by the standards of twenty-something Hollywood: He refuses to roll over and die so that someone younger can replace him. The cad! The monster! Kill him with a radioactive isotope! Or, no, no, even better: Kick him between the legs, right in the career!

That sop to Generation X aside, let us at last consider the biggest, baddest fifties idea in *Godzilla* and its nineties covalent. The prime idea of the fifties monster movie—and of fifties America—can barely be expressed now, so retrograde and slimy has it come to seem. But let us say it loud and clear: that man shall have supremacy over the Earth, its birds, beasts and fishes. It was, we believed and this *Godzilla* advances, our Earth. This is what I admire about this film—like *Independence Day*, it really gives you what it promises. Big intruder comes into the house; we kill it. Hooray, huzzah, way to go! Mess with us and die. If you want to run, you'll only die tired.

That idea is hopelessly out of date. Now Earth is a spaceship, and we humans have merely been entrusted with its stewardship as we pilot our way through the universe with our precious cargo of furry things. Nature is wonderful. Nature is bountiful. We must not work our way upon the face of nature. We are here not to exploit nature but to serve it. But secretly, *Godzilla* doesn't give a damn about nature. Attack us, Jack, we blow you out of your socks, just like we did two years ago when them aliens came down in their mile-wide frisbee and fried the Empire State Building.

Think how rarely this idea is expressed and to what ludicrous ends Steven Spielberg went in the second *Jurassic Park* to avoid mussing the hair of his T. rex. A worm is a cat is a dog is a boy is a dinosaur. Life, no matter the circumstances, is a sacrament. Emmerich pretends he believes this, and he makes all the right sounds, particularly by making certain the movie is devoid of white male authority figures who might seem to take pleasure in making the kill. But he pulls the trigger anyway. Talk about having a cake and eating it, too!

One thing that lets him get away with such apostasy is a nineties idea, and it makes the film distinctly different from a fifties film. It has no subtext. The great monster movies of the fifties—including all the Harryhausen work and the original Toho production—used the monster as a symbol of nature given scaled, puckered, or glisteny flesh; massive claws; and jaws the size of Cadillacs, come to punish us for fracturing the atom and learning how to destroy the planet. That may have been something of a fig leaf for a genre of movies that really took pleasure in the most primitive of cinema spectacle, the pure nihilism of destruction. Nevertheless it gave the movies a cloak of intellectual respectability, and in an era when critiques of our nuclear deterrent were not present in the arenas of public discussion, it might have seemed almost subversive.

But Emmerich and Devlin keep their *Godzilla* distinctly meaning-free. At no point is the beast weighted with significance; he's just a big beast. The end of the Cold War has taken the sting out of bomb fear; but they don't bother to make him a symbol of pollution or ozone depletion or deforestation or any of the other cosmic ills that we have unleashed upon ourselves. He's just a big old green lizard with a prognathous jaw and glittery eyes. That way, secretly, we can enjoy the movie's deepest and most subversive pleasure: Like the boys at the end of *Lord of the Flies*, we can, in our hearts, chant "KILL THE BEAST!" without remorse.

(MAY 25, 1998)

See, it's not really a mummy movie. What it is, is a bald-guy movie. Here are the rules: Mummy movies have a slow-walking, rotting, undead cadaver stumbling around, crushing people. Mummies are stealthy, not fast. You never see a mummy run. Rotting linen bandages by the mile are mandatory. On the other hand, bald-guy movies have some sleek oily grief merchant intimidating with the strength of his glare and the crown of his dome, and then he usually strangles people. I don't know why, your bald guy is usually a strangler.

That's what you find in the all-but-mummyless *Mummy*. Almost no mummies, one very large bald guy. Still, it's difficult to hold this against Universal Studios. How well would you expect a movie called *Bald Guy* to do? These people are not in business to lose money. And anyway, most of the last half of the movie has nothing to do with either bald guys or mummies but with that first-person shooter game called Doom. It's simply an invitation to watch Brendan Fraser blast dusty, smoky holes in shambling apparitions as they come at him in a cellarlike Egyptian treasure chamber.

The movie is fast and furious, shallow, empty, casually racist, merry, jaunty, silly and utterly weightless. It certainly lacks the grandeur of the original from 1932, which starred the great Boris Karloff. This one appears to star Mr. Clean.

Our mummy is the South African actor Arnold Vosloo, playing the Egyptian priest Imhotep. When first glimpsed in a pre-title sequence that could easily be the opening number in *Prince of Egypt*—that is to say, a Universal imitation of a DreamWorks imitation of Disney imitating Cecil B. DeMille—he's trysting with his love lady, who happens to be Pharaoh's mistress. Pharaoh is not happy, and when he confronts the priest and the babe, they kill him.

Priest escapes; babe kills self. Priest steals body, repairs to City of the Dead to reawaken her so they can get it on. Pharaoh's bodyguard tracks priest, mummifies him alive with 300 flesh-eating beetles. Wrinkle: If he is awakened—some mumbo-jumbo has to be spoken at the right time in the right sequence as recorded in the Book of the Dead—he becomes all-powerful. Why? Ancient Egyptian wisdom says: If he doesn't awaken, the movie won't open big in malls from Bangor to Albuquerque.

Enough plot, which hardly matters anyhow. The gist of it is that soon we are in the Egypt of 1926, where Yank soldier of fortune Rick O'Connell (Fraser) teams with the English bro-sis team of Evelyn (Rachel Weisz) and Jonathan (John Hannah) in an attempt to reach the City of the Dead and recover the Book of the Dead, as well as the treasure. Alas, there's another crew of treasure hunters about, friendly competitors,

whose one defining characteristic is that they have very square faces.
They're like refugees from a Dick Tracy comic strip. Occasionally notice-
able in the deep background are plenty of dusky Third Worlders whose
duty is to die screaming in a variety of colorful ways in order to advance
the plot. What is an American adventure movie—or, for that matter, an
American adventure—without a cast of thousands dying out of focus?

Thanks to some really important technical breakthroughs that
have aided our civilization immensely, we are able to see the Mummy
in an unwrapped yet ambulatory stage as a rotting corpse with a bad
attitude. For about the middle third of the picture, he clambers about,
reassembling himself by looting the eyes, tongues, flesh and loin-
cloths of those who freed him. He also has a plague trick and at the
drop of a finger can summon a cloud of locusts, a tide of beetles or a
napalm attack. He even appears able to move the moon into the way of
the sun for a few minutes, but once that trick's finished, nobody ever
mentions it again.

Director Stephen Sommers (who also wrote the screenplay and
must be adjudged guilty on two counts) keeps the thing running fast,
along thirties serial lines. It's all bangbangbang with a comic subtext
(Big American Fraser is stupid but brave; wily bro Hannah is smart but
a coward; big-eyed babe Weisz is sexy but klutzy), and whenever they
can't figure out what to do in the adventure movie, they kill a lot of
people.

In fact, though *The Mummy* probably hopes to be associated with
classy camp thrillers like *Raiders of the Lost Ark*, its unbearably high
body count among the world's people of nonwhite color compels its
entry in a lesser genre, which might be called, however clumsily, "Attempted old-fashioned films that foundered on their flagrant disregard
for human life." The genre highlights would be Tommy Lee Jones's *Nate
and Hayes,* truly despicable, or Tom Selleck's bomb-crazy *High Road to
China*—movie remnants of the age of imperialism that regrettably lin-
gered into the age of anti-imperialism.

In its shallow way, *The Mummy* amuses as it bustles along, littering
the sand with the dead in pursuit of gold. Nearly everybody dies, even,
in the end, some white people. But where the original—one of the great
trio of spooky, splendid horrors of the thirties, with *Frankenstein* and
Dracula—offered stealthy horror and the power of the imagination, this

Mum is only selling the latest in computer morphing techniques. Oh Mummy, poor Mummy, Universal's hung you in the closet and I'm feeling so crummy.   (MAY 7, 1999)

Set in a mucus-rich environment, *Alien: Resurrection* may not be the scariest movie ever made, but certainly is the gloppiest. It's so drippy and slippery you'll feel that you're hiding in Kevin Costner's nasal passages during the filming of *Waterworld*.

But the surprise is not how wet it is, it's how funny. The movie never scales the heights of pure skull-in-the-vise horror that Ridley Scott's original managed. And it never develops the cool marines-vs.-bugs carnage of James Cameron's second installment. But it brings a mordant, crackerjack wit to the world of chest-busting, head-ripping creepazoids from beyond.

This time it's 200 years later, but our heroine is still Sigourney Weaver's Ripley. Could that 8 tattooed on her forearm suggest that she's not quite the original, since the original died at the end of the disappointing *Aliens tiny-three*? And she's not: She's a clone that's been sent in. And so perfectly cloned is she that the scientists not only get a brand-spanking-new Ripley, but they get her black fingernail polish and the alien embryo left in her uterus from the last movie. Pay no attention to the laws of genetics: In space, nobody has heard of Mendel's principles of hereditary phenomena. *Alien: Resurrection* turns out to be far more interested in fiction than science, and it uses cloning as essentially a time machine by which someone from back there can get here.

Here is a deep-space research vessel called the Auriga. Like mad Frankensteins, government researchers (Dan Hedaya, J. E. Freeman, and ever-creepy Brad Dourif) are hot to reproduce the alien from the embryo that Ripley is carrying. They see a need for huge killer bugs, possibly to turn them loose on *Starship Troopers* spider planet Klendathu in a joint sequel down the line. To get it, they have to get her, but they don't realize they have invited two formidable species aboard. One is a giant, clambering head-ripper, and that's the least formidable. After all, it's only a bug.

The other is 6 feet 4 inches (it seems) of cream pale, leather-festooned, cut-muscle Valkyrie warrior queen with acidic blood and the instincts toward aggression of the entire 101st Airborne. Ripley is the superior being, and her attitude toward her fellow earthlings is that they are annoying accidents. They're the true bugs. Weaver plays the role like the goddess Athena on loan to Fox. (I knew Rupert Murdoch had connections, but . . .) And that's the source of much of the humor in the film: her utter, serene superiority to all walnut-faced, desperate men about her.

The film re-creates Scott's original vision of space vehicles not as sleek plastic and stainless steel but as squalid, drippy disasters of plumbing. It's the public-men's-room theory of space flight. And it loves the whole series's fascination with flamboyant gore: People get spattered, spindled, mutilated, and exploded from inside in a number of amusing ways. But structurally, the film bears far more resemblance to another disaster flick than any of the previous *Alien* films. The alien, of course, spawns, and its wretched children bust out to send the ship careening out of control, while scuttling about to devour all the humans. Thus it falls to Ripley and a crew of space privateers, including the incongruous Winona Ryder, to navigate their way across the foundering ship to a smaller lifeboat-style craft: It's *The Poseidon Adventure* with insects.

And speaking of Winona Ryder, what is she doing in this movie? I have no idea. Possibly the filmmakers think her presence will attract the kids who won't be attracted by watching embryos with teeth snap out of the chests of people, or male victims sucked into the huge, wet, gloppy womb wall of Mother Bug. Or perhaps her presence suggests a titillating whiff of a lesbians-in-space thing with Sigourney, but that certainly goes unrealized in the actual picture. No, poor Ryder merely wanders about looking like a perfect white rose in an ordure heap and eventually is connected to the plot in an extremely haphazard way.

A colleague has pointed out that the subtext of the film is birth and all the complications thereof. The laboratory of the ship is really a vast delivery room and the creature, it turns out, has an agenda: she's the Bobbi McCaughey of space bugs, who wants to populate the world with her progeny. The biology seems a little suspicious (no men need apply for stud service), but the film certainly plays with the queasiness the birth process creates in everyone except those in the OB-GYN trade. In fact, to carry it further, the ultimate spawn of the process, which looks like an albino Grinch, is actually dispatched by a method that seems to be a fourth-trimester abortion.

The director, incidentally, is Jean-Pierre Jeunet, the Frenchman famous in art film circles for two highly stylized movies, *Delicatessen* and the *City of Lost Children*.

This one looks a lot like those two and that pretty much sums up *Alien: Resurrection.* It's an art film with bugs that explode out of people's chests. And it's funny. The French, they have a knack, no?

(NOVEMBER 26, 1997)

Silly me. I thought the Nazis lost the war.

But here's the exceedingly strange new movie *Starship Troopers* commandeering 22 million American dollars in its first weekend and certain to make gobs more, while secretly whispering, "Sieg Heil!"

The movie recounts the adventures of a platoon of mobile infantry sometime in the next century as it does battle with a race of arachnid nasties on the far planet of Klendathu. It's an epic of bug blasting, a movie whose script appears to have been the instructions on a can of Raid. And in some profoundly disturbing way, it's Nazi to the core.

I don't mean to suggest that it's political propaganda in the literal sense or that it advocates Nazism. But it's a film that presupposes it. It's spiritually Nazi, psychologically Nazi. It comes directly out of the Nazi imagination, and is set in the Nazi universe.

It hails from what would be Year 64 of the Thousand-Year Reich, a sanitized utopia of heroic, sexless young folk grandly aware of their role as defenders of the known reality and descended from the Nazi pioneer generation of the 1930s and forties. Of course the great Führer has gone to Valhalla, but it's possible that in a home in some mountain fastness, some shiny facsimile of Holy Berchtesgaden, the 97-year-old Heinrich Himmler still dodders about, drooling and filling his Depends with waste, and on the odd clear day when his mind doesn't buzz with Alzheimer's, he remembers with pride the greatness he helped create. In this universe, he has already seen *Starship Troopers* fourteen times. He has been quoted in the *New York Volkischer Beobachter* as saying "Thumbs up!"

Fortunately, back here in grumpy reality, all that was blown to dust, crushed bone and ash back in Year 12, a very bad year for the Thousand-Year Reich and a very good year for the rest of us.

But you couldn't tell that from *Starship Troopers*.

We'll skip the obvious Nazi fashions and the appearances of Doogie Howser late in the film in a black shirt, overcoat, and SS-style cap; we'll skip the stylized swastika that is the mobile infantry's symbol; we'll skip the fact that the movie will soon be abbreviated in the vernacular *SS Troopers;* we'll skip the hazy intimation of a world fascist order contained in the film. Begin with the faces.

At first I thought that the notoriously perverse director, Paul Verhoeven, had a particularly inane imagination when it came to faces. No indeed; he has a very good imagination when it comes to faces. He knows exactly what he wants. So regular are the faces of the "cast"—the acting is so bad, the quotation marks are required—that it clearly represents a conscious decision. The stars, Casper Van Dien, Dina Meyer, Denise Richards, Jake Busey, and Neil Patrick Harris, share this in common: They all look alike.

They have oddly square faces and broad cheekbones, unprominent noses. They're blond or at least fair and boast some of the whitest choppers seen this side of a Dentyne commercial. But it's more than the shape and form: Their faces are also somehow uncomplicated, almost cartoon versions in flesh of actual humanity. Van Dien and Richards are particularly noteworthy in this regard. There's a simplicity and emotionless beauty that's far too vivid to be coincidental. They are generic. And all through the cast you see other iterations of the same principle: smooth, hairless, square, almost idealized faces. Even the odd token black person in this universe has the same bone structure and close-cropped hair.

What's going on? Well, one idea would be that these beings are produced through genetic engineering on an industrial basis, as in *Brave New World* or more recently *Gattaca*. But there's no mention of that in the film. A more insidious possibility relates exactly to Hitler's crazed state: that the size and range of the gene pool has been greatly reduced through some form of "purification." So in an unsettling sense, *Starship Troopers* appears to be set in a post-Holocaust world, a world where the body count didn't stop at 6 million but went on and on and on until only Aryan stock remained.

There are other, deeper issues. One is the movie's obsession that parallels a particularly loathsome Nazi obsession—cleanliness. In fact the Nazis saw their adversaries as representing some form of filth or infection. Their idea of the best world was *Judenrein*, meaning cleansed of Jews. They murdered, in the millions, under the guise of showering. In their perfervid imagination—visible in all their documents and propaganda—Jews and Bolsheviks were seen as eastern "hordes" representing not merely the swarm but the swarm of infection and disease. Look at the concept of *Lebensraum*, living room: Essentially, it is freedom from the filth of crowding.

And that's exactly the obsession with the spiders of Klendathu. In the movie's best special-effects sequence, our heroic platoon stands off hordes of the monsters (who aren't even armed, as a matter of fact, and would seem to be no big deal for any moderately equipped industrialized power with good Krupp and Mauser firepower). The creatures have been imagined horribly as the worst kind of body filth—they are not spiders at all, they are lice, huge infestations of crab lice, with ripping mandibles and piercing claws, who slay by rending their victims into parts. How filthy is that?

At its most visually impressive, the movie seems to recount a Hitlerian fantasy: a platoon of SS men in the far regions of the world standing firm against subhuman hordes, killing them in their millions and themselves dying in the best kind of nobility and sacrifice. The movie has a kind of pornographic relish in its depictions of slaughter. It isn't really set on Klendathu at all, but at Stalingrad.

You can take this even further with just a little research. The best description of the method of *Starship Troopers* came not from the great critics Anthony Lane or Janet Maslin or my brilliant colleague Rita Kempley. Rather, it came from historian Richard Grunberger, who noted that "brutal descriptions of fighting alternated with bathos-dripping 'comradeship.' " That's it perfectly: the utter savagery of the fighting to the last quarter, intercut with the most sentimentalized, infantilized version of human relationships, as reflected in dialogue so bereft of individuality that it could have been written by either a hack or a machine. It's a world where two forms of emotional expression exist: puppy love or death battle.

What Grunberger is describing, however, isn't *Starship Troopers* but a lost work of utter banality titled *Gruppe Bosemüller*, by Werner Beumelburg, a bestseller in Nazi Germany that was representative of a genre called *Fronterlebnis*, the notion of "war as a spiritual experience."

And that is exactly what *Starship Troopers* is selling. Unlike films from a civilized society that see war as a debilitating, tragic necessity, such as *Bridge on the River Kwai* or *Platoon* or *A Farewell to Arms*, this movie sees it as a profoundly moving experience: war as ultimate self-help course.

Its most blasphemous stroke is its inversion of one of the greatest war novels ever written, Erich Maria Remarque's *All Quiet on the Western Front*. This film is explicitly conceived as a rebuke to that great humanitarian soliloquy. It plays with Remarque's opening scene, where a schoolteacher lectures the boys sternly on the duties of manhood, the disciplines of the fatherland, and the glories of war. Believing him literally, our hero Paul rushes to the front, where he discovers the hideous lie his teacher has told him, as millions of other boys the world over are discovering the same lie.

Starship Troopers takes this conceit and literally perverts it. Not only does the teacher (Michael Ironside) tell them of the glories of war, he turns up as their platoon leader, a legendary figure known as "the Lieutenant." Initially missing an arm, he now has a mechanical one; he has been gloriously completed by war. Here, what Remarque treated ironically, Verhoeven treats literally. The lieutenant stoically guides the platoon through its most savage encounters with the spider hordes, and then—this is the film's idea of heavy emotion—is trapped and has his legs ripped off. His stumps spurting blood, he asks our hero Van Dien, who, far from being brutalized by the war, has turned into a butt-kicking NCO, for the ultimate act of intimacy in this world: to kill him. Now Van Dien is man enough to do just that.

That is love among the Nazis: a blast of withering fire through the heart.   (NOVEMBER 11, 1997)

*I*f you pay attention to Steven Spielberg's *The Lost World: Jurassic Park*, you'll note the presence of text, subtext, even urtext. You'll observe the classic structure, the presence of allusion and symbol.

But you won't pay attention. You'll be too busy thinking: Please don't eat me. It's all grrrrrr!-text. For the first half-hour, the movie is pretty crummy. Even Spielberg appears bored with the script's lame setup, its quick evocation of the first movie and its wan establishment of human villains and heroes. Like any fifty-year-old adolescent, he can't wait for the dinosaurs.

And when he gets to them, the movie ceases to bear any relationship to conceits of narrative and becomes a sheer adrenaline spike to the brain stem. You just sit there sucking for ever-diminishing supplies of oxygen, hoping he'll let you go home before you pass out.

As the film opens, a distraught and bedraggled Jeff Goldblum, as chaos theoretician Ian Malcolm, is summoned before Richard Attenborough's biotech magnate, John Hammond, for a mission to a subsidiary dinosaur island near the one nuked at the end of *Jurassic Park*. This island was the actual hatchery, Hammond explains. Malcolm doesn't want to go, being severely traumatized. But, learning his girlfriend, paleontologist Sarah Harding (Julianne Moore) is already there, he agrees. Since the movie has to have a child in jeopardy, a child in jeopardy is located—his stepdaughter, Kelly (Vanessa Lee Chester). She stows away and proceeds to be very, very cute through the remainder of the film.

Once Malcolm and his very small team are on the island, they learn that Hammond's nephew Peter (Arliss Howard) is also there, with a much bigger team first presented as an air cav unit in Vietnam, then as John Wayne's animal capturers from *Hatari*, but ultimately resolved into a hunting party. The head boy is Roland Tembo, the inevitable Brit white hunter (played by Pete Postlethwaite), who wants to put a .470 Nitro Express into T. rex's thoracic cavity. The dinosaurs want neither to be saved nor slaughtered. They just want to eat. End of setup.

Start of movie. Think of a chutes and ladders game between screaming men and large, hungry lizards played in the dark. That's about it.

As a piece of film design, *The Lost World: Jurassic Park* is staggering. Whether he's giving us another ordeal by vehicle hanging off a cliff or watching the 'raptors slither through the elephant grass, trailing wakes of vibration—just like the shark's bubbles in *Jaws*—Spielberg keeps you nailed to your seat.

As always, the real genius is in the tiny details: I loved, for example, a gag where poor Sarah is suspended over nothingness on a cracking windshield. As the fractures quicksilver through the glass, increasing in complexity and emitting vivid cracklings of impending collapse, Ian struggles to reach her. Woman about to fall, man trying to save her: This one is at least as old as *The Perils of Pauline*, but Spielberg has found a way to make it fresh.

And, as always, he appears not to be much interested in his actors. Goldblum may be a small mistake. Always so amusing as the off-lead, he grows tedious as the hero, with that silky way of moving and talking. Moore is far too interesting an actress to be wasted in the one-dimensionalities here. Vince Vaughn, who lived large in *Swingers*, barely registers as the hero's pal.

Ironically, the best performance is reserved for the most scorned role. That's Postlethwaite as the man with the double-rifle. It's been years since hunters have been played as heroic, but Spielberg gives him a quiet dignity and suggests that he represents ideas too complex for the movies. This is a far cry from the usual eco-correct vision of the hunter as a fat-bellied redneck who kills because he's a creep.

But all this is really academic. The hero of *The Lost World* is Spielberg, and the stars are the leaping lizards. T. rex gets a nice run through San Diego, though those with memories of the big beasts that flattened skylines in the 1950s will be a little disappointed that all this big guy does is eat a gas station sign and break a window in a video rental shop. It's the 'raptors you won't forget: what scary little critters they are, fast, lethal, smart, and arrogant.

And Spielberg deserves credit for one last thing: He refuses to sentimentalize them. In primitive ways, the movie is structured around theories of T. rex's familial instincts. Some humans help them, but the big mouths don't care. They don't get it. They don't bond with the humans. They still want to eat them. I like that in a dinosaur.   (MAY 23, 1997)

Some movies do the twist. They stand or fall on their endings. They have no content except the last big reversal. They twist the night away.

So when I say that the ending of writer-director M. Night Shyamalan's *The Sixth Sense* knocked me out of both socks, and I loved that pure moment of revelation, you must bear in mind that—hard as it is to recall now—for the first hour and a half it depressed me.

It's dreary, morose, surly, sullen, dingy. Worse, it's set in Philadelphia. Even worse, it stars, in his sensitive mode, Bruce Willis.

He's a fellow who looks good with the old Beretta clutched in a paw, and a grizzle of three-day beard, and a sneer. You got guerrillas in the mist? Call Bruce, the Orkin Man of international terrorism. He still kills the old way, with gun and fist, and he looks damn good doing it, particularly in a pre-Gable undershirt with those little white straps, the kind that makes the biceps look all bulgy.

But here he's a child psychiatrist—Dr. Malcolm Crowe—with a soft demeanor and a body swaddled in shapeless, dowdy Ivy League clothes. His eyes bleed compassion, his tentative body language announces to the world that he's unsure he belongs. His voice is a mutter hidden inside a whisper. He's marginal.

A tragedy (embittered ex-patient with a gun) that cut him down and crippled him on the best day of his life seems to be the culprit. Now recovered physically, he's not at all recovered mentally. He just doesn't have it together. His wife (Olivia Williams) doesn't listen to him, she may be seeing another man, his thriving practice has shrunk to a single patient, whose therapy is the issue of the movie.

This child, Cole Sear (brilliantly played by Haley Joel Osment), is strangely fearful. Picked on in school, unassertive at home, weirdly weird, he is a travail to his single mother (Aussie Toni Collette) and worrisome to school authorities. Slowly and using his best wiles for empathy, Willis's Dr. Crowe reaches out to make contact. We seem, for a while, to be in a reinvention of a lost sixties genre, the heroic-therapist movie, the masterpiece of which was *David and Lisa*. This movie exhibits the same earnest faith in the power of psychiatry to penetrate, understand and heal; it should be called *Malcolm and Cole*.

Yet the problem, when at last revealed, seems beyond healing. The boy claims that he sees the dead. They are everywhere, and now and then the camera floats over to his point of view, to show us burn victims from the 1930s or colonial serfs dangling at the end of a rope for stealing bread crumbs. But it is testament to Dr. Crowe's humanity that he doesn't download a Prozac Rx on the boy and go play golf. He finds that he believes and that there must be a reason and that in that reason there is a kind of salvation and mercy. That becomes the thrust of the film: What use can this boy be to the ghosts, and what are they to him?

The movie is full of odd touches. The oddest is Collette as the mother; she seems strangely synthetic, unaffiliated with a class or a profession, unrooted in society, like some kind of robot. Her job is never seen, her life is left blank. Is she the source of the emanations of strangeness? And what happened to Daddy? This is never filled in. Is she from a different planet?

Meanwhile, the more the doc struggles to understand and then help the boy, the more his own life unravels. He is feckless, haunted himself. So the film eventually abandons the heroic-therapist model and ventures toward other ground, ever so gently tightening its squeeze. It seems really to achieve something that Stanley Kubrick was possibly groping after in *Eyes Wide Shut*, or that Nicholas Roeg achieved in *Don't Look Now*, which might be called an extreme sense of the bizarre, not as invented by special-effects wizards with unlimited space on the hard drive but in the subtler ways of film craftsmanship. In fact, along with *The Blair Witch Project*, this modestly budgeted but shivery, quivery meditation on the omnipresence of death makes an overblown piece of junk like the 1999 remake of *The Haunting* seem even more worthless and wasteful than it is.

The movie is a maximum creep-out. It's invasive. It's like an enema to the soul as it probes the ways of death—some especially grotesque in a family setting. You leave slightly asquirm. You know it will linger. It becomes a clammy, chilly movie building toward a revelation that you cannot predict.

As I say: I cannot tell you. You'd hate me if I did. I can only say, don't look now, but look sometime.   (AUGUST 6, 1999)

Since time immemorial mankind has worried about three important issues

    a. Is universal peace possible?
    b. Is true love forever?
    c. Could Godzilla beat a space monster?

The answers are (a) No; (b) For others, maybe, but not for you; and (c) Too close to call.

But wait! This just in! For an update on (c), check out *Godzilla 2000* at your local multiplex.

Yes, folks, the tallest, darkest leading man in all Japan is back. He is still big, has all eight of Santa's reindeer's antlers on his back, fission-powered halitosis (all that raw fish) and the look of a Komodo dragon crossed with Lassie. His skin is still green rubber. His eyes are still buttons. When he walks, the earth beneath the Toho back lot still shudders, and he looks—don't spread this around, I'd hate to disillusion the young and start rumors—like a man in a bad monster suit. In this one, he fights a giant-size ugly thing that comes out of a flying saucer that resembles a partially melted stainless-steel Frisbee. Battleground: Tiny Town, Japan.

Sparks fly, fires light, wires crackle, and a number of very nice miniature buildings are trampled into toothpicks. The Japanese, despite the trade deficit and their ability to build fabulous automobiles, still think that a guy in a monster suit is all that is needed for a monster movie.

This one was directed by old-time Godzilla pro Takao Okawara, who proves he hasn't learned a thing over the years. I like that in a man. About the only signs of advanced thinking are occasional images cribbed from *Independence Day*, such as the creeping shadow of death as a big space thing from under the sea (don't ask) hovers over downtown Little Japan.

There are some indicators that Sony intended to release this literal monstrosity as a camp item. For one thing, when the Japanese actors—all trying very hard, no doubt—speak at around 340 mph (based on lip movements) the English soundtrack produces guttural utterances at about 7 mph. In other words, he's probably saying something like "Sir, the space monster's genetic structure is changing owing to its absorption of Godzilla's rapid-regeneration DNA, which we have code-named 'G-1'!" which is translated, for our ears, as something like "Sir, that monster is a crazy goofed-up idiot!"

Somewhere around the 750th repetition, this irony-free deadpan loses its humorous content. Sony would have been better advised to hire some smart young American comics and let them riff into a mike for a soundtrack, after the fashion of Woody Allen's *What's Up, Tiger Lily?* of all those years back.

Godzilla, go home.   (AUGUST 18, 2000)

*E*ven without death rays and Martian fighting machines, the classic science fiction movie that Steven Spielberg's *A.I.* most suggests is *The War of the Worlds*.

The worlds belong to Spielberg himself and to his mentor, inspiration, and the original developer of *A.I.*, the great late Stanley Kubrick.

The two men seem so similar: extraordinary cinema geniuses, driven, perfectionist, powerful, autocratic.

And they are so different.

Spielberg is suburban, sentimental, a believer in happy endings, family wholeness, benevolent aliens that are just a projection of his optimistic worldview. Even if it contains killer sharks, the universe ultimately makes sense; it can be known and understood.

Kubrick came out of harsh New York German-Jewish intellectuality. He's the chess master, the pipe smoker, without a sentimental lick to him, caustic, cynical, cold and analytical. In one of his films, he blew up the world as a joke! The universe is a whirligig of gases and cosmic debris that always conspires to render human nobility and aspiration futile.

So: Spielberg sees the glass as half full; Kubrick saw the glass smashed and ground into your face.

And that struggle fills *A.I.* from start to finish. Kubrick bought the original short story and carefully nurtured and developed it. It is rumored that he enjoyed a secret collaboration with Spielberg; fax machines in closets were involved (how very Kubrick!). When Kubrick died, possibly to escape the reviews of *Eyes Wide Shut*, Spielberg took over the script, rewrote it, produced it, and filled it with his own strengths and weaknesses.

The results is fascinating, if uneven and ultimately rather silly. Problems with the ending, so common these days, dog this visionary film as well.

The original idea has a very specific fifties feel to it, reflecting Kubrick. It's a movie about robots that hails from the days when robots seemed the ultimate expression of human genius, complete with corollary notions that someday artificial life powered by artificial intelligence would fit seamlessly with and ultimately replace humanity. *Blade Runner* has already probed this issue, seeking an answer to the sci-fi writer's classic query: Where does man end and machine begin?

And here's the answer: Who cares? It doesn't matter. Man and machine will never meld, and to pretend that they will is to waste everyone's time. It's so four decades ago.

So *A.I.* is a strangeness: a technically brilliant '00s film full of annoyingly ancient fifties ideas. The movie is full of answers to questions that are seldom asked anymore. Thus it's a film best not to think about, or to pay careful attention to. Just enjoy Spielberg's masterful narrative voice as he pulls you through the odyssey of a science fiction Pinocchio who just wants to be a real boy.

The film is set a few decades after 2001. Most of humanity is gone (the ozone hole got bigger and suntanned billions to death, melting the ice caps and performing ultimate urban renewal on all the coastal cities). But life is pleasant in the small, high-tech, cloistered suburbs where elite survivors live. There, alas, the Swintons, Monica and Henry (Frances O'Connor and Sam Robards), are in mourning.

Their son, stricken with a fatal disease, is cryogenically preserved, awaiting a cure (another fifties idea!). It turns out that Henry works for a high-tech outfit that is in the business of building robots—they're called mechas—so perfect they seem all but human. The one human trait the programmers hadn't been able to hard-wire into their disks is love. But now, under the guidance of Professor Hobby (William Hurt at his most professorial), they've got a prototype of a love-capable mecha.

So David (Haley Joel Osment) comes to live at the Swintons', where his adorable literalism makes him seem like a child raised in a lab. He bursts in on Monica sitting on the toilet, because that big no-no hasn't been drummed into him. But soon enough Monica, who has been fighting it, falls into mother's love with him and he has replaced the frozen Martin.

This is Kubrick's suburbia, not Spielberg's. The house hasn't the messy jumble of a real place, which Spielberg has captured in films like *E.T.* It's a severe, Scandinavian-modern type of place; moreover, the whole gestalt is Kubrickian, from the stately camera movement, to the classic (snaillike) sense of pace, the early-in-their-career use of low-voltage actors (I don't even know who Frances O'Connor is!), and the careful, Flaubertian detail work.

But the emotional turmoil soon unleashed feels Spielbergian: It's from a turbulent childhood with a vanished father and a lot of confusion between siblings. Martin is awakened, cured, and returned home, and suddenly the two boys are fighting for Monica's love, acting out, the whole family disintegrating under stress.

And so Monica faces a shattering decision: She must remove the non-child, whom she loves as much as the real child, from the family. But if she returns him to the company, he will be deactivated, which she interprets as execution. She takes him to the woods and lets him go.

Thus David enters the real world, which turns out to be a history of the future as told by movies of the past. It's part of the carnal London from *A Clockwork Orange* but also the post-apocalypse outback of George Miller's *Road Warrior* films with an overlay of Ridley Scott's incredible evocation of L.A. in *Blade Runner*.

The issue of sexuality is another odd field in which Spielberg's and Kubrick's sensibilities collide. Kubrick clearly reveled in the sexual; his masterpiece *Dr. Strangelove* is full of sexual double-entendre, one of his early succès des scandales was *Lolita*, and his last film, *Eyes Wide Shut*, barely escaped an NC-17 rating. By contrast, Spielberg is Mr. Clean; I cannot think of a single scene in his films where sexuality is significantly addressed.

But sexuality is a theme that runs through *A.I.*, for one of the intriguing aspects of the mechas was their deployment as sex partners. So Jude Law, under slicked-back hair, his handsome features exaggerated by aggressive makeup, becomes David's boon companion in their quest for knowledge. He is a sex professional named Gigolo Joe, though his part in the film is roughly the equivalent to Jiminy Cricket's. Spielberg, who longs desperately to stay in PG-13 territory, never embraces the sexuality implicit in Joe, or even in Rouge City, the town of mecha whores and porn goddesses to which Joe and David head.

For a while the film becomes pure adventure story, as Joe and David, on the lam, join a tribe of lost mechas who are being hunted by exploiters for carnival shows as a protest against the over-mecha-nization of the world, and roam in search of a Blue Fairy that David believes will turn him human, for he has stumbled upon a text of *Pinocchio* and thinks it's a how-to book. It's great fun, as an unlimited production budget allows the filmmakers to conjure all sorts of heretofore unseen sights, including a mecha-hunting vehicle disguised as, yes, the moon.

But ultimately the movie's conclusion arrives, bringing what is certain to become legendary befuddlement. I struggle here not to give any-thing away, but the highly intelligent might want to back off now, for they may divine what it is I'm saying.

It appears to me that Kubrick was intending to reiterate that sense of confused wonder and awe that he brought to the end of *2001: A Space Odyssey*, the profusion of images that carried the dark messages that there were things in the universe that man could not know and that he would have no vocabulary to understand or remember. As Keir Dullea sought the source of the mysterious signals, so does David seek reality and a chance to bond again with his beloved mother. In the first film, this produced a seminal moment in film history: Dullea on one of the moons of Jupiter, sitting in a Louis XVI bedroom. That was Kubrick's methodol-ogy for suggesting the human mind encountering something beyond its scope and recasting it in familiar images.

And so it is with *A.I.* when—I give you no other details purposely—the boy is liberated to full humanity. In fact, he not only represents hu-manity, he has become humanity. If he's not fully human now, he can never be.

But Spielberg couldn't let Kubrick's evocation of this wonder go with-out grounding it in some knowable reality. Thus he invents agents who make the metaphorical transformation realistic and palpable—and silly. In a Spielberg movie, you have to figure that somehow aliens will be in-volved; they will be calming and benevolent, not savage and predatory.

The result is grand but somewhat trivial. The majesty of Kubrick's cold universe has been dragged into the warmth of Spielberg's cuddly one. You want to believe in these two tellers of tales and you want to be-lieve that they could solve their differences to tell one great tale between them, but somehow those differences end up being the most memorable thing in the film.   (JUNE 29, 2001)

I like to think of the great humanist French film critic André Bazin. I like to think of his belief in the truth of cinema, his conviction that through cinema could the world be healed.

Then I like to think of him seeing *Blade II*.

I think it would go something like this:

"AIEEEEEEEEEEEEE-AHHHHHHHHHHHHHHHHH!"

There is no possible adult justification for the picture. It is pure pagan glee, a raptor's fest, a zesty paprika of cannibal stew, stylized toward almost total abstraction, beyond describing, beyond imagining except by its makers.

And that is why it's so good.

Enter here, ye who dare. All others turn back.

What *Blade II* has that so few others of its ilk, or any ilk, do is an actual director. He has a worldview. You may not agree with that worldview, but it's there all the same, and it commands respect for the consistency with which he adheres to it and how its organizing principle permits his oeuvre to cohere.

Here's his worldview: "Let's eat the weak."

No, not exactly Christian or progressive, but you can't have everything. He's Guillermo del Toro, who achieved his breakthrough in 1993 with *Cronos,* and then went American less successfully with 1997's *Mimic.* His last film was *The Devil's Backbone,* a brooding ghost story set during the Spanish Civil War.

This time, freed by a large budget, a major star who gets it, and uncountable gallons of fake blood, he's created something ghastly yet wonderful at the same time.

Derived from Marvel comic books, the movie continues the tale of the half-man, half-vampire Blade (Wesley Snipes), who has become the human champion in the war between the races. But in vampire movies as everywhere, politics intrude; a third subspecies has mutated, and it feasts on vampire themselves, quite effectively. Thus a truce is established: Blade, helped by a vampire special-operations team that looks like a punk garage band that has just looted a National Guard armory, heads out to take down this bad form of vampire.

The setting is Eastern Europe, the production standards high, the violence kinetic and stylized, the acting surprisingly good (with one drab exception); and the plot, while nonsensical if you don't believe in vampires, has a truly intriguing force and subtext. If you're going to make a movie about vampires fighting with automatic weapons in crowded Eastern European go-go joints, this is the way to do it.

It's also amazing how much an actor can contribute, even to an overabundantly effects-driven piece like this. I speak, yes, of Snipes, who is

already so stylized he seems to have stepped from an Egyptian sarcoph-
agus and then gotten a makeover from Aubrey Beardsley, but also of
Ron Perlman. He's Blade's primary antagonist on the ops team, and what
a great performance!

Really, everyone in the movie looks like a Droog or a Druid, yet Perlman manages to give his fellow an extreme individuality. That you even
notice him among the sets and the slaughter and the too many guys in
leather jackets with bald, veiny heads and automatic shotguns is a miracle; that you like him (even though he's the bad guy) goes beyond the
miraculous.

The bald guys are fun, too, one being the master vampire Damaski-
nos (Thomas Kretschmann) and the other his mutant enemy Nomak
(rocker Luke Goss). Alas, the weak link is Leonor Varela, who plays a
vampire with complex family ties; while beautiful, she never seems animated. Okay, so she's dead. Still . . .

Well, anyway: This movie is for a variety of segmented audiences:
children whose souls have been leached by MTV, folks with IQs under
100, geniuses with IQs over 150. You normal people stay away: You
won't get it, you won't like it, and you'll feel violated by it.

(MARCH 22, 2002)

*U*gh! They're hairy and gross. They scamper and flit, all their legs
fluttering and diddling. They squirt sticky stuff. Their faces look
like furry pimples with pincers. No, folks, not movie critics: spiders.

The arachnid pack is the subject proper of *Eight Legged Freaks,* which
recounts the results when inflated tribes of arthropods come out and
boogie. You must say of these creatures that they have good taste: They
eat young men and leave young women untouched. As an old man, I like
that in a monster.

The exceedingly mild David Arquette stars, presumably as a linkage
to the influential *Scream* pictures, as a prodigal son returning to his
hometown, a sort of Battle Mountain, Nevada, of Arizona. It's fallen on
hard times, and this is before the spider invasion. Arquette's Chris Mc-
Cormick, a down-and-out mining engineer, quickly bonds with Sheriff
Sam Parker, the only other sane person in the scabby little town. They

look at each other yearningly. Hmmm, is this the first gay monster movie? No, actually, Sam is a gal, played by B- and TV-movie queen Kari Wuhrer, who's so good in the movie you hope it gives her career a big pop. There's back story involving Chris and Sam, a yadda yadda yadda so predictable it's only sketched, thank God, enough to provide a faint emotional subtext along these lines: When the big spiders aren't trying to eat all the people in the shopping mall, maybe Sam and Chris will finally acknowledge that they are in love.

The setup is classic fifties monster stuff, though a new enabler is deployed. Back then, it was always Our Friend Mr. Atom that either liberated the frozen ancients or mutated the pipsqueak critters into city busters. Now it's toxic waste that causes a tribe of hairy creepers captured by spider freak Tom Noonan (unbilled; he was the bad guy in *Manhunter* all those years back, and directed an excellent film called *What Happened Was . . .*) to get really big fast and go out on the town.

The movie is a lot more interested in amusing you than frightening you. It seems based more on providing the giggly pleasure of the sudden start, when something pops out of nowhere, than on the morbid shock of seeing others of your species stalked and dismembered. In fact, despite a high body count, the movie clings desperately to its audience-friendly PG-13 rating.

If you haven't got it yet, let me explain further. *Eight Legged Freaks* isn't a monster movie, it's a "monster" movie. The quotation marks provide the descriptor of irony. This is postmodern folk art, a tricky transaction in which the work isn't just a story, it's a genre survey, an homage, a meditation, a parody and, oh yeah, while it's at it, still a pretty good story. The spiders, computer-animated, are a lot quicker than the lumbering clay-model city squashers of the past. It is to the monster movie what *Scream* was to slasher movies and *Tremors* was to giant earthworm movies.

Let's let some grad student pursue academic glory on the subject of postmodernism as it applies to monster flicks and note only that the direct antecedent to *Eight Legged Freaks* is Gordon Douglas's brilliant shocker of 1954, *Them!*, which director Ellory Elkayem lovingly quotes by running it on a TV set in the background of a scene. But *Them!* was for real, a film noir of rapacious giant ants eating people in the sewers of Los Angeles. I still wince in pain thinking of great old James Whitmore, as a New Mexico cop, giving up his life to get those kids out. By contrast, nobody really dies in *Eight Legged Freaks*. This one is for play. You have to say: It plays well with others. (JULY 17, 2002)

*T*erminator 3: Rise of the Machines is a $150 million wreck-creational vehicle.

At one point, an evil Terminator drives a 50-ton crane through downtown Los Angeles about 75 miles an hour, attempting to squash a pickup in which flees the father of the future, John Connor. Chasing them is a virtuous Terminator (Arnold Schwarzenegger, of course) in a firetruck (of course). Soon enough, the rules of the road break down—that is, the elemental distinction between street and not-street—and the gigantic machines careen through structures on the left and right, destroying all in their path, tossing Prizms and Neons aside like so many candy wrappers. Wait, it gets wreckier.

The director, Jonathan Mostow, contrives to dangle Schwarzenegger from the crane hook, which—as the crane is no longer moored—is rotating wildly like a dreidel of destruction, taking out buildings left and right, so that the Ahnuld-man is surfing through concrete as he is whipped along. It's a fabulous destroy-o-rama, a lollapalooza of smashing and shattering . . . and this is in the first fifteen minutes!

Is there a story behind all the carnage? Well, looking for one is rather like hunting daffodils on the dirt floor of a demolition derby arena as monster trucks grind each other to fragments and the stench of diesel, 10W40, and testosterone befogs your glasses and inflames your nasal passages. But yes, I believe that at certain moments in all the fun, a story may be identified. Too bad it's not a new one.

A cyborg is sent back to the past (which is our present—that is, now) from the grave new world in which the machines, after a bloody rebellion, are about to be defeated by mankind resurgent. The cyborg's mission is to eliminate the young man who is fated to become the older man who becomes leader of the victorious human forces, before he can become, uh, the leader of the victorious human forces. But from that same grave new world, the humans send a captured, reprogrammed, older Terminator back to act as the boy's protector.

The mild wrinkle that justifies the vehicle-reduction program and the subsequent decibel-increase campaign is that the new bad Terminator is a chick. You may read into that all the latent male castration anxiety at the triumph of the New Woman you want; I suspect that the filmmakers made this choice because they thought it was pretty cool, and didn't think too much more about it.

Supermodel Kristanna Loken embodies this creature in her fleshly appearances, but just as often she's played by Pixels Nos. 8.5 through 13.1 billion, as when she melts like a Popsicle, splatters like a mud pie, atomizes like a cherry bomb or turns her left hand into a Black & Decker No. 4 wide-band power saw. So symmetrical is the human Loken's face, and so utterly empty of emotion, that she might have been designed by a machine for all the difference it would have made.

As for Arnold . . . well, strictly speaking, a film critic is not required. By now he has ascended to the level of pure icon. He is simply there in all his magnificent Arnoldness, grim of jaw, knobby of cheekbone, intense of glare, Wienerschnitzely of accent, and pneumatic of pectoral. Mostow has some fun with him, and he's a good enough sport to play along.

For example, in his introduction, he is, as in the too-serious *Terminator 2*, enjoined to enter a rowdy bar naked in order to acquire a wardrobe. But where *2* used the scene to unleash some head-crushing violence, Mostow puts his fellow into the middle of ladies' night, and all the gals go bonkers when the nude incredible bulk walks in. He then proceeds to the stage—the girls are throwing tens and twenties and I'll bet a coupla fifties and hundreds at him—and removes the leather jeans from a Chippendale dancer, who, by the way, makes the mistake of calling him "honey." It's about as subtle as an outhouse, but it's pretty funny.

Indeed, that's much of the spirit of the film. You can feel Mostow and his writers, John D. Brancato, Michael Ferris and Tedi Sarafian, looting the previous two films, paying homage to lines and images, making jokes off them—"She'll be back," Arnold says of his female opponent—all pleasant grace notes amid the general campaign of destruction. (I think the Russian army lost fewer vehicles in World War II than Mostow does in this film.) Those occasional flashes of wit and sentiment are to be treasured.

Where the film loses energy—if you notice, and you probably won't—is in its evocation of a younger generation of Terminator targets. In the far superior original, the target was John Connor's mother, Sarah, played by Linda Hamilton, which set up a vibration of romantic sacrifice with good guy protector Michael Biehn; in the far inferior 2, John Connor, at about 15, was portrayed by Edward Furlong, an unconventional choice for his body languor and unusual (but appealing) line readings and ironic humor. Though his subsequent career faltered, he was quite charismatic. Now, John, at about 25, is played by Nick Stahl. And although that's not a disaster, Stahl certainly seems generic: handsome, spiky-headed youngster, lacking any particular texture or charisma.

He's teamed with Claire Danes, who, although an accomplished actress, is underused as the generic Girl. She plays one Kate Brewster, who (it helpfully turns out) is fated to become his wife and co-captain in the post-apocalyptic world. Worse still, this bland little romance is connected to the larger story in a narrative convenience difficult to accept. It further turns out her father (David Andrews) is the air force general in charge of the secret computer project that is preparing the way for the war between humans and machines.

As a director, Mostow hasn't the talent for expressive action that the series auteur, James Cameron, did. Cameron was a genius at finding new lines of action so that the whole movie felt astonishing and fresh. The sequel was overblown, but it still exhibited Cameron's genius for unusual movement dynamics. Mostow takes the approach of a Russian general who clears minefields by marching through them; he doesn't focus on individual grace or make the battles personal, emotional, and frightening. He almost never finds ways of isolating his figures in their athletic beauty; he never makes their moves distinctive; he can't find that one killer detail to make the action sequences linger in the imagination, all Cameron hallmarks. Instead, he lets everything go full bore all the time, so the result is the spectacle of endless destruction, amusingly but not emotionally meaningful. By the end of the movie, everything has been trashed, and I do mean everything.

Still, what you feel from *Terminator 3: Rise of the Machines* might be called the good faith of its makers. They've tried hard to honor the spirit of the franchise, not exploit it, and take it to a new level and a surprising destination. They've also kept it mercifully short. If it's not the classic piece of sinew and gristle that *The Terminator* was, it's at least a solidly professional attempt and a pretty good summer movie in the bargain. (JULY 3, 2003) *a*h, the sounds of the Lone Star State. The gently lowing of the cattle. The melodic warble of the Hill Country meadowlark. The soft murmur of a brook cascading through the prairie. The GHHHZZZZIIII-IPPPPPPPPPPPFT! of a chainsaw ripping through a yuppie's tender limbs.

As evidence that we are in a new barbarian age, here's the remake of *The Texas Chainsaw Massacre,* delivered with almost frightening precision. Ugh. Talk about your passionate intensity! Why did it have to be so good? You realize how hard this is on me, to have to tell you what a superb job director Marcus Nispel has done re-creating, yet also revising, 1974's grisly, gristly, protein-centric masterpiece.

Man: meat. Meat: man. Man, meet meat. Meat, meet man. That's pretty much the film in a nutshell. Kids high on grass and life's verdant possibility wander fecklessly into a zone of darkest taboo: people, people who eat people, the luckiest people in the world. Lots of death, lots of eating.

Underneath, what is on display here are two systems of deep American contempt facing each other across a gulf of suspicion and hatred, waging relentless war. It's urban vs. rural, soft vs. hard, educated, tasteful effete elitism vs. cretinous violence. It's red America vs. blue America, with each side representing the stereotype of the other's darkest imaginings.

On the one hand, there's urban, sensual, appetite-driven youth, sweet and innocent yet almost annoyingly vulnerable to predation. They have no idea that upon the darkling plain you are either the eater or the eaten; thus they become the eaten, and, I suppose, a subversive pleasure of the film is watching this process play out. These are five darling youngsters, ripe and firm and adorable, crossing the Texas prairie in a minibus with Alfred E. Neuman's smug mug appliquéd to the ceiling. When you see "What, me worry?" up there, you just know that a turbocharged Stihl buzz blade is going to come a-rippin' through Alfred's smile, amid a spray of sparks, exhaust clouds and shrapnel.

It's all-American hate time! It's a hatefest! Hippie vs. redneck. Those with teeth vs. those without them. Those who say "ain't" ironically, and those who ain't never heard of irony. You want irony, sonny? Here's yore irony—GHHHHZZZZZIPPPPPPPPFT!!!!

Nispel has looked very carefully at Tobe Hooper's original film and seen what was so good about it. It's not just the violence; it's that the camera forever notices things that the poor about-to-be-buzzed kids don't, all these signals that they have entered a grotesque world—little bone constructions, strange, gloppy structures in jaws, hooks everywhere, the drip-drip-drip of mystery liquid, the slightly vacant eyes of the country numb and daft. It calls up, actually, traditions of disturbing photography: people who look a little off, as if they could catch the attention of Diane Arbus; eyes too big, too vacant, manner too hearty, teeth too protuberant.

The scariest of them all, in the new film, may be the sheriff, played by R. Lee Ermey, a squirrelly charismatic who could lead men into combat when he's being good or teenagers into hell when he's being bad. And the cinematographer, Daniel Pearl, does superb work, never quite losing touch with the natural world but conjuring up a tone of appalling menace and squalor with his weird lighting schemes.

The kids are played well enough by actors nobody has ever heard of, with the exception of Jessica Biel, once of TV's *7th Heaven*. She's the only one who really registers, primarily because she's the only one who musters any sort of practical defense to the assaults inflicted upon her.

But this isn't an actor's film; it's a director's film. Nispel, mainly a music vid guy, has all the—oh, I hate to use the word—chops: Like Hooper, he has an extraordinary sense of the meanings concealed in faces and keeps wheeling in grotesques from Pluto and Uranus to populate the screen. A fat old lady in a trailer takes the cake. But Nispel's also got an action jackson, and can put together the mayhem with brilliant suggestibility, as when the legendary Leatherface (played by Andrew Bryniarski) goes on the hunt, his mechanical scythe belching smoke, the sparks flying, the wood splintering, the metal shearing. But Nispel stops short of the hideous; he prefers the disturbing. In his world, the less he shows, the scarier it is.

He has also worked a few revisions, all to the good. Borrowing from *The Blair Witch Project*, he uses the framing device of "found" video, in this case a walk-through by police after the atrocity. He also evens the body count between the slaughterers and the slaughtered, courtesy of the energy of Biel's womanly warrior Erin. (You never saw a fighter with a better stomach, that I'll tell you.)

Those are minor points. The major point is that the new *Texas Chain-saw Massacre* is a GHHHHZZZZZIIIIPPPPPFT! of a ride.

(OCTOBER 17, 2003)

See, I thought it was going to be a big monster movie. You know, some critter or other—huge, scaly, pre- or post-historic and mean as Martha Stewart—goes whup-ass downtown, until a handsome scientist figures out a new ray or vibration or something and puts it down.

Boy, was I wrong. Instead, *Reign of Fire* more closely relates to a now-perished genre that might be called the "Aussie-post-apocalypse-funkadelic-tattooed-mohawked-bad-acting" movie. A mouthful, yes, with only one certifiable masterpiece, *The Road Warrior*, though clones abounded in the mid-eighties.

So although this movie is set in a monster-haunted world, it's not this one, it's in the future. And the monster-tripping-the-light-fantastic-on-the-sidewalks scenario never plays gloriously out. As the movie opens, a few human survivors have retreated to tribal enclaves to survive what the movie sketches all too hastily: the emergence from underground (oh! that's where they went) of a species of biologically dubious flying dragons who eat ash, which they create with the flamethrower glands in their mouths. Bummer.

For some reason—I mean, we can shoot down guided missiles now and then—we are powerless before their onslaught, and they now prevail. In an old castle in the north, a scraggly tribe of surviving Brits huddles around fires and argues whether the future is just bleak or totally damned. The tribe is led by face man Christian Bale, who, helpfully, was present as a tyke when the first of the winged toasting machines emerged from beneath London's Underground. I am not making this up.

All of a sudden, the Yanks are coming, the Yanks are coming, and the only thing wrong with them is that they are overequipped, overfed, and over there. An armored column shows up, clamoring for entrance to the castle. It is led by the cueball-headed Denton Van Zan (Matthew Mc-Conaughey in his best Ahab imitation), a tattooed, pumped-up psycho who loves to kill dragons and yearns to close in on the father-brood in what was once London.

But too much of the film is spent on village politics, as the two entities struggle for control of the castle and humanity, and Bale and McConaughey see who can go further over the top into madness, spit-spray, eyeball-bulging, and bad costume modeling (I give it to McConaughey by a hair).

Finally we get around to some serious monster killing, although a little late. The special effects are good, but when aren't they good these days? As a movie illusion, the digital dragons are far advanced from the cheesy clunkiness of, say, the Japanese *Rodan*, first of the flying monsters. But the movie hasn't a quarter of the charm of the one authentic dragon masterpiece, the superb *Dragonslayer* of 1981.

It's just silly, loud and goofy. The dragon needed a bigger part and the two stars smaller ones. (JULY 12, 2002)

*T*he emotional climax of *Star Wars: Episode II—Attack of the Clones* is fabulous. Soaring and majestic, it reaches deep inside you to strike chords of fond memory, to reaffirm the pleasure and healing power of narrative, to liberate the imagination.

Unfortunately, it comes in the first two seconds. That's when the legendary words "A long time ago in a galaxy far, far away . . ." materialize on the screen and John Williams's familiar music rises thunderously. After that, the movie doesn't go downhill or uphill; it doesn't go anywhere. It flatlines.

Memo to George Lucas: Hire an editor, bud.

You're a great man. So what? You still need an editor. Everybody needs an editor, and nobody needed an editor more than the writer-director of this film. It's too long, it's too dull, it's too lame. Only in its last forty minutes or so, several eons from the beginning, does it leap to the warp speed of kinetic grandeur, and even then it's the grandeur of spectacle, not emotion.

Lucas has previously taken his talking points from the great storytellers and story thinkers of the species: from Joseph Campbell, from

Homer, from Thomas Malory, from Akira Kurosawa, from John Ford, from 4,000 years of tradition of epic voyages and grand adventures. But the mythic source he seems to have based this episode on is . . . *The McLaughlin Group*.

It is inordinately obsessed with politics. Talking heads, some of them green, sit around and say things like, "It's outrageous that, after all those hearings, and four trials in the Supreme Court, Nute Gunray is still viceroy of the Trade Federation. I fear the Senate is powerless to resolve this crisis. On an ontological scale of 1 to 10 representing metaphysical certainty, Mor-ton, do those moneymongers control everything?"

That's almost, but not quite, an exact quote, as the fiery Sio Bibble gets in his licks at a conference between Padmé (also known as Senator Amidala), Queen Jamillia (blue lips), a couple of advisers, and himself in the Naboo Palace. It gets the gist of much of the early blabbering in the film, which is largely stilted political commentary about legislative bodies, parties, maneuvers, treaties, personalities, and reports we know nothing about. It's like reading the latest dispatch on the Mongolian parliament, as reported by Elizabeth Drew in a really cranky mood.

But as for human contact with the story, as for the themes of love and honor, of loyalty to family and tribe and kind, of heroism and sacrifice, wisdom and craven opportunism, there's almost nothing, certainly nothing like those sounded in the first cycle of *Star Wars* films. Not even the action sequences truly stir; too often, they simply resemble *Jetsons* shtick—individual space buggies as sports cars buzzing through Tomorrowtopia—re-created digitally at a budget of billions.

Agh! It's so frustrating to see so much pictorial energy wasted. But then that appears to be where the energy was invented: in an immaculate vision of that long-ago faraway place, which now more than ever has come to resemble a dream in the mind of the smartest teenager of 1935. Even the ships have been retro-ed back to thirties art moderne, and when Senator Amidala's chrome hood ornament of a ship glides in for a rooftop landing, all gleamy, creamy, shiny, and sleek, the sound produced isn't the whoosh of rocket engines but the drone of props. Very impressive. It's like the Hindenburg mooring at the radio mast of the Empire State Building. Strange, but impressive.

What little story creeps out in dribs and drabs never really assembles into a coherent whole; the conflicts are never clarified. I think it goes a little something like this. Senator Amidala (Natalie Portman), who was Queen Amidala in the last one but never mind, journeys to the republic's capital city-planet, Coruscant, to lead opposition in the Senate to some plan to create a clone army to dissuade the growing threats of the Separatists from . . . I'm lost in space already.

Someone tries to kill her. Ka-boom, there goes the chrome ship. The president, Palpatine (who will become emperor), assigns two Jedi to protect her, the master Obi-Wan (Evan McGregor) and his young mentee, Anakin Skywalker (played by *N SYNC star Justin Timberlake—no, no, played by Hayden Christensen, who looks like an *N SYNC kid but doesn't have as much talent). There's another attack on Amidala's life, this time by poison caterpillars, which Anakin lightsabers into sushi, and then that sports-car chase through the corridors of the city 2,000 feet up.

Hmmm, I forget what happens next. Somehow they get separated, the two youngsters on their own, hiding on Anakin's native planet of Tatooine, I believe, while Obi-Wan tracks down intimations he's heard that the clone army has already been built, on a star system whose location has been removed from, er, star system central.

I'll tell you one thing: no star system central, as in, say, MGM, would have built a movie around the dim Americans who haunt this one. In fact, the movie is kind of a laboratory on America vs. British technique. Score: Brits 10, Yanks 0. That's because to the Brits, who work from the outside in, acting is physical mastery of face and voice and body, strategically employed at certain moments for impact. An actor imposes himself on the character, and invents charm and wit and sparkle where none exists. So even the guy playing Palpatine (Ian McDiarmid) is creepy-elegant, and McGregor, athletic and earnest, can even bring a little life to a line like, "I am concerned for my Padawan. He is not ready to be given this assignment on his own yet."

The Americans, on the other hand, are trained to get into the character's mind and imagine as he would imagine, to work from the inside out. But there is no inside here: These characters are nothing but pop-cult props, and that leaves the performers helpless and inert. Natalie Portman has always enjoyed good press, but she was at her best as a child in *The Professional*. She's just overwhelmed here. And even an actual great actor, Samuel L. Jackson, seems ridiculous. He never looks comfortable as the Jedi Mace Windu, in robes and boots, and there's nothing he can do at all with a line like "The Genosians aren't warriors. One Jedi has to be worth a hundred Genosians!"

The *N SYNC kid is even worse. He seems to have wandered in from a Pepsi commercial. No, that would have been Justin Timberlake. Who knows where this dreary boy has been?

There's no reason for the woodenness of the cast other than the director's decision. Has Lucas lost the will to work with good, spontaneous, creative actors? He seems to prefer the closest thing he can get to droids. But it wasn't always so: In the original three *Star Wars* films, Lucas got extremely good work out of Harrison Ford, Mark Hamill, and especially Carrie Fisher. The trio sparkled, and between them was something like chemistry, even in the childishness of the emotional situation. That never happens here: We see handsome children dully repeating memorized lines on dreary soundstages; they seem not to imaginatively see what will be digitally painted in around them.

It is true that eventually *Episode II* springs to some kind of life, when the clones actually attack, as the title promises. In fact, soon enough it's clones vs. droids for control of the empire, but as to the technical difference between a clone and a droid, that I can't tell you, because then I'd have to kill you.

Lucas rather haphazardly just decides to end the movie on a lollapalooza: A rescue (Anakin of Amidala) becomes a romp through a droid factory (clank clank go the stamping machines) which becomes a capture which becomes an execution (by giant crab, no less) becomes another rescue becomes a battle becomes an even bigger battle with ships exploding becomes a series of lightsaber fights between new villain Count Dooku (Christopher Lee, still a legend) and, one by one, Anakin, Obi-Wan and even tiny li'l Yoda, who, animated digitally, turns into quite the fencer.

And then it's over. And not an eon too early. And now for at least three blessed years, peace. (MAY 15, 2002)

*A*t an hour long, in black and white, and starring a miracle-fiber toupee with an actor attached, the material that ultimately became *Star Trek: Nemesis* might have entered the canon as classic TV.

At twice that length, realized at Paramount's most exquisite level of technical excellence and starring a bald guy who can actually act, *Star Trek: Nemesis* is an ordeal for all save the most ardent Treksters. It's a phaser set to stun.

The idea is vivid enough and full of enough intellectual vibration to have been provocative back in the sixties. Our hero is facing diplomatic maneuvering and ultimately mortal space-battle combat against . . . himself. Literally. The Remans (natives of Remus, doncha know) have acquired a DNA strand from Patrick Stewart's Jean-Luc Godard—Jean-Luc Picard, I always make that mistake—and cloned a mini-him. Why? Because, as we all know, the captain of the Starship Enterprise is the world's coolest dude, so this second version will by genetic destiny be high class in the capability department. Alas, Verne Troyer of *Austin Powers* wasn't available to take the role, so they hired someone named Tom Hardy, last seen toting an M-60 through Mogadishu as a confused soldier in *Black Hawk Down*. Yes, Troyer is small and, yes, Hardy is big: Such are great comedy opportunities squandered.

Anyhow, mini-Picard—whose shaven head provides the only real resemblance to Picard—has engineered a coup to take over Remus's brother planet, Romulus, and now is expanding outward to take on Starfleet and eventually the universe. And who is there to stop him but Picard and the big Frisbee with the two flashlights attached?

Clever, no? See how neatly it tracks with an actual social issue, which is the eternal debate over nature vs. nurture? The original Picard, well raised and possessed of healthy self-image, has become the champion of order and decency and good judgment. That same genetic package, raised brutally on Remus (they seem to have trilobites for faces and the dispositions of agitated tarantulas), has grown up evil and ambitious.

But the movie is slower than molasses on the dark side of Uranus. Worse, it's tacky. I know it's supposed to be tacky, for the essence of classic *Star Trek* is its tackiness, but somehow tacky on the big screen isn't the same as tacky on the small. Tiny and blurry on the tube, it's cute and adorable. Blown out to 36 feet by 18 feet, and, worst of all, in actual focus, it just seems depressing.

I feel a rant coming on. Sorry, folks, this isn't going to be pretty. You might want to look away, or at least send the children to their rooms. But . . . really, can't they hire a decent costume designer? To my eyes, those double-knit two-tone sweatshirts with their slight shimmer and complete inability to wrinkle or drape like actual clothes, and those little dweeby badges, and all that short hair and all those freshly scrubbed faces . . . I CAN'T STAND IT! MAKE IT GO AWAY, PLEASE!

And the command bridge of the Enterprise? Give me a break. Does it have to look like the control room of a low-wattage Midwestern TV station? All those little blinking lights? What, is there a fly-into-space knob that has to be set to ON to get the thing to move? Then the fly-into-space light lights up, so we know we're in space. And there must be a cool-sounds knob, too, and a what-Third-World-airport-did-they-loot-to-get-all-those-freakin'-plastic-lounge-chairs knob, too, and that one's set all the way up to 10. Then there's that ersatz techno-yammer. "Sir, aft shield down to 40 percent efficiency. And we've fired all our photon torpedoes!"

Damn the photon torpedoes, I say, full rant ahead. The waxworks sense of it is cloying. It's like visiting an old folks' home when none of the old folks have any connection to you. Demographically, the whole *Star Trek* shebang must skew toward the Alzheimer's generation. We ain't in a country of young men. The movie is almost utterly devoid of youth; the two babes (Marina Sirtis as Counselor Deanna Troi and Dina Meyer as Commander Donatra) could be your grandma, and most of the guys look like they need oatmeal twice a day because their teeth and gums hurt and they want to stay regular. I kept waiting for Norma Desmond to walk in as Miss Space Station, Stardate 10002.

And the sparks. For some reason, dating back to the TV years when special effects were hardly advanced and the budgets minuscule, the *Star Trek* action sequences all involved sparks falling from pipes. That squalid tradition continues, so that in the oh-so-frequent space and phaser battles, rogue phaser blasts and other rays of destruction always bring showers of sparks raining down. It's like the worst kind of sensible suburban Fourth of July.

Then there's the sparseness. For all the size of these big ships, the movie has a small cast and even fewer actual characters. There's no sense of bustle, or teeming activity; it's just a few actors, most of them bad, on big, bad, empty sets. Was the Extras Union on strike or something? There must be seven speaking roles in the whole damned thing.

Even the big effects payoff—the Enterprise vs. a Romulan attack vessel conceived as a giant bird of prey—looks disconcertingly dead. It's just empty imagery, computerized visions of machines whizzing around cyberspace; there's nothing human in it, nothing emotive or resonant.

In the rubble, certain graces should be noted. Stewart, as ever, is utterly professional and always believable. While all about him people like Hardy are overacting and people like Jonathan Frakes as Riker are underacting (possibly because he has almost nothing to do in the film except bark "Retro-designate the photon torpedo attack module!" and fistfight a guy in a rubber mask that somebody left on the radiator overnight), Stewart is acting. It's an actual performance—elegant, crisp, entirely committed. Then there's Brent Spiner as Data, the adenoidal android; I hate the silver goo they paint on his face to signify his mechanistic endo-soul, but he always seems the most human of the characters, and in this film he's the only one to project recognizable emotion.

Rarely in the ten previous *Star Treks* have the movies transcended: that is, widened beyond the narrow scope of the TV cult and all the Trekkie wannabes and reached out to grip a nondenominational audience. Frakes himself directed the best of the second-generation films, *Star Trek: First Contact*, in 1996, just as Leonard Nimoy did the two best first-generation films, *The Voyage Home* (1986) and *The Search for Spock* (1984). The two of them were able to tell tales that had some reach and narrative power. This film, directed by a British yeoman of no particular distinction named Stuart Baird, lacks both. It's for people in costumes, Starfleet Academy graduation rings, and no one else.

(DECEMBER 13, 2002)

*O*migod! It's *Crime and Punishment* in outer space.
It's Dostoyevsky at warp speed.
It's Raskolnikov as a nine-year-old cutie at the controls of a pod racer.
And the Force, for all the mythical flibbertigibbety surrounding it, turns out to be our old friend, long exiled from polite society and after-dinner conversation, the moral imagination.

That, at any rate, is the result of one viewing of *Star Wars: Episode I— The Phantom Menace,* and a largely sleepless night of ratiocination in its wake. Without committing to the specifics of a technical movie review, I hereby issue what we call in the trade a thumb-sucker: An examination (I hope) of the deeper issues of this movie, what its structure dictates to its meaning, and what the future portends as Episodes II and III head bravely forward to the past and bring us to the brink of Episode IV of 1977. (Isn't this where we started all those years ago?)

Gpeorge Lucas, the man-child genius behind all this, has stated publicly that his initial desire was to do a cycle of nine stories in which the only common characters were two androids, C-3PO and R2-D2. Oh, the vainglorious ambitions of youth! But now he's a grown-up, and he sees limits: He can't do everything, especially since he gave himself a nice sixteen-year vacation. The reconfigured plan now will include only six stories, the first three already delivered (in case you've been on Mars: *Star Wars, The Empire Strikes Back* and *Return of the Jedi*) and the second three—chronologically the first three—one-third here as of Wednesday at 12:01 A.M. and the other two installments promised for 2002 and 2005. But it turns out that the cute little robots are of little interest to the older Lucas, and their appearance in Episode I is more like a cameo than a meaningful presence.

And it turns out further that the one figure who will dominate these three films is the same figure who dominated the last three films: Darth Vader (in his good incarnation, Anakin Skywalker), father of both Luke and Leia in the first cycle as well as dark avatar who drove the plot; and, in Episode I, set twenty-five years or so earlier, a mere tot.

He may in fact be too mere a tot. This certainly won't be the last place you read of a critic's difficulties with the performance of young Master Jake Lloyd, who plays the boy Anakin with a kind of unidimensional guilelessness. For this thing to work, the actor playing young Anakin must have that weird greatness of performance that lets us simultaneously see a doubleness within, an ambiguity, a secret but potent imagination. That is a great deal to ask of a child actor, maybe too much. But whatever, poor Jake Lloyd lacks this capacity altogether. There is only an absolute oneness to him, and to see him is not to ponder the potentialities of the human spirit but merely the cuteness of kids. This casting mistake may cost poor Lucas, who financed the film, his pile. It's a dead hole in the middle of all the fun.

There are a great many other flaws in the film, alas. For the record, here's a batch: The central dramatic situation is unclear, a matter of politics that reads like the duller parts of Thucydides' *History of the Pelo-*

ponnesian Wars. Then there's Lucas's obsession with computer-morphed characters who he thinks are cute but simply play dead on-screen. Your eyes just pass over the redoubtable Gungan, Jar Jar Binks, because you know he's not there; he's just blips on a hard drive in some spotless lab in California. Finally, the central characters have no spark of life. The rowdy yapping and bickering that provided the first three films with their human center is missing here entirely, replaced by solemn dialogue that sounds as though it was translated from classical Urdu. Natalie Portman, as the Princess Leia–analogue Queen Amidala, is a particular disaster: She doesn't have spunk. I hate that.

But the problem with the boy is by far the most serious. It's the dead hole at the moral fulcrum of the *Star Wars* chronicles and its most promising line of investigation, its grand inquisition into the nature of good and evil. Lucas has been reading his Fyodor D., it seems: "If man invented the devil," Dostoyevsky postulated, "then surely he invented him in his own image." Did he? Or not? This is the big one.

Why do most of us turn out all right, but some of us, somehow, turn to the dark side? Volumes have been written, and we are no closer to understanding today than we were when the first Hebrew scribe recorded Cain bushwhacking Abel. What explains the Hitlers, the Stalins, the Pol Pots? On a smaller and more intimate scale, what explains the Dillingers, the Charlie Mansons, the Eric Harrises and Dylan Klebolds of this world, who seem to gain pleasure and self-esteem from the crushing of other spirits? What the deep thinkers from A to Z have come up with on this issue may be summed up in the following: nada, nothing, zilch, zero, duh.

But that's the territory the new George Lucas is bravely setting out to navigate, behind all the special-effects trappings and the Jujube-faced computer morphs with Rastafarian accents. And that's what, at heart, the *Star Wars* sweep of stories must ultimately become: an inquiry into the causes of evil. Lucas has done all the groundwork; now only the hard part remains.

For in essence, the *Star Wars* films have taken their key from Dostoyevsky (though visually, each has a different style; the new one is clearly derived from the studio-made Roman epics of the late forties and fifties; it's *Ben-Hur* in outer space) in general and *Crime and Punishment* in specific, with Anakin Skywalker as Raskolnikov, the intellectual who will ultimately will himself to violence and evil.

The general arc of the complete cycle, now visible for the first time, will thus be fall and redemption. Redemption has already been delivered. When first we see him in *Star Wars,* Darth Vader—the name is baby-talk onomatopoeics for Dark Father—is the pure essence of debauched evil. Let's deconstruct this image for a bit and figure out the visual source of his power: He wears a Nazi helmet, a black leather cape, jackboots and stands a good seven feet tall. He strides manfully down corridors and others shrink from him. He dominates with his incisive grasp of the tactical, his eye always fixed on the goal. He is in many ways the best man in the films, surely the most confident, and the most courageous even in a cause that we may abhor. He's a heavy breather announcing his intentions for evil in James Earl Jones's amplified, ominous pre-phone-company voice. And Darth's face: part insectoid, part gas mask, with black, pitiless lenses for eyes. Was ever a Wizard of Ughs there was? No way. It was a superb movie image, instantaneously beamed to the subconscious of the race, where it touched on other deeply rooted memories of evil—from Old Scratch's cloven gait to SS-Reichsführer Heydrich's silky beauty—and rang a loud, insistent bell.

And he recalls that other specialty of the male sex: the difficult man. I think of John Wayne in *The Searchers,* and, in a comic mode, General Buck Turgidson (George C. Scott) in Kubrick's great *Dr. Strangelove,* hoo-hawing as the great bird of prey flaps in low to end the world, or Kurtz (Brando), his sullen baldness dominating the end of *Apocalypse Now.* They are all lost and forlorn, the worst possible fathers, given to their own strumpeting evil vanity, and yet . . . and yet they begot us.

So the movement of the first three films and Vader's crowning moment (and the most redemptive moment, arguably, in movie history) is when the love for his own son overpowers his commitment to evil. He is the one, really, who saves freedom in the galaxy; he reaches out of his caul of menace when he hears his son call him "father," and it's as if eons of crime and murder are shed from his body, and in his last, dying moment, picks up the emperor and tosses him (screaming deliciously) down the cosmic sewer pipe. Wondrous moment! (Wish the old guy had blown up cooler, though.) Total emotional grandeur and the crowning moment in the cycle of the first three films. (Richard Marquand, who directed *Return,* finds a great subtlety by which to communicate Anakin's awakening: It's in the flickering of the light, like the first light of dawn, as it plays across the iron of that heretofore remorseless mask, as the emperor gleefully tries to electrocute Darth's son Luke.)

It's as if the underlying structure of the huge piece had been filched from ever so humble an opus as "Amazing Grace": First he's lost, and then he's saved.

The first three movies show us how he was saved. Now we will see if Lucas can show us how he's lost, and bring off a major masterpiece of popular culture, never mind the preordained box office tally.

There is, admittedly, something limiting about this. Whereas the first three movies were conceived as a quest, these three must almost be an anti-quest. They lead toward the chaos of the galaxy of *Episode IV*, and to get there they must chronicle a man's descent into evil, they must probe his surrender to the blasphemous, his desertion of his wife, his creed, his children, his duties. That is a brave course for a billion-dollar cycle of films to steer, and as Anakin grows and withers, surrendering ultimately to the dark side, the real test for Lucas will be to demonstrate this without losing contact with our emotional connection to the figure.

But it's an interesting course of speculation. What corrupted Anakin into Vader: pride, that manly bringer of self-destruction? Arrogance? Abuse? (An intriguing possibility and the source of many monsters here on banal old Planet E.) Genetic predisposition? Fear? Lucas only knows, and let's hope he can get it together to tell us. If told right, it should be quite a tale.   (MAY 16, 1999)

*T*he *Matrix* is so wild and crazed it requires adult supervision. Thank God, it never got it. It rocks.

Emerging from the sick minds of the Wachowski brothers—these bad boys named Larry and Andy who made their mark with the perverse yet witty lesbo-noir *Bound*—it postulates the following: You (and me and everyone else) are not the lean, sleek creatures our mirrors display each morning. We are the dreams in the soft brain of a cloned baby whose pulpy body is suspended in fluid in a tube, tended by intelligent machines. We are fed a diet of electronic impulses that stimulate us into thinking we live in a place called "here" on a planet called Earth in a year called 1999. In other words, all reality that we experience is virtual reality.

Why do the machines keep us alive? I missed that part. I guess they need our energy to run their garbage disposals, or possibly they require help with their taxes. But humanity dozes onward—it's really 2009—in caverns that look as though they were designed by Attila the Hun's version of Albert Speer, all deco-Gothic-art-moderne-cathedral-esque vault of darkness. Those canisters on the wall? Why, that is humanity—an Alpo display in a cool basement.

Hello, fellow tube-babies! Don't despair. Help is at hand. An intrepid crew of commandos fights to liberate us. Again, my ancient brain is too sludgy with concepts like "logic" and "cause-effect" and "probability" to follow the mechanics of it: It seems that the commando team, led by a genius called Morpheus (Laurence Fishburne), seeks to overthrow the machine order. They live underground, they come up in some sort of ship (again, me no get), and in that proximity to the caverns they can plug into the Matrix and thereby insert themselves into our reality where they seek to awaken us, but are thwarted by "agents" (of the machines) that look like Men in Black but are really Sentient Programs. Meanwhile the agents themselves are searching for ZI-on (as it's pronounced), and the last real city on Earth, or really under it.

The higher eschatology of this is weirdly resonant and titillating; it's like that moment in an eight-year-old's life when he realizes that atoms and the solar system are the same configuration and goes on to wonder if the solar system isn't an atom in a giant's universe! (I still do. That would be neat-o, huh?) What follows is an action movie with mythic overtones in a vernacular of virtuoso tricks and unseen but weirdly familiar vision. It seems like a battle royal in dreamland, where the logic has a nightmare quality to it, a freedom from responsibility and sense that's somehow bracing.

Put another way, here's what follows from this setup: everything. You name it, they stuff it in, a whole vastness of pulp tropes. Commando raids, guns, kung fu, lovey-dovey stuff, betrayal, monsters, punk fashion, neon, torture, explosions, even a few dangerous ideas. Fortunately, the actors are dull enough so that they don't get in the way of the directors.

Our hero is Neo (i.e., "new man"), played by the nice-to-look-at, impossible-to-take-seriously Keanu Reeves. He's okay, not that you'd notice if he wasn't. The others—Joe Pantoliano, Carrie-Anne Moss,

Hugo Weaving, to name most—are also okay, though maybe they weren't, and I didn't notice.

What you do notice is the incredible energy and stylizations of the Wachowskis, who seem to represent the next generation with a vengeance. I have seen the future and it smirks. Is this what the movies are becoming? Well, yes. But at least the Bros. W. do it with the brilliance and zip of the pioneer spirit. Their minds stretched and liberated by the possibilities of cyberspace, John Woo, CD-ROMs, and microwave ovens that can heat a hot dog in 25 seconds, they seem to imagine movie plots in five dimensions, not a mere three, and action in six. *The Matrix* builds to such kinetic momentum that the movie becomes a spike of pure action, and since it's taking place in baby brain reality rather than authentic reality, it's liberated from gravity and sense.

The story is told from Neo's point of view, and it tracks his burgeoning consciousness and his sense of what he can do. Turns out he's "new" in more than one sense. In fact, he might be "The One" who's come to lead the tribe to redemption. (Question: How can these people "save" humanity? Humanity is a toothpaste of DNA and protein in tubes. Are these five people going to break all the tubes and raise a billion babies? Answer: Not given.) So someone has read the Bible and someone has seen *Star Wars* and someone knows who both Odysseus and Gilgamesh are. Is it a movie or a pop quiz on classical mythology?

There's a kind of liberating, almost transforming energy in this film; it lights you up and sends you out all giddy with silliness. You won't quite know what you've seen, but, dammit, you know you've seen something. (MARCH 31, 1999)

*K*ids, kids, kids, quiet down and I'll tell you.

No, it's not great.

No, it's not a disaster.

That leaves two possibilities: Is it really good or is it merely good enough?

Probably more of the latter than the former, though in its last hour *The Matrix Reloaded* acquires something of the force and dynamism that made *The Matrix* a movie to be enjoyed many times over.

Perhaps it's best to think of *Reloaded* not as a movie, but as the first two and a half hours of a five-hour movie that will reach its end in November. That way, you will not be overly irritated as the current chapter pauses to accomplish its many administrative duties. It must introduce new characters and situations that play no part in its resolution, it must set things up for the last installment, and it must leave most of its mysteries unsolved.

Yet the truth is, even if you subtract those dreary necessities from the equation, the film that remains is somewhat disappointing. It certainly lacks the intensity of the first; it has fewer surprises, and its directors-writers-producers-auteurs, the mysterious Wachowski brothers, make far more misjudgments.

But (some of) the fights: still cool.

(Some of) the shoot-outs: still unbelievable.

(Some of) the chases: still awesome.

(All of) the stunts: still fabulous.

(All of) Trinity: still hot.

(Every last pulsating inch, cell, fiber and cuticle of) Monica Bellucci: Well, let me say two words about Monica Bellucci—Monica Bellucci!

And for those who must know, Keanu Reeves: still blankly Zen beautiful, the perfect vessel of hopes and dreams. If this young man ever learned how to act, he'd be dangerous.

Anyway, back in the movie, when it clarifies (it takes a bit of time) the situation is: The machines have discovered the underground site of Zion (where the Earth's last 250,000 free people still live) and are drilling madly toward it to destroy it. In Zion two courses of action are debated: the literal-minded faction wants to intercept the invading diggers and fight a straight-out battle with them, though everybody knows it's a long shot.

But the more metaphysical Morpheus (Laurence Fishburne) believes that the savior of Zion and the ultimate destroyer of the Matrix is The One—you know, that one, Keanu Reeves's Neo—who, on the surface of the planet, can make contact with the Oracle and learn from her how to destroy the machines. In this endeavor he will be supported by Morpheus and the crew of the sub-earth sub *Nebuchadnezzar*, Trinity (Carrie-Anne Moss) and newbie Link (Harold Perrineau Jr.). That ploy is regarded by most as an even longer shot—though, after some political maneuvering, Morpheus gets his way.

There are a couple of subplots. One is Neo's precognition that this mission will end in a dream he's had: Trinity in a free-falling gun battle with an agent, one of whose slugs strike home fatally. And two is that Commander Lock (Harry J. Lennix), head of the rationalists, is now with Captain Niobe (Jada Pinkett Smith) and politically opposed to Morpheus. But she was Morpheus's original squeeze, and his heart still goes thumpa-thumpa for her.

Alas, up front, too much time is spent on internecine Zion politics. Really, who cares, especially when expressed, à la *Star Wars: Attack of the Clones* and every movie ever made about Imperial Rome, in a rhetorical style that might be call High Fructose-Emulsified Purple. "The Council has asked me to speak tonight at the temple gathering," intones old Anthony Zerbe in stentorian voice, in a toga, or is it a breechcloth or a nightshirt? Really, this never works, here or anywhere.

And Zion itself, as movie illusion, is *très tragique:* It looks like an underground city designed by someone who spent too much time in an L.A. grunge club. In fact, everything about Zion kind of bites, including all the nineteenth-century iron doors, the dirt on the floor, the baskets of dates on which the natives seem to feast and, most ludicrous of all, that "temple gathering," which is a kitschy scene of mass-boogaloo hearty-partying through the night. It reminded me of an equally foolish moment in another big movie: when bad Edward G. Robinson led the Israelites astray and back to the golden calf orgy in Cecil B. DeMille's *The Ten Commandments.* This Zion needs a Chuck Heston in the worst sort of way.

Let me pause here to interject a concept: Oh, I wish this film were better! Why does it have to be so annoying? Come on, guys, get it together or you'll squander all of the immense goodwill you achieved with your most bodacious breakthrough film.

Perhaps the most serious deficiency of *Reloaded* is conceptual. Possibly it couldn't be helped. But at the core, the idea of what the Matrix meant—and it was that idea that drove the film to astonishing success and influence—isn't truly reestablished here. I suppose the Wachowskis take it for granted and assume that we do as well, but that's dangerous. It was so useful an idea, so resonant, an equal-opportunity delusion for the secret paranoids that all of us really are: that a secret screen of anti-reality had been imposed by a cabal of mechanical monsters to hide the elemental truth. We're zombies, they drain our electricity, what we see is simply neural responses to pricks inside our brains.

How useful, how flexible, how dramatic, especially as the film built toward that stunning revelation that set the last two acts in particle-accelerator motion. It was a conceit applicable to any oppositional system: libs and cons, Dems and Repubs, old and young, smart and dumb, thesis and antitheses, whatever. It held for everywhere there's an us and a them, which is to say, everywhere.

Though nominally still present in the movie, the central idea is effectively gone. You'd say, gee, if the plot is compelling enough, the fights brilliant enough, the effects effective enough, it doesn't matter. But none of those things is quite true either.

The Wachowskis still use the Hong Kong wire master Yuen Wo Ping to run the fights, but to diminishing effect. In the first hour, too many of the fights are like too many other of the fights. It's always the same structure: Neo, alone, fighting not five men or even ten men, but now fifty or a hundred. As spectacle, this is briefly amusing but it pales rapidly. For one thing, all fifty men look the same: They are Agent Smith (Hugo Weaving), who now has the ability to replicate himself on the principle that if one of him is really cool, fifty will be that much cooler.

Wrong. Fifty Smiths is one-fiftieth as cool as one Smith. Gone is the intense personal animosity between Smith and Neo, and the sense of Smith's overweening superiority, his smugness, his unflappability. He's not a character anymore, he's just an army. Remember that great scene where he complained about the smell of the Matrix and yearned to return to the emptiness of pure mathematics? Great scene; nothing like it at all here.

Gone, too, and very sadly, is any sense of risk. This is cybercombat at its most abstractly meaningless: It's pongs vs. pings, with nothing at stake. Occasionally, when Neo bowls one Smith down a corridor with dozens of Smiths and sends them flying hither and yon, it's funny, but the fights have been mostly emptied of untidy if satisfying aspects like emotion, pain, sweat, effort, and heroism.

Another bad idea: Neo can now fly. O brothers W, why, why, why? If I want to rent *Superman* I'll rent *Superman*; but Neo in his black cape hurtling through the ionosphere faster than a speeding .220 Swift (and baby, that's fast) just fails to impress. It feels—this is an odd term to apply to a movie so full of black leather, latex, and teardrop-shaped sunglasses—cornball.

In its last hour, the movie settles down somewhat. The plot focuses: In the Matrix, Neo is given an assignment by the Oracle that will somehow solve the problem of the diggers' assault. He must reach the source and find the keymaster. Huh? Don't ask me. Something about a Korean guy with a key to a certain room in a skyscraper. Ask someone under seventeen, she'll be able to explain it much better.

In any event, this narrowing of effort leads to the film's two best action sequences, the first set atop a trailer truck roaring along a freeway in which Morpheus does battle with Agent Thompson (Matt McColm) while the careening vehicle tosses small autos this way and that and Trinity, looking ever more like a Buick Roadmaster hood ornament, runs a 9,000-cc motorcycle in and out of the same mechanical chaos. Think of a fight between Mick Jagger and the Man in the Grey Flannel Suit at 80 miles per with Suzy Parker on a unicycle in a parade and you get the idea.

The second—like the climax of *The Matrix*—is a straightforward issue of penetration: The team has to get inside a building. The Agents don't want them inside. Much violence ensues, Trinity risks her foreordained death to save Neo. It's got some hellaciously entertaining stunts, and the topper is that shoot-out in free fall between her and a guy in a suit.

But then the movie stops. It doesn't end, it just runs out of film. Nothing left on the reel. A few issues are solved but others—like why did that annoying kid give Keanu Reeves a spoon?—just hang there, and it'll cost you another $9 in November to find out what the spoon meant and whether the diggers broke through to trip the light fantastic on the sidewalk of Zion. I'll tell you this: You will pay. You will go. You have no choice.   (MAY 15, 2003)

*N*eo, schmeo! In *The Matrix Revolutions*, directors Andy and Larry Wachowski give up on character; instead, they try havoc and let slurp the dogs of war. The film is a soggy mess, essentially a loud, wild one-hundred-minute battle movie bookended by an incomprehensible beginning and a laughable ending.

As a final act and summation of the brilliant *Matrix* and the not-so-brilliant *Matrix Reloaded*, it's utterly inconsequential; as pure spectacle it's almost a hoot but only a little more entertaining, finally, than the Redskins.

For those hundred minutes, we just watch—without reference to Neo (Keanu Reeves), Agent Smith (Hugo Weaving), Morpheus (Laurence Fishburne), Trinity (Carrie-Anne Moss) or any of the other boys and girls—a movie that might as well have been called *Zion vs. the Insect Machines*. The familiar characters are absent from the picture for this long tour of duty, which has many variations but essentially one issue: Gun crews from the underground city try to spray-paint their way out of an onslaught by mechanical creepy-crawlers. You might say the Wachowskis have fallen for the Steve Spurrier fallacy: They've overcommitted to a fun-'n'-gun offense.

The imaginers are not without a certain level of low cunning. They have conceived the machine attack not so much as an invasion or an assault but as an infestation. Thus they play on resonant, universal fears of things that swarm and buzz and bite and have lots of legs and chompy, gibbering jaws. A million tentacled, flying voracious creatures breach the vault of ZI-on (the movie's characters invariably allot the name two full syllables when they speak it), the last remaining human city sequestered somewhere down below, where platoons of manned robots with Gatling-gun fists spit ack-ack and ball tracer at them.

Encased in gigantic mechanistic exoskeletons, the valiant warriors of ZI-on try to kill enough of the flying metal arachnids to survive through the night. It's like the siege of Fort McHenry on steroids from outer space, and the only anthem to be written would be "Praise the Lord and Pass the Ammunition." The illusion is stunningly real, even if it's only happening in geekspace in some anonymous San Fernando Valley bunker where professional entertainment is now manufactured. But you do believe that the hordes swirl and buzz and strafe and the gunners track them and pump them full of glowing slugs amid explosions, collapsing beams, shrapnel, and crumpled-up, unused pages from the script. It's pretty neat.

But you have to ask: Why is this sequence more than an hour long? It could be five minutes and there'd be plenty of time left for old-fashioned stuff like, you know, story and character, both of which are given scant attention over the movie's long, relentless running time. And perhaps then the filmmakers would have gotten around to picking up some of the plot pieces left in the air in the last installment.

But no. The brothers want their battle scene, ahead of the Christmas curve of battle scenes (*The Last Samurai, Lord of the Rings III, Master and Commander: The Far Side of the World,* etc.), so they got their battle scene. It seems to have eaten all their energy and passion.

The movie begins, drearily, with a kind of situation report on where the last film left off: Neo is in a neither-here-nor-there purgatory. The machines are nibbling their way to ZI-on. The council can't decide whether to rescue Neo or commit all its resources to the defense of ZI-on. A spy with a goatee is trying to subvert one of those weird underground submarine ships. (You know what? I never really got those ships. How do they fly? They're not in space, where there's no gravity.) Agent Smith has inserted himself into a Xerox machine and is replicating himself unto infinity. Morpheus and old flame Niobe (Jada Pinkett Smith) are spatting, while officers such as Lock (Harry J. Lennix), Mifune (Nathaniel Lees) and Colt (Peter Lamb) are saying "goddamn" too much and trying to decide on strategy.

Basically, all these stories are put on hold while the Wachowskis lead up to and perform their big war boogaloo. The lead-up is particularly dispiriting: It seems the two boys spent too much time in the den watching *Sands of Iwo Jima* when they were growing up, so their military culture and heroic style has all the stilted stiffness of an old Duke Wayne picture, heavy on the macho gung-hoisms and the stern imprecations of the leaders ("If you let me down, you'll have to worry about the machines—and me!" one officer barks). There's hardly a cliché from War Movies 101 as it was taught in the Republic Pictures back lot in 1948 that isn't exhumed as if it were a new gem. There's even a character called "The Kid."

After the fighting's finally over (whew!), the boys move on to their climax, and it has a sense of a blown budget, and a cast and crew out of energy. I know movies are shot out of sequence, so that can't be right; nevertheless, that's how it feels.

Neo ventures to what is called the Machine City but seems clearly modeled on Oz. The God in the Machine even has a giant face like the Wizard's big green one floating in space, though the Wachowskis aren't clever enough to come up with a man behind the curtain to pay no attention to. But, like Dorothy, Neo is given a task that he must complete and, like Dorothy's, it involves assassination: He must go back into the Matrix and destroy Smith, who is busy taking over the cyberworld and presumably the human and machine worlds next (the logic is a little shaky here).

Which sets up the battle royale: Neo vs. Smith for the world championship. And you have to say the Wachowskis really don't deliver it. I mean, can this knock-down drag-out in the rain really be the climax to seven hours of moviegoing? It lacks energy and style, there's nothing singular to it, and compared with several fights-to-the-death in the recent *Kill Bill*, it's pretty lame. Oh, yeah: kicking and spinning in space, punching and grimacing, but there's nothing special about it. It could be any of Neo and Smith's other fights. It certainly gets nowhere near the intensity of the battle between the two that concluded *The Matrix*.

A lot of other *Matrix* pleasures are gone, too. There's no great, overarching metaphorical idea that echoes; intellectually, the film is less developed than the first edition. Neither Morpheus nor the great Trinity has much to do. Even Agent Smith hardly appears until the end, and when he does, he hasn't anything of the demonic force he had in the original. So, like too many great adventures, from Alexander's conquest of the world to Coppola's *Godfather* saga, the final stage doesn't so much end as bleed out. The only thing remaining is the corpse of our fond memories.   (NOVEMBER 5, 2003)

*O*ther than a distressing lack of quality hair care products, things are fine in Middle Earth. Good is still cute, bad is still monstro-evil, the landscapes still green, the hobbits barefoot and dressed like Victorian squires, the warriors handsome, the milieu kitschy. And ignorant armies still clash by night.

Where are we now? What place is this? We are in myth. It's an artificial myth, invented only in the last century by a fussy Oxford don with too much time on his hands, but it's still convincing, gripping, whole, and nourishing. Certainly of the fantasy film series currently in American theaters—I include *Harry Potter and the Secret Toity* and *Star Trek: Halitosis*—*The Lord of the Rings: The Two Towers* is the best, and not by just a little.

It alone among them transcends. It works as story for the common narrative-starved fool, who needs heroic example and pulsating, vicariously energizing experiences of love and hate. You don't have to be one of those hobbit-like geeks who've lost themselves in this world so intensely there is no other—though I hasten to add that there's nothing wrong with knowing more about Middle Earth than, er, Earth. You can—and this is the cool part—enjoy dual citizenship in the world where trees launch assaults on castles and the one where bills come due. Whichever citizenship you claim, you walk out and you think, that was a hell of a story.

What the director Peter Jackson brings to this second installment is exactly what he brought to the first, which is also what makes, come to think of it, a pretty good middle linebacker: power, speed and cunning. Jackson's not messing around. His commitment to this world is total. He's on a mission from Tolkien, and you either go along or you get trampled.

Of course, one can still track certain irritations. Elijah Wood, as the game little hero hobbit, Frodo Baggins, still relies entirely too much on a single expression: It's that stricken look, as if he's just learned that not only didn't he get into Harvard but he has been banned from ever setting foot in Massachusetts. It's really not acting, it's face-making. Here's how you do it: First, sky-blue contacts. Then, in front of a mirror, make your mouth an open square. Flare your nostrils. Wrinkle that brow. Really, really, squish it up good. Open your eyes to about f/1. Tighten your throat. Suck in your cheeks. There, you are now indistinguishable from the bearer of the One True Ring.

Other shortcomings? The Ents. Ents, not ants. An Ent is a big tree. Or, rather, it is a majestic sentinel of the forest, meant to guard all that is green and good about the world, mainly other trees. But of the brilliant digitized illusions conjured by the film, most of them wondrous and palpable at the same time, the Ents, it must be said, are kind of a disappointment. I mean, come on: They're just trees. Most people will think of the trees that were hornswoggled into throwing apples by the Scarecrow in *The Wizard of Oz;* these guys are taller and tougher and they appear to

have no apples, but they still walk like the kind of tragic human speci-
mens that are over seven feet tall but not coordinated enough for basketball. In other words, they aren't Yao Ming, they are Manute Bol.
Particularly when they march, they just look silly, and when they go to
war, their attack is somehow the least convincing, a letdown in a story
whose strength is that it drags us through the charnel house of medieval
warfare.

And finally, the hair. I suppose if you're shooting three movies back
to back on the other side of the world and it's one of the biggest gambles
ever in the entertainment industry, a detail might have slipped your
mind. In Jackson's case, that little detail was shampoo. He either couldn't
afford it or he forgot all about it. The result is that you never saw so
many greasy, tangled, thorny, wet, lusterless protein brambles as are on
display in this movie. Viggo Mortensen, with a haircut that looks like a
drowned swamp rat floating belly up in a bayou, leads the troop. A man
named Viggo ought to do better than this.

Tell me you don't want plot. You don't, do you? You do. Ach. Well, the
movie takes off directly from where the last one left us, and basically
three plot strains are followed, each strain a journey across Middle Earth.
The team whose formation was the essence of the first film is now broken
up, and we watch as three smaller groups—two teams of two hobbits, and
one team of three warriors—journey across the world, each on a mission,
while various larger forces gather to unleash destruction.

The gathering storm is the unification of the dark lord Sauron (still
unseen, but whose menace is felt everywhere—and in No. 3, Jackson had
better deliver, but good) with the lesser monster Saruman the White
(Christopher Lee, on leave from the disappointing *Star Wars* second
gen). It's Saruman who's unleashed his legions of grown-from-mud
warriors called Uruk-hai—they look like a DNA combo of WWE heavy-
weights and large, grumpy pigs—upon some other Middle Earth town-
ships and shires, namely Rohan. (Gee, do you think I'm copying this
from some Web site?)

Team A of hobbits consists of Frodo (Wood) and Sam (Sean Astin).
Frodo has the One Ring, and his job is to get across Middle Earth and
penetrate the topless towers of Mordor and there dump the ring into a
volcano to destroy it and restore harmony to the world. But he must do
this without wearing the ring, which would corrupt his character.

Team B in the Hobbit League is Merry (Dominic Monaghan) and Pippin (Billy Boyd), who are going somewhere that no Web site seems to know. They are the ones who get caught up by the Ents, and when war breaks out, it is they who leverage the Ents into a counterattack against one of the towers.

Because I have no imagination for little critters, I preferred the third team, comprising warriors Aragorn (Mortensen), Gimli (John Rhys-Davies) and Legolas (Orlando Bloom). They could have sailed in from that old Viking dragon ship on the beach there, or perhaps they came with those Huns and their yurts off the Asian steppes, or possibly they fought with the Green Berets at Tan Phu, the Spartans at Thermopylae or Henry at Agincourt, but, no doubt about it, they are the soldiers and their business is war.

And that's really the business of *The Two Towers* and the business of director Jackson. In the end it's a medieval battle rhapsody and you can pretend the Uruk-hai are demons from the mud of hell or Flemish mercenaries from beyond Hanover in the year 1642, and it really makes no difference at all. It's men in mud and rain, at a castle keep, in armor with spears and swords, and it's a long, long day's dying.

Jackson's imagination is most vividly provoked by the extreme nature of Bronze Age battle, for the last hour of *The Two Towers* is pure combat and it's mind-blowing. The scene is Helm's Deep, a castle moored against a rock escarpment that takes the full force of the Uruk-hai attack, while our three human heroes and the Rohanites stand fast. Some won't be able to watch the hackings and gougings, and some (e.g., moi) won't be able to look away.

But beneath it all is the same issue that defined Tolkien's life, the battle between Western democracy and monsters who wanted to destroy it. Read into it what you want, or read nothing into it, but it's really the oldest story of all. It's the one about a band of free men on a hilltop with nothing to get them through the night but their belief in themselves and their cause and the long steel they carry in their scabbards.

(DECEMBER 17, 2002)

*I*t may help if you know an orc from a Ringwraith or Aragorn from Gimli or Gandalf from Maiar. Yeah, and while you're at it, you might learn how the politics of the Second Age differ from the politics of the Third Age, and how Sméagol degenerated into Gollum but at key moments his essential Sméagolism bursts through, and why it is that Elrond reminds you of *The Matrix*. All that is fine.

But here's basically enough to get you through *The Lord of the Rings: The Return of the King:* There's us and there's them. They want what we have. We're not about to give it to them.

What we have is called civilization, and to defend it we will fight a war to end all wars, except for the war after that, and the next one, too. But anyway: *Return of the King*, like many epic fantasies, decodes into straight combat stuff. We fight a big fight over here to keep from being overrun; meanwhile, our commandos try and sneak in and deliver a death blow over there. Okay, so instead of wearing camouflage tunics and carrying M-4s, our special forces ops have big hairy bare feet and dress like extras in *H.M.S. Pinafore*.

But it's the same as it ever was, and when it's over everybody comes home to celebrate except that there's too much fatigue, melancholy, shame, loss, and residual fear for the great feelings to last for long. So it ends with as much rue as glee, and some old soldiers fade away. And there's that sense that maybe, as terrible as they were, those were the best years of our lives.

Of course, on this side of the trenches, not all our allies are, strictly speaking, human. We're in Middle Earth, after all, not on Earth. Our side includes dwarves, hobbits, elves, and wizards, and everybody looks as though they just stepped out of a Maxfield Parrish painting. Hey, it's Tolkien. What did you expect?

J.R.R. Tolkien, famously, was a World War I veteran. He saw men die in the thousands in the mud of the Somme (where he fought); to my knowledge, he never wrote about it directly, and he never became one of the strident, bitter antiwar novelists of the 1920s; he didn't publish his first novel until 1937, and it was called not *Goodbye to All That* or *A Farewell to Arms* but *The Hobbit*. Possibly he believed too fervently in metaphysical systems to consign the slaughter he'd witnessed to existential nothingness, and then, later, the slaughter he experienced vicariously as a citizen of Britain during the war it fought 20 years later. It had to mean something, and one way of looking at *Lord of the Rings* is to imagine the old combat-scorched don using words as therapy for the pain of those war memories.

So in his great books and in Peter Jackson's great movie versions, there's a kind of subsumed memory of the Great War underneath it all. You see it on the battlefields, such as the one at Pelennor Fields, the climactic engagement here. It's an endless field of ruin, desolate and despairing, blown with smoke and dust. It's the Somme—where 60,000 young English boys ran into emplaced German machine gun fire—as distilled through some sort of fantastic imagination and reconstructed in fairy tale form. But still, it's the Somme. Grim-faced men doing their duty against overwhelming odds, not particularly happy about it, wishing deeply to be somewhere else, but willing to follow the dictates of duty, which means death.

And the battle turns, so it works out, on something that every Great War vet must have thought about at moments of crisis on the battlefield. Suppose, he must have thought, all the men who died here, suppose suddenly now, in the day when Heaven was falling, the hour when Earth's foundations fled, suppose we were helped by our own dead, who would rise and carry the day. Men who've seen a lot of death would necessarily think that; and so it is that Aragorn arrives with the Army of the Dead, and turns the tide against the dark hordes from Mordor.

You don't have to love hobbits (I don't) to love this, but nevertheless it's true that the one thing Jackson does brilliantly is capture the exhilaration, fatigue, heroism, and despair of war. He looks at it as something not ennobling but exhausting, more ordeal than crusade but—completely necessary.

So this film is mostly war. It builds, skillfully, toward that big kill-off at Pelennor Fields, which it re-creates with almost unbearable intensity. You may want to laugh, of course: There are flying lizards and really big elephants, and guys without faces under their armored visors and even a fleet of eagles that comes to the rescue at a key point. Yet you cannot laugh because the battle is so intense and the stakes so high, and Frodo and Sam and Gollum are getting so close to Mount Doom.

Underneath everything—all the quasi-mythic names, all the Christian symbolism, all the Arthurian idylls, all the beasties and races and shires and dells, all the sentimentalizations of the English countryside and the memories of the battlefields of the Great War—*The Lord of the Rings* in general and *The Return of the King* in specific is a species of drop-dead melodramatic plotting. Tolkien and his representative on Earth, Jackson, really know how to get a tale roaring down the tracks.

Yet paradoxically, this final installment seems somehow less densely plotted than the other two, possibly because some of the main characters are now dead, and some of the subplots (like the two other hobbits in the story, Merry and Pippin) are folded into the battle story. Basically, we're down to two stories, cutting between them at precisely dramatic moments for maximum tension.

In one, men and elves and dwarves deal with the invasion from Mordor, as the Mordorian army swarms toward Minas Tirith, imagined as a great Escheresque structure in the mountains overlooking the plains of Pelennor. There, political realities must be faced, as various men, dwarves, and elves decide whether to join in the crusade, various fathers and sons quarrel, and leader-in-waiting Aragorn (Viggo Mortensen, still in need of a bottle of Breck) deals with his own apprehensions about his legacy of kingliness.

Meanwhile, that smaller unit of hobbit-commandos—this is Frodo (the ultra-alarmed Elijah Wood) and the ever more heroic Sam (Sean Astin)—have bonded with the sincerely insane Gollum (who originally found the ring when he was a hobbit, as the first few minutes show us) and are creeping ever closer to Mount Doom to throw the damned thing, which only Frodo can hold without being corrupted, into the volcano's fiery maw.

If there are flaws in the film, they seem to be flaws inherited directly from Tolkien's original conception, rather than newly minted movie flaws. One is that Sauron, the Lord of the Rings himself, the Dark Lord, Gorthaur, Annatar, the Black Hand, He, Lord of the Dark Tower, the Nameless One (he sure has a lot o' names for a Nameless One), isn't personified. In *The Two Towers,* he was fronted by Saruman (played by eternal dark lord Christopher Lee) and that was helpful, for it gave you someone to hate.

In this version, Sauron has taken the form of the Lidless Eye, and he looks like something off a secret Masonic document, an eye bathed in fire and floating in space. Like the many effects in the film it's impressive, but it's static. We want a villain whose ritual death will delight us. (On the other hand, when someone takes out one of the Ringwraiths by driving a sword through his face, I liked that a lot!) Watching what is essentially a structure tip into the flames lacks dramatic impact.

A second annoyance is the occurrence so soon of a battle after the big one at Pelennor Fields. In the actual book, there were nine battles in twenty-six days, but Jackson rearranges or consolidates. Still, it feels like not enough or too much. Aragorn leads troops to the Black Gates, that is, to actually assault Mordor proper, as a diversion from Frodo's mission. It feels anticlimactic and somewhat hastily arrived at.

Then, finally, there are the endings, all six of them. I suppose if you're essentially making one 558-minute movie you're entitled to six endings. And for the members of the cult, each of those endings ties up a storyline and will produce unbelievable poignancy. For us outsiders, it seems like too much of a good thing. You keep awaiting the wondrous magical elven words "The" and "End" to bring the enchantment to a finish. Instead your mind's eye produces "But Wait: There's Still More Stuff!"

But all those are minor rants: The big fact is that *The Return of the King* puts you there at Waterloo, or Thermopylae, or the Bulge, any desperate place where men ran low on blood and iron and ammo, but not on courage.   (DECEMBER 16, 2003)

Seven

TOONS

*T*h-th-that's not all, folks.

Th-th-there's more.

Looney Tunes: Back in Action, the crazed and wonderful continuation of the great Warner Bros. cartoon tradition at feature film budget and length, is delightful, delicious, and destructive. It makes one indisputable point, rich in philosophical and political meaning, a vast epiphany that we ought to all, every last one of us, understand and memorize: It's Daffy Duck's world and we're just visiting.

Mr. Duck is in fine form, and his considerable intelligence informs and illuminates *Looney Tunes;* moreover, it's wonderful to watch him relate with his costar Bugs Bunny.

Redford/Newman, Matthau/Lemmon, Laurel/Hardy, Duck/Bunny—we are talking fabulous screen pairings, the exquisite, instinctive pas de deux of ego as reflected in sublime comic timing, physical awareness, and interspecies mind-meld.

As for the humans in the cast—hmmm, were there any? Oh yes, if memory serves, Brendan Fraser has a good-hearted lark as the lunky D. J. Drake, a wannabe stuntman who was formerly Brendan Fraser's stand-in but was fired by Brendan Fraser for getting too much screen time in *The Mummy* (that's typical of this film's inside-movies sensibility). Then there's Jenna Elfman, who looks like Ann Coulter chilled on Prozac. She's a studio exec—the "vice president of comedy"—who fires Duck and then, when the new Bunny film just doesn't seem to work, must rehire him for the Brothers Warner (played by the identical Stanton twins, Don and Dan, who were, respectively, an asylum guard and his

T-2000 duplicate in the twin-rich *Terminator 2: Judgment Day*). But Duck has vanished.

Actually, he's headed off to Vegas with Drake to rescue Drake's father, the movie actor and spy Damien Drake (Timothy Dalton), who has been kidnapped by agents of Acme Corp., an evil corporation headed by psycho CEO Mr. Chairman (Steve Martin), who . . .

Well, a watched plot never boils, so let's let this one simmer away as it morphs into a completely meaningless parody of a globe-hopping, lesser Bond picture. The primary virtue of *Looney Tunes: Back in Action* is the dexterity with which it captures the spirit of the great Warner Bros. cartoons of the forties and fifties, wherein the director-animator Chuck Jones, the preeminent Bunny and Duck auteur (Mel Blanc just did the voices), really invented the cartoon as narrative-busting, frame-shattering, gravity-defying bomb. He brought a spirit to the flickers that could only be expressed in one word: anarchy. That impulse toward helter-skelter, an oft-troubling thing, representative of the nihilism the bitterly disconnected feel toward the world about them, does have its uses, but almost none of them is political. In the context of the animated film, it is a most wondrous force. As director Joe Dante (no stranger to anarchy—*Gremlins* was his great hit) unleashes it, it destroys everything and makes us laugh all the time.

Thus, at its best, Looney Tunes is a hymn to chaos, and Duck and Bunny its high priests. These boys can wreck anything, and have a good time doing it. To see them loose in the Louvre, that citadel of the permanent, the valuable, the sacred and the perfect, is priceless. As animated creatures, they are free to enter the paintings on the wall and, within those paintings, to absorb those painters' styles. To see a cartoon icon screaming next to Edvard Munch's iconic yellow-green wailer on that bridge in a duet of angst is a pure, fabulous toot. And we get the following delirious spectacle: a pointillist Bugs being pursued through *Sunday Afternoon on the Island of La Grande Jatte* by a pointillist Elmer Fudd, amid women in bustles and monkeys on leashes and lounging dogs and French-looking guys in weird jockey hats. Somewhere Georges Seurat is spinning in his grave, but I know of a guy who grew up with a copy of that painting hanging in his living room who hasn't stopped laughing.

Another gambit gets the characters to Area 52, which, as someone explains, is the real top-secret research site in the Nevada desert; Area 51 was merely the cover story. Anyhow, in this place they come across and are eventually attacked by a fleet of cheap fifties movie monsters, including the guy in the gorilla suit wearing the diver's helmet. Why, even a black-and-white Kevin McCarthy, carrying a pod and screaming, "They're coming!" wanders in, seemingly straight off the set of *Invasion of the Body Snatchers*.

The movie is made technically possible by computer-generated imagery, which enables—as in *Who Framed Roger Rabbit*—the animated characters to acquire depth, weight and substance. In olden days, combining the animated and the real never quite worked because the dimensionality was strikingly different: Here, Mr. Bunny and Mr. Duck can occupy the same space as Mr. Fraser and Ms. Elfman in a totally captivating illusion. It seems real in the movie sense—that is, as if you are watching a photographed document.

But possibly the true genius behind this movie is an old-fashioned kind of genius: That would be the writer's. Larry Doyle gets animated humor and timing to an exquisite degree, possibly honed by all his years writing for *The Simpsons* and *King of the Hill*. He brilliantly works in fabled figures from the Warner canon, including Tweety Bird and Sylvester, Pepe Le Pew and of course that Sisyphean figure of futility, Wile E. Coyote, who, as he must, continually disappoints his employer, Mr. Chairman. Doyle and Dante are clearly guys who get the sound and the fury of the Looney Tunes world, and we're all the better off for it.

(NOVEMBER 14, 2003)

*T*reasure Planet answers a question that to my knowledge has never been asked before, possibly because no one cared: What kind of a thirtieth century would the eighteenth century make?

The issue isn't likely to be on anyone's Must-Figure-Out-Before-Dinner list, but the answer, contained in the new, lovely Disney animated feature, is nevertheless quite interesting: The eighteenth century makes a splendid thirtieth century.

That's the film's continual source of delight. The directors, Ron Clements and John Musker, and their staff of 34,598 technicians use *Treasure Island*, the venerable boys' maritime adventure by Robert Louis

Stevenson, as the template for a projection into some far-distant future when ships still sail and pirates still close and grapple and things still burn and sink.

Like the four-masters of yore, plying the majestic blue seas of the Atlantic laden with cargo or hungering for plunder, these four-masters ply a blue sea of stars to exotic atolls hanging in space. The conceit, which works surprisingly well, is based on solar energy, so that one doesn't put nine sheets to the wind but nine sheets to the light particles and, thus filled, the solar sails pull the stately craft through the ether. They solve the air problem simply by ignoring it.

It's all quite vividly imagined, down to the tiniest details. The camera (or excuse me?—whatever it is, as they don't use cameras anymore, do they?) floats upward to a crescent moon above the surface of Jim Hawkins's home planet, only to find it's a crescent all right, and also a moon, but artificial: a curvilinear spaceport whose design imperatives hail from the works of Hogarth, not Lucas. It's full of dense alleyways and crooked, raggedy little houses, and the great vessels lie moored at a dock town as hustling and bustling as any in the oeuvre of Errol Flynn. What, no Olivia de Havilland?

Well, yes, there is an Olivia de Havilland, except she's, er, a cat—the sexy Captain Amelia, as purred to life by Emma Thompson. That's another conceit, and one that is borrowed from Lucas's *Star Wars*: that this eighteenth-century future is populated not merely with human beings but also with creatures evolved from house pets, as well as all manner of Canteena-style weirdos, none of whom, of course, dress in spandex and powder-blue space cadet unis, but in homespun linen, thigh-high boots and broad piratey caps, the swirling, caparisoned excesses of eighteenth-century fashion. What a mix! It shouldn't work, but it does.

The story is purloined neatly from Stevenson and will be more or less familiar to all who've encountered that Scottish lad's spinnings over the years. The key dynamic—surprisingly modern, given that Stevenson was writing in the 1880s—is the ambiguous relationship between the adventurous young Jim (voiced by Joseph Gordon-Levitt) and Long John Silver (Brian Murray), who, this time through, is a cyborg, with gizmos for eyes and an Eddie Scissorhands right paw. But Silver is still the ship's cook, still a secret plotter against the ship's captain and first mate. He knows that young Jim has come into possession of a certain map to a certain planet some months' solar-sail away, and with his hearties (all aboard as ship's crew) Silver plans to mutiny and take the planet's legendary treasure for himself.

The Jim-Jim thing is a great relationship, because it gets so vividly at the tides of emotion that spew and fume in the straits between father and son, or young men and older men. The father loves the son, but he also hates him. He wants him to do well, but he also doesn't want to be defeated by him. He takes pride in his courage and spunk and will defend him to the death—and then will try to kill him to advance his own ends.

Stevenson, of course, was no stranger to the duality in man, as he made clear in *Dr. Jekyll and Mr. Hyde*. That duality runs through this tortured relationship as well, and if Murray's giant, hobbling bloke isn't as memorable as the classic Robert Newton in Disney's first *Treasure Island* (1950), he's nevertheless a formidable being.

The Clements-Musker team is one of Disney's most successful, numbering among their hits *The Little Mermaid* and *Aladdin,* as well as the lesser *Hercules*. One of their strong points is speed, as lit up at key points by a star turn. Thus, as drama, this *Treasure* is fast, playful and rather shallow, but when it seems in danger of foundering, they pump it up with a brilliant vocal performance by Martin Short as "B.E.N.," who was a human being named Ben when Stevenson invented his presence on the island. Now, of course, the marooned man is a robot. But he's really not— he's just Martin Short, and although this isn't the place for my long-planned, definitive essay "Martin Short: God or Merely Godlike?" he really takes the movie over, after the fashion of a similarly incandescent Robin Williams, in *Aladdin*. Clements-Musker don't allow Short to riff the way they let Williams, so the performance isn't as free-form. But it's really fabulous; Short, one of the masters of the language of showbiz irony, manages to delight kids and adults, though in different ways.

The other Clements-Musker specialty is action. *Treasure Planet* has at least three mind-blowing sequences combining various forms of animation seamlessly and creating a truly thrilling illusion of danger. Possibly they overuse flame as a menace, but in deep space, you're far more likely to burn than drown, right?

Treasure Planet boasts the purest of Disney raptures: It unites the generations, rather than driving them apart.   (NOVEMBER 27, 2002)

*H*e's flying.

Look at him way up high and suddenly there he is, flying. He can soar, he can weave and what's more, he's not even trying.

This is . . . Tarzan?

Yes it is, at least according to the new animated Disney take on Edgar Rice Burroughs's fabled character. The film sees the ape man more as the Peter Pan of a never-never land (never existed, never will) than as a chest-beating avatar of white superiority. He's no avatar, he's an aviator. This Tarz is a magical sprite who zips through the ether with the grace of the Red Baron in defiance of that nasty reality called gravity; he sprinkles the fairy dust of eternal innocence.

The movie is great fun if weightless as its central character and denuded of ideas. To save consideration of the awkward issues threaded into the DNA of Burroughs's concoction—colonialism and racism, for example—the movie simply eliminates all native peoples from its universe. This does simplify things, and leaves plenty of room for delight rather than tragic reflection. And it opens up other possibilities; think how much trouble could be avoided in a *Lawrence of Arabia* without those pesky Arabs, or *An American in Paris* without those rude Frenchies.

Still, the delight—chiefly the delight of pure bravado execution—is considerable. Animation is so evolved as both an art and a technological process, particularly as the old-style imagination for character grace and nuance is seamlessly meshed with new-style computer concepts so brilliant as to be mind-boggling, that the whole thing dazzles.

In the best sequences, Tarzan uses vines for lift, but once he gets into the arboreal highway he uses the sheer power of self-belief for propulsion and negotiates from vine to vine and limb to limb with aerobatic smoothness. I believe he even does an Immelmann turn. Or, now and then, the skies turn metaphorically to seas and he becomes a surfer-dude riding a green, chlorophyll-filled forest canopy conceived as vast pipelines for him to veer this way and that. Hard on the feet? Well, not if you're animated. At such moments, *Tarzan* produces almost giddy pleasure, the cutting so quick and vital and rhythmic it takes years and pounds off you. I suppose if you're under six, you return to a fetal state.

The movie that sets up and fills space between these brilliant sequences is possibly not quite up to those standards but far from stupid. It begins with a story of origins, following as the baby Brit marooned on the African coastline (or possibly the coastline of an artificial islet somewhere in the greater Orlando area) is then orphaned by a leopard and saved from death by a mother ape, herself mourning over a lost child. (Yes, there is death in this world; later, Tarz gets even with the big cat with a most unapelike tool called a shiv.) Thus he's raised by the big apes—Glenn Close and Lance Henriksen are the majestic if somewhat one-dimensional parents. And who does he grow up to be? Someone hulking and brutish? Not these days, kids.

He grows up to be lithe and quick rather than densely muscled and powerful, though his calves and wrists (perpetually hanging downward as he necessarily apes the apes), accumulate all the fast-twitch muscle fiber. Somehow, he ends up with—this must be breeding—Lord Byron's magnificently chiseled profile, and, again because it's a cartoon, he stays untouched by dirt, mud, greasy hair, or halitosis. His voice is read with sensitive anguish rather than bull-moose intractability by Tony Goldwyn (most famously, the bad guy in *Ghost*).

Dignity turns out to be the hallmark of ape culture, which is portrayed with the gravity of a rabbinical college. The family issues are familiar: As a hairless one, the boy can never impress father Kerchak while being adored by mama Kala. The Disney people do stoop to vulgarity in their trademark "comic sidekick" routine, with the strident Long Island blasts of no less a mini-Merman (or, since Merman was small and she is big, perhaps that should be maxi-Merman) than Rosie O'Donnell as Terk, Tarz's best pal. A mistake, I think.

The movie ceases to be ethnography and becomes a story when the girl arrives. This is Jane Porter, daughter of Professor Porter. The two of them have come to study the apes, not on a safari (can't have a safari without native gun bearers, and there are no natives, remember?) but under the stewardship of a white hunter type named Clayton, who looks like Basil Rathbone on androstenedione. The character animation, by the way, is superb; look particularly at the elegant yet expressive simplicity of Jane's face, and the magic of the lines that give it such life, the entire illusion richly amped by a charming Minnie Driver reading the lines in a wondrous Victorian virgin titter.

The rest? Chutes and ladders, near-misses, fall-down-go-booms, a few mild musical numbers behind the mild voice and music of Phil

Collins. The dilemmas are equally mild: Will Tarzan return to England or stay with the apes? Will the wicked hunter capture the apes? Will Tarzan get to first base with Jane? All are easily solved—that is, if you can be persuaded that an elephant could shinny up a rope.

This Tarzan doesn't bellow, he kvetches; he doesn't dominate, he persuades; he doesn't rule, he seeks consensus. He isn't the king of the apes, he's a citizen of the animal planet. (JUNE 18, 1999)

*I*f you were under the misimpression that Sinbad was a character in *1001 Arabian Nights*, the New DreamWorks variation on that old story will set you straight. According to the gospel of SpielbergKatzenberg, the heroic sailor is a character conceived in 101 Hollywood nights at Spago.

Sinbad: Legend of the Seven Seas, in fact, has nothing whatsoever to do with Arabic culture or any culture. The story has been cut loose from its historical moorings and transpires in a world that never was, as overseen by gods who never were, in lands that never existed, hard by seas that were never wet.

Chalk it up to a spirit of planetary ecumenism. And, of course, the businessman's practical grasp of market realities. But I, for one, will mourn the passing of the old tribalisms; I liked the exciting specificity of a divided world. It was nice when the Japanese had samurai, the English knights, the Arabians harems, and the Greeks goddesses. This new mulch of place and thing may be safer but it sure is duller—and maybe it's not even safer.

So the New Sinbad—voiced, however improbably, by the very Yankee Doodle–dandy Brad Pitt—plies a sea that encompasses a Fiji and a Syracuse but not an Alexandria. He is haunted by a god not called Allah or Buddha or God but, improbably, Eris. Eris? Yeah, and she's voiced by Michelle Pfeiffer—you know, of the Valley Pfeiffers.

Eris is the Goddess of Chaos. Why would there be a Goddess of Chaos? I have no idea. She just likes to mess people up. Remember the fast, beautiful bad girl in high school? Eris is her, all grown up to be a goddess. So, just because it's her nature, she decides to diddle with the humans under her domain. She's like a kid dropping firecrackers on an anthill.

Her plot is to steal something called the Book of Peace, some sort of hazily defined religious gimcrack that keeps the cosmos on an even keel. What religion was that again? Anyway, first she bribes Sinbad to steal it, and when he fails, she steals it herself. Through plot manipulations left over from an Errol Flynn movie, he is forced to go recover it in the Land of Chaos, or his friend Proteus (Joseph Fiennes), the prince of Syracuse and Sinbad's boyhood friend, will get a neck tuck courtesy of a headsman's scimitar. Ew.

So off sails Sinbad to the edge of the world, with his colorful crew and the stowaway Marina (voiced by Catherine Zeta-Jones in a throaty vibrato), Proteus's fiancée, and on to the land of Chaos. Epic quest? Ordeals? Myths-R-Us? Joseph Campbell, call your agent.

Yes, it's ridiculous, but on its own terms, *Sinbad* works pretty well. The DreamWorks animation unit is staffed by ex-video game pros (like co-director Patrick Gilmore), and they know how to tell a tale in images and to keep the thing moving along. The same studio honed its craft on *Shrek*, so there's a tradition here. The action sequences have a videogame immediacy to them, particularly the sword fights, of which there are many.

As a technical accomplishment, the film does one thing brilliantly and another thing not so brilliantly. The brilliant thing is its combination of hard and soft cartoon forms; in other words, the traditionally cel-animated characters are set to play in a computer-animated world of forms and shapes, with spectacular success. The integration is superb.

On the other hand, the DreamWorks pencil-pushers are at their worst in articulating the mouths of the characters as they speak. The lips move primitively up and down as if the speaker is saying "Urk, urk, urk, urk," yet out comes "But Proteus will die by nightfall if we don't find the properly primed wind to propel our purple sails toward the topless towers of Syracuse." Then there's another problem, which may be only in my head. I have an ear for voices, so when I hear Brad Pitt, my mind produces an image of Brad Pitt, but that's not Brad Pitt up there, it's some kind of Howard-Keel-wannabe-from-*Kismet* look-alike. That disconnect—it's particularly the case with the Sinbad and Eris characters—keeps interfering with the illusion on-screen.

Finally, a comment about audience. Much as I enjoyed its daffy energy, I have to wonder: Whom is this movie aimed at? It seems to make more sense as a show reel for the animators than a crowd-pleaser for the masses. It's certainly not hard-edged enough for the teenage audience that will flock to *Terminator 3* this weekend, but it's possibly too vigorous and dark for the very young audience. Moreover, it doesn't have much in the way of an engaging musical score of hummable tunes. It seems like a movie carefully engineered for an audience of exactly nobody.

(JULY 2, 2003)

*L*ittle-known fact about Stalinist Russia, 1926, courtesy of *Anastasia:* There was no food but there was a surprising abundance of Maybelline eyeliner.

How else to explain the almond definition of Anastasia's vaguely Orientalized eyes in this beautiful idiot of an animated movie? She doesn't look like a Russian princess at all, but more like the teenage Cher.

Though it's from Twentieth Century–Fox, *Anastasia* shows us a very Disney Russian Revolution, so Disney that, oops, they forgot the Communists. The movie is a dream, a peach, and a lie. It works fabulously as spectacle, at least marginally as story, and as history it's bunk.

Of what importance is history, you ask, if it makes my little girl smile? There's no answer to this question, really, but one must ask directors Don Bluth and Gary Goldman why they chose to call it *Anastasia* and set it in the century's central drama if they meant to completely ignore that history. They could have called it The *Missing Princess* and set it in Graustarkia, Ruritania, or on the Island of Guavabuto.

Bluth and Goldman are ex-Disney animators who left the studio in a huff in 1979 because it had abandoned the classic, voluptuous, painterly stylistics of *Snow White* and *Dumbo* for a cleaner, cheaper modern look. Since then, they've bounced from studio to studio trying to out-Disney Disney, and this is one time they may have succeeded.

On the other hand, they may have cheated.

The hardest thing to animate convincingly is human movement. But it becomes considerably easier if you trace it—and, using human beings as "live action reference," Bluth and Goldman have clearly filmed some of the film's complex action, then based their images on those sequences. So the movie is an odd hybrid: It seems animated, it has all the stylizations of animation, yet the human movement is so realistic that your brain picks up on it subconsciously, sending little signals of weirdness up to the conscious. It's continually . . . not annoying, so much, but notice-able.

The story is an infantilized, sanitized version of the 1956 film starring Yul Brynner and Ingrid Bergman (she won an Oscar). A White Russian finds an orphan to pass off as the only survivor of the murdered Romanov clan, making her heir to a treasure that her father, Czar Nicholas II, had hidden in Paris banks before the revolution. To qualify, she much pass muster before another surviving royal, the dowager empress. But what seems a mere scam soon proves troublesome: She may be the actual princess and the con man may be in love with her.

With Meg Ryan and John Cusack voicing the roles, Anastasia and Dimitri have been simplified from the Bergman-Brynner cosmopolitan wariness into twentysomethings, with faces as uncomplex as Ohio cheer-leaders. It's not particularly believable, but it certainly makes box office sense.

The movie evokes the terrifying events beginning in 1916 in highly spurious form, then cuts to 1926, where the con man Dimitri is recruit-ing a young woman to play Anastasia in his scam. Fate throws him to-gether with the amnesiac orphan Anya, and they journey from St. Petersburg (which was then called Leningrad, though the movie never notices) to Paris and the scrutiny of the dowager empress, along the way bedeviled by the spirit of the Mad Monk Rasputin, who in limbo has sworn to destroy the Romanovs. (More historical absurdity: The Ro-manovs promoted him; it was nobles who murdered him.)

One can see the material's fascination for the animation team: great set-pieces of the lavish glories of Czarist Russia, the thrills of escape, the tenderness of young love, the mystery of the girl's identity, the melan-choly of a lost world, the chance to re-create not merely "St. Petersburg" in 1926 but, more promisingly, Paris.

But there are pitfalls, too: the depressing business at Yekaterinburg in 1918 when Bolshie goons took Mr. and Mrs. Czar and all the little czars and czarinas into the cellar and spattered their brains on the bricks. Not exactly your typical musical number.

So Anastasia is peeled off from her family at the railway station and the fate of her parents and siblings is never referred to again; they're simply gone. That seems okay. But the actual revolution itself is strangely handled. It's ascribed entirely to the curse by the mad monk, who "spread unhappiness through the land." Other than a hammer and sickle on one guard's babushka, there's not a single reference to the political system that replaced Mr. and Mrs. Czar and its monumental cruelties. There's no reference whatsoever to the Romanov's culpability in the debacle, or to the idiotic bloodbath known as World War I, which made the whole thing possible and set the century up for eighty more years of conflict. The brothers Lenin, Trotsky, and Stalin go unmentioned.

This creeps me way out. The museum of history is full of tragedy, cobwebs, and corpses. Somehow attention must be paid to the great campaigns of death that shaped the century and haunt us to this day. To pretend it's not there, even in so innocent a vehicle as this, feels indecent, as if a reliquary is being burgled by hucksters.

But let's put that aside. Kids under 10 will love *Anastasia* as a colorful spectacle, though the very young might find the final confrontation between Anastasia and Rasputin on a Paris bridge somewhat intense, as it borrows elements from both Prince Charming's battle with the dragon in *Sleeping Beauty* and the "Night on Bald Mountain" from *Fantasia*.

The vocal performances are okay. Ryan and Cusack are incongruously American—every other Russian character speaks with an accent—but as there's no requirement for internal logic in animation, it's not bothersome. Ryan hardly registers as anything beyond generically spunky; Cusack overregisters as Cusack, so you see his own face, not Dimitri's visage, when he speaks. The musical numbers are all right, but they have a fifties feel to them, a sense of the static; the numbers in such recent Disney products as *Beauty and the Beast* or *The Lion King,* driven by dazzling editing, are much better.

So here's my quote for the movie ad blurb: "*Anastasia* isn't terribly bad! In fact, it's almost all right!" Twentieth Century–Fox advertising department, go for it!   (NOVEMBER 21, 1997)

*I*s *The Prince of Egypt* a good movie or the most expensive Sunday-school filmstrip ever made? My enthusiasm for Western man is so primal that I lean toward the former. Really, so much of it begins with

Moses: the concept of freedom, the sense of the worth of the individual, the idea of God as an abstract ideal of morality instead of a batch of dog-faced bullies, commandments 1 through 10, even that inconvenient one about the neighbor's wife, and the coolness of beards. Oh, and also: Judaism and Christianity, democracy and baseball, to say nothing of Shakespeare, Bogart, and Faulkner.

The new animated feature from DreamWorks SKG gets that. If nothing else it's a wonderful essay on the meaning of freedom and the courage it takes to wrestle it from despots. In that sense, it feels more political and cultural than religious. You don't see faith systems in opposition so much as idea systems.

Primarily concerned with the first part of the Book of Exodus—you know, the part with all the special effects—it leaves out that dreary forty years in the wilderness and, being aimed at families, equally omits the shimmy-shim-sham danced about the feet of the Golden Calf. We begin by watching Baby Moses basket-surf the Nile, to be rescued by an Egyptian princess. He is raised to privilege in the court as brother to the Pharaoh to be. Upon discovering his true Hebrew identity, he suffers a crisis, flees, and returns with the best slogan ever written: Let My People Go. When Pharaoh won't listen, God sends bugs and frogs. The people are ultimately let go, but then Pharaoh goes after them. There's no revisionist carping about Red/Reed Sea translation confusion: This is the big wet one, baby, and Moses parts it as neatly as Elvis parted his first hairdo for Ed Sullivan. When Pharaoh and his boys lumber in their chariots across the same passage, only Charlie Tuna is around to listen to their complaints.

The movie's proudest accomplishment is that it revises our version of Moses toward something more immediate and believable, more humanly knowable. This is not the time and the place to bedevil Charlton Heston, who after all can't really help being Charlton Heston. But his famous 1956 movie *Moses* was a reflection of a time that invested most of its authority in the severe white male, an unbending paragon of morality, strength, and wisdom. Watch the news for seven or possibly as long as eleven seconds and see how far that one has fallen!

But this Moses, voiced by the less than imperial Val Kilmer, is less iconographic and more human. This Moses doesn't seem to be posing for Mount Rushmore, and you could never ski down his cheekbones. Wiry and Semitic, he's a man beset with doubts, who feels himself completely unworthy. When he discovers his secret heritage, he reacts more like Woody Allen than an NRA president: He gets mopey, depressed, and self-loathing. He wants to be hugged.

Without going too far into this matter, it seems clear that this Moses reflects the personality of his creator, DreamWorks co-founder Jeffrey Katzenberg. Possibly he represents a little of Katzenberg's more famous partner, Steven Spielberg, as well. Heston's Big Mo was a vision of the annoyingly Caesarean Cecil B. DeMille, a bald tyrant who stomped around movie sets in jodhpurs and cavalry boots like some sort of Crimean War general about to order the Light Brigade to charge. He believed in the principle of absolute authority—his own—and he directed with the subtlety of a man carving an angel out of a lump of coal with a chisel.

The second virtue to *The Prince of Egypt* is a superb performance. It's amazing how a great actor can dominate a project without even showing his face. I refer not to Kilmer, who is appropriately unassertive in the role, nor to the absurd Valley Girl stylings of Michelle Pfeiffer as Tzipporah, Moses' wife. Hard to believe Moses' wife went to Redondo Beach High School!

No, the reigning vocal genius of *The Prince of Egypt* is Ralph Fiennes as Rameses, the non-blood brother of Moses' upbringing, inheritor of the throne. It is to the production's credit that he's given a motive—his fear of being the "weak link" in pharaonic succession, of failing the empire of his fathers and his sons. But this Pharaoh, like the Moses of his opposition, is a man, not a symbol, and in Fiennes's reading we hear the tragedy of a king born out of time, shackled to a set of beliefs that are crumbling daily, still in tragic love with a brother who has outgrown him. In the fight of his life, he's overmatched and he doesn't even know it: He's not going against Moses, he's up against the Big Guy Himself.

How do you fight plagues? How do you fight frogs in the billions? What about locusts—DDT is still 3,000 years in the future. And that, of course, gets to the third triumph of this surprisingly short, intense film. It really rides the possibilities of animation out to the limits. The design seems drawn from some of Gustave Doré's scarier prints, and the sense of both the monumental and the inspirational is well evoked. When God sends flames to light up the Egyptian night, they glow with the incandescence of hell on Earth. When the Red Sea parts, it ascends to heaven, a great backlit wall of undulating, light-diffusing water.

Likewise, the Egyptian architecture has been cleverly created to carry a message. Its geometric mass and density almost beyond human measure aptly invoke a world with many followers and but one leader, who in his own mind thought he was beyond human and nearly a god himself. It's the architecture of human delusion, grandly evil in its assumption of the ruler's right to command the totality of social obedience.

Raise a man in monstrous buildings, and he becomes a monster. So it is with Pharaoh. By contrast, Moses, shorn of the grandeur of architecture that assails Heaven, glimpses man on the horizon and something above. He becomes more human: humbled, doubting, pathetic and, given his persistence in the face of those doubts, truly heroic. That's what *The Prince of Egypt* finally is: a hero's biography.   (DECEMBER 18, 1998)

*H*ere's a good one. Wile E. Coyote chases Road Runner over hill and dale, and is closing in. Boy, is he excited! Finally going to get that pesky critter! He's so close. He's just about to pounce and . . . Road Runner stops. Say, what the hey? Road Runner looks down. Omigod, they've run off a cliff, and Coyote has been so obsessed with his quarry he hasn't noticed he's standing on air. Oops. Down he goes, smaller and smaller and—

SPLAT! Little puff of dust from the impact, far below.

That is so cool. I laugh every time. That Wile E. Coyote, he always gets faked out.

Now here's another one. The 40-foot tall, 4,000-pound Hulk, all green fury and knots of fast-twitch muscle fiber, is locomoting so crazily across the landscape that not even army helicopters can keep up with him. Bounce-a-bounce he goes, giant supersonic hops over the same hills and dales of the American Southwest, and pretty soon he outdistances the choppers and their annoying mini-guns and Hellfire missiles, and so he stops.

He just stops. On the old dime. See, he's coming in at a 45-degree angle, he has to be going at least 350 miles an hour to outdistance those gunships, but he stops . . . cold. Hmmm. Whatever happened to that old one about law of inertia, by which bodies in motion tend to remain in motion? Here's what would really be involved in a Hulk-stop from a pedant's point of view: He'd have to brake with his feet each time he hit the ground and desist in the power blasts from his calf muscles, and his bounces would get smaller and smaller and finally, some miles from the initial decision to stop, he finally would stop. Somehow I don't think old Sir Isaac, rusticating dreamily back at Cambridge in the seventeenth century while he decoded the universe for us, ever figured on the Hulk's trick, that sudden, physics-defying STOP. His brain, as rare and eloquent and refined as it was, simply would not have been supple enough to wrap around the Hulk's sudden halt. It wouldn't have been softened by fifteen years of computer-generated imagery.

So here's a question that occurs to me—a man slightly over the age of twelve—but will occur to no men under the age of twelve: Why is what happens to Wile E. Coyote funny—then, now, always—as well as inventive and provocative and memorable, and what happens when the Hulk declares himself done with bounding just annoying? You see it and you think, or maybe you don't think, you feel something like: Oh, come on!

It has to do with the interaction of two separate systems. The first is the internal limit of each movie world (or the lack thereof), and the second is our human perception of that reality as played against our index of the expected. When we see a cartoon—like Road Runner and the Coyote—we understand and accept the conventions. We have entered a special zone of the imagination where much of the pleasure is in seeing the immutable laws of physics broken merrily for comic effect. That has been an animated staple for a hundred years. The idea that Coyote's response to gravity is conditional to Coyote's awareness of gravity is always funny and never perplexing. We have grown used it, and we rapidly decode the indicators—the two-dimensionality of the figures, the stylizations of the facial and body information, the flatness of the backgrounds—and without making the decision consciously, we adjust. In fact, we adjust so fast it's not even noticeable.

Yet the conceit of *Hulk* and all the computer-generated imagery movies like it is exactly the opposite: It is to represent not a cartoon world where we accept as convention the lack of real-world rules, but to represent a photo-realistic world, with its assumption of real-world laws, and then subvert those laws—gravity and physics for starters, but biology as well—in realistic-seeming ways with which the mind must grapple, adjusting eventually to the brute fact that seeing is not believing anymore. This is much easier before age twelve than after.

Here's what happens: Our eyes register the more specific shapes of the beings and machines and grade them as "real"; we perceive the space that they occupy and the backgrounds in such detail that we again call it "real." In fact, our eyes have been utterly fooled by what appears to be realistic, but which, in fact is not realistic, where the rules of physics are no more applicable than in the cartoon's simpler world. The Hulk can land instantly because the Hulk doesn't really exist in a real world but only in that realistic computer-generated world. We're really peeking onto a hard drive where some highly skilled technician has coded a complex digital system to create that which could not be.

As any number of old scientists say at the end of any number of old monster movies, more or less, "Perhaps there are things in the universe that God does not want man to know."

That is the glory and the frustration of computer-generated imagery, which seems to represent something strangely new as it takes over the nation's screens in the summer. The motion picture is no longer a document of photography; it has been liberated from photography, for better or worse, while at the same time much of its bewildered audience (guilty, guilty) clings to the nerve pattern perceptions of the photographed.

Of course those deep-brain playing fields have long been a target of filmmakers, but rarely have they been hit so powerfully. One of the most primitive of filmmaking impulses is the impulse to fool. As early as 1901, the French fantasist Georges Méliès was hoking together a movie about a cannon that fired a rocket that hit the Man in the Moon right in the eye. He had made a breakthrough. He created a moving picture of what seemed real but clearly was not. If he hadn't made this discovery, someone else would have, to be sure. But he was the first to understand the camera's ability to frame a fantasy and transfer it to the world of the photo-real.

We take it for granted now. It was big then. And it wasn't long after that that filmmakers stumbled on the magic of stop-motion animation, by which objects (usually dinosaurs) could be built in both miniature with some degree of flexibility, and then manipulated, one dreary frame at a time, through the photography process until, when the film was run in real time, a semblance of motion was delivered. And so cities were crushed by dinosaurs and giant squids and this town even suffered the indignity of a large flying saucer right where it hurt the most, cantilevered sideways into the Capitol dome. (Hah! Take that, Baltimore! You never were cool enough to merit monstro-destruction in the fifties.)

But still, those devices were different at some deep level. It wasn't only the crudity (seen today, Ray Harryhausen's great monster pics of the fifties seem so campy) but the self-imposed rigidity of concept. These filmmakers were moving the illusion of the fantastic into the real world, but in the real world (actually, the photo-realistic world), they hewed to the real rules: gravity, physics and so forth. In fact, a theme in fifties monster pix was just that: The invaders might have been from the past or the future or a different galaxy or Mars, but they were ultimately defeated by some principle of Earth science that they had overlooked. In *The War of the Worlds*, it was bacteria, which the super Martian intelligences, studying Earth from afar, had not been aware of. In *The Beast from 20,000 Fathoms* and again in *It Came from Beneath the Sea*, it was some principle of nuclear physics as manifested in a weapon. Finally, in the oh-so-fabulous *Earth vs. the Flying Saucers*, it appeared to be radio waves of some sort. The science was always a little hazy, but at least it was science.

The coming of the computer to filmmaking changed all that, possibly in ways yet to be tracked, with results whose ramifications have yet to be noted. But it started so innocuously; who could have known we were on the edge of a new world?

I should right now stop and give you a good, quick, down-and-dirty description of the technique of CGI. Sorry; it won't happen. I won't because I can't. They just do it by magic, and here's a sample of the prose used to describe the process: "They developed another frame buffer that used 1,000 lines; they also built custom graphics processors, image accelerators and the software to run it. This development led to the first use of computer graphics for motion pictures in 1973 when Whitney and Demos worked on the motion picture *Westworld*." Image accelerators? Graphics processors? Dorothy, I have a feeling we're not in Kansas any more.

By most accounts, the early CGI was used to inscribe backgrounds of scientific regularity and precision, as in *Westworld*. It gave the first-generation *Star Wars* movies an eerie reality, although at some point in the filming George Lucas devolved to detailed models, images of which were placed on digital backgrounds. At first, then, CGI was a labor-saving device, rather than a creative one. It provided backgrounds against which either models or subtler, hand-drawn animated figures could cavort. The illusions of space and depth were breathtaking, reaching their most spectacular example in the ballroom sequences in Disney's *Beauty and the Beast* of 1991. This was seen as a refutation, among other things, of CGI's biggest failure to date: the earlier Disney catastrophe *Tron*, from 1982, whose conceit was that it actually took place within a cyberworld, and the "heroes" and "villains" (on bikes, if memory serves) were actually competing programs. It proved a costly lesson, along the following lines: It doesn't matter how radical the new technology is if the oldest of software—the story—is substandard and without a point of human emotional contact.

But by 1995, it was possible to do a whole movie in CGI. That was the Disney hit *Toy Story*, which unified a great story with great vocal performance (by Tom Hanks and Tim Allen) with then state-of-the-art filmmaking. Still, caught up as you were in the thrust of narrative, a certain deep-brain part of you insisted on laying the template of "cartoon" on the action. You knew it wasn't a cartoon because, of course, the objects had weight and size and clearly appeared to occupy space in a way that a cartoon figure never can. Yet at the same time they weren't quite real. They were in some half-world. They had weight and occupied space but lived a stylized existence. The feeling they evoked was weirdly dislocating. No vocabulary quite existed to describe it; the lab boys had far outstripped the language boys in invention. Yet we hadn't really left the cartoon world and its assumptions. We'd just souped it up, made it faster, cooler, more realistic but still not very realistic.

Indeed, so successful was this version of CGI that it spawned a whole genre of cartoonlike CGI films; one of them, *Finding Nemo*, is emerging as one of the big hits of the summer. In some way, however, cartoonified CGI doesn't represent anything new.

What provokes me is what might be called—I coin a phrase here—the hard cartoon of CGI, of which *Hulk* is a primary example, but far from the only example. In fact CGI has become the dominant mode of movie reality with not only *Hulk*, but also *The Matrix Reloaded* and *X 2* still big on the screens and both *Terminator 3: The Rise of the Machines* and *Pirates of the Caribbean* set to launch shortly, and the presumably biggest film of the year, *The Lord of the Rings: The Return of the King*, set for December 17. The mind boggles, the eye stumbles. It's everywhere, it's everywhere.

And hasn't it become boring? That fooled eye, somehow, yearns for other pleasures. Fool me once, shame on you, fool me twice, shame on me. Aren't we there yet?

Why do these giant films no longer do the trick? Part of the reason is sameness. You can build only so many pixelated armies and pixelhorrific monsters and pixelbland damsels and pixelinfinite landscapes before it becomes unremarkable. One has only to look at other Hollywood passions to see how quickly they fade, like 3-D. Sooner or later the audience returns to story. It always has, it always will.

But there's another thing. I take some pleasure in it: It's that the eye, though seemingly fooled, really hasn't been. At some level, we realize that what we are seeing is not there. Our eyes are coded to notice animal movement. That's part of the genetic heritage of the hundreds of thousands of unremembered years on the cruel Neolithic plains. We respond, at some level, to the authentic vitality of a creature moving, whether as prey which we must pursue and kill to feed our families, or as vestigial relic of that long desperate time. And when we see the Hulk climbing over the hill, we know it's phony. We know it can't happen, it didn't happen, it won't happen. We know it can't hunt us and we'll never hunt it, so at a certain level, it becomes irrelevant. It's big, it's green, it's dull. Just like most CGI.　　　　　　　　　　　　　　　(JUNE 29, 2003)

Eight

A LAST VISIT
TO THE VALENCIA

*T*here were two movie theaters in our town.* One was stately, sedate, tasteful and plush. I recall grand staircases carpeted with imitation red velvet, walls of polished tile, lots of rippling silk brocade hanging everywhere, indirect filtered lighting that created an illusion of starglow. It wasn't a movie house, it was a cathedral. It seemed to demand respect and obedience.

This was the theater our parents went to and the one to which, on certain ceremonial family occasions, they took us along, where the no-talking rule was strictly enforced, and our ties were clipped on, our fingernails examined for filth, our teeth and ears scrubbed. It had the sense of both Sunday school and a mansion. It represented, I suppose, our parents' view of America, and the movies it presented reinforced their philosophy.

It was big on the MGM product, on musicals, on historical recreations, the occasional high-end comedy. It's where the big movies played, after they'd parked in a Loop show house for a few months. It's where you met the stars up there, twelve feet high in the soft wash of Technicolor, Charlton Heston, Rory Calhoun, James Cagney, Lauren Bacall, the young Marilyn Monroe.

The other theater was, for a time, only a rumor. Its allure was illicit, low, salacious. It's where the "other" movies played.

---

*Oops. When I wrote this piece in 1997, I forgot about the Coronet. I had it right in the Introduction.

Now, as an adult, I know that it was merely a B-house, home to the lower end of the spectrum of the nearly endless train of 600 or so films made each year in the early fifties, before television got big and turned most such places into parking lots. I know that Universal and American-International and Republic pictures played there, cheapo melodramas, gangster pix. I know that rereleases showed up (*Armored Attack*, for one, a retitled version of Lillian Hellman's pro-Soviet *North Star*, sent back to the world as a mea culpa with a Cold War coda tacked on) and the endless, disreputable westerns. The movies arrived two at a time, on double bills, changing each week—*Hell on Frisco Bay*, *Seven Men from Now*, *Francis the Talking Mule*, *Rogue Cop*, *The Creature from the Black Lagoon*—never overstaying their leave by a single day.

But in 1953, its pleasures were yet untasted by a certain seven-year-old child. He is towheaded, frightened, the younger kid in a neighborhood of bigger kids. He feels powerless in all aspects of his life, except for the nightly torture he dishes out to his two younger brothers as an expression of his only advantage on the species.

One night during the summer of '53 he is watching television, which is then a square tube mounted in a monumental mahogany console, roughly 600 pounds in weight; it look more like an organ or some kind of religious artifact than the daily conveyor of *The Howdy Doody Show*. He sits there, largely vegetable, mind dull, as always frightened.

The house is ruled by a father. By the structures of the time, the father's role is to rule. It is unquestioned. As one TV series points out, he knows best. Society is the fact organized around the sanctity of his wisdom, the authority of his strength. He runs the family.

Likewise, in his profession, the father answers to a dean. It could be a supervisor, a manager, a senior partner; it just happens to be a dean. The pattern of family organization is repeated in the larger society, all of which somehow fits into a still larger pattern until the entire culture is regulated. Nobody would call this wrong, because no vocabulary exists yet for such a judgment.

This pattern has its temptations. The order it guarantees is not unpleasant: The boy walks clean streets under a vault of elms to school without fear or even the concept of fear. He understands that somehow the world is safe in meaningful ways—that is, if the Russian Bisons don't sneak over the ice cap and drop their A-bombs, but of course that's why we have a DEW line and F-89 Scorpions, all-weather jets with missile pods on their wing tips, so the possibility is just a titillation of doom that will never really happen. Life is uneventful, well organized, a system of moving from here to there by exact, known steps. There is no doubt about anything and you have no ability to imagine what you are surrendering to such a system.

Many people miss it still.

So here sits the boy; there blares the television, black-and-white.

"What monstrosity has man's atomic curiosity unleashed in a frozen arctic wasteland?" asks the television, behind an image of a frozen crest set ashiver by . . . by . . . something.

The boy sits up, ceases ever so slightly to be a vegetable.

"What creature patrols the green depths in its inexorable voyage toward its ultimate confrontation with the petty species called man?"

There's a flash of something large and glistening, distorted by a rain-smeared window; then a silhouette of something large resting its forepaws on a lighthouse. "Aieeeeeeeeee!" the paltry humans scream, rushing down the spiral staircase as the structure cracks around them.

"What horrors," demands the narrator, "are soon to be visited on the mightiest of human metropolises?"

And with that we see panic in the streets, a single brave cop firing upward at an unseen colossus until a shadow opens like a black orchid and overwhelms him in a flash of indistinct motion.

"Opening this Friday at a theater near you."

Suddenly this child of the fifties knows something: He has got to see this movie.

The theater was called the Valencia. It was four blocks south of the Varsity—the grown-up theater—on Sherman, across from Walker Bros. and the Toddle House, two institutions that issued a primitive fifties version of fast food. The theater nestled in the greasy miasma of the burger joints and was utterly unmemorable from the outside.

Enter, however, as I must have for the first time in 1953, with Muerney Green and Wyatt and Chris James and Brenda Harris, and get beyond the stench of ancient popcorn butter and melted Jujubes, past the old soft drink machine, and what you saw was a castle.

Movies at the Valencia weren't a religion, as they were at the Varsity, but an empire. The screen nestled in a crenellated fortification, complete with towers and turrets and keeps and windows, all of it no doubt papier-mâché but to our eyes wondrous. It somehow removed the movies—the whole experience—from the province of parents, that is, the province of adults, from society, really from control.

Freedom? Imagine the pleasure of it. Liberty? Liberty like a drug! Liberty like a rush of exuberance, a ray of hot bliss pouring down from heaven!

I must be careful not to make too much of this. Things never happen in reality with the clarity that they do in recollection. Symbolism is rarely apparent when it's happening.

Still, I do know that the first movie I ever saw alone—that is, with other children, not with my parents—was *The Beast from 20,000 Fathoms*. I know also that it so overwhelmed me I sneaked back two days later and saw it again, after spinning some easily penetrated fib, for which I was severely punished by my father—and punishment in those days routinely meant physical violence. I recall that it cost a dime. (A dime! Can it have cost a dime?) I even recall the undercard of the double feature, another cheesy thriller called *The Magnetic Monster*, which had to do with a runaway nuclear reaction in some kind of undersea laboratory.

Best of all was a moment that still manages to stir me, even in the most routine strip-mall shoe-box multiplex. It's the moment that brings back all the pleasure of that first, and still deepest, sense of freedom—the moment when the lights drop and out of the dark thrusts a spear of light. It is only images projected on an expanse of glass-impregnated paper of a certain size by a lamp of a certain wattage, of overattractive people who are overpaid doing things that are absurd.

But it's also a piston driving an extraordinary sense of possibility. For that spear of light frees not the images on the celluloid, but the viewer's imagination. Free at last, great God, free at last! There is no father there to supervise, no mother to tidy, no teacher to correct, no older boys to frighten, no younger brothers to torment, no Reds to blow you off the face of the Earth.

The beast walks. He crushes the city. The buildings topple, the cop is devoured, the army arrives. There are no limits to imagining—somehow you learn this instinctively.

For better or worse, you begin to recognize the possibility of a life that will someday be your own. (JULY 1, 1997)

INDEX

Movie titles and pages in bold denote reviews.